CAIRO

THE CITY VICTORIOUS

Max Rodenbeck has lived in Cairo off and on for 20 years. He is a correspondent for the *Economist*.

Max Rodenbeck

Cairo

The City Victorious

PICADOR

First published 1998 by Picador

This edition published 1999 by Picador
an imprint of Macmillan Publishers Ltd
25 Eccleston Place, London SW1W 9NF,
Basingstoke and Oxford
Associated companies throughout the world
www.macmillan.co.uk

ISBN 0 330 33710 6

1 3 5 7 9 8 6 4 2

A CIP catalogue record for this book is available from the British Library.

Typeset by SetSystems Ltd, Saffron Walden, Essex
Printed and bound in Great Britain by
Mackays of Chatham plc, Chatham, Kent

TO K.K.

We shall omit from our history the tales invented by Herodotus, and certain other writers on Egyptian affairs who deliberately prefer fables to fact, and who spin yarns merely for the sake of amusement. We shall, however, set forth the things written by the priests of Egypt in their sacred records, which we have examined diligently and minutely.

Diodorus Siculus, *the Library of History*, first century BC

𓊖 is the hieroglyphic symbol for a city, showing a wall surrounding crossroads.

Contents

An Orientation ix

1. Beginnings 1

2. Dead Cities 25

3. Cities of the Dead 56

4. Mother of the World 91

5. Medieval Decline 123

6. The Phoenix Caged 148

7. Where Worlds Collide 173

8. Conflict and Fusion 204

9. Keeping the Faith 235

10. High Life, Low Life 263

11. The Voice of Cairo 308

Glossary 343

Bibliography 349

Index 372

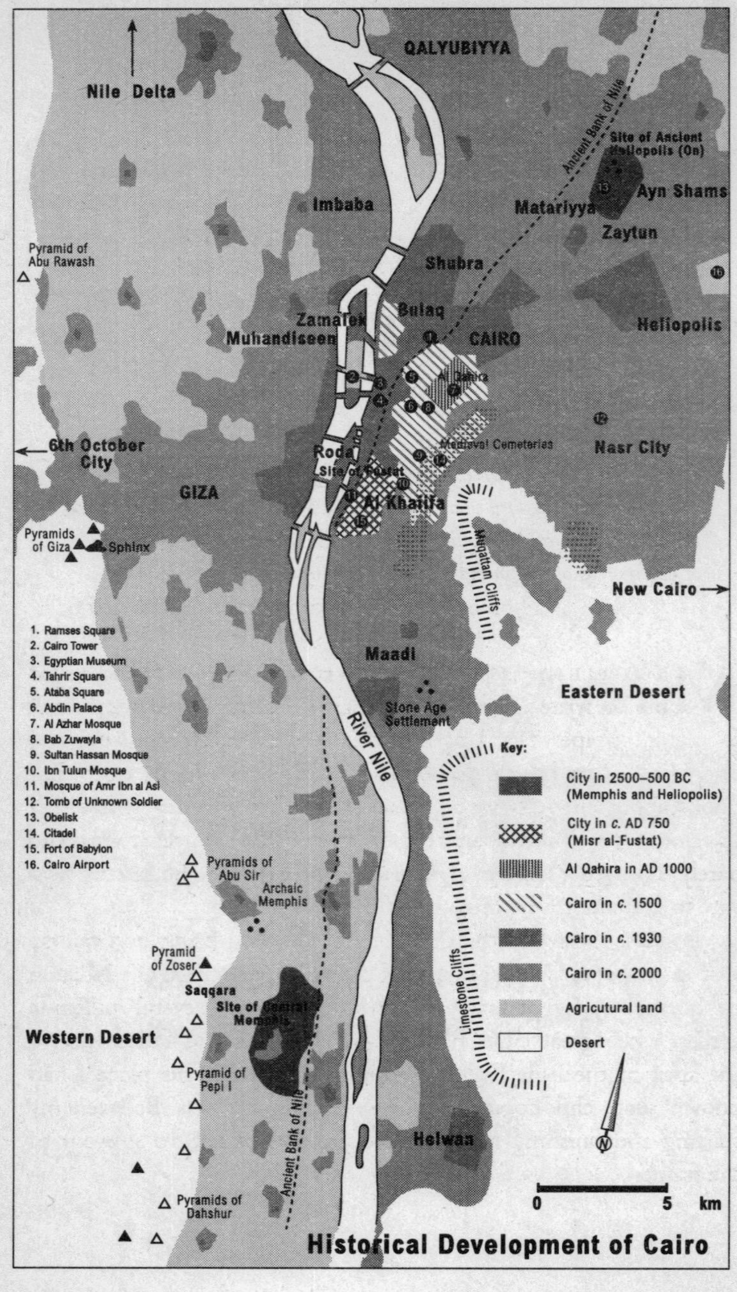

QALYUBIYYA
Nile Delta
Ancient Bank of Nile
Site of Ancient Heliopolis (On)
Ayn Shams
Matariyya
Zaytun
Imbaba
Pyramid of Abu Rawash
Shubra
Bulaq
Zamalek
Muhandiseen
CAIRO
Heliopolis
Al Qahira
Medieval Cemeteries
Nasr City
6th October City
Roda
Site of Fustat
GIZA
Al Khalifa
Pyramids of Giza
Sphinx
Muqattam Cliffs
New Cairo
1. Ramses Square
2. Cairo Tower
3. Egyptian Museum
4. Tahrir Square
5. Ataba Square
6. Abdin Palace
7. Al Azhar Mosque
8. Bab Zuwayla
9. Sultan Hassan Mosque
10. Ibn Tulun Mosque
11. Mosque of Amr Ibn al Asi
12. Tomb of Unknown Soldier
13. Obelisk
14. Citadel
15. Fort of Babylon
16. Cairo Airport
Maadi
Stone Age Settlement
Eastern Desert
River Nile
Key:
City in 2500–500 BC (Memphis and Heliopolis)
City in c. AD 750 (Misr al-Fustat)
Al Qahira in AD 1000
Cairo in c. 1500
Cairo in c. 1930
Cairo in c. 2000
Agricutural land
Desert
Pyramids of Abu Sir
Archaic Memphis
Pyramid of Zoser
Saqqara
Site of Central Memphis
Western Desert
Limestone Cliffs
Pyramid of Pepi I
Helwan
Ancient Bank of Nile
Pyramids of Dahshur
0
5
km
N
Historical Development of Cairo

An Orientation

Every year a little deposit of mud is left by the Nile on its banks, and every year sees deposited upon the counters of the London booksellers the turbid overflow of journalizing travel. Alas! It has not the usefulness of the leavings of this sacred river.

Thomas Gold Appleton, *A Nile Journal*, 1876

Mr Appleton is right, which is why when a friend urged me to write a book about Cairo, I said *tsk* and went back to my waterpipe. Yes, I agreed, this was a magnificent city, and one whose story has rarely been told with sympathy or truth. But books about cities, I argued, were of two kinds. They were either travelogues or histories, and I knew that, while a travel story could barely skim the surface of Cairo's depth, a straight history was sure to founder in the immensity of the city's past.

Besides, there was the question of where to begin in a tale so vast in scope as Cairo's. Fourteen centuries ago, when the Muslim conquerors of Egypt made this their capital? Or several millennia earlier, when great cities had already bloomed and faded here at the apex of the Nile Delta? And where to end? This place I had known since childhood was changing elusively fast. Between my starting and finishing its portrait Cairo was certain to slip out of the frame.

Then, perhaps I had come to know the city all too well. If Cairo was, in the words of its great novelist the Nobel laureate Naguib Mahfouz, like meeting your beloved in old age, then was I to tell about her wrinkles, her bad breath and worse taste, and her unfortunate habit of shouting at the servants? Because just as one could expand on the city's wonders – its pyramids and minarets and showbiz glitter – one could also mutter over its noise and pollution and sheer, bewildering, annoying clutter.

The fact was that after a twelve-year stretch of living in Cairo, most of which was spent in enchantment, I was falling out of love. The city was changing, and what it was changing into disturbed me, as it disturbed most Cairenes that I knew. I felt increasingly estranged from what was becoming a harder, more impatient, less tolerant city of ugly new buildings – a place far removed from other Cairos I had known.

I FIRST ARRIVED here at the age of two. What I remember is heady colour bursts of bougainvillea crimson, jacaranda violet and flame-tree red, and the glistening blackness of olives at the Greek grocer. I remember the crackling urgency of backgammon dice in cafés and the tooting insistence of human, animal and motorized traffic. I recall the glamour of seeing *Lawrence of Arabia* open at that art deco jewel of a cinema, the Metro on Sulayman Pasha Street, and the sheer fun of hurling potatoes into the gap-toothed maw of a hippo at the zoo (still elegant then, with its pathways in Portuguese mosaic and lemonade served beside the still-lush lotus ponds). I remember the peculiarity of that cartoon mountainscape of pyramids on the western horizon, and the taxis – those high-sprung jalopies in harlequin black and white whose radios moaned a single song by the city's great diva Umm Kulsoum, then at the climax of her fortunes. 'You are my life,' she crooned over and over, as the Nile's sunset sheen flickered through the treacly jungle of banyan trees lining the Corniche. 'You are my life that dawned with your light.'

I didn't understand the words then. That particular light dawned much later, when I returned to study Arabic here, worked as a reporter, and discovered the Mother of the World – as Egyptians fondly call their capital – in all her shambolic grandeur and operatic despair. The city seduced me. Her depth seemed limitless, whether by the measure of time or the fortunes of her people or the mystery of their ways. Layers overlapped effortlessly: the ancient and the new, the foreign and the native, the rich and the poor. Worlds mingled in the bookstalls along the edge of the Azbakiyya Gardens: the works of Enver Hoxha next to a score by Puccini beside an Armenian body-building manual on top of the *Thousand and One Nights*. They mingled in the streets, where the barefoot incense man swirled his censer from shop to shop, collecting a *shillin* or *barīza* from their keepers in exchange for a blessing. Brandy-swilling leftists at the Café Riche spun tall plots to tease eavesdropping, hookah-puffing secret police. Refugees out of Africa rented their bodies at the Borsalino discotheque to key-jangling spivs and Israeli agents and German engineers and backpackers straying from the road to Kathmandu. On the weathered marble floor of a fourteenth-century mosque, under the coffered and gilded ceiling, a turbanned sheikh dozed over his holy book. Young couples cooed at the chipped tables of the venerable Groppi Tea Rooms. They ignored their neighbours, the painted old birds in laddered stockings who had lost the will to migrate back to Salonica or Trieste or wherever it was they had come from, and so reminisced in ragged Levantine French about Cairo's Roaring Forties – and when the waiter turned his back slipped scarce sugar cubes into their tattered Hermès handbags.

In time the old birds at Groppi went extinct, along with most of the variegated cosmopolitans whose world had closed in after the 1952 revolution. The Nileside banyans fell to road-widening schemes. Secret police began to do their mufti in beards and robes. They now hunted not harmless leftist barflies, but the new breed of violent zealots who buzzed with pious anger and chiselled busily at Cairo's old civility. A chorus of full-volume Koranic cassette sellers invaded the Azbakiyya bookstalls. Instead of weeding out these noisy intruders, the dullard city government abolished the market altogether.

I grew wary of exploring the city. Each successive visit to its old core – the zone of grand medieval mosques and palaces and bazaars – brought fresh evidence of further decay: marble buckled off walls, ancient minarets toppled into neighbouring houses; and in the markets plastic shoes and pharaonic T-shirts replaced camel-hide slippers and satin kaftans. Strolling one day downtown – in what used to be the 'European' Quarter – I discovered one favourite café transformed into a tawdry jeans outlet and another replaced by a burger bar called Madonna's. The National Hotel, whose crusty, broken-keyed piano bar once boasted a preposterous coterie of Second World War vintage prostitutes, was bought and torn down by an 'Islamic' investment company. When its pyramid scheme went bust the site remained a gaping parking lot.

It was not just my own proprietorial sensibilities that made this breakneck defoliation sad. Everyone from Shukri the ironing man to Ahmad the tailor to Dr Sabri the dentist felt it, and moaned about it. The weather had never been humid like this, they agreed. The streets had never looked so scruffy. The Cairene character itself, they chimed, had altered. People were now sanctimonious, rude and grasping where once they lived only for laughs. Those who could were simply leaving. Embarrassed clusters of would-be émigrés huddled outside foreign consulates. Even Usta Mahmud the mechanic, a gruff fellow more interested in feeding stray cats than in servicing cars, took off to live with his son in Jersey City, New Jersey.

After a particularly scorching, frustrating summer I joined the exodus.

AN ORIENTATION

'He who drinks the water of the Nile is destined to taste its sweetness again.' The proverb is something of a cliché to Egyptians, but I couldn't help recalling it as my plane touched down at Cairo three years later. The idea of the place had made me uneasy, but all hesitation evaporated with the first sniff of the city's hot night air, with the welcoming image of a soldier sleeping in an airport corridor and the familiar feel of playful bustle as taxi hustlers swooped like seagulls on to the crowd of dazed travellers at the airport's exits. As the impressions flooded in, I knew without a doubt I was home. The place was tatty, yes. It was grubby and noisy too. But Cairo fitted snug as an old shoe.

Right away I knew, too, that I must write this book. There lurked a faint recollection of how the ancient gods had kept Menelaus dawdling by the Nile on his way home from the Trojan War. 'And so he tarried, for he had not paid their due of sacrifice,' is how Homer explained the strange reluctance of Odysseus's friend to return to Sparta. I felt that in some similar sense I owed an offering, however flawed, to this city which had given me so many stories and whose people had been so unfailingly kind.

Besides, my brief hejira had renewed my appreciation of Cairo. Other places may have been neater, quieter and less prone to wrenching change, but they all lacked something. The easy warmth of Cairenes, perhaps, and their indomitable insouciance; the complexities and complicities of their relations; their casual mixing of sensuality with moral rigour, of razor wit with credulity. Or perhaps it was the possibility this city offered of escape into other worlds: into the splendours of its pharaonic and medieval pasts, say, or out of its bruising crowds on to the soft, gentle current of the Nile – even if the tapering lateen sails of the river feluccas did now advertise Coca-Cola.

And then, reading into Cairo's past, I saw how foolish it was to fret about its future. How silly to imagine that this great town – this *Ur-Stadt* if there ever was one – could ever decay beyond repair. The fact was that not one generation in Cairo's five millennia of incarnations had failed to whine about decline, and still the city endured.

Cairo's ancient stone guardian, the Sphinx himself, had been known to complain of neglect. According to the 3,000-year-old stone inscription between his paws, the Sphinx appeared in a dream to a young prince who, exhausted by a desert gazelle hunt, had fallen asleep in his shadow. 'My manner is as if I were ailing in all my limbs,' moaned the idol. 'The sand of the desert upon which I stand has reached me.' The Sphinx vowed that if the prince dusted him off he could have the god's kingdom on earth 'at the head of the living'. The Sphinx kept his promise. The prince was to rule Egypt as the pharaoh Tutmosis IV.

The plaintive tone echoed in medieval times, when Cairo was reborn as the greatest of Muslim cities. Here is a certain Sheikh Badr al-Din al-Zaytuni, complaining in verse about the sultan's closure of the Birkat al-Ratl, a seasonal lake outside the great city walls where fifteenth-century Cairenes had whiled away autumn evenings on torchlit pleasure boats:

The eater of opium found constant delight . . .
While the mirth of the drunkard was at its height.
Goblets brimmed beneath the full moon . . .
While poets sang to the gentlest of tunes.

Now time has erased these haunts . . .
O eyes, shed tears of grief, O heart endure!
And God's favour bless those days of joy when Cairo was secure.

And here was the French novelist Pierre Loti, who reckoned at the turn of the last century that the city had grown too modern. It had lost its *Thousand and One Nights* allure: 'What is this? Where are we fallen? Save that it is more vulgar than Nice, or the Riviera . . . [the] great town – which sweats gold now that men have started to buy from it its dignity and its soul – is become a place of rendezvous and holiday for all the idlers and upstarts of the whole world...'

Loti was wrong. Cairo may have lived through periods of bad as well as good taste. (Actually, much of what Loti saw as vulgarity is now considered fine stuff and worthy of preservation – like the *beaux arts* and neo-Islamic architecture of the European Quarter.) The city may have plundered many of its own riches or wantonly scarred them or let them tumble into ruin. But it has never sold its dignity or its soul. This is, after all, the place that endowed the world with the myth of the phoenix.

It was to ancient Heliopolis, the oldest of Cairo's many avatars, that the bird of fabulous plumage was said to return every 500 years, to settle on the burning altar at the great Temple of the Sun and then to rise again from its own ashes. Time and again, Cairo too has risen from its ashes. It has survived countless invasions, booms and busts, famines, plagues and calamities. Through them all the city has ultimately remained, as in its classical Arabic name, al-Qahira – The Victorious.

It was this resilient fluidity, above all, that I wanted to explain. To do so required neither a history nor a descriptive travelogue. It demanded a narrative that would fuse the two, and that would let the city tell its own story through the voices of its old gods, of its stones and chronicles, and of its lovers and critics through the ages down to the present. The writing would be difficult, but, if the story were to loop and tangle and digress, well, that too would be in the character of Cairo.

A GAS STATION marks the site of the old Shepheard's Hotel on Gumhuriyya Street. Jitney cabs honk and jostle in the roadway out front, driven by under-age barkers who lean out the sliding doors shouting '*Kit Kat! Kit Kat!*' (They refer not to the Kit Kat, which was a Second World War nightclub on a houseboat across the river, but to the adjacent mosque which adopted the name and happens to be where this minibus route terminates.)

A hundred years – a mere drop in the Nile-flood of Cairene history – separate this scene from another.

Then, silent Nubian waiters in satin kaftans swished among the tables on Shepheard's streetside terrace. They bore whisky-sodas to officers of the occupying British army, who retired here after a hard day on the polo grounds of the Gezira Sporting Club. They served hibiscus teas to tarboosh-topped pashas and beys of Cairo's upper crust, who talked cotton prices and political scandal. But the grand old Victorian pile also drew customers of another kind. Shepheard's was a key port of call for what wags dubbed the Imperial Fishing Fleet, by which they meant the flotilla of debutantes who set out from Home each winter with the express aim of trawling for a husband in the British colonial service.

It was here that my great-grandmother Alfreda made her catch. One afternoon in the spring of 1895, Alfreda Eppes and her sister Josephine joggled towards Shepheard's, perched side-saddle on twin white donkeys with henna-stained manes. The ladies were proud Virginia gentlewomen. In the months since embarking on this grand tour, since leaving their ancestral estate by the lazy river James, they could claim to have seen something of the Old World. But in truth it had been most trying, this day of perusing Oriental sights in the company of importunate dragomen and donkeyboys. And now, in front of the hotel, the dainty memsahibs were engulfed in a human squall. Fiercely moustachioed hawkers pressed in, proferring all manner of unwanted goods, from hippo-hide whips and horsetail fly whisks to flowers, stuffed crocodiles, live leopards and boa constrictors, sandalwood boxes, beads, tarbooshes and – by the sour account of a contemporary traveller – 'images of ancient gods made 3,000 years too late to get into the tombs of the pharoahs'.

Shepheard's famously huge, pistol-packing Montenegrin door-man was too far off to usher the ladies to safety. (Seven years later he was to be arrested for firing his gun point blank into the pestiferous crowd of natives.) And now all pretence of dignity slipped away as Alfreda's donkey stumbled. Encumbered by voluminous skirts, great-granny spilled into the dust in full view of the terrace voyeurs.

But rescue was at hand. A gallant Englishman, stopping in Cairo on his way back from India, happened on the scene. Young Herbert now leaped forward, doffed his cork-lined solar topi and assisted the young lady to her tight-laced feet. A romance was born. After much hot pursuit – and some hard bargaining with Alfreda's father, to whom Limeys were only a slice less crude than Yankees – Herbert carried Alfreda to Bombay as the wife of an officer in Her Majesty's Indian Civil Service.

To tell the truth, family legend is unclear about whether my great-grandparents' Donkey Incident took place at Shepheard's Hotel or out at the Pyramids. Or, indeed, whether Alfreda actually tumbled from her mount (his version) or rather impressed her suitor by nimbly leaping off it (hers). However it may have been, the unshakeable fact is that I owe my existence to a certain anonymous donkey of Cairo. So I trust that the many friends who encouraged and abetted the making of this book will forgive my extending foremost gratitude to that irascible beast.

Hard on his hooves comes Stephen Hubbell, without whose patient prompting *The City Victorious* would most surely have been vanquished. William Lyster gave generously of his time and invaluable wisdom. Antony Sattin and Carol Janeway provided much useful guidance. Grateful thanks are due to my parents, John and Elizabeth Rodenbeck, for bringing me here and for their enduring interest in Cairo; to Michael Jones, for pointers on the topography of the early city and on the Ancient Egyptian language; to Hassan Abuseda, Ziad and Daisy Bahaeddin, Muhammad Ben Ahmed, Alice Brinton, Adel Fahmy, Paul Geday, Maria Golia, Bill Hamilton, Cathy Healey, Marise Hilal and the staff of Estoril, Sonallah Ibrahim, Barry Iverson, Siona Jenkins,

Dr and Mrs Hassan Khalil, Dr Phillip Mansell, Magdi Mitwalli, Mia Monasterly, Samir Morcos, Trevor Naylor, Dr Hassouna Saba, Mona Saba, Adel and Mahmoud Sabet, Norbert Schiller, Hana Sholkamy, David Sims, Pierre Sioufi, Nihal Tamraz and Mercedes Volait; and to the night shift at the Grillon.

I also owe a tribute to the many scholars who have travelled the same path, or parts of it, before me. I often found myself skirting around subjects for the simple reason that previous writers had already treated them with unmatchable thoroughness. Besides, I would hate to subtract one bit from the pleasure of discovery that any Cairo enthusiast will find in works like the novelist James Aldridge's classic biography of the city – published thirty years ago and strangely never reissued – or the scholarly urban histories of Janet Abu Lughod and André Raymond, or Susan Staffa's excellent social history of the medieval city, or Diane Singerman's masterful study of modern society in the traditional quarters, or the incredibly prolific productions of historians David Ayalon and the great Gaston Wiet. This list could go on much longer, but then its place should really be at the back of the book, where indeed it will be found in the shape of a bibliography.

Above all, I owe an immense debt to the fortitude and intelligence of Karima Khalil, who shepherded this work unswervingly through deserts and green valleys alike.

Cairo, November 1997

CHAPTER ONE

BEGINNINGS

Now the eighth descendant of King Osymandias . . . founded Memphis, the most illustrious city in Egypt. For he sought out the most fitting site in the land, the place where the Nile divides into the Delta; wherefore it came to pass that the city, situated, as it were, at the gateway to Egypt, was master of all the commerce passing upstream to the country above.

Diodorus Siculus, *The Library of History*, first century BC

ABU ABDALLAH MUHAMMAD Ibn Battuta set out from Tangier on the second day of the month of Rajab in the seven-hundred-and-twenty-fifth year of the Hejira. He was twenty-two years old and overpowered, he would later recall, by a burning need to enter the illustrious sanctuaries of Mecca and Medina. He travelled on foot mostly, taking a full year and a half to cover the 4,000 miles between his home town by the Straits of Gibraltar and the Muslim holy places of Arabia. Yet when his pilgrimage was complete Ibn Battuta's thirst for adventure still raged. He was not to go home, in fact, for thirty years – not before seeing at first hand the Arab cities of Jerusalem, Damascus and Baghdad and the Christian emperor's capital at Constantinople; not before coasting African reefs to slave-trading Zanzibar; before sliding by sledge across the frozen realm of the khan of the Golden Horde to the splendid cities of Bokhara and

Samarkand; before scaling the Hindu Kush and descending to the humid plains of the Indus and Ganges; not before serving as chief Malikite cadi of Delhi and as ambassador from its fierce and capricious sultan to the court of China, which he reached by way of Ceylon, monsoon-drenched Sumatra and the bustling port of Canton. Ibn Battuta would not rest in sleepy little Tangier again until he had seen all of the known world (aside, of course, from the crude and violent lands of the Western Christians). Wishing to reach the very edges of civilization, he would not be satisfied until he had toured the delightful but doomed towns of Muslim Andalusia in the north and the gold-rich city of Timbuktu across the Sahara to the south.

Ibn Battuta followed a simple rule in all his 75,000 miles of wandering: he vowed never to travel the same road twice. Yet there was one town he stopped at no fewer than five times. It was a matter of course that he should, since this was not only the largest and richest city of the age and the capital of the mightiest kingdom, it was also the crossroads of the busiest routes of trade and pilgrimage from east to west and north to south.

Cairo was, quite simply, the navel of the world. It dazzled Ibn Battuta like no other city. To his secretary Ibn Juzayy he was to dictate this encomium:

> Mistress of broad provinces and fruitful lands, boundless in profusion of buildings, peerless in beauty and splendour, she shelters all you will of the learned and the ignorant, the grave and the gay, the prudent and the foolish, the noble and the base ... Like the waves of the sea she surges with her throngs of folk, yet for all the capacity of her station and her power to sustain can scarce hold their number. Her youth is ever new despite the length of days. Her reigning star never shifts from the mansion of fortune.

When Ibn Battuta first arrived, in the year AD 1326, Cairo was indeed at a peak in its fortunes. For three centuries it had been the greatest of Muslim cities. But this town was already ancient long before the coming of Islam. Successive cities had grown, flourished, decayed and been reborn on this site beginning no less than 4,000 years before. The town was so old that its inhabitants even at the start of that barely conceivable antiquity believed that this was where Creation itself had taken place.

The spot where the Ancient Egyptians said life began looks an odd choice today. It lies out in the ragged north-east suburbs of the great city, not far from the end of a metro line. Industrial plants jostle here with ranks of dwellings slapped together in raw red brick and slung with washing. Heedless of momentous happenings in ages past, shoppers haggle by the butchers' stalls and pyramids of melons that enliven the main street until it peters out abruptly in a fenced-off acreage of flat brown dust. The emptiness, in this city where land is coveted like gold, is eerie.

The barren land is the site of a long-gone town called On.* Gone, that is, except for a lone monolith, a single shaft of solid pink granite that soars defiantly out of the rubble. This is a 4,000-year-old obelisk, the last of an avenue of obelisks that once led to the great temple of On. Its stone siblings are gone, succumbed to different fates; they toppled and were broken up for stone, or got hauled off whole as trophies, dubbed Cleopatra's Needles, and then were shipped away down the Nile and across the sea to grace stripling cities by the murky rivers Hudson and Thames.

Further back, at the beginning of time itself, nothing existed of Cairo or On or of anything else. There was no River Nile even, the Ancient Egyptians believed. The entire universe was a colourless, proportionless ooze. And then, for no reason in particular, out of this shapeless element something solid formed. It swelled into a mound in what was to become the courtyard of

*On is the biblical version of a name ancient Egyptians probably pronounced 'Yunu'.

the great temple of On. The mound was later called the Benben, and was stylized as a pyramid.

Out of this Benben rose the sun, taking the form of Atum, the creator god. He was a glowing orb atop the pyramid, or a flaming phoenix, perhaps, or maybe even a man-shaped god – the fluidity of ancient myth makes his image difficult to grasp. Whatever his form, Atum stood here lighting the emptiness. Then, say the sacred texts that the priests of On inscribed in pyramid-tombs across the river to the west, Atum aroused himself 'so that he should create orgasm'. He engendered twins. From his nose snorted Shu, the fiery god of air. From his mouth flew Tefnut, the vaporous goddess of moisture who still gives her name to the Arabic word for spitting. Shu and Tefnut begat Geb and Nut – earth and sky – who begat the rest of the nine chief gods of On: Osiris, Isis, her sister Nephthys and the outsider Seth, who burst unexpectedly from Nut's womb. Witnessing the result of his exertions, Atum burst into tears. His tears became mankind, and populated the world.

This is what the priests of On said happened here. But the priests of Memphis, a rival city whose ruins lie across the Nile, twenty miles off at the opposite edge of modern Cairo, disputed their version of events. It was not Atum of On, they asserted, but Ptah of Memphis who created the world; not Atum the sun, but Ptah the 'beautiful of face' who conceived of all, then uttered it into being with his Word, and fashioned man in his image.

Yet even before On and Memphis had advanced enough to quarrel, another seminal event occurred in their vicinity.

The scheming god Seth was the villain of Ancient Egyptian myth. A fork-tailed canine with a long, drooping snout, he stalked the rim of the valley, bellowing and howling and stirring up sandstorms. Seth was the master of the Red Lands – the desert – but he was a lonely god. In his solitude he envied his brother Osiris, happy ruler of the Black Lands watered by the Nile. Seth conceived a plot. He held a banquet. After wining and dining his brother, he jokingly invited him to lie down inside a beautiful box. No sooner had Osiris climbed in than Seth slammed the lid closed and heaved the box into the great river. The goddess Isis, grieving, searched high and low for the body of her beloved brother. Finding his corpse on the shores of what is now Lebanon, she impregnated herself with his seed. Isis gave birth to falcon-headed Horus.* The child grew up, nurturing dreams of vengeance, amid the reeds of the Nile Delta. When he came of age Horus set out to track his murderous uncle.

But Seth was lusty as well as cunning. His winsome young nephew pleased him. When he came upon the falcon-headed youth at a place between On and Memphis that the Egyptians later called Kher'aha, the Site of the Battle, Seth assaulted Horus. The two gods rolled in the dust of the Nile bank, transformed into hippopotami. They fought for three days and nights, maybe even for years. Seth plucked out Horus's eagle eye, but Horus tore off his uncle's testicles. In the end Thoth, the baboon-like (but sometimes ibis-headed) god of wisdom and writing, intervened. He retrieved the eye of Horus. He held a trial at On, or perhaps Memphis, and the fighting gods were reconciled.

Like all good myths, this most ancient one prisms into numberless versions. Sometimes the fight of the gods is glossed as a complicitous carousal. More often Horus represents the triumph of outraged justice, which is why the falcon or eagle or phoenix became a sign of victory while the forked tail of Seth evolved into a mark of Satan.† Modern scholars wrangle as much as the

* Other accounts say Horus was born before Osiris's death – or even identify him as Osiris's brother. Still more versions add a long chapter to the myth in which Seth captures Osiris's body again, chops it up, and scatters the parts over Egypt. Isis then wanders high and low to gather the parts and make her lost lover/husband/brother whole.

† The mythical imagery of ancient Egypt endures in surprising places. For instance, the US $1 bill transmits such snapshots of early Cairo as the victorious Horus in eagle form and the Benben pyramid surmounted by a sun-like eye.

ancients over the details, but concur that the story of the battle of the gods symbolized religious and political fusion. It may illustrate the struggle between the early kingdoms of Upper and Lower Egypt, and their subsequent unification. Then again, Seth and Horus may represent the conflict between the settled people of the Nile Valley and nomads from Asia, the arrival of whom some antiquarians say was responsible for catalysing advanced civilization here 5,000 years ago.

The point is that Kher'aha, the mythic site of the battle between Seth and Horus, was where the great metropolis of Cairo sprawls today. At the confluence of continents, at the narrow neck of the Nile Valley just before it spreads into the flat water-maze of the Delta, this has always been a place where elements mingle and cultures collide. Invaders have come and gone: the Asiatic Hyksos, Libyans, Ethiopians, Assyrians, Persians, Greeks, Romans, Arabs, Turks, French, British and recent hordes of tourists. The cities here have risen and fallen, but always this spot has been the crucible of Egypt's fate.

LEAVING ASIDE MYTH, science asserts that permanent settlement started at Cairo near the end of the last Ice Age. It was then, around 10,000 years ago, that global warming scorched the grasslands which once bordered the Nile Valley, sending their rich wildlife of elephants, lions and giraffes scurrying into the African hinterland. It diminished the river, taming its 10-million-year-old habit of scouring a deeper and deeper gorge in its hard bed of Eocene limestone. Instead, the Nile now flooded once a year in late summer, rising by twenty feet to fill the narrow valley from desert to desert. Receding in the autumn, it deposited silts eroded from the distant volcanic mountains of Ethiopia. The silt thickened by a millimetre a year, forming a loamy and rich soil that is today some thirty feet deep.

Together these changes brought about the end of hunter-gatherer cultures that had flourished in what is now the Sahara. By necessity these palaeolithic wanderers – many of whose 150,000-year-old flint blades have been found near On – settled in the valley for good. With time they learned to husband animals and raise crops. They discovered how to fashion pottery and bricks for the building of walls. As the Egyptians' technical skills improved and so allowed wealth to accumulate, larger towns grew up elsewhere in Egypt. Still, in the region of what would become Cairo there seem to have been only a scattering of villages.

Seventy years ago archaeologists excavated a neolithic site near Maadi, a leafy Cairo suburb half an hour by metro from the remains of On. On the edge of the desert, behind what is now a satellite tracking station, they uncovered the traces of a densely settled village surrounded by sturdy walls. Aside from fine pottery they found delicate vessels bored out of basalt, woven textiles and slate palettes for mixing cosmetics that were skilfully carved in relief with designs of plants and animals. Here, in about 4,000 BC, the dead were buried with a few favourite possessions. Their bodies were laid down on their right sides facing the rising sun, just as they are in Cairo to this day.*

Of those early villages in the region, On appears to have been the most important. Mythology and recorded history suggest that it may have been the locus of a solar cult and a centre of astronomical observation from the earliest times. Though archeological details are scanty, the scientific skill of On's ancient inhabitants has helped some scholars to posit a specific date for the town's beginnings: 19 July 4241 BC. At 4.58 a.m. to be precise – which is to say at the moment when Sirius, that brightest but shyest of stars in the northern heavens, peeked over the dawn horizon at the latitude of On.

What allows such a precise guess is the fact that the

* Sceptics, of course, may note that the modern dead intend to face Mecca, not the sunrise.

astronomers of On appear to have solved one of nature's puzzles far in advance of anyone else. They noticed that while the 'natural' calendar that follows the cycles of the moon makes a year of only 354 days, the solar year is longer. The sun scale was more in tune with the needs of seasonal agriculture (not to mention sun worship), but it was tricky finding a fixed point from which to calculate its year. Stargazers remarked that in the late spring Sirius hid for two and a half moons, then leaped into view in midsummer, just when the river began to overflow its banks. From one rising of Sirius to the next was exactly 365 days, a span that seemed to match the solar cycle. The Egyptians divided this solar year into twelve months of thirty days each, with five extra days for an annual festival.

Having launched their elegant calendar, however, the Egyptians soon found they were losing one day every four years. The trouble was that the earth dawdles maddeningly. It took not the neat 365 days that the astronomers of On expected, but 365¼ for it to revolve around the sun. (Much later, when the Romans decided to adopt the Egyptian calendar, Julius Caesar hired an Alexandrian named Sosigenes to solve this problem. He came up with the idea of leap years. This was clever, but then he bungled the Egyptians' symmetry by juggling the lengths of months into our current irregular terms.) The loss of these quarter-days meant that the Egyptian calendar slipped slowly out of sync. Its New Year fell on the exact same day as the rising of Sirius only in four years out of every 1461 Egyptian years.

From a work called *De Die Matali,* by the second-century Roman writer Censorinus, nineteenth-century scholars knew that one of these exact coincidences took place in about AD 142. Calculating back in time, they surmised that Sirius's rising and the Egyptian New Year had coincided in around 1320, 2780 and 4241 BC. Since the Pyramid Texts, inscribed when these structures were built in the twenty-fifth century BC, showed an already thorough familiarity with the 365-day calendar, the only conclusion to draw was that its use must have begun at the earlier date. The civilization of On, wrote the great American Egyptologist James Henry Breasted a century ago, thus furnishes us with the earliest fixed date in the history of the world.

Egyptology being an inexact science, many of its scholars question this chronology. Their chief quibble is that the calculation of a calendar would have required the use of writing, a skill which does not seem to have developed until a thousand years later.

IN THE FOURTH millennium BC the various city states north and south of On coalesced into two kingdoms. The long, thin realm of Upper Egypt stretched the length of the valley southwards to the furthest navigable reaches of the Nile at Aswan. To the north, the marshy plain of the Delta became the kingdom of Lower Egypt, with On at its southern border. In this murky age the two halves of the country fought a see-saw war. Time and again their armies stomped across the site of modern Cairo – in the footsteps, so to speak, of Seth and Horus. The struggle concluded at last, in about 3100 BC, with the conquest of the Delta by the king of Upper Egypt.

Unification seeded the genius of Egyptian civilization. Royal patronage poured into the arts of peace, not war. More elaborate systems of government required more sophisticated record-keeping, and so spurred the invention of writing. History itself began. Among the first things history recorded was the establishment of a royal capital. In a move of great foresight, Menes, the semi-legendary unifying king and founder of the First Dynasty, chose to build his city at the frontier between the two lands. Rather than picking On, which was on the right bank of the Nile and so exposed to attack from the East, he chose a virgin site twenty miles south-west on the left bank, just upstream from the forking of the Delta. To protect this new city from the Nile's flood waters Menes had it ringed with canals and levees. Battlements surrounded the city, too, giving it its first name, the White Wall – a name which also evoked the royal colour of Upper Egypt.

This city was to endure until the age of Islam, which is to say for three and a half millennia or thirty-four of the forty-six varied dynasties that have ruled Egypt down to the present.* For most of that time it was the commercial and administrative capital, the home of royal palaces and tombs, of coronations and jubilees, of the highest courts of law and of the finest artisans. The White Wall contained the royal treasury and the standard weights and measures of Egypt. It was here that the chief Nilometer for recording the river's rise and fall stood, and where the major garrison and fleet were maintained. With a population which may have surpassed 100,000 during peaks of prosperity, the city's size was unrivalled in the ancient world, at least until the short-lived efflorescence of Mesopotamian Babylon in the seventh century BC.

Six dynasties after Menes the Ancient Egyptian capital adopted its most enduring name, Men-nefer – meaning Lasting and Beautiful.† Much later the Greeks corrupted this to Memphis.

In the thousand-year span of those first six dynasties – the period of Memphis's greatest ascendance – Egyptian civilization blossomed. This era witnessed the elaboration of state administration and court ritual, the establishment of fixed legal practice and religious doctrine. It saw the refinement of skills like shipbuilding, metalworking and the use of stone for sculpture and

*Some historians may dispute the reckoning of forty-six dynasties, insisting that, instead of being categorized as two dynasties, the Roman and Byzantine eras should be divided into more distinct periods – such as the Julio-Claudian, the Flavian etc.

† This epithet seems to have transferred to Memphis as a whole from the name of a Sixth Dynasty pyramid built at Saqqara for the pharaoh Pepi I (*c.* 2250 BC.) The full name for the tomb – and for the adjacent palace and worker settlement that would have thrived during his reign – was Men-nefer-Pepi, meaning The Beauty of Pepi Endures.

building. The conventions of Egyptian art, its proportions and perspective, were set to last until the coming of Christianity. They reached their earliest, and many would say finest, expression in the great pyramids and other tombs and temples of Memphis. So dominant was the capital that the country as a whole became known to the outside world from the name of Memphis's centrepiece, the massive, fifty-acre temple complex of its patron god Ptah. Hut-ka-Ptah, the House of the Ka (or essence) of Ptah, was rendered by the Babylonians as Hikuptah. The Greek ear heard this as Aigiptos, and so, by way of Latin, we reached Egypt.

While Memphis ruled the land, its older twin retained prestige in religion. On's Temple of the Sun was even more richly endowed than that of Ptah. Its priests were renowned for their skill in science and magic. Their version of belief became the dominant doctrine in Egypt, providing the philosophical underpinnings for the pharaohs' divine kingship as well as for conceptions of the afterlife. This is why, when the Hebrews wanted to show how well the biblical Joseph had fared in Egypt, they said he had married none other than the daughter of the high priest of On, Potiphar.* The Greeks, who called On Heliopolis in honour of its sun worship, said that Solon, Pythagoras, Plato and Eudoxus had all studied there. It was they who first acknowledged that it was the priests of Heliopolis who devised the earliest solar calendar.

Ancient conceptions of time were sophisticated indeed. The idea of eternity so preoccupied the Egyptians that their language expressed subtly distinct forms: while *d—t* (the lack of vowels in hieroglyphics renders pronunciation speculative) described absolute changelessness, the term *n—h—h* signified cyclical recurrence. River, sky and desert were eternal, but so in their way were the works of man. Memphis and Heliopolis both shifted their

*Potiphar is most likely a Hebraization of the Egyptian Pa-di-ef-Ra, meaning He Who is Given to (the sun-god) Ra – undoubtedly an appropriate name for a servant of God.

positions by a few miles this way and that, following human fashions as well as the restless snaking of the Nile's banks. Both ultimately faded. Time flattened the Benben mound of On into fields; its agents dismantled the House of the Ka of Ptah and dispersed its priests. But by the measure of *n—h—h* the city or cities here have been unquestionably eternal.

The route from Memphis to Heliopolis, slashing upwards from south-west to north-east, remains the major traffic axis of twentieth-century Cairo. Now, of course, it is diesel barges that ply the Nile, not papyrus skiffs and long-nosed gondolas of Phoenician cedar.* Six-lane highways flank the river. No fewer than ten major bridges cross its 500-yard width at Cairo. Near ancient Heliopolis jets swoop into the busiest airport in the Middle East. On the pyramid-studded desert plateaus of Giza and Saqqara overlooking the site of Memphis, tour buses disgorge thousands of visitors a day. In between the two ancient cities, all across the plain of Kher'aha and beyond, surges a sea of humanity 12-million strong. Having endured 5,000 recorded years under 500 rulers, Cairo remains the greatest metropolis in its quadrant of the globe.

TALL BUILDINGS ARE no novelty to Cairo. Its loftiest medieval minarets are 250 feet high, and even the apartment houses of a thousand years ago were commonly seven or, by one account, up to fourteeen storeys tall. Skyscrapers by the Nile now rise to three or four times that height – which is to say to about the same height as the taller pyramids just down the road at Giza. Like those impressive forebears, they offer tremendous views – but are accessible by elevator rather than by a steep, perilous and indeed illegal clamber over weathered stone.

* Such as the gorgeous, 140-foot barque intended for the pharaoh Cheops's journeys in the afterlife. This oldest boat in the world is preserved intact in a museum by his pyramid at Giza.

Yet the classic panorama of Cairo remains the one that enchanted Orientalist painters a century ago. On smogless days the vista from the esplanade at the Citadel, Cairo's mammoth crusader-era fortress, is stunning. It is from here that centuries of rulers surveyed the city at their feet (and occasionally, in times of trouble, from where they fired cannonshots to subdue its unruly people). But the view encompasses more than the buildings and streets of today's city. It embraces the sweep of time itself.

Far to the west across the visible sliver of Nile a dense, toothy jumble of yellowed apartment blocks recedes almost to the horizon. That horizon is the Sahara, whose empty immensity stretches 3,000 miles from here to the Atlantic. But then there, on the desert escarpment ten miles away, looms a peculiar shape: a neat triangle. It is the Great Pyramid of Cheops at Giza, erected in 2550 BC. And off to its left, past a brood of forty-storey modern colossi in the southern suburbs, you can just make out the ridges of the even more ancient Step Pyramid at Saqqara, which is said to be the oldest free-standing man-made structure in the world. In fact the whole soft line of desert where the sun will set, between Giza and Saqqara and for miles on either side, is a sawtooth sierra of ancient tombs, among them scores of lesser pyramids. For two and a half millennia it served as the graveyard of Memphis's kings and nobles.

Of the pharaonic capital itself, nothing can be seen from this vantage but a dusty carpet of palmtops down in the valley below the Step Pyramid. The date groves enfold the few stubs and chunks of Memphis that have not subsided into the quicksilt of the valley floor. And even these scant remains threaten to vanish now, not into the ground but under the brick and reinforced concrete of expanding Cairo.

Closer at hand – only two miles from the Citadel – a long, deep range of tall buildings bounds the course of the Nile through the city. These are the chain hotels, government ministries and offices and luxury apartments that cluster in the modern city centre. When Memphis still flourished this now costly land was largely under water, but the Nile has furrowed new channels since then, pushed and pulled by the build-up of silt. Perhaps as recently as 2,000 years ago it divided here into the two main branches of the Delta; that divide is now fifteen miles further north. Nearer our times the river spilled over much of this terrain in the flood season, making it unsuitable for building. The stabilizing of the river banks at the end of the nineteenth century coincided with Cairo's emergence from medieval isolation. The subsequent boom transformed this part of town into a zone of carriage roads and elegant Italianate villas. But the city has again mutated. The roads are traffic-clogged, the villas largely replaced by apartment blocks that run the gamut of twentieth-century style, from *beaux arts* to high art deco to futurist and Stalinist and brute-faced steel and glass.

Along the Nile to the left, the scale of buildings diminishes until we reach a curiously barren spot, a flat plain studded with greying mounds, with here and there a wisp of smoke. This scarred ground is the likely site of the battle of Seth and Horus. But these dung heaps smother other battlegrounds, as well as vestiges of a city which was yet another of Cairo's illustrious forbears. As Memphis declined, this city grew first as a Roman and later as a Byzantine garrison town. When Muslim warriors surged out of Arabia in AD 640, it was the fall of this fortress after seven months' siege that clinched their conquest of Egypt. The Caliph's governors made this place, which they called Misr al-Fustat, the seat of their rule.* They apportioned encampments

* They called the town Misr al-Fustat to distinguish it from Misr al-Qadima, or Old Misr, which was then the name given to fading Memphis. Misr was the ancient Semitic term for Egypt; hence this new capital, like Memphis, shared its name with the country as a whole. Fustat was most probably an Arabization of the Greek *fossaton*, meaning a moat, perhaps because the Arab army had camped 'beyond the moat' of the Byzantine fortress.

for each tribe in the victorious Arab army, and within a century a great city had grown up here – a city which would soon overshadow all others in the realm of Islam.

A thousand years ago the Persian geographer Hudud al-Alam described Misr al-Fustat as the wealthiest city in the world. An Arab contemporary, the Jerusalemite al-Muqaddasi, said that its citizens thronged as thick as locusts. As centuries passed, however, the rich and powerful sought more spacious quarters further north in the open plain stretching towards the ruins of ancient On. By the time Columbus sailed for the Indies – hoping, like his Portuguese competitors, to find a new route to the east and thus break the spice monopoly of the sultans who reigned from this very Citadel – Misr al-Fustat was nothing but a rubbish tip for the great and prosperous city of Cairo.

Turning right to follow this migration of fortunes, we come to the scene closest at hand. This is the fabled medieval Cairo of bazaars and domes, and of minarets: the stubby spiral at the ninth-century Mosque of Ahmad Ibn Tulun, the elegant tiers of Sultan Hasan's fourteenth-century *madrasa*, the sharp, pencil-pointed towers of the Ottoman period, the twin bulbs atop Bab Zuwayla – the eleventh-century gate where long ago the heads of criminals were hung and a troll was said to lurk behind the massive door. Or rather what we see here is what is left of the medieval city. Splendid mosques and palaces survive by the dozen, evoking the long summer from the tenth to the sixteenth centuries when Cairo was the biggest and richest city west of India.* But every month a high-rise sprouts to block the view, or else another quaint old house tumbles down on top of its inhabitants.

So we come to the north, where the valley opens out as if under the press of people and the full scale of Cairo, still the

*Constantinople, seat of the Byzantine emperors, continued to outshine Cairo for some time, but its star waned rapidly after the crusaders betrayed and sacked the city in AD 1203 and 1204.

largest city of Islam, of Africa, of the Mediterranean world, becomes clear. Here the metropolis sprawls a good twenty miles, swamping ancient On and its forlorn remaining obelisk, filling suburbs like working-class Shubra and the prosperous new Heliopolis, each of which holds more people than the capital city of any nearby country. Far away, barely visible at the cutting edge of this urban juggernaut, tower blocks stride out into the sand and factories devour the precious black soil of the Delta.

NATIVE CAIRENES TEND to leave such monumental views to tourists. In a sense they have to. The all-devouring nature of today's megacity militates against reflection, against long perspectives in either time or space. The dimensions that frame life here are far narrower.

Cairo is, according to the United Nations, the most densely populated large urban area in the world. Overall, this city packs 70,000 people into each of its 200 square miles, confining its citizens more tightly than does the bristling little island of Manhattan. In central districts like Muski and Bab al-Shaʿriyya the density is 300,000 per square mile, a figure that soars in some back streets to a crushing 700,000. By and large these numbers throng not tower blocks but alleyfuls of low-rise tenements that differ little from the housing stock of, say, a thousand years ago. In such conditions, with three and sometimes five people to a tiny room, families take turns to eat and sleep. Schools operate in up to three shifts, and still have to squeeze fifty, sixty or sometimes eighty students to a class.

The pressure of people touches every aspect of life in Cairo. It drives the price of land as high as $500 a square foot, making millionaires out of speculators while stifling youthful dreams of independence. It overburdens public services and so litters thoroughfares with uncollected waste, but it also limits crime by cluttering getaway routes. Crowds draw in business, creating a rich and varied market that generates money to embellish the city with the facilities and monuments which sustain its sense of greatness. But they force compromises: to relieve traffic, concrete flyovers brush past medieval walls; to provide housing, apartment buildings supplant gardens.

Crowding squeezes Cairenes out of their homes. But where to go? There are precious few green spaces. Until a recent crash programme the city had only five square inches of parkland per inhabitant, which is to say less than the area covered by the sole of one adult foot. Rather than standing like flamingos, Cairenes take to the streets. They turn sidewalks and roadways into zones of commerce and entertainment, converting them piecemeal into playgrounds and restaurants and open-air mosques. The street is where some 40,000 homeless children sleep, and where all the people of Cairo engage in combat with the city's million motor vehicles and 5,000 donkey carts.

Combined with the dust that blows ceaselessly off the desert, heavy use gives the city a cosy patina of age. It burnishes knobs and handrails to a greasy smoothness, cracks tiles into shards, and tints walls to a uniform dun colour that ignites into gold in the soft, slanting light of late afternoon. Sidewalks buckle under the weight of feet. Staircases in grand *beaux arts* buildings sag, their marble steps eroded into slippery hollows. Advertising tattoos every surface with Arabic's elegant squiggle. Neon spangles rooftops, mingling with antennae and the upturned domes of satellite dishes.

The air itself is saturated with the things of man. Deep-frying oil and fresh mint overlie the musk of freshly slaked dust and the sweat of transpired fenugreek that is so cloying it sticks to paper money. The human urge to be noticed floods the whole sound spectrum with noise, from *'Allahu Akbar'* blasting off every mosque megaphone to insults hurled from the other end of the Arabic alphabet. The noonday din at one Cairo intersection is a rock-concert-equivalent ninety decibels. No wonder. The average car is fifteen years old, and ill-tuned. Drivers honk with tic-like compulsion, as if to refrain from doing so would stop the world from turning. Everyday chit-chat is partaken in bellows and guffaws, punctuated by backslaps and riddled with the witty repartee for which Cairo's earthy argot is a perfect medium.

If voices are worn, so are faces. Statues in the Egyptian Museum from the Old Kingdom (2600–2180 BC) often appear like close cousins of the commuters milling at Cairo's central bus station, just outside the museum's heavy iron gates. But while the exquisitely sculpted pharaohs and scribes have a smooth-browed solemnity, the bus fares bear a weathered look – a look that tells of hardship endured with patience, of dreams unrealized. Cairenes age early. Indeed, many an adolesence is spent labouring in cramped workshops. (The figure is 16 per cent of children aged from six to fourteen, which makes perhaps 300,000 child labourers in the city.) Many adulthoods expire in the drudgery of juggling two or three jobs to get by.

Yet the preponderance of careworn expressions and the resigned unhurriedness of the crowd belie another aspect of Cairo's people. Perhaps because so many have been poor for so many generations, they are quick to seize any chance of diversion. Jokes form a kind of currency, such that a wisecrack from the most importunate beggar may bring instant reward. The jibes can be cruel, but more often are not. In fact few cities are so relaxed, so accommodating, so disdainful of merely impersonal relations. Loneliness, that bane of city life in the West, is almost unknown.

The crowding makes for noise and stress, pollution and social tension. The carnival atmosphere can be grating if you are not in the mood. Cairenes themselves complain. Yet secretly, complicitously, they are by and large addicted to living cheek by jowl with a never-ending spectacle. Meet an exile in some far corner of the world – which typically will be one of those spotless towns, say

Vancouver or Frankfurt, that attracts Cairene deserters by sheer oppositeness – and the first thing you will hear is that compared to home, it is *bland*. 'These streets are so empty,' whined a chain-smoking Egyptian woman I met in sleepy, well-ordered Tunis. 'And they're full of...' she winced, releasing a little puff of indignation, 'trees!'

This explains why the Cairene idea of a holiday is not to escape from the throng, but to take it with you. On Muslim feasts day-trippers mob the double-decked steamboats that churn downstream to the park at the Nile Barrage, where the river forks into the Delta. Before the ships have even slipped their dock in the centre of the city, boom boxes are cranked up. Scarves are slung around hips. The clapping starts, and for the whole hour-long journey revellers belly dance in a spontaneous combustion of fun.

The fact is, this city that is so astoundingly old is also surprisingly young. In the past century its population has swollen by a factor of twenty-five. Crowding is twice what it was in 1950. It is three times the level of 1920, when the city housed barely a million people. A third of Cairenes are under the age of fifteen. Few remember the statelier ways of a mere generation ago, let alone give more than a passing shrug for ancient glories. Except, that is, when it comes to investing the aura of the pharaohs to prime the lucrative curiosity of foreign tourists.

ASIDE FROM THE odd New-Ager enraptured by obelisks, nobody in Cairo believes any more that life began here. Other creation theories are current – Islamic ones for the vast majority, biblical ones for the six in a hundred Cairenes who are Christian*; and even, though rarely, secular ideas like evolution and the Big Bang.

*Most of Egypt's Christians belong to the Coptic Orthodox Church – whose name, like Egypt's, stems from the old name for Memphis, Hikaptah, House of the Ka of Ptah.

But if Cairo is no longer perceived as the actual site of Creation, it is still, to its people, very much the centre of things.

In Egypt, all roads lead to the capital – which is logical since nearly half the country's cars and half its industry are here. One in four Egyptians lives in Greater Cairo, and many more aspire to. They have sound reason. Cairenes live longer and eat better than their country cousins. Income per person is 25 per cent higher, the proportion of poor 30 per cent lower, and only a third as many children under the age of five die of disease. In impoverished Upper Egypt the literacy rate is only half of Cairo's. There are no Egyptian daily newspapers outside Cairo, and the score of dailies printed here devote scant space on their innermost pages to all that happens elsewhere in the country. Even in sports Cairo reigns supreme. Its Ahli and Zamalek clubs have monopolized Egypt's national soccer championship for all but two of the last fifty years.

After 5,000 years of civilization, Egypt's political system remains pyramid-shaped. Cairo sits indomitably at the pinnacle. Its Ministry of Irrigation decides which farmer gets how much water for his crops. Its Ministry of Religious Affairs chooses who is to deliver sermons in which mosques, and what they are to say. Its Ministry of the Interior picks the mayors for all Egypt's 4,000 villages. The president, who resides here, appoints the governors of all twenty-six provinces and the heads of all twelve national universities, four of which, naturally, are in Cairo.

Until the last century all farmland in Egypt belonged in theory to the country's rulers. The lion's share of profit from the world's richest land was sucked into the capital. Even today, although farmland is nearly all privately owned, the state retains title to the 96 per cent of Egypt which is desert. The decisions about what to do with this vast holding – whether, say, to sell it to investors or to hand it out to cronies of the ruling party – are largely made by the civil servants of Cairo's 2-million-strong bureaucracy.

The city's dominance echoes in the language itself. Misr – the word derived from the same roots as the biblical *Mizraim*, or Egyptians – is still the common Arabic name for the city. And just as Memphis was once confused with Egypt as a whole, to this day the name for Egypt in Arabic, Hebrew, Turkish, Persian, Urdu or Hindi is also Misr.

Nor does the sway of Cairo end at Egypt's borders. To 250 million Arabic speakers and I billion Muslims, Cairo retains a mystique, a stature, a reassuring gravity that no other city can match. Sure, the imported symbols of New World monoculture flourish here: brand-burger fast-food outlets, discos, theme parks and the rest. But, unlike many Third World capitals, Cairo has the depth to generate its own fashions. It projects its own rhythms and language far and wide. The cassette-tape call to prayer wafting over a Javanese village was most likely recorded by one of the honey-tongued Koran reciters of Cairo. The music pulsing through the heat of a Moroccan Kasbah came from here, too, as did the satellite-borne soap opera enthralling a Kuwaiti financier's air-conditioned harem.

When Arabs think of Cairo, they think of it as a repository of Arabness: the seat of the greatest universities, the largest libraries, the biggest-circulation newspapers, the most vibrant pop culture – and even of the busiest camel market in the Arab world. The million Arab tourists who come every year rarely bother with Cairo's antiquities. They head instead to theatres, to cinemas and literary watering holes, to swank gambling casinos and glitzy nightclubs. They go to cafés to soak up the sound of Cairene slang and eavesdrop on the latest jokes. They flock to concert halls for the toniest in classical Oriental music, and swarm street kiosks blaring the sassiest Arabic rap. They come because, worn as she is, Cairo still draws the best talent in Arab arts.

As a minor example, take belly dancing (or, as practitioners prefer to call it, Oriental Dance). A quick survey of Cairo night-spots finds performers of a dozen nationalities: Lucy at the

Parisiana, Katya at the Andalus, Suzy and Yasmina at the Versailles, Bushra at Casino al-Mawʿad (which translates as The Rendezvous) to name a few. Among these tinselled, gyrating houris are Russians, Americans, Lebanese, Germans, Tunisians and even the occasional Israeli star. Of course the native dancers claim that no one can feel the music like they can. The foreigners are too skinny, not generous enough in shoulders and hips. Their studied technique lacks the effortless control that makes or breaks a star. Nor does anyone, yet, make the money that top Egyptian performers do. Such sums rise to a reputed $10,000 a night – enough to pay the annual wages of ten traffic cops, and another reason why Cairo is the undisputed belly-dancing capital of the world.

Glitter of a different kind draws another sort of fan. All the fabulous treasure of Tutankhamun – including among other things in solid gold the young king's sandals and toe- and finger-caps, his sceptre, face mask and coffin – comprises a minor fraction of the 100,000-odd objects displayed at the Egyptian Museum. The jewellery of Queen Weret, unearthed just south of Cairo in 1994, looks sparkling new after 3,700 years underground. Her anklets – in alternating bands of coral-coloured carnelian, sea-blue lapis lazuli and sky-blue turquoise clasped with gold in the form of cowrie shells and lions – evoke the exquisite taste of the court at Memphis. But Weret's funeral trousseau, complete with a purple amethyst the size of a soap bar, must compete with dozens of other cases overflowing with jewellery from the royal tombs of Saqqara, Giza, Abydos and Tanis. Room after room of sculpture in granite, porphyry, diorite and marble gives the lie to claims that Ancient Egyptian art is formulaic or dull. A lonely-looking statue of an Assyrian king, brought by invaders of the eighth century BC, only highlights the talent of the Egyptians. Its crude proportions project brute force, whereas the Egyptian statuary all around seeks to inspire not fear but respect for wisdom and refinement. Old Kingdom reliefs of dancing girls and pleasure excursions under the influence of wine and the narcotic lotus make one wonder whether man's subsequent 5,000 years of travails have produced any advance in the quality of life.

Even small items of everyday use show a brilliant simplicity of design. Among the oldest objects are flawless drinking vessels bored out of the hardest stones. A delicate pair of sandals woven from palm fibres echoes the sleek curves of the 4,700-year-old solar boat housed a few miles away by the Great Pyramid at Giza. A toy bird carved from wood in 600 BC is, uncannily, shaped like a jumbo jet, down to its aerodynamic wing-tips. The funerary portrait of a wealthy Memphite matron of the second century AD, complete with earrings, necklace and elegant coiffure, is the very picture of a Cairene society hostess in the 1930s.

So it comes as little surprise that the lure of Cairo is almost as old as the place itself.

The poets of Ancient Egypt waxed at length on the charms of their capital. In one papyrus a traveller dreams of the city as he floats downstream to meet his beloved. The river is wine, he says, and Memphis a chalice of fruits set before Ptah, the God Who is Beautiful of Face. 'The like of Memphis has never been seen,' declares a text from the New Kingdom (1565–1085 BC). It goes on to extoll the city's full granaries, its pleasure lakes dappled with blossoming lotus, and its confident community of foreign merchants. The scribe enthuses over the amusements on offer at Memphis, such as a show of lady wrestlers or the sight of noblewomen relaxing in their gardens.

The *Thousand and One Nights,* that ancient kaleidoscope of stories within stories, also singles out this city for praise (perhaps understandably, because, though the work evolved out of Indian and Persian originals, much of it was composed here during Cairo's medieval heyday). In one tale, a Jewish physician treats a man in Damascus who relates the story of his life. The narrator describes how as a youth, in the great mosque of Mosul on the banks of the faraway Tigris, he listened entranced to his father and uncles talking after Friday prayers. They sat in a circle, he relates, enumerating the marvels of distant lands. Then one of his uncles said, 'Travellers tell that there is nothing on the face of the earth fairer than Cairo.' And his father added, 'He who has not seen Cairo has not seen the world. Its dust is gold; its Nile is a wonder; its women are like the black-eyed virgins of paradise; its houses are palaces; its air is temperate; its odour surpassing that of aloes-wood, and cheering the heart: and how could Cairo be otherwise, when she is the Mother of the World?'

After hearing this description, the storyteller says, he passed the night sleepless with longing. As soon as he came of age he travelled abroad with his merchant uncles; as soon as he could he slipped their caravan and ran off to Cairo. And that was the beginning of his story.

CHAPTER TWO

Dead Cities

Egypt shall gather them up, Memphis shall bury them.

Hosea 9:6

These people regard the span of life as a very short time and of little importance, and instead devote themselves to the long memory bequeathed by virtue. This is why they call the houses of the living mere hostels for brief sojourn, but give the name of eternal abodes to the tombs of the dead.

Diodorus Siculus, *The Library of History*, first century BC

THE NILE IS a well-mannered river. It flows out of Africa at a stately but firm three miles per hour. Nine days out of ten a countervailing wind blows down from the Mediterranean. The arrangement might have been designed expressly for pleasure cruising in the low-slung, lateen-rigged feluccas that can be hired by the hour along the Cairo Corniche. The current tugs them downstream. The wind, which in springtime brings a whiff of Delta orange blossom into the city, tows them back. This soft Nile breeze is so reliable that the Egyptians' hieroglyph for travelling south or north simply pictures a boat with its sails full or furled.

But sometimes – in April especially – the wind changes

ominously. Brewing up from east or west, it sweeps the desert blustering into the city. Stifling hot and teased with whirlwinds, the sandstorms counterpoint the river, serving to remind Cairo that even as the water of life flows through its centre, death lurks at the edges of the valley. Cairenes need reminding. The city's ceaseless urban racket casts an amnesiac spell. It is easy to forget how close the utter empty silence of the desert lies.

FOR FOURTEEN CENTURIES the district of al-Khalifa has marked the city's meeting with the desert. Half tumbledown houses, half tombs, al-Khalifa nestles between the towering walls of the Citadel and the grander natural bastion of the Muqattam, the 650-foot-high desert cliff that closes in the valley from the east. The district is known for its many famous graves, for its prison and its colourful criminals, and for the even more colourful comic parade – complete with transvestites and parodies of politicians – thrown together every year in honour of one of the Prophet's great-granddaughters, who is buried here.

It is also known for its Friday street markets. One of these, Cairo's chief emporium for pets and exotic animals, stretches along a shambling track that forks towards the Muqattam cliffs. The commerce begins with creepy sea creatures – tubfuls of scrabbling, antennae-wagging lobsters and crayfish, whose keepers shout their Arabic names: '*Gambaree! Istakooza! Istakooza hayyaa!*' The crowd quickly thickens. Soon small boys thrust out liquid-filled plastic bags, out of which peer lazily curious tropical fish. Glass-walled tanks parked in the roadside dust restrain dense coils of land snakes and water snakes and frogs and lizards. A tiny green chameleon hangs by its tail from a black-cowled crone's little finger, its two-toed feet groping daintily at the thin air. Stacked nearby are a caged mongoose, a weasel, hamsters and a pansy-like bouquet of Siamese kittens. Next door an angry monkey rattles its chain. Feathered creatures follow: Congolese parrots in party colours, trays of squeaky orange fuzzballs that are day-old chicks, parakeets, mynah birds, and a bevy of hawks crammed all together and lunching on scraps of raw, crimson meat. Next to them a spook; a giant and scruffy old stuffed owl that is missing one ear. But suddenly a fearsome eyelid flips open and glares contempt. A small girl screams.

Dogs of every breed yap and whimper. The birds chirp and coo, the cats miaow, a donkey hee-haws lusty indignation, and the seething crush of people, excited by all the animal frenzy, haggles and cajoles and backslaps with almost demonic vigour. A motorcyclist cleaves wildly through it all, looking like the devil himself in a leather balaclava helmet, revving and tooting his horn. An occasional sonic boom shifts the dust and shoots free pigeons into flight; it is from the nearby quarries blasting ever deeper into the limestone cliffs.

Over all the mad music there echoes a persistent rapping, chipping noise. This steady percussion seems to beckon from an alleyway leading uphill, away from the crowd and towards the cliffs. A dozen steps away from the market an eerie quiet falls, as if someone has flicked a switch and extinguished Inferno. The alley opens on to a bright desert of ochre walls, rubble and yellowing tombs. A spent syringe lies on the ground beside a fallen headstone. Far up above, clapped against the cliff face like a lunatic prince's sandcastle, the long-abandoned monastery of a heretical dervish order glowers.

The only sound now is the rhythmic chinking noise. It grows louder and the rhythms link, run in unison, and then separate again. A feral cat saunters through a gap in a wall where someone has daubed 'God is Great' in blue paint. It wanders into a wide yard littered with lumps of stone. On the far side three figures armed with hammers and chisels chop at a great coffin-sized hunk of rock.

This scene of primitive industry is absorbing – evocative like a distant echo of the very beginnings of the city. How many millions of times, one can only wonder, have men like these gone through the same simple motions – positioning the wedge, swinging the mallet, dragging and levering heavy blocks of limestone – at this very spot? After all, the many Cairos have not once paused from cutting away at the quarries that edge the foot of the Muqattam, not since the ancients learned to carve out their stone; to shape it and haul it off to build walls and temples and above all tombs, those innumerable monuments to the dead of all ages which enshrine the memory of the many cities that have risen, flourished and fallen here down to our own times.

THE QUARRYING BEGAN 5,000 years ago, soon after the unifying pharaoh Menes founded the city of Memphis just across the river from here. By the time of the Third Dynasty, four centuries later, the limestone of these cliffs had become the building material of choice; when anything was made to last, it had to be in stone. The other primal element at hand – the creamy silt deposited by the Nile – went into the making of bricks, the use of which was relegated for ever after to ephemeral things like houses.

This is one reason why little is left of Cairo's earliest forebears. Rain and time and the annual Nile flood have simply washed the brick dwellings of Memphis and Heliopolis away. What survive are what the ancient Egyptians called The Castles of Eternity: the stone sepulchres of kings and nobles. Their greatest splendour is to be seen on the opposite side of the valley from the Muqattam, along the desert rim west of Memphis where the sun sets. There above the flood plain lies the sandy realm of Sokar, Memphis's guardian god of tombs. His memory lingers in the modern name of Saqqara, the site which marks the centre of the sprawling, fifty-mile-long cemetery which grew, over the 3,500-year lifespan of Memphis, into the most immense necropolis the world has ever known; and which remains today an inexhaustible archaeological mother-lode.

The people of Memphis rated stonemasonry as important an invention as writing – so important that they ended by turning their first builder in stone, the Third Dynasty minister Imhotep, into a god.* Imhotep deserved the kudos. An inscription found at Saqqara ascribed an impressive list of titles to him: Chancellor of the King of Lower Egypt, Second to the King of Upper Egypt,† Administrator of the Great Palace, Hereditary Lord, High Priest of Heliopolis, Builder, Sculptor. But the proof of Imhotep's genius was not just scratched in stone. It was fixed in eternity, for this was the man who built the first pyramid.

Before Imhotep, the grandest of the pharaohs' tombs were massive, ingot-shaped bunkers made of brick. Already they expressed a concern with eternity, but Imhotep's patron, the pharaoh Zoser (*c.* 2670–2650 BC), demanded something more comfortable for his afterlife. He wanted a monument that would not merely endure but would also tower over Memphis and encapsulate the glory of his kingship. Imhotep's inspiration was to build a standard tomb, but square at the base and cased in white limestone, and then to pile on top no less than five more, of diminishing size, to the dizzy height of 200 feet. This innovation achieved nothing less than a monumental linking of worship for the sun-god Ra – whose cult had largely superseded that of the creator god Atum at Heliopolis – with veneration of the ruler. The pyramid was both the pharaoh's staircase to the sky and a colossal image of the sun's rays fanning on the horizon.

On a clear day the six massive storeys of Zoser's Step Pyramid can still be seen from twenty-five miles away. Closer inspection

* Full deification did not come until the waning of Ancient Egypt under the Greek-speaking Ptolemaic Dynasty (323–30 BC). The Greeks associated Imhotep with Asklepios, their god of healing.

† The pharaohs of unified Egypt retained separate titles to the former independent kingdoms. The ruler himself embodied their union by wearing the emblems of both Upper and Lower Egypt, and by symbolically reuniting the country in jubilee festivals held at Saqqara.

reveals that nearly all the original stone casing has gone. But if Imhotep's masterpiece is worn, careful reconstruction has brought back some fine details in the vast surrounding compound he built. Vestiges of the limestone enclosing walls – they frame an area the size of twelve Manhattan city blocks – have convinced archaeologists that Imhotep playfully meant them to echo the White Wall of the city of Memphis down below. Similarly, inside the jubilee court by the pyramid itself, the row of graceful chapels he built recreate in stone the varied building techniques of different parts of Egypt: here a limestone column looks like bundled reeds; there a ceiling evokes palm logs laid side by side. And beyond the jubilee court where Zoser and his successors ritually reunified Upper and Lower Egypt by tying lotus and papyrus reeds around a stake, beyond the high stone walls crenellated with cobra heads, spread acre upon desert acre of smaller pyramids and untold numbers of lesser tombs, many of which remain undiscovered – including Imhotep's own.

Refinements followed quickly on Imhotep's triumph, such that within a century the greatest pyramid builder of all time, the fourth Dynasty pharaoh Seneferu (2575–2551 BC), was raising multiple pyramids that were both bigger and sleeker in profile. Seneferu ordered no fewer than four of them: one at Meidum, thirty-seven miles upriver from Zoser's tomb, a small one at Seila a little further on, and two big beauties at Dahshur, just south of Saqqara, where they could also be admired with ease from the palace at Memphis. Seneferu's determination to get it right demanded the shifting of some 9 million tons of stone, with no wheels and no pulleys yet invented to ease the load. His efforts were not entirely successful. The outer limestone casing at Meidum collapsed, exposing the stubby tower of the core. His first attempt at Dahshur was also too ambitious. Halfway through construction the foundations began to crack, so the angle of its slope was abruptly dropped from sixty to forty-three degrees, creating a neatly bent shape that may appear daring and attractive to the modern eye but apparently failed to satisfy the pharaoh. Chastened by failure, Seneferu's workers played it safe on their last try at Dahshur. His final pyramid rises to its height of 340 feet at the gentlest of angles.

All this back-breaking practice was put to good use by Seneferu's son Cheops (more accurately pronounced Khufu, but the Greek version, Cheops, is more familar). This pharaoh chose a new and even more spectacular site for his tomb. His pyramid on the plateau of Giza, just north of Saqqara, was to be the biggest, the most perfect, the most incontestable proof of the magnificence of the court of Memphis. Imagine the builders' panic when they heard the contract specifications: stack 2.3 million stone blocks of an average weight of 2.5 tons to a height of 480 feet upon a thirteen-acre base whose squareness and levelness must be accurate to within a thumb's width. The sides must slope at an exact 51° 52′ to a precisely centred point. Carefully encase the whole in a smooth sheath of finest white Muqattam limestone such that joints several yards long are invisible, or at any rate not thicker than a sheet of papyrus. Bury me inside. Let visitors to the plateau of Giza admire our might, our skill, our faith in our gods, until the end of time. And let them ponder how this Great Pyramid was made.

There has been no shortage of pondering ever since, and still no modern engineer has tabled a leak-proof explanation of how such a man-made mountain could be built in the thirty years of Cheops's reign – which is to say, at a pace of one mammoth stone block put in place every two minutes (not to mention the fact that at least seventeen other pyramids of varying size were erected during the Fourth Dynasty's brief century-and-a-quarter span). Some Egyptologists suggest that the scope of the project was so huge, the task of mobilizing men and *matériel* for it so challenging, that the building of Cheops's pyramid must have greatly strengthened the centralized bureaucracy that made Egypt the most enduring of ancient states.

The Greek historian Herodotus, who stopped at Giza 2,000 years later, says that the priests of Heliopolis told him Cheops was an appalling tyrant who had driven 100,000 men to labour at the task. Modern scholars say such a number of workmen was possible, but probably only a third as many were required full-time. Moreover, apart from some Middle Kingdom (2050–1780 BC) texts that speak of Cheops as bloodthirsty, there is little to indicate that the workers endured particular hardship. Many were probably recruited during the annual flood, when the farmers' fields were under water anyway. In that season the Nile brimmed to the edge of the desert, allowing ships to carry stone clear across to Giza from the Muqattam quarries. A permanent staff of skilled craftsmen – some 4,000 of them – were housed in a specially built village just next to the site, and were probably decently fed and paid. Even Herodotus admits that the recorded outlay on the workers' radish, onion and garlic rations alone was some 1,600 talents or 9,600,000 silver drachmas.

Furthermore, dragging mammoth stone blocks is evidently not as hard as one might think. An archaeologist's experiment with a replica sledge has shown that six men can easily pull a six-ton rock over level ground. Uphill would be more difficult, but then much of the undressed stone for the pyramid's interior structure came from the nearby desert, not from the Muqattam cliffs across the river. As for the quarrymen who did work these cliffs for the pyramid's outer casing, their graffiti bear no suggestion of excessive hardship. Scrawled in red ochre on numerous blocks, the quarry marks are simply proud advertisements not unlike some modern brickmaker's identifying stamp. One of them reads, 'The Craftsmen-gang. How powerful is the white Crown of Cheops!' Perhaps these stonecutters were hoping that praise for the king would earn them an extra radish or two. But what, then, of 'The Drunkards of Mycerinus' – the name of a work crew associated with the builder of the third great pyramid at Giza?

Relying on his priestly informants, Herodotus had no evidence to dispute their stories of Cheops's legendary wickedness. The Greek was told, for instance, that Cheops was so greedy he sold his daughter's sexual favours. Her pyramid – the middle of three baby ones that stand next to her father's – was said to have been built with the proceeds of her whoring, the payment being a one-ton rock for every trick. Moreover, both Cheops and his successor, Chephren – builder of the second of Giza's three colossal pyramids – had themselves buried secretly elsewhere, for fear that their wrathful subjects would never let them rest in their graves.

Like tourists of all ages, Herodotus was duped by glib native guides, who in this case did not care to admit that their ancestors' tombs had long since been plundered, which was why the pyramids were empty. But even Herodotus scorned to believe the tale related by another credulous ancient, the geographer Strabo. Touring Giza in 24 BC, this citizen of Rome was told that the smallest of the three main pyramids – which archaeologists attribute to Cheops's grandson Mycerinus – was in fact a monument to a Greek courtesan named Rhodopis. This lady of many charms, he explained, was the mistress of Charaxus, a rich Greek wine dealer in the Egyptian city of Naucratis who also happened to be the brother of the poetess Sappho. When Rhodopis was bathing in the Nile one day an eagle snatched one of her sandals, carried it to Memphis, and dropped it square into the pharaoh's lap. 'Struck by the shape of the sandal and the singularity of the accident,' continued Strabo, 'the king sent over the country to discover the woman to whom it belonged. She was found and brought to him, and he made her his wife. At her death she was honoured with the above-mentioned tomb.'

These tales – the last of which clearly presages that of Cinderella – represent just a very few links in the chain of pyramid fable that has entertained Cairenes right down to the present. The early Christians declared that the structures were not tombs but rather the granaries of Joseph, raised by the Biblical dream-reader to spare Egypt from famine. Jews have asserted it was *their* ancestors who laboured at the pyramids, before Moses released them from slavery.* Medieval Muslims said it was the ancient prophet Idris who built them, to preserve all knowledge from the Flood (Idris being identified with both the biblical Enoch and the Greek Hermes, who in turn was linked to the Ancient Egyptian god of wisdom, Thoth). A thirteenth-century Arab treatise attributed miraculous powers to the Great Pyramid of Cheops, so that an adulterous couple who dared to profane its inner chambers were 'Cast along the ground, and dyed in a Phrensie' (as a seventeenth-century English translator phrased it). Modern fantasists have claimed the structures are giant water pumps, or observatories, or radios to receive the wisdom of outer space. And so the pyramids have continued to fulfil their purpose, being stairways to every changing conception of heaven.

A MILLENNIUM AFTER Cheops, quarrymen still chiselled at the face of the Muqattam. The stone-built tombs of Memphis's nobles remained sumptuous. The detailed scenes of daily life preserved by the shallow relief carvings on their walls, though not as perfect as the Old Kingdom reliefs nearby which depict the workshops and pleasure gardens of Memphis with cartoon-like clarity and humour, have amazed generations of visitors to Saqqara. Together they formed one of the most complete pictorial records of any civilization in history. But grand pyramids had fallen out of fashion. Try as they might by adding sphinxes and layers of pink granite and other flourishes, no one could top Cheops. It may have been that the kings no longer wielded such absolute sway; that they could not summon and supply 100,000-

*Most historians believe that the Hebrews only appeared in Egypt 1,200 years later, when they may have worked to build a city in the Eastern Delta for the Nineteenth Dynasty pharaoh Ramses II.

strong armies of workers. It was also true that in the interim the priests of Memphis and Heliopolis had learned a trick or two, and now claimed that a few correctly inscribed spells could do the work of a pyramid in terms of allowing the soul to commune with the gods.

At a time when the finishing touches were just being put to Stonehenge, Egypt and Memphis's fortunes had already fallen and risen again, and still Muqattam limestone was in great demand. Ahmose, the founder of the Eighteenth Dynasty [1570–1320 BC], reunited a country reeling from foreign invasion and two centuries of unrest. In restoring the temple of the capital city's patron god, Ptah, he had this inscription carved at a quarry just south of al-Khalifa:

> His Majesty gave the order to open the rock chambers anew and to cut out thence the best white stone of the hill country for the houses of the gods, whose existence is for endless years, for the house of the divine Ptah at Memphis.

Jump forward a millennium or two. Rome has long since fallen. Europe wallows in its Dark Ages. Memphis is forgotten, but the temples of the mighty new city of Cairo – angled south-east to Mecca now and not towards the rising sun – are still being built of Muqattam limestone. So are the walls and towers of the Citadel, by the hand of thousands of captured Christian crusaders. And so are the splendid tombs of Cairo's Muslim rulers and holy men.

Another leap in time brings us to the present. Open your eyes to the crump of a distant dynamite blast. Follow the line of the Muqattam cliffs fifteen miles to the southern limit of the city and a foaming white cloud belches skyward at a place called Tura. It is smoke from the factories that devour the same old stone and pulverize it into Portland cement, but which are so badly tuned that they spew a million tons of the product into the air every year – enough to blanch the whole surrounding district with a ghostly volcanic ash. Much of modern Cairo is built of this cement. So is the very last of the city's tomb pyramids – actually a hollow pyramid-frame whose four huge slanting legs are carved in angular Kufic script with the names of fallen Egyptian soldiers. It dates from AD 1980, and was built to commemorate the unknown soldiers who died in wars against Israel. One of its occupants, however, is all too well known: Anwar al-Sadat, that late pharaoh of Egypt who died in a hail of bullets a few yards away while saluting his army on parade.

THEN AGAIN, THIS rock which the workmen of al-Khalifa chisel at so diligently may not be from the Muqattam at all. It might be translucent yellow alabaster, or grey marble from the Eastern Desert, or pink granite from Aswan. Perhaps, in the character of the city, it has been cannibalized from a nearby and long-neglected tomb. The possibility is not that remote. One of the bibles of Egyptology, the seven-volume *Topographical Bibliography of Ancient Egyptian Hieroglyphic Texts,* lends it historical weight. This catalogue of inscriptions hides enlightening gems. Here are some entries from a chapter titled 'Monuments and Re-used Blocks Found in the City of Cairo':

> Grey granite column of Amenophis III [1391–1353 BC] usurped by Merneptah [1224–1214 BC] and Setnakht [1196–1194 BC], probably from Heliopolis not Memphis, found in an 18th Century house in Cairo ... now in the British Museum.

> Part of lid of black granite sarcophagus of P-ar-kap [*c.* 500 BC] Persian, used as threshold in Mosque of Kikhya [eighteenth century AD] at north end of Abdin Street.

> Green basalt stele with remains of trilingual decree of Canopus (almost illegible), year 9 of Ptolemy III Euergetes I [239 BC],

used as a threshold in the Mosque of Amir Akhur [AD 1504] now in Louvre.

Fragment of recumbent Sphinx of Pepi I [2289–2255 BC], found in Haret el Roum [the *ḥāra* or quarter of the Greeks] east of the Mosque of Al Muayyad.

Quartzite jamb of Sesostris I [1971–1926 BC], probably from Heliopolis, in house opposite Coptic Church . . .

Black granite obelisk of Ramses II [1290–1224 BC], re-used by Merneptah and Sethos II [1214–1204 BC], perhaps usurped from Middle Kingdom [2050–1780 BC] . . . used as threshold in a house in Cairo, now in Berlin Museum.

And these are just a few of the recognizable pieces, the ones with still-legible inscriptions. The point is that Cairenes have always quarried their own tombs and temples for choice bits of stone. The evidence is manifold. Whenever old pieties lost their sheen, the stones lost their significance and reverted to mere merchandise. For instance, from the earliest times it was common for nobles to inscribe their tombs with protests of innocence. "I have never cheated; I have never lied" – such is the gist of these pleas to the gods of the afterworld. But, by its very denial, an Old Kingdom inscription at Giza reveals how widespread one sin was: 'I never brought anyone else's property to this tomb . . . I built it in return for all the bread and beer I gave to the workers . . . I gave them much linen, too.'

New Kingdom tomb builders at Saqqara stole blocks from Old Kingdom sepulchres; not even the godly Imhotep's constructions were spared. In the fifth century AD some of the same stones were then incorporated in a Christian monastery. When that was abandoned, peasants plundered it to build houses in the fields over the ruins of Memphis. Romans tore off the smooth limestone casing of the Giza pyramids to grind it up for plaster, just as a millennium earlier Ramses II had reused granite from the site.

Muslim masons of the eleventh century found that decorative blocks from Heliopolis slotted nicely into the inner ramparts of the Cairo city walls, where the reliefs of hippos and crocodiles – they can still be seen at the city gate of Bab al-Futuh – must have puzzled and amused generations of bored soldiers. Nearly every column in all the hundreds of medieval mosques in the city was recycled from some pagan temple. Other ancient columns were sliced like loaves of bread into discs and inserted into the stone marquetry of pavings and walls. Mosque thresholds, too, were often choice pharaonic plunder, placed so that the faithful could trample on the beliefs of idol-worshippers before shedding their shoes and entering the house of Allah.

Abd al-Latif of Baghdad, an erudite physician who visited Cairo at the end of the twelfth century AD, was appalled to find no less a personage than a son of the great sultan Saladin (better known to Arabs as Salah al-Din) engaged in quarrying ancient sites. Courtiers had convinced the prince to tear down the smallest of the three main Giza pyramids – that of Mycerinus/Rhodopis – and sell the stone to contractors. Abd al-Latif came upon the team of demolishers eight months into their labours. The doctor's memoirs showed he was not impressed:

> After remaining on this spot and spending all their money, as their toil and fatigue continually increased while their resolution dwindled and their strength wore out, those of the commission were forced, shamed and censured to abandon the undertaking. Far from achieving their design, all they did was to spoil the pyramid and show manifest proof of their inability. Contemplating the mass of stones collected by this demolition, one may imagine the pyramid ruined to its foundation. But on looking at the structure it seems as if it had suffered no injury . . .
>
> Witnessing the extreme difficulty experienced in dragging down a single stone, I questioned one of the foremen as to whether, if offered a thousand dinars to replace just one of the

> stones in the position it was in before, he thought himse[lf] competent to the undertaking. His answer was that were he offered that sum many times over, he would never be able to accomplish the task. This he affirmed with an oath.

Seneferu's pyramids at Dahshur and the big three at Giza – Cheops and Chephren and Mycerinus – have lost their starkly elegant smoothness. But at least sheer bulk has preserved their shape enough for them to remain the most instantly recognizable structures in the world. Their relations fared far worse: of nearly a hundred other pyramids in the field that stretches from Abu Ruwash just north of Giza to Illahun sixty miles south, most are little more than dunes of rubble. Three such mounds rise from the edge of the valley at Abu Sir, between Giza and Saqqara. The temple walls and corridors and subsidiary courts of just one of them, the pyramid complex of Sahure (2458–2446 BC), originally boasted a mind-boggling 12,000 square yards of carved limestone reliefs. Of these a mere 180 square yards have survived, and most in pretty rough condition.

It would be nice to think that stolen stones were always put to good use, but this was not the case. Some destructions were malicious. In AD 1378 a Sufi sheikh known as Sayim al-Dahr – the Perpetual Faster – attacked the face, ears and nose of the Giza Sphinx in a fit of iconoclastic zeal. The ancient idol took revenge, so Arab chronicles say, by blowing a veil of sand over the bothersome village at his feet, whereupon the peasantry lynched the skinny Sufi.*

Long before, other great monuments had fallen to organized vandalism. The Assyrians sacked Memphis in the seventh century BC. The Persian emperor Cambyses, who conquered Egypt a century later, was so enraged by an attempted uprising that he

* This incident was reported by the medieval chronicler Taqi al-Din al-Maqrizi. Subsequent generations blamed Mamluk soldiers or French troops under Napoleon for defacing the Sphinx, but there is no evidence against either.

wrecked the ancient Temple of the Sun at Heliopolis to its foundations. And not only did he slaughter Memphis's sacred Apis, a live bull which was kept in the Temple of Ptah and worshipped as a manifestation of the god, but, as Herodotus tells us, he also 'Broke open ancient tombs and examined the bodies.'

Cambyses' morbid curiosity was hardly unique. The pyramids, of course, had long since been divested of their human contents. As the city of Memphis declined, the villages that took its place found tomb plunder a useful supplement to farming. The mummy-grubbing was to continue through the advent of Islam and down to the present.

The rewards could be surprising. Abd al-Latif of Baghdad recounts this gruesome tale:

> A credible person told me that, joining once in a search for treasures near the pyramids, his party found a tightly sealed jar, on opening which and finding honey, they ate it. One of them noticed a hair that had stuck to his finger: he pulled it towards him and a small infant appeared, the whole of the limbs of which seemed still to have preserved their original freshness . . .

The fashion for digging up mummies peaked in the sixteenth and seventeenth centuries, when by a grisly twist of credulity Europeans came to believe that the gooey interiors of the rotted corpses had healing powers. Formed into a poultice, this *momia* was thought to make an excellent remedy for cuts and bruises. Some prescribed that it was best swallowed. One Vincent le Blanc of Marseilles, writing of Saqqara in 1660, said,

> 'Tis where the greatest part of Mummy, or flesh buried and roasted in the sand is gotten, which the wind uncovering, the next passenger brings to town for sale, it being very medicinable. Here you see a dead man is often more serviceable to the living than the living themselves; yet some approve not of the physick.

A compatriot of his, a certain Monsieur de Thevenot, wrote an all-too-believable account of his own visit in 1654 to what he calls the Village of the Mummies. The villagers near Saqqara were, he says, 'Very greedy of Money, and spare not to do any thing so they may come by it. And as they fancy, that the Franks carry always a good deal about them, when they have them in their Clutches, they squeeze them all they can...' Having paid the grand sum of eight piastres to be shown a fresh mummy pit, Thevenot was lowered into a hole in the ground which had plainly long since been exposed. His guides extracted another piastre for the job of chopping open the coffin he found in the tomb, and then the mummy inside was so decayed that the only salvageable parts were its hands. These the tourist took home with him to France.

Thevenot had reason to complain. A few years earlier the Roman antiquarian Pietro della Valle had paid a mere six piastres for the privilege of removing two intact, perfectly wrapped mummies from Saqqara. Not only this, but his prizes both bore exquisite portraits of their owners. One showed a young man with curly black hair and beard dressed in a long linen robe adorned with gold and jewels. On his belt was inscribed the Greek word '*Eupsychei*', meaning 'Farewell'. The other portrait appeared to be of his wife. Her picture was lavished with similarly rich adornment, including rings on every finger. A century later della Valle's descendants sold these two rich citizens of Roman Memphis to a German nobleman. He carried them to Dresden, where these first discoveries of what were to be known as Fayoum Portraits can be seen today at the State Museum.

The rise in mummy prices reflected a sad truth. Happy to keep the apothecaries of Europe supplied, Cairene merchants had plundered the ancient necropolis to such effect that they were running out of bodies. This proved but a minor obstacle. The mummy traders found that fresh corpses would do perfectly well. They bought the unclaimed bodies of criminals and the indigent, stuffed them with pitch, and left them in the sun to ripen. This profitable ruse lasted, we are told, until one dealer's disgruntled slave betrayed his master to the governor of Cairo. The Ottoman pasha had the whole profession clapped in irons.

It was around this time, too, that some savvy Cairene huckster produced *The Book of Buried Pearls and of the Precious Mystery, Giving the Hiding Places of Finds and Treasures.* This Arabic tomb robber's manual detailed magic formulae for outwitting the jinns who guarded ancient tombs. It gave precise directions to mountains of jewels and a bottomless well of silver which it claimed was sunk deep inside the Great Pyramid. The book was still circulating early in the twentieth century, having been, as a curator of the Egyptian Museum claimed at the time, the greatest single cause of damage to the country's antiquities.

The Romans avidly collected pharaonic knick-knacks, which explains why Rome prickles with thirteen obelisks – more than any city in Egypt. Augustus Caesar himself launched the fashion. Soon after defeating Cleopatra and her lover Mark Antony in 30 BC, and so ending Egypt's independence, he ordered the twin granite obelisks of Tutmosis III to be removed from the Temple of the Sun at Heliopolis. These early spoils were not to make it to Rome. They remained stuck at Alexandria for nineteen centuries before crossing the seas as gifts from Egypt to London and New York.

Such faraway capitals were already awash with pharaonic loot. Like so many classical tastes, Egyptomania had revived in Enlightenment Europe. Napoleon Bonaparte, for one, was inspired by the romance of Egypt. His Egyptian campaign failed miserably in military terms, but it did succeed in rousing Western lust for the East. The passion was soon to rise to fever pitch. In 1824 the brilliant French scholar Jean François Champollion broke the code to hieroglyphics, using the clue of a trilingual inscription that one of Napoleon's officers had found near Rosetta. After 1,500 years of mystery, Ancient Egypt was suddenly comprehensible. Wealthy Europeans, led by the consuls of Britain and France at Cairo, competed now to extract the richest prizes from ancient sites. Their unrestricted scavenging formed the basis of the great collections of Paris, London, Leiden and Turin.

Egypt's own nineteenth-century rulers proved equally keen for spoils. The disdain of the good Muslim for paganism, however, made them less discriminating. In their impatience to catch up with the West they sacrificed countless ancient monuments on the altar of progress. A dozen entire temples vanished for ever during the single decade of the 1820s, among them those at Armant and Elephantine, at Antinoe and Ashmunein. The ancient stones, consumed in lime kilns and crushed to provide mortar and plaster, rose again as the chimneys of provincial factories and as walls for the palaces of pashas in Cairo.

It was not until 1857, with the founding of the antiquities museum at Cairo by the pioneering archaeologist Mariette Pasha, that the wholesale plunder diminished. By the end of the century guards protected the major sites. The vast Memphite necropolis ceased to be seen as a mere mine. Instead, it was to be exploited for tourism and scholarship. Even so, in 1880 a hundred camel-loads of stone per day were being carried into the capital from the pyramid of Cheops's son Djedefre near the village of Abu Ruwash. Only a public outcry prevented the great Giza pyramids themselves from being quarried to build the first dams on the Nile, the Delta Barrages to the north of Cairo, which were completed in 1891. And right into the early twentieth century farmers continued to level the humus mounds covering ancient Memphis, having found that the city's remains made excellent fertilizer.

Jeremiah was right, for once. The doomsaying biblical prophet had warned that God would smash 'the images of Beth

Shemesh that is in the land of Egypt' and would burn with fire 'the houses of the gods of the Egyptians'. The 'images' of Beth Shemesh, which in Hebrew meant House of the Sun – i.e. Heliopolis – were indeed destroyed.* The site of the sacred Benben stone, whose worship dated back to prehistoric times; the home of Ra the sun-god, whose temple once owned 100,000 acres employing 12,000 peasants; the place where legend claimed that Thoth had invented writing; the On of the Bible where Joseph wed the daughter of the high priest Potiphar; the centre of mathematics and astronomy where the first 365-day calendar and 24-hour clock were devised and where the finest minds of Greece studied – of all this glory all but the merest traces vanished. The only intact piece of ancient Heliopolis to endure was its one lone obelisk.

As to this survivor, Diodorus Siculus states that it was one of a pair of obelisks erected by the pharaoh Sesostris I. This king went suddenly blind, says the ancient Sicilian geographer, and seeking a cure he consulted an oracle. 'Adore the god of Heliopolis,' the oracle told him, 'and sight will return when you wash your eyes with the urine of any wife who has never known a man outside of wedlock.' It proved easy enough to have obelisks raised as a sign of devotion, but the second part of the bargain was harder to fulfil. Poor old Sesostris had to burn many an adulteress alive, including his own wife, until at long last a certain gardener's spouse passed the rinse test. The pharaoh married this chaste dame, concludes Diodorus, as soon as he regained his sight.

The truth is more prosaic. The Ancient Egyptians were never

*Jeremiah 43:13. 'Images' may also be interpreted as 'pillars' or 'obelisks'. Jeremiah ascribed their destruction to the Babylonian king Nebuchadnezzar, who attacked Egypt in 591 and 567 BC. However, the deed may have been committed a century earlier by Assyrian invaders or a few decades later by the Persians. The Hebrew Beth Shemesh endures in the name of an adjacent district of modern Cairo, ʿAyn Shams. 'Shams' means sun in Arabic – it was also the name of the pre-Islamic Arabian sun-god. 'ʿAyn' means an eye or a spring, but here it may simply be an adaptation of the name 'On'.

so archly misogynistic as Diodorus would have us believe. Besides, inscriptions on the surviving obelisk state simply that it was one of a pair built to commemorate the thirtieth jubilee of Sesostris in about 1940 BC.

What is most certain is that the obelisk watched the city around it disappear. Its twin fell some time in the twelfth century AD. The broken pieces no doubt ended up in some unknown walls of Cairo. But already when Strabo saw Heliopolis 2,000 years ago, he could dismiss it as a deserted mound: 'It is said that anciently this was the principal residence of the priests, who studied philosophy and astronomy. But there are no longer such a body of persons or such pursuits.' So the lonely monolith stood for twenty centuries among fields, a helpless sentinel at the northern approach to Cairo, impassive to the glories of succeeding armies of Arabs, Crusaders, Turks, Frenchmen and Britons who all camped at its foot, until the obelisk suffered the final indignity of being engulfed in a dingy suburb of the brash twentieth-century metropolis.*

The end came far more gradually for Memphis than for Heliopolis. The fortunes of Egypt's first capital oscillated across thirty dynasties of pharaohs. At times other towns held greater sway. The royal court itself moved repeatedly. Often, as in Sesostris's time, it went to new precincts that were virtually suburbs of Memphis, but sometimes the pharaohs installed themselves far away. Judging by Cairo's later history, one may suppose restless rulers were propelled by the hope of escaping the congestion and intrigue of Memphis. In his effort to introduce the radical idea of a single, all-powerful god, the eighteenth Dynasty pharaoh Akhenaten (who reigned from 1379 to

* Until the 1940s, however, the obelisk remained a site of annual pilgrimage. Joseph McPherson, a British officer in the Cairo police, recorded that peasants from nearby villages gathered here at dawn on the day of the spring festival known as Sham al-Nissim to watch the sun rise.

1361 BC) tried to shake off the power of the established priesthood by building a new capital at Tel al-Amarna in Middle Egypt. A hundred years later Ramses II held court in the eastern Delta. Thebes, far to the south, had already served as capital and had also replaced Heliopolis as the seat of the most powerful priesthood in Egypt. Among the many great temples of Thebes in Ramses's time, Karnak alone boasted an endowment of 583,000 acres worked by 87,000 peasants. New Kingdom pharaohs, including Tutankhamun, preferred to be buried at Thebes's Valley of the Kings rather than at Saqqara.

But Memphis's position at the head of the Delta still made it, as Diodorus says, 'the gateway to Egypt, the master of the commerce passing upstream to the country above.' Its port of Peruw-Nefer (which rather charmingly meant *Bon Voyage*) was the busiest in the country. The pharaoh's palace in the centre of town, close by the Temple of Ptah, was the seat of Egypt's administration for most of the time – if not the preferred residence of the king himself. Both great institutions, as well as the city's vast necropolis, were added to by successive rulers down to the thirtieth and last wholly Egyptian dynasty. Ramses II had two colossal statues of himself erected at Memphis. The highest offices of Egypt's bureaucracy must still have been based there in his reign (1304–1237 BC), to judge from the fact that many of the greatest nobles chose to be buried at Saqqara. Ramses's son Khaemwes, who as crown prince assumed the title of high Priest of Ptah, was himself entombed in the desert overlooking Memphis. Half a millennium later the Twenty-sixth Dynasty ruler Apries (589–570 BC) built a vast new royal palace just north of the Temple of Ptah. (Sadly, he built it in mud brick, so all that remains today is a large hummock of higher ground amid fields.)

When Herodotus passed through in 450 BC Memphis had been reduced to a provincial capital within the vast Persian Empire. Yet it remained a cosmopolitan city. Herodotus mentioned prosperous quarters of Greeks, Indians, Canaanites, Medes,

Sumerians, Scythians and Kurds. The Phoenician deities Baal and Astarte had long enjoyed their own temples here. The presence of Levantine traders was so familiar that the Egyptian word for haggling was 'to speak like a Syrian'. All these foreigners transmitted Memphite customs and beliefs far afield. The Greeks, for instance, derived their picture of what happens after death from the topography of Egypt's capital. The crossing of the river Styx to Hades was modelled, wrote Diodorus, on the dispatch of funeral barges from Memphis across a lake that separated the city from the Saqqara necropolis, a lake which he describes as 'surrounded by beautiful meadows and canals, with lotus and flowering rushes'.

Alexander the Great captured Egypt's ancient capital in 332 BC. Unlike the Persians, who had scorned Egyptian beliefs, he took care to woo the Memphites. He organized games and concerts. He paid tribute to the sacred Apis bull. But he also inadvertently sealed the fate of Memphis by founding Alexandria. The port city became the seat of the dynasty established by the emperor's general Ptolemy Soter, who grabbed Egypt as his slice of Alexander's legacy. The Ptolemies' three-century reign transformed Alexandria into a rich metropolis that was the pre-eminent city of the Hellenistic Age.

While Memphis faded by comparison with this upstart rival, the inland city did share in the prosperity that Ptolemaic rule brought to Egypt. Its large Greek community fared especially well. One can see this by the profusion of Greek papyri describing bustling trade in such things as slaves, glass, bronzework and the sweet white wine that Memphis was famed for – including one third-century shipping document that details a bribe of ten drachmas paid to the city's chief customs inspector. Far from staying aloof, the Greek-speaking Ptolemies were sensitive to their position as alien rulers. Recognizing Memphis's centrality in Egyptian tradition, they made a great show of patronizing its temples and shrines. They enlisted the Apis bulls into a new, amalgamated deity – Sarapis – whose cult became a sort of official religious doctrine. The Temple of Ptah, now associated also with Sarapis, Isis and above all the now deified Imhotep, god of wisdom and healing, was once again the most popular pilgrimage site in Egypt. Supplicants would sleep within its precincts, then pay one of the city's many professional seers to interpret their dreams. It was here, too, that Ptolemaic kings continued to be crowned, and with the full pomp of their Egyptian predecessors.

Indeed, the event recorded by the key to the cipher of hieroglyphics, the Rosetta Stone, is the gathering of the entire priesthood of Egypt at Memphis for the Receiving of the Sovereignty by Ptolemy V Epiphanes Eucharistus in 196 BC. In the form of Ptolemaic decrees, the inscription is in three languages: ancient hieroglyphics, the more current demotic Egyptian script and Greek. The text amounts to a sophisticated public-relations pitch, showing clearly how concerned the rulers were to placate their native subjects: 'Inasmuch as the king is well disposed to the gods,' it reads, 'and inasmuch as he has lightened taxes, amnestied rebels and defended the country; has restored temples throughout the land; has given gifts to and made arrangement for the burial of sacred bulls – because the king has done these things, henceforth higher honours will be paid to him and to his ancestors.'

No number of honours, however, could save the Ptolemies from the rising power of Rome. The hungry Roman Empire's swift fleets and disciplined army made Egypt, with its temptingly large agricultural surplus, an easy plum to pick. The fourteenth and most famous ruler of the Ptolemaic line, Cleopatra VII Philopator, used all her wiles to hold off the growing challenge. Her affair with Julius Caesar worked to Egypt's benefit for a time. After his murder, Cleopatra gambled on an alliance with the rebellious Roman general Mark Antony, and lost. With her lover's fall at the Battle of Actium, the last queen of an independent Egypt knew she was doomed. Cleopatra sealed herself in a tower and pressed the poisonous asp of lore to her breast. Octavian – later the Emperor Augustus Caesar – captured Alexandria, extinguished the Ptolemies and declared Egypt his personal possession.

It was at around this time that Diodorus Siculus visited Memphis, which he described as having a circumference of seventeen and a half miles. A century later Strabo said that Roman Memphis remained large and populous and was 'inhabited by mixed races of people'. He judged the Temple of Ptah (which he associated with the Roman Vulcan or Greek Hephaestus) to be very sumptuously constructed. The former palaces were, however, in ruins.

Modern archaeology corroborates the ancient geographers. Ptolemaic remains on the east bank of the Nile show that Memphis had expanded enough for its suburbs to take root across the river, where the Arab capitals of Egypt were later to grow. Drill core samples taken from Memphis's own vast, sunken ruin field have exposed Roman-era vestiges outlining a city the shape and size of Manhattan. Roman Memphis may have stretched for twelve miles along the west bank of the Nile, reaching right up to the outskirts of the modern district of Giza.

But three slow-motion calamities were to stifle the ancient capital during the Roman era. Instead of installing a garrison in Memphis itself, Augustus housed his legions on the opposite bank of the Nile. Later emperors built a major fortress just downstream from here at a site facing the northern suburbs of Memphis. This was called Per-hapi-on, which in Egyptian meant the River House of On – i.e. the port of Heliopolis. Babylon, as the Romans mispronounced the place – making it easy to confuse with the Mesopotamian city – not only commanded an easy river crossing by way of the island of Roda, it also straddled a canal which linked to waterways that the later pharaohs had cut to the Red Sea. A city of camp followers soon grew up at this strategic spot, and commerce began to drift away from Memphis.

Just as old money and power abandoned the city, so did the old religion. The emperor Augustus had dismissed the Memphites' customs as folly. How could they, he sneered, worship cattle? Roman disdain took concrete form in the expropriation of all the temple estates that had paid the salaries of Egypt's priesthood. In other ways the new rulers were tolerant. Some temples were restored and some cults were promoted – the Egyptian goddess Isis, for instance, became popular throughout the empire. But Egypt's old religion, being based on the idea that the pharaoh was man's link to the gods, with the priests being merely his representatives, could hardly thrive when the pharaoh/emperor was a Latin-speaking foreigner who lived in Rome and didn't take his godly role very seriously.

The decline of old ways helped Christianity to gain an early foothold in Egypt. Not only was the new religion considered subversive by the Romans – which made it attractive in the eyes of Egyptian nationalists – but much of its imagery merged comfortably with Egyptian beliefs: the infant Jesus with the child Horus, Isis with the Virgin Mary, the death of Osiris with the martyrdom of Christ, the symbol of the ankh or Key of Life with the cross. Nor did it hurt that the Holy Family was said to have passed through Egypt on its flight from King Herod, tracing a trail of future Egyptian pilgrimage sites that included Heliopolis and a spot on the now fashionable east bank of the Nile, just opposite Memphis.

Still, Christianity's hold was not, at first, very firm. Mark the Evangelist, Egypt's great missionary and patron saint, may have been martyred at Alexandria in AD 63 for preaching against the adoration of the Apis bulls at Memphis, yet the travelling Roman emperor Hadrian remarked in a letter home from Egypt in AD 134 that he had seen 'those who call themselves bishops of Christ devoting themselves to Sarapis'.

By the end of the second century, however, the ancient cults were expiring. Their priesthoods slowly dispersed. Christianity began making such rapid inroads that the alarmed Romans mounted a series of persecutions in which 144,000 Egyptian Christians are said to have perished. The trauma was so ghastly that the Coptic Christian calendar begins in AD 284 – the inaugural year of the emperor Diocletian, who was credited with the worst excesses. But the terror produced a backlash. Within seven years of Diocletian's death the Roman emperor Constantine had himself converted to the new religion and moved the seat of the empire to Byzantium. By the Coptic year 103, fanatic monks under orders from Patriarch Cyril of Alexandria had stormed and desecrated the last of Egypt's pagan temples, probably including that of Ptah at Memphis.

Finally, and most irreversibly, the gods of nature themselves abandoned Memphis. Like a restless snake the Nile shifted a mile eastward in its bed, leaving the port of Bon Voyage high and dry. The whole Delta pushed north, so that the branching of the river was now several miles downstream from the ancient capital, closer to the Romans' Babylon. Old dykes that had long protected the city fell into disrepair, and the softened mud of the valley floor began to swallow its gracious stone structures whole.

By the time the Arabs arrived in AD 640, under the banner of Islam, Memphis was little more than a ghostly shadow of the thriving garrison town on the opposite bank. Babylon, not Memphis, was the seat of an important bishopric. It was the fall of Babylon after a seven-month siege that marked the fall of Christian Egypt. And it was here, outside the walls of the Roman fortress, that the Arabs established their capital – their commander, Amr ibn al-ʿAs, had preferred the sumptuousness of Alexandria's abandoned palaces, but his master, the caliph Omar, had recognized the strategic importance of Cairo's site. The conquerors called the new city Misr al-Fustat, and as it grew and prospered the name of poor Memphis devolved first into Old Misr and then was forgotten altogether.

During his sojourn at Cairo six centuries later, Abd al-Latif of Baghdad sailed across the Nile to Memphis. What the learned Arab saw provoked this reverie:

> Notwithstanding the vast size of this city and its great age, and in spite of the efforts by various nations to wipe out its most minute traces by shipping away the stones and materials of which it was built, by wrecking its buildings and mutilating the images with which they were adorned ... still its ruins present a combination of wonders which confounds the understanding. The more the whole is considered, the greater the admiration it inspires. Contemplating these vestiges of antiquity, a thoughtful man is disposed to forgive the error of the vulgar who believed that the ancient mortals who constructed them were gigantic in stature, or that they could make stones obey their commands by striking them with a wand.

Imagine the eloquent doctor's dismay were he to see the site today, because the last few centuries have proved the cruellest of all. Aside from its spectacular desert necropolis, there is practically nothing left of Memphis itself. Undulating earthen mounds, a colossal statue of Ramses II, a few other choice rocks and the faintest traces of the great walls of the Temple of Ptah are all that mark the spot. The city's ancient foundations lie sixteen feet underground, which is to say in the swampy and corrosive underworld below the water-table. And now even the lush palm groves that shade the whole vast site are under threat. As Cairo swells, walls of apartment blocks are advancing on Memphis. The cliffs of stone, and indeed the whole mineral element, seem set to triumph over the green of the valley.

How far the mighty have fallen. And even the less mighty. Leaving the Muqattam stonecutters to their work and plunging back into the squawking jungle of al-Khalifa's animal market, one can't help thinking how much better some of these caged creatures would have fared if only they had lived a few thousand years ago.

The monkey on his chain, for instance, might have spent his days mooning about some temple at Memphis, coddled, pampered and revered as a living incarnation of Thoth. On his death he would have been expensively embalmed and mummified. His name, place of birth, date of burial and a prayer for his salvation would have been written on his coffin, which would have been carried in procession to the Catacombs of the Sacred Baboons at Saqqara. There he would have lain in comfort until tomb robbers or Egyptologists found him.

At Memphis, falcons, bulls, cats and even dogs were maintained in style as living images of beast-headed gods. It was not only Apis bulls that were venerated in life and death, but also their mother cows. Two full years of preparation were required before a dead holy cow could at last be sent to the underground Resting Place of the Mothers of Apis at Saqqara, mummified and beautified with a gilded face mask. As for the sacred ibis birds, archaeologists have given up exploring the extremities of their catacombs, because they are simply too vast: multiple passages 30 feet wide and 165 feet long are packed from floor to ceiling with pottery jars of bird remains. The whole undertaking quarter of Memphis – the priests and bearers, the oil boilers, spice blenders, pitch and cartonnage makers, linen weavers, painters, writers and illustrators of funerary texts, amulet makers and so on – must have worked overtime for centuries to stock these vaults with their bizarre contents of an estimated 2 million bird mummies.

The city's animal afterworld has suffered a cruel decline since the end of paganism. For people it has not been so bad. Standards never again rose to the height of pyramids. In fact, as early as 1000 BC the unwary or illiterate risked being swindled by the sleazier morticians of Memphis, who cheated by painting coffins with bogus glyphs instead of proper instructions from the Book of the Dead. (The fakes looked like modern forgeries – just like the hieroglyphic gobbledegook churned out by the souvenir industry, in fact. The puzzled archaeologists who found them wondered at first if someone had played a practical joke on them.)

But you could still obtain a decent mummification in 450 BC: Herodotus says the undertakers displayed wooden models of three grades of mummy. Impressed by the chemical ingenuity of the Memphites, the curious Greek spared no detail in his description. Having ghoulishly elaborated a first class mummification he continued:

> When, for reason of expense, the second quality is called for, the procedure is different: no incision is made and the intestines are not removed, but oil of cedar is injected with a syringe into the body through the anus, which is afterwards stopped to prevent the liquid from escaping. The body is then pickled in natron* for the prescribed number of days, on the last of which the oil is drained off. The effect of this is so powerful that as it leaves the body it brings with it the stomach and intestines in a liquid state, and as the flesh, too, is dissolved by the natron, nothing of the body is left but the skin. After this treatment it is returned to the family without further fuss.

It is a relief to find that the mummy-munching Europeans of later times were not quite so cannibalistic as one may have feared. In fact scientists believe that the extraordinary state of preservation shown by the mummies on display at the Egyptian Museum owes as much to the dry desert climate as to feats of chemistry. The Egyptians' preoccupation with death did, however, secure a kind of immortality. The tomb reliefs at Saqqara and Giza, with their scenes of farming and industry and worship, have enabled scholars to conjecture the fine minutiae of working life in Memphis: how beer was brewed and wine pressed; how linen was manufactured;

* Sodium sesquicarbonate. The salty substance is found in abundance in the desert between Memphis and Alexandria.

how fashions in clothing and hairdressing changed; how keelless ships were built and bronze was smelted; what games and musical instruments were played.

After Herodotus, Memphis's undertaking industry sank into serious decline. Its last important client was the thirty-three-year-old Alexander the Great. His body sojourned there for fifty years before being sent, properly pickled one presumes, to the great city on the coast which he had founded. Grand-scale tomb building slowly petered out after Alexander. The Greek and Roman elites who mastered the country had more modest funeral habits than the natives, indulging in fine portraiture of the dead rather than tomb construction. (The Egyptian Museum boasts an unrivalled collection of these superb and eerily lifelike Fayoum Portraits.) Then, when Christianity took hold, all the old customs were renounced. The Egyptian Church cultivated an image of fierce asceticism. Saintliness in its eyes was achieved by spurning the luxuries of the imperial court at Byzantium, by never washing or eating, by holing up in a desert cave, by wearing coarse garments; and certainly not by splurging on your tomb.

Still, some of the old habits must have lingered. Soon after they brought the new religion of Islam to Egypt, the Arabs found it necessary to ban funeral practices they saw as excessive, such as the hiring of professional mourners. Then, following an uprising by the Coptic Christians who still made up the majority of Egyptians two centuries after the Muslim conquest, the caliph al-Mutawakkil punished the rebels with discriminatory laws. Infidels were henceforth forbidden the use of horses. They were obliged to wear distinguishing clothes as a mark of shame. The strictures were enforced with varying severity. But one punishment – perhaps the most severe of all in the eyes of Cairo – never lapsed before modern times. The graves of non-Muslims were to conform to Islamic precepts, ruled the caliph. They were to be 'indistinguishable from the earth around'.

CHAPTER THREE

CITIES OF THE DEAD

One mile distant from Cairo is a city which is not walled, is as large as Venice, and has tall structures and short ones . . . Every Saracen and townsman has a building in this city. In the short ones they bury their dead, and in the tall ones all the lords who own them give alms to the poor every Friday.

Emmanuel Piloti the Cretan, *c.* 1440

CAIRO IMPRESSED IBN Battuta more than any other city. It is odd, then, that his 2,000-page travelogue devoted just a scant few lines to describing the place. The peripatetic Moroccan skimped even on the Pyramids. They were, he insisted, round at the base and shaped like cones – thus revealing that in five visits to Cairo he had never bothered to cross the Nile and take a closer look.

Ibn Battuta probably judged that his fourteenth-century readers were well enough acquainted with the city and its pagan monuments. To an educated Muslim the more impressive marvels were not pyramids, but tombs of more immediate relevance. The Muslim cemeteries south of the great city were, he wrote, a place 'of vast repute for blessed power'. Cairo's great and good had erected here a whole parallel city of domed chapels that looked like houses surrounded by walls:

> They construct chambers in them and hire the services of Koran readers who recite night and day in beautiful voices. Some build a mosque or a *madrasa* [a college of Islamic law] by the side of their mausoleum. They go out every Thursday evening to spend the night there with their children and womenfolk and make a circuit of the famous sanctuaries ... The market people take out all kinds of edibles ... The cemetery contains ... an uncountable number of graves of men eminent for learning and religion, and in it lie a goodly number of the Companions of the Prophet and of the leading figures of both earlier and later generations ...

Ibn Battuta went on to list all the famous graves he had visited. He was showing off his piety, of course, but in visiting the tombs he was also being a conscientious tourist. In his day the cemeteries of al-Khalifa were an established place of pilgrimage, especially for those Muslims unable to afford the journey to Mecca. A profusion of specialized guidebooks catered to visitors even in the thirteenth century. They listed famous sights, described the proper rituals associated with them, and recommended itineraries to take in such attractions as the tombs of the Holder of the Prophet's Cloak; of Antar, carver of the Prophet's pulpit; of Muhammad's jeweller and standard-bearer; and of one of his suckling brothers – as well as a preserved footprint of Moses. According to Cairo's foremost medieval chronicler, Taqi al-Din al-Maqrizi (1364–1442), the graveyard in his day was the most popular pleasure resort in Egypt.

Clearly, Cairo's fascination with the dead had somehow overruled the Prophet's explicit injunction against showing them undue reverence. In fact, a spectacular revival of tomb building had followed the arrival of Islam in AD 640. And just as the funeral monuments of Saqqara and Giza recorded the city's earliest incarnations in stone, so were the tombs of the holy men and rulers and chief citizens of the Muslim era to chronicle its fortunes right down to the present.

A MIRROR TO Memphis's ancient necropolis spreads all around the animal market of al-Khalifa, stretching north and south for five miles along the foot of the Muqattam cliffs. Its mightiest sepulchres are domed, not peaked in pyramids. Denser and more democratic than its pagan forebear, and very much alive, this City of the Dead also tells parallel histories: one spiritual, the other earthly.

As one heads upstream, away from the city and deeper into the cemetery, the animal market dwindles to a last few pigeon hobbyists. The beastly babble fades into the domestic patter of a quiet suburb. Order is restored. Streets run straight and dignified between the walls of family tomb plots. Behind wrought-iron gateways are house-like structures of one storey, with here and there a dome signifying the tomb of someone more important, such as the ninth-century mystic Dhu'l-Nun al-Misri or the twentieth-century singer Umm Kulsoum. The older tombs are in stone. Newer ones are of fine pink brick which shows a care for quality that all but rich Cairenes rarely bother with in houses. Window grilles and open doorways reveal interior courts festooned with bright-coloured laundry. Women sit circled on mats around TV sets and primus stoves, while bare-bottomed toddlers play hide-and-seek among the cenotaphs.

No one knows exactly how many people live in the tombs. Estimates range from 50,000 to ten times that number – it is as hard to say as it is hard to define where the tombs end and the living city begins. The fact is that, like the Memphite necropolis in its heyday, Cairo's City of the Dead has always been home to a shifting population. Some of the tomb dwellers, especially the paid guardians and their families, have lived here for generations. Others, pushed by poverty, have moved in more recently to take advantage of the graveyards' open skies and proximity to the modern city centre. The number of squatters has swollen as Cairo itself has expanded, its unstoppable growth turning cemeteries which once marked the shore of the desert into islands surrounded by denser human habitation.

Off to the left, a funeral procession shutters in and out of view down successive perpendicular alleyways. It hurries at a murmuring trot: these funerals are speedy affairs, since Muslim custom demands burial before sunset on the day of death. Besides, the burden is heavy. The pall-bearers jostle antlike under the bier, whose swaddling of undyed cloth turns it into a monster larva. Volunteers relay forward to shoulder their share. The Koran reader in his dark grey kaftan and rounded, blue-tasselled fez scuttles along with the rest. He is preparing in his mind, one supposes, the instructions he will give to the deceased on how to answer the interrogating angels of the grave, Munkar and Nakeer, who will come to torment him after dark. The sombre caravan slips past. It is not numerous; the dead man is neither rich nor famous.

Down to the right, into a narrower lane, and a ramshackle flea market is open for trade. Sellers squat against the walls with their wares spread before them: used baby shoes, broken bathroom fittings, a yellowed sheaf of movie posters, a few links of chain, a pram with one wheel. Goods from neighbourhood workshops vie for a place in the dust too: TV aerials concocted from old tin cans, waterpipes jerry-rigged out of fly-spray canisters, shopping bags sewn from plastic fertilizer sacks. A straggle of buyers shuffles and pokes.

Abruptly there are buildings of two and three floors instead of tombs. More people – a crowd almost – accumulate in the well-shaded footway. The alley opens, debouching into a wide street where a small carnival is under way. Leaning towers of paper cones ring pyramids of yellow lupin seeds mounded on brightly painted wooden pushcarts. Vendors amble about tooting horns and touting plastic toys and tinfoil party hats. A tatterdemalion rocket ride that has been welded out of oil drums cranks slowly into a spin, its cargo of tiny tots squealing delight.

This is the *mawlid*, or annual festival, of Muhammad Ibn Idris al-Shafiʿi, a Muslim jurist of the ninth century whose great mausoleum is the centrepoint of the tombs of al-Khalifa. This sheer cube of a building capped with a high, metal-clad dome rises austerely out of the festival clutter like a dusty Duomo. But this is no longer the monument Ibn Battuta described as enjoying an immense revenue – 'an exceedingly fine piece of architecture and exceptionally lofty'. Like any folk shrine worth its salt, the building has been so overlaid with additions and accretions that little of the initial artistic intent remains. Its potency now is spiritual, not aesthetic.

Or that is what one must guess, surrendering one's footwear to the quick-fingered shoekeeper at the door and stepping inside to be swarmed in the sudden gloom by a whispering hush of supplicants. They are women mostly, enveloped in the black shrouds of the poor, fragrant with the musty sourness of close rooms and scarce water and misfortune. Some press up close to the elaborate wooden screen surrounding the saint's cenotaph, directly under the dome, and mumble prayers for health or forgiveness. Others stalk purposefully around the perimeter in imitation of the circling of the Black Stone at Mecca – and perhaps even in a distant re-enactment of fertility rites around the Benben stone at Heliopolis.*

FOLLOWING A LONG career as a leading jurist of his age, Imam al-Shafiʿi died at Misr al-Fustat in AD 820. During his lifetime

* Ancient rituals do endure: at the tomb of Sidi Uqba a few hundred yards away, barren and unmarried women gather on Fridays to influence fate by turning seven times around a pillar while casting seven stones over their left shoulders.

scholars had worked to fix a legal code for Islam based on the Koran and the sayings and acts of the Prophet. The ulema – the men of *ᶜilm* or science, which is to say Islamic learning – had reached consensus on some matters of law but differed on others. Al-Shafiᶜi gained fame by seeking compromises. He argued that, while the school of Malik ibn Anas (a jurist who lived at Medina in AD 716–95) stuck too rigidly to the letter of sacred texts, the rival school of Abu Hanifa (who taught at Kufa in Iraq and died in AD 767) was excessively free in its interpretation. Shafiᶜi proposed instead an amalgam of the two, and this middle path soon developed into a separate school of law. He also systematized the science of jurisprudence. Shafiᶜi's methodology, if not his interpretations, were accepted by all the schools of Islamic law.

Although in modern times the domain of religious law has been limited – in Egypt, at least – to areas like inheritance and marriage, the moderate Shafiᶜite school still predominates in the city. (Which is one reason why there is no hand-chopping, flogging or lapidation here, as imposed by the Saudis, who are avid followers of Ahmad Ibn Hanbal, the founder of the last, and sternest, accepted school of Sunni law, who died at Baghdad in AD 855.) More about legalities later. The point is that Imam al-Shafiᶜi is an important figure in the Islamic civilization of Cairo, a man whose credentials for a kind of sainthood are sound. This is more than can be said for many of the 300-odd other Muslim holy men and women whose tomb shrines pepper the traditional quarters of the city.

Take the most popular saint of all, the Prophet's grandson al-Husayn. The noble provenance, piety and notable death of al-Husayn are beyond dispute – indeed his murder, at the order of Caliph Yazid in AD 680, became one of the central dramas of Shi'ite Islam.* But it is a well-known fact that the martyr's body

* The word Shiᶜite comes from the *shiᶜat Ali,* or partisans of al-Husayn's father Ali, who was Muhammad's cousin and son-in-law. Shiᶜites believe in the divine right of Ali's family to rule – a right contested by the majority of Sunnis.

was buried in Iraq. All Cairo can lay claim to is the poor fellow's severed head, and even that claim is tenuous. The grisly relic was said to have travelled first to Damascus, then to Ascalon in Palestine. Not until 1153 was it whisked to Cairo, to save it from advancing Christian crusaders. But then at least one medieval source declares that this was not al-Husayn's head at all, but his grandson's.

Regardless of doubts, the funerary mosque of al-Husayn remains Cairo's most venerated shrine. It is where politicians have themselves shown praying on TV and where, once a year and every night for a full week, a million-strong crowd gathers to celebrate al-Husayn's martyrdom. It may be that the Shiʿites of Iran mark the saint's death by public weeping and self-flagellation, but Cairo's *mawlid* devotees, joined by the thousands of country folk who pour into the city to snooze and brew tea in the medieval alleyways surrounding the shrine, come for fun as much as for devotion. The revelry begins after dusk, gaining momentum far into the early hours. Fair-goers jive and joke and test their skill in shooting galleries and trials of strength. Some, drawn by the rhythm of drums and the whine of reed flutes, join ritual dances in the dozens of marquees set up by different Sufi brotherhoods. Others press into the shrine itself to gain the saint's *baraka* or blessing, while Breughel-faced beggars and weasel-featured pickpockets work the throngs outside.

One night, while squeezing through the crowds some distance from the saint's tomb, I felt a clutching at my sleeve. I looked, and found the blind eyes of a stooped old man beseeching me. In a thick country accent he begged me to lead him to al-Husayn, and as I piloted him through the noise and confusion he kept repeating, 'Ya Husayn! Praise be to God!' When we merged in the fervent crush at the door of the shrine I felt him tremble with anticipation. His hand slipped down to mine, which he kissed and raised to his forehead. 'May the Lord preserve your sight, my son,' he cried before vanishing over the threshold like a bird released from a cage.

But why is it that Cairo, whose Muslim faith is solidly of the orthodox Sunni kind, should venerate this Shiʿite martyr? And, for that matter, how is it that some Muslims have also come to sanctify the tombs of the Prophet's friends and relations, not to mention sundry jurists and sheikhs and fakirs? The answers lie in the matrix of tensions which have always characterized Islam – between literal and allegorical readings of Scripture, between pristine ideals and less tidy facts, between the demands of the faith and the will of rulers; in short, between the Word of God and the needs of man.

Edward Lane, an English Orientalist and student of this city, reported 170 years ago that even as Cairo's Muslims, Christians and Jews abhorred one another's doctrines, they happily shared each others' superstitions.* Like the earlier creeds, Islam had to grapple with enduring pagan instincts, including a common yearning for physical closeness to the deity. Jews found this, perhaps, in the covenants that God is said to have given them as his Chosen People. Christian belief adapted to pre-existing faiths wherever it went, then channelled pagan idol worship into a reverence for icons of its own elaborate cast of martyrs and saints. Abjuring both exclusivism and graven images, Islam sought more personal intervention.

This is what the *mawlids* are, in essence, about. They revolve around the tomb of a person who, by some sign or other, appeared

* The London *Jewish Chronicle* of 20 July 1906 carries a letter from one Herman Loewe describing the Jewish *mawlid* of Ben Ezra in Old Cairo. Local Muslims and Copts enthusiastically joined the celebrations, he says. The rowdy, drunken crowd inside the synagogue 'went mad' when the Ark bearing sacred scrolls was opened. The fervent mob knocked the author to the ground in the rush to 'snatch and carry away' a sacred scroll. 'I crept out of the synagogue, bruised, gasping and dazed,' he continues. 'Outside, the feasting was going on as before, but it had now developed into an orgy, and there were some very unpleasant features connected with it . . .'

to his contemporaries to be a *wāli* – one close to God. To be near one so blessed, even after his death, is therefore to approach the divine. There is a whiff of something very ancient here, as the Egyptologist Sir Gardner Wilkinson noted over a century ago: 'The remark of Herodotus, that the Egyptians could not live without a king, may find a parallel in their impossibility of living without a pantheon of saints. And, notwithstanding the positive commands of Islam to allow no one to share any of the honours due to the deity alone, no ancient or modern religion could produce a larger number of divine claimants.'

Yet some *mawlids* embrace an element of Bacchanalian excess that seems completely at odds with their declared purpose – let alone what the textbooks of monotheism have to say. To cite an obscure but diverting clue, back in 450 BC Herodotus witnessed a festival of Dionysus just north of Memphis. A procession of ladies marched down a village street, each toting an effigy of the god that was fitted with outsized genitals on a hinge. The simple mechanism allowed the ladies to wag the penises provocatively by tugging on a string. Now, earlier in the twentieth century Joseph McPherson, an officer in the Cairo police, came across a parade in a village just outside the capital. It was the festival of a local *wāli,* he discovered, and on this day the villagers chose their handsomest lad to lead a parade. Carried stark naked through the streets on a sort of throne, the youth had a cord tied to his penis which an accomplice would jiggle to keep his virile member erect.

Such goings-on have long brought on to *mawlids* the opprobrium of the orthodox – as well as the scepticism of the educated classes. This is why they have grown increasingly rare. Yet the *mawlid* of Sayyida Zaynab, the sister of the martyred al-Husayn, and Cairo's second most popular saint, still maintains a reputation for lewdness. On the Big Night hundreds of thousands of youths in high spirits cram the wide square in front of her shrine, not far from the city centre.

There were too many for comfort on a recent visit, so I

looked for diversion in the alleys and side streets. Peasant families huddled here around gas lamps and charcoal braziers, inviting all and sundry to join them for tea or a meal or just a chat. Wider spaces were filled by colour-patterned marquees put up for the occasion by varied orders and lodges among the seventy-odd Sufi brotherhoods registered in Egypt. Every tent housed its own band and singer of *dhikr* – odes in love of God. The overall noise may have been a clashing, amplified chaos that could be heard for miles around, but inside each tent the dervishes concentrated solely on their own guide and rhythm and music. A few wore city clothes – some suits and ties even – but most, having travelled here from all across Egypt, wore country *galabiyyas*. Eyes squeezed tight in trance, the dancers hurled their shoulders this way and then that, back and forth in time with the beat, some swaying, some thrashing, some hopping as if on coals, their ecstasy mounting higher and higher as the tempo quickened.

Sellers of popcorn and party hats plied the pushing crowds gathered outside, and around the shooting galleries and boat-shaped swings that whooping daredevils rocked into continuous, dizzy whirls. A magic show occupied a trailer that was camouflaged under lurid hoardings showing lightning bursting from a dwarf's fingertip, a turbaned impresario with voodoo eyes and a scantily dressed dame reclining voluptuously in minaret-high levitation. The barker, a languid youth in a Ronald Reagan T-shirt, paced up and down with a mike, packing in kids with a seamless harangue promising sights never seen before and Susu the talking head.

The next marquee was a mystery. There was no sign of what the show might be, but the raptest jamboree of adolescent boys I have ever seen thronged the narrow entrance like a swarm of hornets, craning and shoving to get in and get close. An enthralled, musk-laden urgency seemed to charge their faces. The squirming then stopped abruptly, and the boys stood still as a tenor wail wafted through the flimsy canvas walls. The voice moaned and undulated, heaved and panted, sighing through pitch after pitch in a spectacular and apparently endless crescendo of oohs and ahs. As the spine-tingling caterwaul went on and on it slowly dawned on me that the entertainment these youths had paid a *rial* for was a kind of aural pornography. What held them in such utter and unaccustomed reverence was nothing less than an impersonation of the wildest cries of female arousal.

The *mawlid* of Sayyida Zaynab is, through no fault of the lady herself, known for rowdiness. Most of the several score others that Cairo celebrates are far tamer, offering fun of the innocent, family kind alongside religious worship. Whatever form they take, *mawlids* clearly exist to fulfil irrepressible needs. This explains why they have survived the scorn of officials and clerics for centuries. But *mawlids* endure only as long as the memory of their *wāli*. Although new ones have continued to crop up even in the twentieth century, many have passed from the calendar of the city. These days, sadly, they are under renewed pressure. Commercialization has combined with a loss of neighbourhood feeling to take the spirit out of many of the smaller *mawlids*. More portentously, a puritan movement has increasingly taken hold of Islamic discourse. In contrast to the *mawlid* crowds, its disciples tend to express primordial urges with less joy and more anger.

IT WOULD BE misleading to imply that *mawlids* are simply a relic of pagan forms of worship.

Although Cairenes had venerated Muslim holy men from the earliest age of Islam, the big boost for sainthood did not come until 350 years after the Arab conquest. Until then Egypt had been a province of the Abbasid Empire whose seat was in distant Baghdad. Cairo – or Misr al-Fustat as it was still known – was merely a provincial capital, an industrial town lacking the splendour of a court.

In AD 969 a new and radically different dynasty swept in from

Tunisia and wrested Egypt from Abbasid control. In contrast to the caliphs of Baghdad – Sunni Muslims whose legitimacy sprang from their descent from the Prophet's uncle Abbas – the upstart dynasty claimed a purer provenance, direct from the Prophet's daughter Fatima. The so-called Fatimids were Shi'ites, and so believed that one man in each generation of a certain line of descent from the Prophet held a semi-divine authority to interpret the will of God. Conveniently, this infallible imam was none other than the reigning Fatimid caliph.

Thinking to seclude their court from their subjects, the Fatimids founded a royal precinct a few miles north of Misr al-Fustat. The walled, one-and-a-half-mile-square city was to be an exclusive zone of palaces and parade grounds and private gardens – a sort of precursor to the Kremlin or to the Forbidden City of Beijing. Heeding the advice of astrologers, they called the place al-Qahira after the planet Mars the Triumphant. (Italian traders, with that inability to pronounce that has so often recurred here, soon garbled the name into Cairo.*) This was the beginning of the city's golden age. Fustat still prospered, but over time it became a mere satellite of ever-expanding Cairo. For 500 years, under the Fatimids and their successors, Cairo would be the capital of an empire that embraced the holy cities of Mecca, Medina and Jerusalem – an empire whose ever-changing borders nudged at one time or another the Taurus Mountains in the north, the Tigris River in the east, the Yemeni highlands in the south, and the coasts of Sicily in the west.

Yet the Fatimids faced an immediate problem. The people they ruled – those who were not Christian or Jewish, that is – were overwhelmingly Sunni Muslims. Moreover the Fatimids' purported descent from the Prophet was widely disbelieved.

* The English word garble, incidentally, is Arabic in origin. *Gharbala,* meaning to sift, passed by way of Cairene spice merchants into the Italian *garbellare,* which meant to sort or select.

When the conqueror al-Muᶜizz li Din Allah – the name means Glorifier of the Faith of Allah – entered Misr al-Fustat on horseback, it was said, an upright citizen had challenged his claim to the title of caliph. Al Muᶜizz thereupon drew his sword. 'Here is my lineage,' he declared. Then, scattering gold coins from his purse, he continued, 'And here is my proof.'

The Fatimids harboured no illusion of winning wholesale conversions to Shiᶜism. In any case their version of the creed, influenced by later Greek philosophy, taught that true religion was beyond the understanding of the simple-minded masses. So, rather than antagonize their subjects, the Fatimids set out to dilute their faith with folk belief. Several acknowledged members of the Prophet's family were already buried and venerated at Cairo. These, and the remains of other ancestors which al-Muᶜizz purposefully carried with him to his new capital, were now furnished with fancy shrines. Ostentatious alms-giving encouraged devotional visits to these family tombs. Soon the habit of the few became the custom of the many. Tomb visiting became so popular, in fact, that the sixth Fatimid caliph, al-Hakim, was reportedly only narrowly dissuaded from bringing the body of the Prophet himself to Cairo from Medina.

After 200 splendid years – years in which Cairo emerged as the greatest city in Islam – the Fatimid regime declined into decadence and intrigue. Christian crusaders, installed now in Palestine, threatened the Abode of Islam. Seeking allies against the invaders – even Shiᶜite heretics – in 1168 a Sunni general by the name of Saladin (or, more properly, Salah al-Din al-Ayyubi) arrived from Syria to enlist support from the foundering Fatimids. To his surprise, Saladin found it easier to shunt Cairo's rulers aside and take command of their empire himself.

Saladin had no genealogical pretensions – he was in any case of Kurdish, not Arab, origin. Instead, he claimed legitimacy from his upholding of Sunni orthodoxy. Pledging allegiance to the Abbasid caliphs of Baghdad, he took for himself the lesser title of

Sultan. Saladin stamped out Shiʿite practices by locking up or executing the entire Fatimid court. Reintroducing the old schools of law, he built new colleges and imported Sunni professors from the East to staff them. He opened the imperial precinct of Cairo to the public, requisitioned its palaces for his officers, and ordered the construction of a new and more secure royal residence. This was to be the Citadel, whose turrets and minarets still grace Cairo's skyline.

Just as the Ptolemies had accommodated Memphite beliefs, Saladin's successors saw the wisdom of respecting popular custom. Cairenes continued to revere the illustrious dead – excepting, of course, the later descendants of the Fatimids.* The new rulers encouraged them by restoring the Imam al-Shafiʿi's shrine, which had fallen into decay along with those of other early Sunni jurists and scholars. They paid officials to oversee Friday tours of Sunni-sanctioned tombs, and even instituted a police force to prevent immoral behaviour in the cemetery, which was apparently common. Saladin's nephew al-Kamil al-Ayyubi (1218–38), a statesmanlike sultan who infuriated both Christian and Muslim extremists by agreeing to share control of Jerusalem with the crusaders, occasionally took part in tomb tours himself. He may have been assisted by the publication of guidebooks such as one by a certain Muwaffaq al-Din ibn Uthman which advised pilgrims not to kiss the holy men's tombs because this was 'a Christian habit'.

The Ayyubids also encouraged Sufism, the Islamic mysticism that was taking the thirteenth century by storm. Named after the rough *ṣūf* or wool garments its early adherents wore, this new religious approach softened the edges of dry orthodoxy by

* Later – in the fourteenth century – a property speculator had the Fatimid family tomb by the shrine of al-Husayn demolished. The bodies were exhumed and dumped in the dung heaps outside the city walls. The site of the tombs became the Khan al-Khalili, which to this day is Cairo's chief bazaar for jewellery, handicrafts and tourist knick-knacks.

incorporating esoteric beliefs. Among them was the idea that certain sheikhs became *wālis*. (The proper Arabic plural is actually *awliya*). Like the pharaohs and like the Shiʿite imams, perhaps, these masters grew so close to God that they became vessels for the divine. They could intercede with the Almighty or simply – by touch or speech or thought – dispense his *baraka*. Not surprisingly, these powers were believed by some to follow their sheikhs into the grave. And so yet another constellation of holy tombs began to sprout.

Again, some were the tombs of sheikhs who had well-earned reputations for miracles, or especial kindness or learning. But popular demand for folk heroes led to the elevation of some very suspect characters. For instance, the eighteenth-century historian Abd al-Rahman al-Jabarti described a contemporary of his called Sheikh Ali al-Bakri, who earned a reputation for holiness by wandering about the city naked and babbling. Seeing the potential, Sheikh Ali's brother set himself up as a manager and collected pious donations. Sheikh Ali grew enormously fat, wrote al-Jabarti:

> Men and women, and particularly the wives of the grandees, flocked to him with presents and votive offerings which enriched the coffers of his brother. The honours which he received ended not with his death. His funeral was attended by multitudes from every quarter. His brother buried him in the mosque of al-Sharaibee ... and frequently repaired thither with readers of the Koran, *munshids* to sing odes in his honour, flag-bearers, and other persons who wailed and screamed, rubbed their faces against the bars of the window before his grave, and caught the air of the place in their hands to thrust it into their bosoms and pockets.

Forty years later, Edward Lane remarked that whenever he passed the tomb of Sheikh Ali his servant would touch the bars of its window with his right hand, then kiss his fingers to obtain a blessing.

Lane and al-Jabarti were not alone in scorning such excess. One eighteenth-century governor of the city, when told that a mosque keeper had attracted a following by claiming his goat was an incarnated saint, had the animal roasted and served to its owner. At the end of the nineteenth century the government banned the *dawsa*, a Sufi practice whereby the sheikhs of some orders tested the faith of disciples by riding over their prostrate bodies on horseback. But Cairo's rulers usually preferred to accommodate popular fervour. Early in the eighteenth century angry mobs had forced the authorities to banish a preacher who dared to attack saint worship. Long before – in the fourteenth century – the killjoy cleric Ibn Taymiyya sparked a protest march of 500 Sufis with his railings against 'innovation' in the practice of Islam. Famed for his severity – he once kicked over a backgammon board in a Cairo street because he disapproved of games, and argued that not just women but pretty adolescent boys too should be veiled from public view – Ibn Taymiyya was eventually locked up in the Citadel. Ironically, on his death he himself was revered for a time as a saint. His tomb in Damascus became a place of pilgrimage.

Nowadays Ibn Taymiyya has stopped turning in his grave. Islam's new fundamentalists have revived his puritan ethics.

GIVEN MEDIEVAL CAIRO'S fascination with tombs, unpopular rulers found it expedient to buy favour by embellishing famous shrines. Imam al-Shafiʿi's, for instance, was restored seven times. But the more ambitious of sultans then went a step further: they began to build monumental tombs for themselves.

The idea was helped by a foreign influence. From the eleventh century onwards the Turks flooded into the Islamic world, joining the same great flux of peoples from the Central Asian steppes that brought the Huns to the Danube, the Tartars to the Don and the Mongols to the gates of Damascus. They arrived in Cairo mostly by way of the slave markets, where Turkish boys in particular fetched high prices for their fair skin, straight hair and horsemanship. Turks were already famed as warriors. Aside from their fighting tradition, they carried with them a custom of burying their chieftains in elaborate tombs – a custom that reflected, perhaps, the nomad's yearning for permanence.

The last of the major Ayyubid sultans, Saladin's great-nephew al-Salih Ayyub (1240–49), was a hard man and a stickler for loyalty. He warred against his cousins, was said to have had his own brother strangled, and distrusted his son so much that he dispatched the boy to the Anatolian marches at the furthest corner of his kingdom. Al-Salih's character disposed him to heed these words of Nizam al-Mulk, an eleventh-century wazir of Baghdad who was admired as the Machiavelli of his age: 'One obedient slave is better than 300 sons; for the latter desire their father's death, the former long life for his master.' And so al-Salih indulged himself in importing a whole corps of superb slave boys from across the lands of Central Asia and the Caucasus.

They became known as Mamluks, which meant those who are owned – as distinct from the terms *garya* and *ghulam,* which referred to ordinary girl and boy household slaves. After rigorous training in court etiquette, Islamic sciences and all the martial arts, the slave recruits were freed. But even as adult soldiers they were expected to remain loyal to their master, to be servants to his household and brothers in arms with their fellows, bound by an indomitable *esprit de corps.* In time the Mamluks – as they continued to be called as freedmen – became a proud military caste much like the samurai of Japan. Equipped with the latest in Eastern military technology – including stirrups and the recurved composite bow, a Turkish invention which was much lighter than the longbow but nearly as powerful – these sword- and lance-wielding horse-borne archers soon made mincemeat of the lumbering crusader knights.

It was in the midst of a campaign in the Nile Delta, where

the Franks under Louis IX had landed in the hope of pressing on to Cairo, that Sultan al-Salih Ayyub died of a fever. His wife Shagar al-Durr, a Turcoman slave who had been a gift from the Abbasid caliph, took the chief of the Mamluk guard into her confidence to conceal the sultan's death. The pair maintained the fiction for two months – long enough for al-Salih's son to be recalled from northern Syria to assume command. The ruse succeeded. The Franks suffered a resounding defeat. Louis was captured and ransomed for a million gold dinars. But the former sultan's Mamluks, flush with victory, resented his son's haughty ways. They bridled particularly at his promotion of African eunuchs to the highest positions. Shagar al-Durr was angry too; the boy rashly demanded that she hand over her jewels. And so al-Salih's Mamluks murdered their master's son.

Precarious as her position was, Shagar al-Durr managed to complete the *coup d'état*. For eighty days she ruled as sultana – the rarest of feats for a woman in medieval Islam.* The outraged Abbasid caliph, who was of course her original owner, dispatched a stinging note from Baghdad: 'Since no *man* among you is worthy of being sultan I will come in person and bring you one. Know you not that the Prophet – may he be exalted – has said, "Woe unto nations governed by woman?"' Determined to legitimize her rule, Shagar al-Durr married the chief of her husband's Mamluks and had him proclaimed sultan. No fool she: she first had him divorce his wife, Umm Ali. Not only that, but she continued to hold the reins of power herself.

All went smoothly for seven years. The growing corps of Mamluks stifled rumbles of dissent from partisans of the Ayyubid family. A hapless six-year-old cousin of al-Salih Ayyub was named as co-regent, a clever move to give the appearance of continuity. Shagar al-Durr then played a propaganda trump. She built a

* The only other case is that of Princess Balqish Jehan Raziya of Delhi, who reigned in that city from 1236 to 1239 before being murdered by her jealous brother.

splendid mausoleum for her deceased husband. Shunning the cemeteries, she placed it on the site of the former Fatimid palace, smack in the middle of the busiest thoroughfare in Cairo. (It still stands in the bazaar of the brass merchants, next to the soaring gateway and minaret of the law school that al-Salih himself had built earlier.)

Shagar al-Durr had secured her legitimacy for a time. One day, however, she learned that her Mamluk husband was planning to take a Turkish princess as a second wife. (Technically he was allowed four.) Jealousy, and the notion of this slave soldier scheming to forge dynastic ties on his own, drove her to violence. She summoned him to the Citadel. The officer, wary of her temper and fearful because an astrologer had told him he would die by the hand of a woman, had to be cajoled into leaving a polo match in the western suburbs of the city. His instincts were right. Five assassins stabbed him fatally on the way to the palace.

It was said that Shagar al-Durr realized she was doomed, and so crushed her jewels in a mortar to stop them ever falling into the hands of another woman. Soon after that, Ali, her Mamluk husband's son by his first wife, stormed the palace with a furious band of his father's troops. They hauled the sultana from her quarters and flung her at the mercy of his mother. Umm Ali – who had been divorced from her dashing officer in favour of Shagar al-Durr – struck her rival and hurled insults before having her female servants strip the ex-sultana and beat her to death with wooden bath clogs.* Then, as the fifteenth-century historian Ibn Iyas recalls, 'She was dragged by the feet and thrown from the top of the moat naked, with nothing but a garment around the waist. She remained there in the moat for three days, unburied, until, it is said, one of the rabble descended under cover of night

*Umm Ali, incidentally, gave her name to a dessert made from hot cream and nuts – perhaps because the pleasure of eating it is akin to the sweetest revenge. A dairy shop only a stone's throw from the tomb of al-Salih Ayyub makes a speciality of the dish.

and cut off the sash of her garment because it was of red silk with a circle of pearls and because it smelled of musk.' At length Shagar al-Durr was buried in her own magnificent tomb. She had built it, with admirable foresight, in a choice spot near the shrines of the female saints Nafisa, Ruqqaya, Atika and Sukayna.

In 1258, less than a year after Shagar al-Durr met her end, Mongol hordes razed the caliphal capital of Baghdad, building pyramids of skulls in its place. Genghis Khan's wild cavalry rolled the captured caliph up in a carpet and trampled him to death. Remnants of the Abbasid family fled to Cairo, whose Mamluk slaves-turned-masters had became the only force capable of resisting the Mongols. For two and a half centuries thereafter the Mamluks, having established a rigidly militaristic regime that perpetuated the tradition of martial servitude and advancement, kept the once omnipotent caliphs at Cairo as puppet popes. So low did the Abbasids' fortunes sink that, for lack of a fitting tomb of his own, one of the last of their number was laid to rest beside Shagar al-Durr, his great-great-grandfather's slave girl.

Inside the chamber under her dome, a mosaic in cut glass adorns the curve of the niche that indicates the direction of Mecca. In a poetical allusion to Shagar al-Durr – whose fanciful name means Tree of Pearls – it shows a tree bearing fruit formed by little pieces of mother-of-pearl. The wooden cenotaph nearby carries this apt verse:

> *O ye who stand beside my grave, show not surprise at my condition.*
> *Yesterday I was as you. Tomorrow you will be as me.*

SHAGAR AL-DURR HAD set a new standard. From her time onwards every Cairene grandee or grande dame invested in a domed mausoleum as soon as their career permitted. As she had done with her husband's tomb, they attached them by preference to pious foundations; schools or mosques or hostels for dervishes – whatever would best enhance the patron's image as a champion of the faith. With time, the fashion transformed the processional streets of the Mamluk capital into the avenues of funerary foundations that one sees today, their narrow roadways dwarfed, Wall Street-like, by soaring domes and minarets.

Cairo's architects quickly grasped their Turkish overlords' desire for dramatic effect. Their designs evolved to emphasize verticality: inset panels, monumental portals and striped stonework drew the eye upward to the ever-taller minarets. The increasing density of the city stretched the skill of its builders further. Staggered façades cleverly exposed the buildings' main features to the street. Ingenious floor plans squeezed perfectly proportioned and Mecca-oriented inner courtyards into the most irregular of plots. The sepulchral domes themselves grew in size and sophistication. Muqattam limestone replaced brick, and then was cut to form ridges which were refined into elaborate geometric patterns so that the last domes of the Mamluk sultanate became the carved tapestries of starbursts and interlaced flowers which are best seen today in the great cemeteries east of the city walls at the tombs of the fifteenth-century sultans Barsbay and Qayt-bay.

It was not merely fashion that pushed the Mamluks to morbid heights of tomb building. Sudden, violent death was all too common among the ruling elite of former slaves. Out of fifty-three Mamluk sultans between 1257 and 1517, nineteen were murdered, assassinated or executed. Only ten died in office of natural causes; the rest were deposed. The Mamluk system, whereby the sultan granted fiefdoms to his generals in return for their maintenance of private armies, concentrated all the wealth of the sultanate, which is to say of Egypt, of Syria and of the Arabian littoral south beyond Mecca, in the hands of a few great amirs. Since their holdings reverted to the state when they died, these generals were encouraged to spend while they could. Hence the temptation to build tombs – reinforced, perhaps, by hopes that one day the people of Cairo would forget their dastardly deeds and turn them into saints.

It was not too far-fetched a wish. Across from the tomb that Shagar al-Durr built for her husband, the Mamluk sultan al-Mansur Qalawun was to undertake a far more ambitious construction. His work perfectly embodied the character of the Mamluk regime, combining ruthlessness, extravagance and aesthetic refinement with a craving for popularity. Qalawun had the current tenant of the chosen property, an Ayyubid princess, turfed out. He then had the city's finest artisans rounded up to help with demolition and rebuilding. The sultan's soldiers forced hapless wayfarers – even distinguished sheikhs – to carry stones. Despite popular indignation, which was so great that the sultan's propagandists felt obliged to spread the tale that it was not taxes but rather a secret treasure found on the site that paid for the building, the whole immense structure was completed in a single year. On its opening in 1285 courageous clerics at first declared prayer there unlawful. When one was finally coaxed into delivering an inaugural sermon he used the occasion to blast the sultan for his tyranny.

Qalawun intended his monument to establish his own and his city's glory beyond all question. To appeal to the common people, it housed a free hospital that was endowed with the best doctors and druggists of the age. The college of medicine and Islamic law next door catered to the educated classes. For the sultan himself there was a fabulous tomb chamber. Faced with intricately carved stucco, lined with panels of polychrome marble and with stone puzzled into endless repetitions of the name Muhammad, the whole was topped by a great dome raised on granite pharaonic columns with Corinthian capitals pilfered from the declining city of Alexandria.

The mausoleum, one of the most beautiful the medieval city preserves, took as its model the Dome of the Rock in Jerusalem.

The Mamluks had recently recaptured this third holiest shrine in Islam from the crusaders. There, a gilded dome covered a boulder from which the Prophet Muhammad was said to have sprung on a winged horse in a miraculous night flight to the seven heavens. An octagonal ambulatory surrounded the sacred stone itself. In Qalawun's mausoleum in Cairo a similar gallery – ready-made for pious circumambulation – ringed instead the cenotaph of this former slave who had risen by strength and cunning to rule the wealthiest realm west of Samarkand. A body of prized eunuchs mounted guard to ensure proper respect, just as at the sultan's harem in the Citadel. The tomb chamber protruded into the roadway, where passers-by could bless the sultan in his grave and profit from the paid Koran readers who chanted night and day from its windows.

Qalawun's origins and his unpopularity while he ruled were eventually forgotten. He was never elevated to sainthood, but he did found the closest thing the Mamluks ever had to a dynasty. His sons and grandsons continued to rule – and to build spectacular tombs – for a further century before their own Mamluks ousted them. His hospital treated patients for hundreds of years – at the rate of 4,000 a day in its fourteenth-century prime. Its reputation eventually faded. Before crumbling entirely, the hospital became an insane asylum, and this was replaced in the nineteenth century by an eye clinic.

But the magnificent tomb still stands, its dome and minaret dominating the most monument-packed stretch of street in the city. Tourists are the only visitors now, but reports from the last century say it was even then still believed that the only certain cure for headache was to rub the stone turban atop Qalawun's cenotaph.

THERE WAS ANOTHER, darker, reasoning behind the medieval tomb-building frenzy. The custom of visiting and worshipping in graveyards was also an act of appeasement. It came in response to the anger of the heavens witnessed by Cairenes as famines and epidemics ravaged their city again and again throughout the period of its greatest splendour. The cemeteries did not just grow: they expanded in sickening waves.

Nature's whim had always made the level of the Nile a matter of intense public concern. The earliest Muslim governors had built a Nilometer on the island of Roda facing Misr al-Fustat. (It went out of use only a century ago, but still stands on the southern tip of the island.) In the late summer flood season, heralds wearing yellow bandannas would run through the city to announce the day's reading. Shopkeepers tipped them gratefully, since the river level affected both prices and tax estimates. When it reached the required sixteen cubits, the government could be sure of a plentiful harvest and full coffers. If it rose too high or fell short, trouble was at hand.

This happened repeatedly between the tenth and fourteenth centuries, often with appalling results. So dreaded was the temper of the river that when the Arabic grammarian Ibn al-Nahas strolled along its bank humming to himself one day in AD 950, some alert citizen took him for a sorcerer. Imagining that the scholar was casting spells on the river, the vigilante hurled him into the water, where he drowned.

When a disastrous drought came in AD 967, the ensuing disorder eased the Fatimids' conquest of Egypt. The Nile's capriciousness was indiscriminate, however. The Fatimid caliph himself suffered from the calamitous seven-year dearth of 1065–72. In those years the city succumbed to panic. Bread, say the chronicles, was auctioned at an unbelievable twelve dinars a loaf,* – a price so far beyond the reach of the poor that some were said to have resorted to fitting meat hooks to ropes so as to

* Although the whole scale of values has changed, rendering comparison highly speculative, a Fatimid dinar would be roughly equivalent to $200 today.

fish unlucky pedestrians off the street and eat them. The historian al-Maqrizi says the caliph al-Mustansir was forced to sell precious objects, furniture, horses, arms and eventually all the movable contents of his palace. When he was reduced at last to squatting on a mat on the floor of his throne room and living off charity, the women of his court fled. The Shiʿite princesses set off for the rival Abbasid city of Baghdad, 'their hair dishevelled, howling with hunger', only to fall outside the walls of Cairo and die of starvation. Al-Mustansir's humiliation now touched bottom: the caliph was forced to pawn ornaments from the tombs of his ancestors.

Al Mustansir's possessions cannot have brought in very much. Al-Maqrizi – who, as a Sunni cleric, admittedly had it in for Egypt's former Shiʿite masters – tells us that at the height of the famine a wealthy widow pawned a necklace which had cost her 1,000 dinars. All it fetched was a sack of flour. The unlucky lady hired guards to defend her pathetic prize, but even so a mob attacked them outside the city gates and relieved her of all but a fistful. This she made into a biscuit which she carried to the door of the caliph's palace. 'People of Cairo!' she shouted to the crowd that gathered, 'Blessings on our master al-Mustansir. Providence has proven the goodness of his rule, since I have bought this biscuit for 1,000 dinars!'

The poor lady's scouring sarcasm – and her tone is still typical of Cairene protests – was to no avail. There was no uprising. The caliph, rescued by the arrival of his army from Syria, went on to rule for another twenty-five years. His dynasty survived another century. The tribulations of al-Mustansir, moreover, were to pale in comparison with the horrors that befell Cairo thirty years after the fall of the Fatimids.

The visiting doctor Abd al Latif of Baghdad witnessed these at first hand. As it became clear that the flood of the year 1200 was insufficient, he relates, all those who could afford to abandoned Egypt altogether. Those who could not took refuge in the capital and shared its ghastly fate;

> For when the sun had entered the sign of the Ram the air was corrupted, the plague and contagion began to make itself felt, and the poor, pressed by famine ... ate carrion, corpses, dogs and the excrement and filth of animals. This went on for a long time, until they began to eat little children ...
>
> When poor people began to eat human flesh, such was the horror and shock that these crimes became the chief topic of conversation ... But soon they grew used to such things, and developed quite a taste for these detestable foods, and saw men make it their ordinary nourishment, to eat as a treat, and make reserves of it ...
>
> A large number of people crossed to the island of Roda and hid out in mud huts from where they hunted passers-by to kidnap them. The authorities were notified and set out to kill them, but the cannibals escaped. There was found in their huts a huge quantity of human bones. A man who is honest told me they counted 400 skulls ...
>
> As for the number of the poor who perished from exhaustion and hunger, God alone knows ... This should be regarded as a slight example ... for the intelligent to realize the horror seen at Fustat and Cairo: in the streets where I trod, there was no single one where the feet or the eyes did not meet with a corpse or a man in the throes of mortal agony, or even a large number of people in this unhappy condition ...
>
> They carried away ... from Cairo each day between 100 and 500 bodies ... At Fustat the number of dead was incalculable: they could not inter them, but contented themselves with throwing them outside the town. In the end there were no more people even to lift them and they remained in the market, and between the houses and shops ... The greater part of the town was depopulated ... I have been told there had previously been at Fustat 900 makers of rush mats, and

> there remained only fifteen. One could not but apply the same proportion to the other crafts.

Abd al-Latif goes on to say that the number of registered dead in the two years of famine – that is, those who were properly buried – was 110,000. He believed the total to be far higher.

At that time Misr al-Fustat and Cairo, though only a few miles apart, were rival cities. Most commerce and industry still centred closer to the Nile at Fustat, even though a serious fire had ravaged the town at the end of the Fatimid era. (The fire was deliberately set by a Fatimid wazir, who feared that advancing crusaders would use unwalled Fustat as a vantage point for attacking the imperial enclosure of al-Qahira.) Cairo, with its finer houses and government offices, was just beginning to dominate its forebear. The famine accelerated the decline of Misr al-Fustat. Abd al-Latif says that its abandoned buildings were plundered for wood and fittings. In better-policed Cairo, meanwhile, property prices fell to one-sixteenth of their previous value, which must have encouraged survivors to move in.

Cairo recovered. It grew rich again, and its population had probably doubled by the time the Grim Reaper returned a century and a half later. In 1347 slave traders from the Black Sea brought with them something far deadlier than a cargo of future Mamluk warriors: the Black Death. The plague infested the whole of the known world, but nowhere was it fiercer than in Cairo. Over two years it wiped out an estimated one-third of the population. The number of victims, al-Maqrizi records, surpassed 1,000 a day:

> A man would sense that he had fever in his body. Then he would feel nauseated and spit blood, with death following. One after another the people of his household would go after him until all of them had perished. As everyone left alive was sure that he would die of the disease, all of the people prepared

> themselves for the end, increasing their charities, making expiation and turning to worship.

In the wake of this epidemic, says Cairo's pre-eminent chronicler, you could walk the busy mile between the two old city gates, Bab Zuwayla and Bab al-Futuh, without once being jostled.

It was a blow from which the city might have recovered – like the towns of Europe – if only the disease had not struck repeatedly, and often in the pneumonic form, which is far more contagious. Between 1347 and 1517 there were 55 plague outbreaks, among them 20 epidemics. From 1517 to 1894 the plague was reported in 133 years, with 33 major epidemics. While the population of Europe grew from the fourteenth century onward, Egypt's declined. In 1800 it was a third of what it had been at the time of the Arab conquest 1,200 years before. The devastation was economic as well. Revenue from Egypt's land tax in 1500 was a mere quarter of its level in 1200. Fewer Mamluk slaves could be bought and equipped, and of these many succumbed to the plague, which in itself meant a significant loss of capital. This whittling away of the sultanate's army and resources was one reason why the invading Ottoman Turks found it so easy to overrun the Mamluk realm at the beginning of the sixteenth century.

Cairo boasted the greatest army and proudest citadel of the age, but it was utterly defenceless against disease. Fatally, ruler and ruled alike continued to ascribe the plague to heavenly anger. Fanaticism and superstition flourished. During an outbreak in 1438 the sultan was assured by a sheikh of the al-Azhar mosque that 'If fornication spreads among men, the plague appears among them, also if women adorn themselves and walk in the streets ...' Until a public outcry forced him to relent, the sultan banned women from leaving their homes.

Life somehow went on amid the misery. The city survived. Some of its citizens prospered: the mystics and astrologers and

Koran chanters, the undertakers and sellers of the victims' flea-infested clothes, which seventeenth-century European visitors were appalled to find for sale in the markets. And, of course, the tomb builders.

Alexander Kinglake, author of the travel classic *Eothen*, arrived in 1835 to find himself a fearful witness to one of the last devastating plagues. Most Europeans had chosen to flee the city, but this foolhardy Briton stayed. During a sojourn of only three weeks his landlord, his banker, the doctor who treated him for a fever, a magician he hired, his donkey driver and the brother and sister of his household servant all died of the disease:

> When first I arrived at Cairo the funerals that passed daily under my windows were many, but still there were frequent and long intervals without a howl ... these intervals became less frequent and shorter, and at last the passing of the howlers from morn to noon was almost incessant. I believe that about one half of the whole population was carried off by this visitation.

He was wrong. According to official figures it was only a quarter of Cairo's 250,000 people.* But still one can understand Kinglake's astonishment when he found, in a busy cemetery outside the city, swings and festival tents set up for a *mawlid*.

CAIRO HAD ATTAINED the pinnacle of its fortunes when Sultan al-Nasir Muhammad ibn Qalawun died of old age in the year 1341. This son of the hospital-building Qalawun had ruled continuously since the beginning of the century – a record never surpassed by any Mamluk sovereign. Despite his cruelty – he had some 150 of his amirs killed and thousands of lesser opponents tortured by the most diabolical methods – al-Nasir Muhammad's

* Four years before, cholera had carried off another 36,000 Cairenes.

reign had been an interlude of peace and prosperity. In wealth, size and power Cairo was unrivalled in the known world. The Ottoman Turks to the north were not yet a threat; the Mongol menace from the east had receded. Christian Europe now sent merchants, not warriors, to the Mamluk capital, which reaped phenomenal profits from its monopoly of trade with the Orient. The sultan himself cashed in handsomely. By a redistribution of fiefdoms which he had forced on his amirs, five-twelfths of the empire's revenues – including the tax receipts of Mecca, Damascus and Aleppo and the tariffs of Jedda, Alexandria and Tripoli – now flowed directly into his coffers in the Citadel. Al-Nasir Muhammad's eleven daughters received a dowry of some 800,000 gold dinars each. His fourteen sons were the wealthiest men in the world.

They were not so fortunate in other ways. During the six short years that followed al-Nasir's death, murder and intrigue eliminated five of his sons from the succession. Soon after their brother Hasan, a freckled, red-haired boy of twelve, acceded to the throne in 1347, the Black Death struck down a third of his capital's people.

Ironically, the youthful Sultan Hasan found himself richer than ever. As whole families were erased, thousands of victims died intestate. Their property reverted to the ruler. Perhaps in the hope that an act of piety would appease God (or maybe encouraged by courtiers seeking commissions and kickbacks), Hasan decided to spend this hoard on the most gigantic religious edifice yet seen in Islam. It would not be complete, of course, without the most glorious royal tomb to grace Cairo.

The site Hasan chose was across from the polo ground below the sumptuous Striped Palace his father had built in the Citadel, from whose windows he could watch the progress of construction. The work began in 1356, and for five years thereafter the treasury haemorrhaged funds at a rate of 1,000 dinars a day. The building's lavish ornamentation reflected the eclectic outlook of the Mamluks' imperial city. Its mammoth sunken doorway, capped with a stone semi-dome carved into stalactites as intricate as the inside of a pomegranate, mimicked the portals of Seljuk mosques in Anatolia. Chinese porcelain inspired the stone-carved lotuses and hyacinths that flanked the great doors, which were of burnished bronze worked into a mesmerizing pattern of starbursts. The stone door frames of the interior, tiered in black and white stripes, showed the influence of Muslim Spain. Twenty-seven shades of marble from across the Mediterranean paved the courts and chambers and fountains inside. Yet the whole projected an austere aesthetic and a scale so powerful that it could only have been at home in the great, bustling capital that was Cairo.

Sultan Hasan's combined mosque, *madrasa* and tomb covered 10,000 square yards. It had walls of cut limestone 130 feet high, with minarets towering 150 feet further. They were so lofty, in fact, that when one of them collapsed before completion it was said to have crushed 300 onlookers. This single building contained four complete apartment buildings providing free lodging to 500 students along with a salaried staff that included two physicians and a surgeon as well as professors, calligraphers, a professional incense burner, six prayer-leaders, fifty-one prayer-callers and 120 Koran readers. The dormitories, six storeys high and placed at the corners of a vast central courtyard, surmounted a ground floor incorporating kitchens and wells in addition to an arcaded market two acres in area whose rents were to pay for maintaining the institution. Colossal vaults opened off the sides of the courtyard between the colleges. The one facing Mecca was deeper than the others, panelled with marble marquetry and bordered with a stucco frieze of lotus blossoms spiralling around a Koranic inscription in ornate Kufic script.

Daringly, the gold and silver inlaid doors flanking the prayer niche opened on to the sultan's own domed tomb chamber. Turning to Mecca, the faithful would worship facing Hasan's cenotaph. The idea was that, just as his subjects had prostrated themselves before him when he was alive, so they would bow their foreheads to the ground before him after his death. But this peculiar vision was not to be fulfilled. Sultan Hasan made the fatal error of trying to curtail the power of both his generals and the court eunuchs. As the intrigue mounted, the sultan, now aged twenty-six, fled the Citadel. He was hunted, captured hiding in the city, and killed. The whereabouts of his body were never revealed.

And in fact his mosque never was completed to the last detail: to this day you can see the marks made by master stonecarvers who sketched in designs which were to be finished by apprentices. Sultan Hasan's monument to the plague was, however, so sturdily built that rebels later used its roof to fire catapults and artillery at the Citadel. At least one wary sultan had the front steps demolished to prevent access, which is one reason why it is so well preserved – right down to the brilliant gold inlay of the tomb doors which has miraculously survived intact.

The Mosque of Sultan Hasan still towers above all the other mosques of Cairo. Its stern façades, with their astoundingly modern-looking vertical panels of windows, still seem intent on warding off the disease raging outside. And when you slip off your shoes and penetrate the interior the spell of the place still holds. A dark corridor disorientates at first, sending you left and then right and then left again, tantalizing you with other passages, other possibilities, before drawing you to a rectangle of light that opens on the tremendous volume of the courtyard, where you blink and stand humbled by the scale and perfection of this vision of peace.

A CENTURY AND a half after Sultan Hasan, the Mamluk sultanate fell. In the dark year 1517 the great new empire of the Ottoman Turks overwhelmed Egypt. An occupying army marched into Cairo.

The city was again reduced to provincial status, a town ruled by Ottoman governors rather than its own kings. Constantinople, its old rival, had triumphed, and, as successive Ottoman sultans embellished their capital on the Bosporus with palaces and domes and minarets, the monuments of Cairo's lost golden age grew tarnished with neglect in a constant reminder of the city's fallen state.

Tombs crumbled in the outlying parts of the City of the Dead. Their ruins merged with the grey refuse heaps that now smothered long-abandoned quarters of Misr al-Fustat. Beginning in the sixteenth century, travellers began to report that in this melancholic wasteland crowds of curious Cairenes gathered once a year. They came to a spot where an ancient Coptic martyr was said to have been buried, for it was here that an eerie spectacle unfolded. On the appointed day, the bodies of the dead were said to emerge, to sway for a time in a silent dance, and then to disappear again into the ground. As a French adventurer by the name of Carlier de Pinon related in 1579, some of the corpses were whole, some in parts – 'as all the inhabitants of Cairo testified, and as I was particularly assured by my host, a man by no means superstitious'.

A century later this *danse macabre* had somehow moved across the river to the ruins of Memphis.* But it no longer fooled some. Certainly not the sceptical Englishman George Sandys, who offered this account:

> A day or two after, we crossed the NILUS from Cairo. Three miles beyond on the left hand we came to the place where upon Good Friday the Arms and Legs of a number of men appear stretched forth of the earth, to the astonishment of the multitude. This I have heard confirmed by CHRISTIANS, MAHOMETANS, and JEWS, as seen upon their several Faiths. An imposture, perhaps contrived by Water-men who,

* The word *macabre* may itself be of Cairene origin, deriving from the Arabic *maqābir*, one of the army of terms meaning tombs.

> fetching from the MUMMIES whereof there are an inconsumable number, and keeping the mystery in their Families, do stick them overnight in the sand, obtaining thereby the yearly Ferrying-over of many thousands of Passengers.

Sandys may have got it right. The curious phenomenon had faded from the annals of the city by the eighteenth century.

Nowadays the only mummies to be seen lie safely under glass at the Egyptian Museum. Plagues and famines are, happily, unknown to modern Cairo. Nevertheless, the rites of death keep a powerful hold. Political demonstrations rarely raise big crowds in this cynical city, but the funerals of the famous draw thousands. When the greatest pharaoh of modern times, President Gamal Abd al-Nasser, died in 1970, the 2 million followers of his cortège nearly caused the Qasr al-Nil Bridge to collapse. And Cairo has continued to honour heroes with magnificent tombs: the nationalist leader Saad Zaghloul lies in a splendid neo-pharaonic temple; Nasser in a neo-Mamluk funerary mosque; President Anwar al-Sadat under a pyramid of cast concrete. (King Farouk, however, was parked in an obscure family tomb in the dead of night, the regime which overthrew him apparently acting on the ancient instinct to punish one's foes even in the afterlife.)

So casual about other things, Cairenes are strikingly punctilious in the rituals of condolence. Friends not only will drop everything to rush to a funeral but will also mark the end of the forty-day mourning period and the anniversary of someone's passing. The death notices in *Al-Ahram*, the city's newspaper of record, run to thirty solid columns a day and often more: the saying is that a person cannot have died if their death goes unmentioned in *Al-Ahram* – which incidentally means 'The Pyramids'. Ladies of leisure often turn straight to the back of the paper so as to plan their daily agenda of condolence visits. (Besides, the form of the notices is intriguingly thorough. Every member of the bereaved family is listed, along with their place of work and their relation to the deceased. For anyone hoping to unravel the knotted web of family alliances which binds Cairene society, the obituaries are a uniquely penetrating tool.)

If a single trait can describe Cairo's people, it must be their enduring, life-giving nonchalance. And where does it come from? One drowsy denizen of a Cairo bar, a psychiatrist by day, assured me that obsession with the afterlife – even to the exclusion of daily travails – explains all the city's mysteries. 'Everyone here, you see, lives inside his coffin,' he said. 'We are all half mummies ... and half gods!'

CHAPTER FOUR

MOTHER OF THE WORLD

We arrived in Cairo on Sunday, June 17, 1481. I had come to see the Cairenes and their deeds. However, if I were to write about its wealth and its people, all of this book would not be sufficient. I swear that if it were possible to put Rome, Venice, Milan, Padua, Florence and four more cities together, they would not equal in wealth and population half that of Cairo.

Rabbi Meshulam of Volterra, quoted in E. N. Adler, *Jewish Travellers*

JACOB SAPHIR, A Talmudist who has wandered far and wide collecting alms for the Jewish poor of Jerusalem, is used to trotting about on donkeyback. The year is 1864, and this is the third time in as many years that the Lithuanian scholar has hired one of these mountable taxis to ride the carriage road south to the riverside suburb now known as Old Cairo. Leaving behind the last of the Ottoman Rococo palaces that Egypt's cotton-rich rulers have recently built for themselves, he crosses a bridge over a canal and passes the massive intake tower of a sixteenth-century aqueduct. From here Saphir can see, far off to the right at the tip of the island of Roda, the conical roof of the Nilometer. Perhaps the sight inspires a reverie: local legend holds that a tree by the ancient building marks the very spot where the daughter of

Pharaoh found the infant Moses among the bulrushes. But Saphir's thoughts may turn instead to more recent events. Barely two years have passed since the Englishman John Hanning Speke announced his sensational discovery of the source of the blessed river at faraway Lake Victoria.

The traveller presses on, skirting the high walls of a Coptic monastery. Off to the left, between the first tumbledown houses of Old Cairo, he spies a long, low structure which the Baedeker identifies as the mosque built by Amr ibn al-ʿAs, the Arab general whose army captured Egypt and founded the city of Misr al-Fustat in AD 640. An unglamorous building, its rough squareness evokes the simplicity of early Islam. Ashen dung heaps undulate behind the mosque, burying the traces of Amr's city and stretching to the distant dome of Imam al-Shafiʿi's tomb, which stands silhouetted against the Muqattam cliffs. Pursuing his course, Saphir arrives at last outside the much-eroded walls of the Roman fort of Babylon. Its moat is long gone; its broad, round towers are sunk in the ground to half their fifty-foot height. Saphir must dismount, trip down a dusty slope, and stoop to pass through a low doorway that gives access to the cramped warren of lanes inside the fort.

For a thousand years a little synagogue has stood in a cul-de-sac at the back of Babylon, sharing the shelter of the Roman walls with a clutter of equally ancient churches and monasteries. It is the oldest and most venerated synagogue in Cairo, but most of its congregation moved long ago to the Jewish Quarter in the city itself. With only twelve impoverished and – as Saphir was to note – scarcely observant Jewish families left in Old Cairo, it is hardly surprising that their temple should appear rather desolate and neglected. But Saphir is undeterred. He is hoping that this time the synagogue's keepers will let him look into a closet where there is rumoured to be a great hoard of ancient manuscripts.

The keepers of the Synagogue of Ben Ezra usher this rare visitor inside. Would he like to touch again the ancient Torah which, they say, was written by the hand of Ezra the Scribe and carried to Egypt by the Prophet Jeremiah to save it from the ravages of Nebuchadnezzar? Saphir declines. It took a great deal of cajoling and baksheesh to see the scroll last time. He would like instead to explore the temple storeroom. But no, say the guardians, it is *mamnū͑* – forbidden – and, besides, the room is guarded by a deadly snake.

Saphir is well prepared. He has, he declares, the permission of the highest rabbinical authorities in Cairo. Not only this, but he is a skilled charmer of snakes, and moreover is protected by an amulet. This he displays – although it is nothing but the commonest of mezuzoth – and then, to greater effect, he jingles his purse. The keepers produce a ladder. Saphir clambers high up on to the roof of a tall, narrow chamber. Lowering himself in through a gaping hole, he comes to rest on a dust-smothered mound of fallen masonry and paper. Amid the chunks of stone and wood are crackling leaves of parchment and papyrus, scraps of inscribed leather and crumbling bindings.

SAPHIR WAS TO be disappointed. 'After I had laboured for two days and was covered with dust and loose earth,' he wrote in his diary, 'I picked out several sheets of different old scrolls and manuscripts, but I did not find any use or information in them – WHO KNOWS WHAT LIES UNDERNEATH! – for I was tired of searching.' He was never to know that the hole in the roof opened a panoramic view on to life in the greatest trading city of the Middle Ages.

Saphir had in fact penetrated the intact Geniza (or treasury) of Ben Ezra. Since the synagogue's last restoration in AD 1041 nearly all the papers of the city's Jewish community* had been

*More accurately, of the so-called Palestinian Jews, as opposed to the smaller Karaite and Iraqi Jewish sects, which had separate institutions at Cairo.

thrown higgledy-piggledy into this musty, two-and-a-half-storey-high lumber room, because by tradition any document in Hebrew letters, or any that might bear the name of God, had to be preserved. Aside from countless pages from sacred texts, the trove contained thousands of more mundane documents, the bulk of them from the tenth- to thirteenth-century heyday of Misr al-Fustat, before most of the city's Jews made the short move to al-Qahira. Court depositions nestled among deeds and titles and contracts, letters and petitions, business accounts and inventories, religious questions and rulings; in short, the Geniza held the most complete documentation of any medieval society that has ever been unearthed.

Manuscript collectors got wind of Saphir's find soon enough.* As Ben Ezra's keepers found that their musty papers could be exchanged for fresh cash, scraps and bundles began to filter out of the Geniza. Some quarter of a million fragments in all fluttered away as far afield as St Petersburg, Paris, Budapest and Philadelphia. By 1913 not a single snippet was left in Cairo.†

It took scholars decades to begin making sense of the stash. Their task was complicated by the peculiar writing habits of the Jews of Fustat, who mostly wrote their vernacular Arabic in Hebrew script, but sometimes wrote Hebrew in Arabic script and later, after the arrival of refugees from Spain, wrote occasionally in Ladino, the now-forgotten Yiddish of Iberia, or even in pure Castilian. Gentile documents in Arabic, Coptic, Latin, Syriac,

*Saphir published his memoirs in Hebrew in 1866. This may have alerted treasure-hunters to the Geniza, but there is evidence that leakage had begun before that.

†The bulk of the Geniza documents ended up at Cambridge. There, in 1896, the reader in Talmudics had humoured two stern Scottish sisters by agreeing to look at a manuscript they had recently purchased in Cairo. He opened their package expecting some bazaar forgery, and gasped. The document, a unique copy of the lost Hebrew text of a book from the Apocrypha, was priceless. He rushed to Cairo, where he charmed the Jewish community into allowing him to carry off all that remained of the Geniza.

Aramaic and also Georgian had somehow crept into the Geniza as well, adding to the intricacy of the puzzle.

The paper mosaic that slowly emerged pictures a prosperous and astonishingly cosmopolitan trading society. Ties of family and trade linked Fustat to Andalusia and to Samarkand, to Yemen and even across the Indian Ocean to the Malabar Coast and Ceylon. This was a society where, in 1016, a rabbi of Qairawan in Tunisia could send a letter by public post to Fustat enquiring what to do about the inheritance of a native of Baghdad who had died, 4,000 miles from home, in Morocco. Or where the Supreme Cohen of Jerusalem would write to announce the imminent arrival of a trader from Iran bearing the recommendation of a mutual friend, a merchant in Seville. Or where an order would be received from one Nahray Ben Nissim, a Tunisian trader in 120 different commodities, for a number of fine crystal wands for the application of kohl.

The bankers of eleventh-century Fustat issued promissory notes and offered loans at interest, as invoices and deeds from the Geniza show. Doctors made patients sign disclaimers before performing operations. Traders sold on credit. At Fustat you could purchase a one-forty-eighth share of a property in the city. You could buy a slave by instalments, as we know from a letter to the chief rabbi of Cairo at the end of the twelfth century – who was none other than the great reformer Maimoun Ibn Musa, better known as Maimonides, author of the *Mishna Torah* and the Arabic philosophical classic *Dalālat al-Ḥāʾirīn* or *The Guide for the Perplexed*. The petitioner asked what action to take against a man who had purchased a slave from him at a price of twelve and a half dinars, to be paid at one dinar a month, and then absconded. We do not know what Maimonides answered. Part of the charm of the Geniza is its piecemeal randomness.

Sometimes the documents thrust the people of Fustat into startlingly sharp focus. We know, for instance, precisely what a certain Ali of Tripoli, a stitcher of animal skins, looked like in

1136. His rental contract – for a house and garden with a fountain 'on the shore of the blessed Nile' – comes complete with an elaborate written portrait, a formality which was apparently as indispensable then as the multiple photos demanded by Cairene bureaucrats today. Ali emerges as a middle-aged man of 'reddish-brown complexion'. He has a smooth, slightly wrinkled forehead, light hair between his eyebrows, dark-brown eyes, a hooked nose and a round beard. His top right incisor is missing.

Under the laissez-faire rule of the Fatimids (969–1171), Fustat – with its growing twin city of Cairo – became the major emporium of the Western world. The Geniza documents evoke the profusion of wares to be found in its eleventh-century bazaars: copies of the *Thousand and One Nights* (as we know from a bookseller's inventory), mosquito nets from the Egyptian Delta, reed mats from Alexandria and Basra, opium of Asyut, silk turbans from Muslim Spain and Sicily, Yemeni mattresses, Baghdad cloaks, Armenian carpets, Abyssinian hides and ostrich feathers, Chinese porcelains, perfumed Tunisian soaps, copper vessels from Mosul, swords of Damascene steel, Koran stands of Indian teak, Byzantine brocades, Baltic amber, pearls from Muscat and rubies of Ceylon that might have been shipped by Maimonides' own brother David, who traded in precious stones before his tragic drowning in the Indian Ocean. And there were the local manufactures: exquisite coloured glass which a Persian traveller praised as being like emeralds in clarity and brilliance; glazed porcelains so fine as to be translucent – including excellent imitations of Chinese Tang and Sung ware; paper – as yet unknown in Europe and so cheap at Fustat that confectioners and fruit sellers wrapped their goods in it; indigo, sugar, and twenty-six varieties of flax, the best of them reserved for the Fustat linen which was so delicate that a caliph of Baghdad likened it to the white film which lines the inside of eggshells.

The gold dinars minted in Fatimid Cairo made their way to the ends of the known world, becoming the standard currency of the age. The city's Arabic trading terms accompanied them, and so helped refine the rough, earthy English of Chaucer. There was *fustian*, the tough blend of *cotton* – from the Arabic *qutn* – and linen made at Fustat. There was the *dimity* of Damietta, the *damask* of Damascus, the *gauze* of Gaza, the *muslin* of Mosul and the watered silk of Baghdad's Atabi quarter known as *tabby* cloth. There was soft *mohair* and delicate *chiffon*; and the *camisole*, the *ream*, the *sash*, the *sequin*, the *mattress* and the *sofa*. A shipment leaving Fustat might comprise *jars* of *camphor* or *syrup* or *sherbet*; *sugar*, *candy* and spices like *cinnabar*, *caraway*, *carob*, *cumin* and *sesame* seeds, enough to fill a *magazine* or *arsenal*, and certainly to require payment of a hefty *tariff*. An *admiral* of the highest *calibre* might command the vessel. Having consulted his *almanac* and imbibed a *carafe* brimming with an *elixir* of *attar* of *jasmine* when the sun reached its *zenith*, he would have himself *massaged* with a gentle *drubbing* before the *mizzen* mast, to the accompaniment of a *lute*.*

While Egypt luxuriated, Europe was lurching to the end of a dark age. Beginning with the Synod of Toulouse in 1229, which established the network of spies and witch trials known as the Inquisition, the Catholic Church escalated persecution of heretics, Jews and Muslims. Like the Jews of Switzerland in the Second World War, the 7,000 fortunate Jews of Fustat grew to dread the influx of refugees from across the Mediterranean. Not only were many of these newcomers uncouth, they were also destitute.

*Mohair – made from finest goat's hair – derives from the Arabic word *mukhayyar*, meaning 'chosen'. Chiffon, the flimsiest silk, comes from *shafāf*, meaning transparent. Crimson=*kirmiz*; azure=*azraq*; blouse=Pelusium, a port city in the Eastern Delta; camisole (and the French *chemise*)=*qamīs*; ream=*ruzma*; sash=*shāsh*; sequin=*sikka*; mattress=*maṭraḥa*; sofa=*ṣuffa*; jar=*jarra*; camphor=*kāfūr*; syrup=*sharāb*; sherbet=*sharbāt*; sugar=*sukkar*; candy=*qandi*; cinnabar=*zunjufr*; caraway=*karawiya*; carob=*kharrūb*; cumin=*kammūn*; sesame=*simsim*; magazine=*makhzan*; arsenal=*dār al-ṣinaʿa*, meaning a House of Industry; tariff=*taʿrifa*; admiral=*amīr al-baḥr*, or Lord of the Sea; almanac=*al-manākh*; carafe=*gharrāfa*; elixir=*al-iksīr*; attar=*ʿiṭr*; jasmine=*yasmīn*; zenith=*samat*; massage=*masaḥa*; drub=*daraba*; mizzen=*mizān* or balance; lute=*al-ʿūd*, the ancestor of the guitar.

They could not afford the tax of one to four dinars a head that Egypt's rulers imposed on their non-Muslim subjects – a tax which the local community would be obliged to pay on the immigrants' behalf. A letter in the Geniza – sent from a citizen of Alexandria to the chief justice of Fustat's Jews, Hananel Ben Samuel, and dated 15 May 1235 – reveals anxiety over the bigger tax burden: 'A boat has arrived from Marseilles after a voyage of twenty-five days. Moses, the parchment-maker, who travelled on it – you know him – told us that a huge crowd of our co-religionists prepare to come. May God guard us from the troubles they cause!'

LIKE MEMPHIS IN Herodotus' time, Fustat in the eleventh and twelfth centuries was a city where races and creeds mingled peaceably on the whole. Aside from the constant influx of slaves, the cross-currents of war and commerce and religious devotion brought waves of foreign immigrants. The Fatimid army, for example, was made up of Berber, Sudanese and Turkish brigades. The palace guard, 10,000-strong according to the eleventh-century Persian traveller Nasir Khusraw, was a sort of Foreign Legion of mercenaries, with each corps wielding its national arms. Khusraw described the Fatimid court as a haven for political refugees. Lords and princes of the Maghreb, Yemen, Byzantium, Slavonia, Nubia, Ethiopia and Georgia, he said, as well as sundry men of letters, received stipends from the caliph. 'They live at court like ministers of state,' wrote Khusraw in his *Safarnameh*. 'With nothing in particular to do they wander about, chat with each other and retire to their quarters.' Four hundred years later, the Flemish traveller Joos van Ghistele described having met, among others in a few days at Cairo, a Christian renegade from Valencia who worked as a translator, a Prussian from Danzig employed as an officer in the sultan's treasury, three Mamluk soldiers from Bordeaux, and a jeweller from his own native city of Ghent.

Because of its position on the route to Mecca, Egypt drew pilgrims from across Islam. Many, like the Tunisian-born scholar Abd al-Rahman Ibn Khaldun in the fourteenth century, ended up staying to study or teach in the well-endowed colleges of Fustat and Cairo. Al-Azhar, founded by the Fatimid caliph al-Muʿizz, was the oldest of these. It maintained separate lodgings for Moroccans, Syrians, Turks and Red Sea peoples. Christian and Jewish pilgrims, too, made the city a stopping-place on the route to the Holy Land.

But it was above all trade that gave Egypt's capital its international cast. The Italian port of Amalfi established a permanent delegation at Fustat in AD 996. King Roger II of Sicily, whose father had wrested their island kingdom from Fatimid control and who was so curious about Cairo that he sent the Arab geographer Abu Abdallah Muhammad al-Idrisi to report on its marvels, signed a trade pact with the Fatimids in 1143. Commercial treaties with Ceylon, Venice, Florence and Genoa followed in Mamluk times, when the commerce in Eastern spices reached its height. So prosperous was a spice-trading guild known as the Karimis that they acted as lenders of last resort to the government itself. When a chief of the guild by the name of Nasir al-Din Balisi died in 1373, his sons inherited a trading network with agents in India, Yemen, Abyssinia and Mali – as well as a legacy valued at a million gold dinars. Later, during Ottoman rule, Cairo was the linchpin of the international coffee business, importing the beans from Yemen and exporting them to Europe. Its famous luxury bazaar, Khan al Khalili, became a prosperous merchant colony of Persians and Turks.

In the barrierless world of medieval Islam it was easy for foreign Muslims to set up shop in the Egyptian capital. For infidels there were obstacles. The *jizya* – the tax on non-Muslims which was abolished only in the mid nineteenth century – was a serious burden. Since its revenue dwindled over time as the proportion of Muslims rose, police grew stricter in checking Christians and Jews for annual certificates of acquittance. Without a tax certificate you could not travel. Families were held responsible for absent members. Non-payment meant imprisonment.

The Geniza reveals, however, that Fustat's minorities were troubled less by persecution than by the everyday concerns they shared with their Muslim neighbours, the major ones being the price of bread and the level of the Nile. Property deeds show that there were no ghettos in Fustat. Jewish-owned houses usually adjoined Muslim and Christian property, and Jewish merchants often had Muslim partners. Christians and Jews worked in a range of professions, from doctors and wine dealers – there was even a Street of the Winesellers in Muslim-ruled Fustat – to high posts in government and lowly crafts like mat-weaving.

Being themselves from a Shi'ite sect which most Muslims considered heretical, the Fatimids naturally sympathized with minorities. Repeated decrees declared the caliph's beneficence, such as one of 1134 which promised 'to guard those of the People of Protection who are included in this Kingdom and to cover them with the cloak of compassion and mercy'. The Fatimid government hosted feasts to mark Christian holidays. It not only paid the salary of the head of the Jewish community but also occasionally funded the building of churches and yeshivas. Although the wealthiest merchants and officials tended to be Muslims, Christians and Jews rose to prominence. Three generations of court physicians were Jewish. Numerous Fatimid wazirs were Christian, as were most officials in the caliphate's complex fiscal bureaucracy.

Resentment at such apparent favour did bubble over at times, as in this verse composed by a Fatimid poet by the name of Rida ibn Thawb:

These days the Jews have reached their dream
They're rich; they reign supreme . . .
O Egyptians, here's my advice to you
Turn Jewish, since the heavens have turned Jew!

With the close of Fatimid rule in 1171, sentiments like these would express themselves with growing frequency in outright persecution. Still, Cairo's minorities never endured the horrors perpetrated in contemporary Europe. No sect here – with the exception of the Fatimids' own sect, the Ismaili Shi'ites – was ever hounded to extinction like the Jews and Muslims of Spain or the Cathars of France.

In times gone by, when stones threatened us, we wandered from place to place,' wrote Maimonides in his *Responsa*. 'But by the mercy of God we have now been enabled to find a resting place in this city.' The city he meant was Fustat, yet in his time Fustat was declining. Before being overthrown, the Fatimid government – itself cosily ensconced a few miles off in well-defended Cairo – had torched outlying quarters for fear that unwalled Fustat would fall into the hands of the crusaders. The famine of 1200 depopulated Fustat further. But it was the gravity of political power that exerted the strongest pull. The Fatimids' successors had opened Cairo to commoners, while themselves moving to the towering Citadel they had built at its south-east corner. Business gravitated to the new seat of administration. Maimonides himself wrote to a friend complaining of his need to commute daily to the court of Saladin, where he – and his son after him – served as the sultan's chief physician: 'I do not return to Misr [al-Fustat] until the afternoon. Then I am almost dying from hunger. I find the antechambers filled with people, both Jews and Gentiles, nobles and commoners . . . I dismount from my animal, wash my hands, go forth to my patients and entreat them to bear with me while I partake of some refreshment.'

As Fustat had absorbed Memphis, Cairo subsumed Fustat. The common people's name for Egypt's capital – Misr – now applied to Cairo. Fustat became known as Misr al-Quadima or Old Cairo, which was exactly what Memphis had been called until its last traces vanished sometime in the fourteenth century. But Fustat did not disappear as completely as the pharaonic city. Instead it became a suburb of Cairo, a genteel rival to the bustling new port at Bulaq, a few miles north along the Nile.

Medieval Cairo was in fact a continuum of three cities. The great body of al-Qahira, placed well back from the Nile's undulating flood plain, stood on the two legs of the northern and southern port suburbs. Saladin's Citadel, with its palaces and government *dīwāns* and barracks and stables, formed the city's head. It was at first separated from al-Qahira's massive southern gate, Bab Zuwayla, by a mile of open land, but the grand mansions of courtiers and generals soon filled the space. Bab Zuwayla's rounded towers lost their defensive function. They now straddled the Qasaba, the main commercial street running north to the gates of Bab al-Futuh and south towards Fustat. Al-Qahira eventually burst its walls to the north and west, too, sprawling into fields and towards the Nile at Bulaq.

WHETHER MUSLIM PILGRIMS, Jewish scholars or Christian traders, medieval travellers agreed on one thing: the scale of Cairo was incomparable.

Khalil al-Zahiri, a Persian who saw the city in the fourteenth Century, swore that it was ample enough to fit the ten largest towns of his own country. Writing in 1384, a Florentine traveller by the name of Leonardo Frescobaldi said that more people dwelled on a single Cairo street than in all of Florence. The number of vessels docked at the port of Bulaq, he claimed, was equal to three times the shipping in the harbours of Venice, Genoa and Ancona combined. A generation later Emmanuel Piloti, a Cretan-Venetian whose silk and wine import business flourished at Cairo for twenty years, said the city was simply the largest in the world: 'It has a circumference of eighteen miles, within which live people without number ... It is in the very greatest prosperity of any city ...' Cairo was four times the size of Venice, said another wandering European. Seven times Paris, parroted a third in 1483, who went on to say it took him twelve full hours to ride a horse around its periphery.

The Cairo that new arrivals saw must have seemed as strikingly urban, in its scale and density and sensibilities, as New York or Hong Kong does today. Its population may have reached half a million or more before the great plague of 1348, making it the biggest city the Western world had seen since the decline of Rome.* From a distance it was said to look like a lofty mountain. Buildings of ten and, by one account, even fourteen storeys towered over streets only a few yards wide and crowded 'thick as locusts' with wayfarers. A single such tenement might house hundreds, even thousands, of people: two old schoolmates, say the chronicles, met by chance after thirty years' separation, only to find that they had lived all that time in the same building. Al-Maqrizi recorded the construction of an immense structure whose ground floor was a caravanserai and whose upper storeys contained 360 apartments housing 4,000 tenants.

Land values rose so high that architects grew skilled at squeezing their buildings into odd-shaped plots, chamfering corners, retracting entrances, and angling towers and windows to maximize their exposure to the streets. Off the main thoroughfares

*Precise figures for Cairo are disputed, but there is no question it outsized Mediterranean rivals. Rome at the height of its empire may have had a million inhabitants, but in AD 1500 its population was a mere 40,000. Paris was Europe's greatest city in that year, with perhaps 200,000 people. Constantinople had 100,000; London half that number.

such tactics were useless. With houses packed tight and leaning closely overhead, many alleys were dark enough for bats to fly in daytime. Fresh air itself was at a premium: the better houses were fitted with wind-catchers to scoop in the cool northern breeze. High ceilings, fountains, marble floors and open courtyards with north-facing verandas completed a natural air-conditioning system. Such ingenuity was of no use to the poor, however. Numerous visitors remarked on the large numbers of homeless. 'One sees many living on the city outskirts in tents, in pavilions, in holes and wells,' wrote Joos van Ghistele in 1483. 'For the lack of dwellings they cannot live in the city.' This was despite the fact that rent for a simple house could be as low as a few dinars a year – and as high as 800 for a stately mansion on a prime site in twelfth-century Cairo.

The city's great size tested medieval logistics in the extreme. Cairo's distance from the Nile made the supply of water problematic. Quenching its thirst, reported al-Maqrizi, required the constant labour of some 10,000 water-bearers. Their fleet of donkeys and camels plied ceaselessly between the Nile and the city to fill its private cisterns and public fountains by subscription. A similar number of itinerant caterers provided hot food, because the high cost of fuel in unforested Egypt meant that few could afford their own kitchens. Instead Cairenes bought grilled lamb from trays carried on the turbaned heads of public stewards, or roast chickens that had been reared in incubated batteries – a technology which never failed to impress European visitors. (An interesting resonance: Ptolemaic records from the third century BC show that public lentil-soup kitchens did a roaring trade at Memphis.)

Al Maqrizi counted 12,000 shops on the Qasaba alone,*

* The Qasaba – which evocatively means a funnel or gorge or throat – threads the northern and southern gates of Cairo. However, each section of its four-mile length has a different name: e.g. the Brassmakers, the Tentmakers, the Sifters, Between the Palaces, and so on.

and 87 separate markets in the city as a whole. On the outskirts these traded in general merchandise, but towards the city centre specialization was the rule. Boutiques selling inscribed ivory combs clustered near the Mosque of al-Azhar. Next door was the market for costly Siberian sable, lynx, ermine and squirrel furs. Arms, from laminated Khorrasani bows to chain mail to gold-and-silver inlaid swords, were sold between the mosques of Sultan Hasan and al-Maridani. The Bab Zuwayla – the former southern gate of Fatimid Cairo which had been overtaken by urban sprawl so that it now marked the symbolic heart of the city – itself hosted food stalls for sweets and a little market for musical instruments that was said to be a meeting place for libertines. Markets towards the northern gates of Bab al-Futuh and Bab al-Nasr furnished such things as saddlery and cloth, songbirds and of course slaves.

At least until the introduction of plantation slavery in the New World, the Cairo market was unrivalled in the quantity and variety of its human merchandise. Brought by caravan from the Sudan, Arabia, Syria and Libya, and by ship across the Red Sea and the Mediterranean, thousands of slaves – up to 10,000 a year even in the 1860s – changed hands here. Most were destined for domestic servitude in the city itself. Yet, aside from one slave uprising in the late fifteenth century, when several hundred stableboys revolted, fled across the river to Giza, and elected their own mock sultan and court, there is no evidence that the institution of slavery here was ever as intolerably cruel as in the Americas. Slaves were allowed to own property. It was not unusual for them to accumulate great fortunes: on her death in AD 1024 one slave girl of a Fatimid prince left a legacy valued at 400,000 gold dinars. Cairene merchants commonly shipped goods in the care of trusted slaves, and posted them as agents in far-off ports. While children born of concubines were automatically free, masters often liberated their slaves because doing so was considered an act of commendable piety.

Prices in the fifteenth century ranged from ten dinars for a serving maid to several thousand for the handsomest swordsman or shapeliest dancer (which compares sadly with the 30,000 dinars that Sultan al-Nasir Muhammad blew on a magnificent horse in 1320). Among Mamluks – boy slaves of good soldier stock – the most prized were fierce Tartars (typically 140 ducats a head, says Emmanuel Piloti), then Circassians, then Greeks, followed by Albanians, Slavs and lastly Serbs – a snip at seventy ducats apiece.* Seekers of concubines enjoyed a similarly wide choice. Abyssinian girls were prized for the reputed hotness and snugness of their 'pearl-boxes of ruby-depth', by one randy Turk's account. Buyers with other tastes could pick from narrow-eyed Mongols to flaxen-haired Caucasians. But caution was advised: dealers dyed blonde hair black because it fetched a better price.

Cairo expressed its merchant savvy in other ways. In 1324, 500 slaves, each bearing a tube of gold coins weighing 500 *mithqals* (about five pounds), heralded the arrival of Mansa Musa, king of Mali, bound on the pilgrimage to Mecca. Their heavy burden proved to be the African sovereign's small change: a hundred pack camels followed, every one loaded with three *kantars* – about 300 pounds – of the precious metal. Yet so thoroughly was Mansa Musa fleeced at Cairo that on his return from Mecca he was obliged to borrow 50,000 dinars from an Egyptian spice merchant.

Twelve years after Mansa Musa's visit, by which time the price of gold had yet to recover from his flooding of the market, Cairo shopkeepers still boasted of how they had milked the pious potentate and his train. 'One of them might buy a garment for five dinars when it was not worth one,' Ibn Fadlallah al-Umari, a Syrian traveller, was told. 'Such was their trustfulness that it was possible to practise any deception on them.' Another chronicler confirmed the account. The Africans, he related, thought their money was inexhaustible. But they were astounded 'at the

* A Venetian ducat was more or less equal in value to a gold dinar.

ampleness of the country and how their money had been used up, so they grew needy and resold what they had bought at half its value'. Back beyond Timbuktu, said al-Umari, Cairo's greed had so tarnished its reputation that were the most learned doctor of religious sciences to confess that he hailed from that city the Malians would treat him with contempt.

If Cairo itself was splendid, its court was nothing less than magnificent. Impregnable walls that stretched nearly two miles in circumference enclosed a veritable city inside the Citadel. Its mosques and markets vied for space with palaces and prisons, arsenals and stables, and the treasury, royal mint and Hall of Justice. In the fourteenth century, under the Mamluk sultan al-Nasir Muhammad, the Citadel's kitchens turned out some twenty-five tons of food a day, and for one splendid banquet served up 3,000 sheep, 600 cows and 500 horses while consuming a hundred tons of sugar for the desserts and sherbets.

Aside from its vast staff of state officials, the castle housed the sultan's two 'families' – his slave army and his army of wives and concubines and children. Each was meticulously chaperoned by a liveried and fiercely hierarchical corps of eunuchs. The Northern Enclosure quartered the royal Mamluks. These youths, whom the sultan's agents would have selected from the finest Turkish, Mongol and Slavic stocks, lived here in twelve barracks, each of which was said to have a capacity of 1,000 men. Secured out of sight behind the Southern Enclosure's Gate of the Veil, meanwhile, were the five Noble Dwellings where the sultan's harem lived. Al-Nasir Muhammad's four legal wives each maintained a household of her own, complete with children and slave girls. The fifth great hall was reserved for his 1,200 concubines.

Successive European visitors swore they had never seen any court to match the Mamluk ruler's in pomp and wealth and size. Felice Brancacci, a Florentine diplomat, expressed the impact of such magnificence in a breathless account of an audience with Sultan Barsbay in 1422. Having been told to rise at dawn, he wrote, his embassy was left to wait for hours on the polo grounds outside the Citadel gates. At last they were conducted in and closely escorted upwards through an endless sequence of courts and vaulted passages packed with neatly uniformed royal guards. After being searched for weapons 'down to our hose', he writes,

> We arrived at the sultan's quarters, having climbed eight full flights of stairs guarded by more Mamluks. These last were equipped with lances tipped with many points so as to resemble halberds, and they clashed these together over our heads as we passed.
>
> The room which we now entered was divided like a church into three naves separated by stone columns. It was paved with marble marquetry and covered with a carpet over most of its surface. Facing the entrance was a sort of stage with a stair on either side. On this stage, seated right on the boards, was the sultan. He was dressed in white linen . . . a man of thirty-eight to forty years with a brown beard. Immediately behind him stood a great number of his Mamluks. One held in his hand a sword and its scabbard, another carried a ewer, a third carried high on his shoulder a tube, a fathom in length and an inch in width, all of gold coins . . . The disposition of the whole vast assembly brought to mind a triumphal scene such as one might see in a painting. On every side were musicians playing the viol, the rebec, the lute, hollow instruments and cymbals, all together and accompanied by singers.
>
> Myself, my eye dazzled and ears deafened, aside from kissing the floor at every step, I make no claim to describe this with any order. What is more each of us found himself seized at the shoulders by two men and treated like pack-animals: each time they wanted us to kiss the floor they deafened us with shouts in their language. In this way they made us kiss the ground seven or eight times. When we were some fifty yards from the sultan we were stopped and the noise ceased. They

> told us to be brief for this first interview, during which at every moment three glinting hatchets were brandished over our heads. We had hardly told our interpreter a dozen words to introduce the matter when we were interrupted. 'Enough! Enough!' And while making us kiss the floor, they conducted us in retreat to the entrance...
>
> I note as a detail that in presenting the letter of Our Lordship, we kissed the document and held it before us for a moment. The official that took it grunted in our faces over the letter, then slapped us each with it well and good...
>
> Everywhere we were told that never had Frankish ambassadors been given such a good welcome...

Brancacci was later given a far warmer private reception. His mission was a success. The sultan granted Florence trading privileges.

And in fact Cairo could hardly be considered an inhospitable town. Entering the massive eleventh-century gate of Bab Zuwayla even now one gets a sense of the conveniences afforded to medieval travellers.

Inside the passageway itself, the tall grilled window on the left was once a platform for public Koran chanters, whose job was to bless passers-by with the word of God. A few steps on, a public drinking fountain catered to wayfarers of the Ottoman period. The upper floor of the small building was devoted to a Koran school for children. Pious benefactors endowed hundreds of such institutions in the city, so heeding the Prophet's saying that the two greatest mercies are water for the thirsty and knowledge for the ignorant.

A large caravanserai, a typical example of the seventy-odd merchant hostels that al-Maqrizi enumerated in the city, stands next door. Largely collapsed now, its upper storeys once provided lodging for travellers. The courtyard, now congested with shops and workshops, was originally an open trading floor where caravans could unload their goods. Just beyond is a public bathhouse – one of fifty-two listed by al-Maqrizi – while across the street rises the great tomb, mosque, college and dervish monastery of the fifteenth-century sultan al-Mu'ayyad Sheikh, where incidentally al-Maqrizi worked for a time as a professor of Islamic traditions. Sparrows chirrup and flitter among the trees in its spacious courtyard, accompanying the snores of the weary faithful who for over 600 years have used the mosque for their afternoon snooze. No fewer than six more free-tuition colleges of Islamic science – dating from the thirteenth to the sixteenth centuries and now preserved as tourist attractions – line the street to the north, as well as the scant remains of the massive charity hospital of Sultan Qalawun.

This thirteenth-century structure was only one of several free hospitals in the city. The earliest, a full 400 years older, was paid for by a tax on the slave market. Its inmates were to be kept under care, it was stipulated, until well enough to consume a whole roast chicken. The foundation charter of Qalawun's hospital was similarly detailed: it specified, out of a total annual budget of 50,000 dinars, a precise sum for the purchase of palm fronds to fan the feverish. Priority of treatment was to be given to 'the most needy, the unlucky, the weak, the helpless and the wretched'. Doctors made rounds twice a day, touring the separate wards for different diseases and supervising the in-house apothecary.

Most such institutions were financed by a form of endowment trust that developed to exploit loopholes in Islamic inheritance law. Because the law divided legacies in strict mathematic proportion, properties tended to disperse quickly. Owners who wanted their estate kept intact after their death, or perhaps favoured one of their descendants, would form a *waqf*, which meant literally to put a 'hold' on their property. So long as the property's revenues were devoted to a charitable purpose, the benefactor could then appoint whomever he wished as the salaried executor of the *waqf*. The trusts were theoretically held in perpetuity, and had the added advantage of being – again theoretically – immune from confiscation by the government. By the year 1339 the income from 130,000 acres of farmland, as well as from a good chunk of urban real estate, was devoted to the upkeep of Cairo's fountains, schools and hospitals. By the end of the eighteenth century a fifth of all Egypt's arable land – some 600,000 acres – was held in *waqf*, including one small property, endowed in the thirteenth century, which provided for the daily feeding of Cairo's stray cats.

THE SCALE OF medieval Cairo, combined with the complete veiling of half its people – namely women – allowed for a very modern degree of anonymity. One visitor in 1390 said the Qasaba was so packed on an average day that he assumed at first there was a wedding or funeral in progress. Moreover, he noted with delight, the crowding made it possible to pursue young boys or women without attracting notice.

Perhaps the predator was less perceptive than he thought. It was at around this time that ladies of fashion adopted male dress. As al-Maqrizi explained, this was 'because the love of men spread among the nobles so that their women tried to make themselves look like boys in the hope of capturing the hearts of their menfolk'. The scandalized sultan forbade ladies from wearing turbans.

Such blandishments reflected a firm belief that women needed to be controlled and protected for their own good. The veil was de rigueur. This was not so much because of any Koranic injunction as because it was thought to preserve men from temptation, which was something that the truly masculine man was assumed to be unable to resist. Women, conversely, were assumed to be predisposed to tempt. This was why the law stipulated that so long as a man had paid his dowry in full he could forbid his wife from leaving his house. In the fourteenth century, one Cairo sheikh was held up as a model because he obliged his wife to inform him of every single thing she did in his absence. Even if she had only moved a jar from one shelf to another, the sheikh had to know, because he, as her husband and her better, was responsible before God for her deeds.

Al-Maqrizi reveals just how zealously female chastity was guarded in an anecdote about the tomb of Tatar al-Higaziyya, who was one of Sultan al-Nasir Muhammad's daughters. This enormously rich lady's *waqf* endowed salaries for several Koran readers as well as a staff of eunuchs who were to keep constant vigil at her tomb. One of the Koran readers devised a classic Cairene ruse to avenge some slight. He denounced a fellow reciter to the chief eunuch guard. The cheeky fellow, he whispered, had snuck into Lady Tatar's tomb chamber in a scandalous state, without wearing his drawers. Enraged, the chief eunuch had the bewildered fellow dragged before him and flogged as he shouted, 'You dare enter the presence of Her Ladyship without underwear!'

Some visitors, however, reckoned that the women of Cairo enjoyed a fair degree of freedom. Observing crowds of ladies heading daily to the city's cemeteries, the Danish traveller Carsten Niebuhr noted in 1761 that they went 'on pretence of performing their devotions, but in reality for the pleasure of walking abroad'. One of the attractions of the graveyards, indeed, was that by custom women removed their veils there. Why not? After all they were among family, even if these male chaperones were dead.

Far in advance of the West, Islamic law accepted female property ownership as a matter of course. A quarter of the *waqf* deeds that survive in Cairo's archives from the years 853 to 1516 are in the name of women. Certain professions were reserved: hairdressers, professional mourners, marriage-brokers, midwives and purveyors of fashions and cosmetics were all female. Some women worked as merchants, and even as religious teachers and ascetics who staffed the city's several Sufi convents. At least one tough lady gained fame as the leader of a neighbourhood gang. Aziza the Beast, as she was known, ran a protection racket near Bab Zuwayla in the nineteenth century; her skill at delivering knock-out blows with a butt of the head kept shopkeepers in terror.

The female ideal, however, was absolute, pampered indolence. According to the fifteenth-century traveller al-Hasan al-Wazzan al-Zayyati, better known as Leo Africanus, the upper-class ladies of Cairo were so wary of their reputations that there was not one who would deign to spin, or sew, or cook: 'When the husband is at his shop, his wife dresses up and perfumes herself, then takes a donkey and rambles about town visiting parents and friends.' Men had to keep on their toes, too. It was true that a wife was legally obliged to accede to her husband's request for intercourse, but then it was also possible for a wife to proclaim before a judge that her husband was impotent. This was a 'very frequent' cause for divorce, says Leo – and he is backed up by documentary evidence in the form of a court ruling from 1341. For whatever reason, divorce was common: the daughter of one Mamluk amir married six times, while one of the later caliphs' daughters had five successive husbands. Records from the Cairo religious courts in 1898 show that there were three divorces for every four marriages in that year.

Among the ruling class, alliances between families were often sealed by intermarriage. Writing in the 1820s, this is how Edward Lane described the influence that a higher-status wife could wield on her husband's behaviour:

> It is not uncommon for a wife who is the daughter of a man of higher rank than her husband to exercise a severe degree of tyranny over the latter: and the case is generally the same when a pasha, or other great personage, gives a slave of his own harem in marriage to one of his officers. She will not allow him to have any concubines; but considers all female slaves as her own; and may even carry her authority so far as not to permit

> those who have the least pretensions to beauty to remain in his presence when he visits the harem; or will oblige them to veil their faces. Some adopt a different course: they pretend not to object to the husband's having concubines; but when any one of them becomes a favourite, and the wife is neglected, the latter contrives to remove the object of her jealousy by means of poison.*

Then, as now in Cairo, whiteness and plumpness were considered the twin traits of feminine perfection. The first of these was easier to achieve, since veils shielded women of class from the disfiguring rays of the sun. Getting fat was another matter. So pressing was the need for fullness, say the chroniclers, that Muslim parents forbade their marriageable daughters to fast during the month of Ramadan for fear of putting off suitors. One Ibn al-Hajj, a Moroccan critic of Cairene wiles, informs us that patrician ladies of the fourteenth century ate fattening food at bedtime, making nightcaps of breadcrumbs mixed with nuts. Some swore by a concoction of crushed beetles, while the real fanatics even sipped human bile in the belief it increased the appetite.

Medieval Cairenes were clearly obsessed with appearance. Under their gauzy black veils and pillarbox hats and white overcoats, under linen camisoles and silk pantaloons and bejewelled slippers, women of leisure were commonly tattooed, body-painted, nail-polished in red lacquer, lipsticked and rouged, hennaed and expensively perfumed. At one stage the fashion was for enormously long sleeves that required as much as 92 cubits of cloth.† The government felt obliged to ban this extravagance, but intervened again in 1472 to demand the wearing of tall hats – 'at least a third of a cubit high' – instead of indecently short

*I owe this passage to the scholarship of Jason Thompson, who has excavated unpublished work from Lane manuscripts in the British Library and the Bodleian.

† 1 cubit = 18–22 inches.

ones. (Knowing Cairo, one may speculate that some manipulative Mamluk official had cornered the market and spotted a profit in high hats.)

When sectarian rules were enforced, as they were when public tolerance was on the wane, Muslims wore white turbans, Christians blue, Jews yellow, and the tiny sect of Samaritans red. Each of the many Sufi orders had its own colour of turban too, tending to greens and blacks and crimsons. Dress denoted rank as well as faith. There were special uniforms with special headdresses for every class of court official, from slipper-bearers to heralds to scribes. The highest honour of the Mamluk state was to be given ceremonial robes by the sultan. The linens and silks and furs, the gold-studded belt and fine saddle and armour that made up such a gift had a value equivalent in modern terms to a luxury motor car.

Small wonder that perhaps the most bemoaned change that came with the fall of the Mamluk sultanate in 1517 was the decline in sartorial splendour. To wear the tall red felt hats around which the Mamluks wound their turbans became an offence punishable by death. The conquering Ottoman troops that ransacked the city, complained one Cairene witness, were not only drunk but ill-clothed, wearing silly conical hats and slovenly uniforms 'such that one could not distinguish among them between master and servant'. Worse yet, to a Cairene accustomed to staining his whiskers with henna and perfuming them with civet, many were beardless.

THE MEDIEVAL CITY'S social calendar provided plenty of occasions for ostentatious display. At the hippodrome below the Citadel, each Mamluk amir's private army and the sultan's royal troops showed their mettle at weekly polo matches and archery contests. Aside from the local saints' days and Muslim feasts, a great yearly festival marked the departure of the pilgrimage caravan to Mecca. Another celebrated the height of the Nile flood. On this Day of Plenitude the sovereign would sail the royal yacht to the island of Roda to anoint the measuring pillar of the Nilometer with musk. Then, at his signal, workers would demolish a dike built across the *khalīj* or drainage canal that linked Fustat to Cairo. A doll representing the bride of the river – a sort of model sacrificial virgin – would tumble into the current as the unleashed waters surged up the channel into the city to the sound of kettledrums and cannonshot. In the evening, revellers took to the stream in illuminated boats. On this day, says the prudish al-Maqrizi, the water of the Nile became polluted with shameful sins: 'There were many murders by drunken men, and forbidden things were done openly.'

Al-Maqrizi's disapproval was not shared by earlier chroniclers. A witness to the Christian feast of Epiphany on 10 January 942, the historian al-Masʿudi, describes a scene of cross-confessional fun. The city's ruler had ordered a thousand torches erected on the Fustat river bank, and a thousand more facing them on Roda. 'Muslims and Christians by hundreds of thousands crowded the Nile in boats, or in kiosks on its shores, all eager for pleasure and vying in equipage, dress, gold and silver cups, and jewellery. The sound of music played all about, with singing and dancing ... It was a splendid night, and most people bathed in the Nile, knowing full well that it is a cure for all disease.'

After every military triumph, parades would march down the Qasaba to show off captives and booty. Following the sacking of his realm by the Mamluks in 1426, King John of Cyprus was dragged through Cairo in chains. The townsfolk jammed so close together and cheered the spectacle with such zeal, says the chronicler Ibn Taghribirdi, that a man could not hear his companion's words. But the observer drops an inadvertent clue about the nature of Cairene crowds when he adds that on this occasion they gathered spontaneously, 'without being sent there for the purpose by anyone'.

Taverns lined the leafy banks of the *khalīj*. Pleasure boats cruised the many seasonal lakes around the city, which were favoured haunts for lovers of music and imbibers of hashish, opium and wine. Though spurned by the pious, such vices brought hefty revenues to the state. In the early fourteenth century taxes on wine and prostitution – another strictly regulated industry – brought in a reported 1,000 dinars a day. For a time the governor of Cairo himself controlled the city's prostitution rackets. Indeed, complained al-Maqrizi, so greedy were the Mamluk state's tax collectors that women of ill repute resorted to ambushing potential customers and holding them to ransom. The trade flourished particularly in the western suburbs and near Bab Zuwayla. By the sixteenth century the district of Bab al-Luq alone could boast some 800 ladies of the night. A Turkish tourist of the time assures us that they excelled in uttering voluptuous, raucous cries and in making slow coquettish motions 'like an Arabian horse that has slipped out from under its rider'.

Cairo offered more innocent pleasures too, in abundance. The gardens between the city proper and the Nile charmed Joos van Ghistele in the fifteenth century – particularly the banana trees which he had never seen before: 'Lords, ladies and merchants pass their time in these gardens and orchards, some in houses, some in tents, some in pavilions ... They have food and drink brought, and all that they need. One sees many ladies come to walk about and visit relatives, and to amuse themselves such that, in truth, they live there as in paradise.'

Hucksters and showmen of all kinds gathered near the lakes of Azbakiyya and the Birkat al-Fil, just outside the city walls: geomancers, astrologers, shadow-puppeteers, storytellers, acrobats, baton-twirlers, the professional farters known as *zarrat*, flame-spitters, stone-swallowers and the like. In 1517 Leo Africanus saw trained fleas and dancing camels at Azbakiyya. A donkey act particularly caught his fancy:

> Having danced awhile, the trainer speaks to his donkey. He tells him that the sultan needs all the donkeys of Cairo to carry stones for some building project. Tumbling to the ground, the donkey raises its hoofs in the air, puffs out its belly, and shuts its eyes as if dead. The mountebank wails to his audience and asks for its help to buy another. The collection made, he continues: 'Don't believe my donkey is dead. He just wants me to buy him a treat with *your* money.' Then, turning to the beast he tells him to get up. The donkey does not budge. He delivers a fine volley of blows; the animal doesn't flinch in the slightest. So the man starts up his nonsense, saying, 'Gentlemen, may it be known that the sultan has issued the following edict: tomorrow all the people of Cairo must come out to cheer my triumphal entry. I command that all the prettiest damsels of the city should be mounted on fine donkeys fed with barley and the sweet water of the Nile.' Hardly has the showman uttered these words when the ass bounds to its feet, haughty and seemingly pleased as Punch. The mountebank goes on: 'True, the sheikh of my alley* asked that I lend my gallant steed to his wife, who is old and ugly.' At these words the donkey, apparently endowed with human intelligence, lowers its eyes and hobbles away as if he has gone lame. 'So you like pretty ladies, then?' The donkey nods its head. 'Well,' says the trainer, 'there are plenty here! Show us who you like best.' The donkey trots around the circle of spectators. He chooses the loveliest and touches her with his muzzle. The whole crowd shouts, 'Hey, Mrs Donkey,' to tease the woman, while the mountebank rides off on his ass.

One of the earliest known theatrical productions in Arabic, a play for shadow puppets by the thirteenth-century writer Ibn Daniyal, celebrates this Cairene *demi-monde* of entertaining conmen and grifters. 'Curious and Strange' (*ʿAjīb wa Gharīb*) are the two

* The alley or *ḥāra* was the principal urban subdivision of Cairo until the nineteenth century. Each *ḥāra* had its own sheikh or boss in charge of keeping order, collecting taxes and so on.

central characters of this rollicking skit, which takes place outside Bab Zuwayla. Curious is a Tartuffe, a swindling preacher, while Strange makes a living by faking blindness and epileptic fits and by peddling bogus amulets. The unsavoury pair introduce a string of other lowlife characters: a snake-charmer, a Sudanese clown, a sword-swallower, a self-mutilated beggar and so on. Each one bewails his lot, but then with a snigger and a swagger reveals how he has suckered the credulous burghers of Cairo.

A roguish lot indeed, even in the midst of calamity: in 1517, after his slovenly troops had wrecked the city, the Ottoman sultan Selim the Grim was treated to an entertainment. A Cairene puppeteer re-enacted for him the capture and execution of Tumanbay, the last Mamluk sultan of Cairo. Faithful to the real event at Bab Zuwayla, the puppet master had Tumanbay's hanging rope snap twice before his puppet expired. Selim the Grim was pleased; he was even seen to crack a smile. The haughty Turk rewarded the entertainer with 200 dinars, and took him home to Constantinople so his son – the future Sulayman the Magnificent – could see the show.

MEDIEVAL CAIRO SUFFERED scourges we think of as modern. Air pollution was a problem even in the eleventh century, if we are to believe Ibn Ridwan. This respected physician to the Fatimid caliph al-Mustansir said smoke from bathhouse boilers was so thick at Fustat that patients were advised to move to the suburbs. (Bathgoers, however, were spared pollution of another kind: their girl and boy bath attendants were forbidden by law from eating garlic or onions.) The good doctor recorded his complaints in a book on the bodily ills of Egypt. Today's Cairenes would find his observations oddly apt: 'In the evening, especially in the summer, a troubled, blackish vapour hangs over the city. The dust, which is irritating to the throat and dirties clothes in a single day, is particularly thick when there is no wind in the air.'

And this was despite a municipal ordinance that forced shop-keepers to dampen roadways to keep the dust down (a custom that still persists).

Traffic was so bad that rules were imposed to relieve congestion. Just as today, they were habitually ignored. In accordance with a tradition ascribed to the Prophet Muhammad, streets were supposed to be wide enough to allow two fully laden camels to pass. But constant encroachment meant that police frequently had to demolish obstructions. Road users were required to pass on the left; water-carriers to seal their goatskins so as not to splash. Animals with heavy loads were to be equipped with alarm bells, and combustible freight like tinder and straw was banned from the main streets altogether. Nevertheless Ibn Saʿid, a poet from Granada, got stuck in a Qasaba pile-up in 1241, when an ox cart loaded with stones blocked a minister's cavalcade. 'The wazir stopped, and the scurrying became intense. There were cookshops in this place, and their smoke blew into our faces and on to the robes of the minister. The passers-by, I among them, nearly expired.' Away from the main thoroughfares, in the dusty back alleys where ministers – then as now – were unlikely to tread, such jams were frequent.

There were few wheeled vehicles in Cairo before 1800. Strange though it may seem, camels had rendered carriages obsolete: the humped beasts required no surfaced roads, needed fewer people to look after them, and carried comparable loads. While the highest-ranking ladies travelled in litters slung between two camels, public transport within the city was almost entirely by means of donkeys. There were some 20,000 of them in the fourteenth century, by al-Maqrizi's estimate. From taxi ranks at all the city gates and in the major squares, a whole day's hire could be arranged for pennies. Most visitors praised the convenience. It was quite possible, claimed Alexander Kinglake a century and a half ago, to write a letter on the pummel of one of these ambling mounts. Not everyone was so charmed. Six centuries before my great-grandmother, the poet Ibn Saʿid had a spot of trouble with the donkey business:

> At Bab Zuwayla I saw more donkeys than can be found in any other country. They were for the use of going [from Cairo] to Fustat. My companion climbed on a donkey and motioned me to do the same. But I refused [until] he told me that Egyptian notables did not find this degrading; and indeed I noticed jurists, cloth merchants and distinguished persons all riding the beasts. I followed their example, but while I was just getting myself properly seated the donkeyboy signalled to the animal, who charged off, kicking up a blackish dust that blinded me and soiled my clothes. What I had feared then happened. I fell into the black swirl of dust.

Ibn Saʿid had reason to be unhappy. The ground on to which he tumbled was likely to have been littered with refuse, for despite its antiquity, Cairo had never mastered the trick of cleaning itself.* Despite the daily passage of night-soil collectors, the medieval city's streets were filthy.

The effects over time of accumulating waste need not be imagined. They can be seen in the old quarters of modern Cairo, where centuries of detritus – and the straw sprinkled on top to make roads passable after rains – has built up street levels as much as twenty-three feet in a thousand years. Passing through Bab Zuwayla today, one walks at the height where an eleventh-century camel rider would have been.

When Napoleon arrived 200 years ago he captured a city that had literally sunk into itself. Where it was not hemmed by tombs,

* Even in ancient Memphis garbage collection was ineffectual. Its streets were free of the modern scourge of plastic containers, but scraps of papyrus and broken crockery were left in roadbeds for archaeologists to find 3,000 years later.

Cairo was rimmed for most of its circumference by hundred-foot-high mountains of debris where generations of townsfolk had dumped their waste outside the walls.

Although most of these were cleared in the nineteenth century, the medieval dustheap behind the venerable Mosque of al-Azhar and beyond the old hashish market of al-Batniyya still stands. It is an impressive sight, stretching for a mile in length and rising to an astounding fifteen storeys, swamping the great stone ramparts of the imperial Fatimid city. It is a monument in garbage to the endurance of Cairo. And also a testament to its medieval wealth, for as al-Maqrizi relates:

> In the capital of Egypt, they say, refuse to the value of a thousand gold dinars is cast on the dung heaps every day. They refer to ... the clay pots used by sellers of milk and yogurt, and by poor folk at food stalls. They are thinking, too ... of the wicker racks used by cheesemakers, and of the paper cones used by druggists, and the string which ties the bags in which provisions like grain are sold, etc. Because, once these packages have been taken home from the markets, they are thrown away ...'

CHAPTER FIVE

MEDIEVAL DECLINE

The first thing that astonishes a stranger to Cairo is the squalid wretchedness of the Arabs, and the external splendour of the Turks.

R. R. Madden, *Travels*, 1825

LONG BEFORE NAPOLEON arrived to find Cairo ringed with mounds of waste, a different breed of foreign invader had knocked at the gates of the city.

In the spring of 1167 an army of Christian crusaders rode into Egypt from Palestine. Having met little resistance from the now feeble forces of the waning Fatimid dynasty – indeed, the Egyptians had hinted at the desirability of joining the invaders in an alliance against Syria – it pitched camp outside the formidable northern walls of Cairo. In the morning an embassy comprising two gallant knights, Sir Hugh of Caesaria and Sir Geoffrey Fulcher, dismounted their chargers in front of Bab al-Futuh, the caliphal capital's Gate of Conquest. A silent escort of foot soldiers brought them into the city, marching them down the processional street of Bayn al-Qasrayn* past the buttressed minarets of the

*Bayn al-Qasrayn means Between the Palaces, a reference to the Eastern and Western Palaces of the Fatimid caliphs that flanked the street. The palaces were long ago replaced by Mamluk funerary institutions, but the name for this stretch of the Qasaba endures – even into the title of a work by the novelist Naguib Mahfouz. All

great mosque of Caliph al-Hakim and the exquisitely carved stone façade of al-Aqmar, the moonlit mosque. At length they reached the vast parade ground between the two caliphal palaces, and were admitted into the 4,000-roomed Eastern Palace itself.

Willam, the contemporary archbishop of Tyre who recorded their reception in his *History of Deeds Beyond the Sea,* said that the Christian soldiers' amazement grew with every step: this, at last, was the land of milk and honey which Pope Urban II had evoked, a century earlier, to inspire his followers to holy war. The caliph's chief wazir escorted the knights through halls guarded by Sudanese swordsmen, along mosaic paths in gardens where fountains played, through cloisters with gilded ceilings, past kitchens stocked daily by fourteen camel-loads of snow brought from Mount Sinai, and through menageries filled with parrots and giraffes and other exotic animals 'such as the mind of the sleeper might conjure up in the visions of the night; such, indeed, as the regions of the East and South bring forth, but the West sees never, and scarcely ever hears of'. At last they were ushered into the throne room, where a gold- and pearl-embroidered curtain swept dramatically aside to reveal the infallible imam of the Ismaili Shiᶜites seated on a golden throne. To the horror of the court, Sir Hugh insisted on shaking hands with the eighteen-year-old caliph. Al-ᶜAdid, the last of the Fatimid line, proved more courteous than his courtiers: he even removed his glove for the handshake. His diplomacy paid off. The infidel embassy accepted his terms. For the paltry sum of 200,000 dinars, they agreed to leave Cairo alone. The very next day the Christians marched back to Palestine with their loot.

And so the city was spared the fate of Jerusalem. When that

---

that remains of the palaces are some finely carved wooden lintels that can be seen in Cairo's Islamic Museum.

Fatimid provincial town had fallen in 1099, the crusaders had revolutionized Middle Eastern warfare by massacring its entire civilian population.

In the subsequent two centuries the Christians tried repeatedly for the greater prize of Egypt. They sacked its port cities of Alexandria and Damietta in 1149. They captured the town of Bilbays, just forty miles north of Cairo, in 1168, and slaughtered its inhabitants to a man. The Fatimids held them off with bribes and promises. When that didn't work they allied first with the Christians, then with the Sunni Muslims of Syria. But in the end the Shiʿite dynasty grew too weak to survive. Racked by schisms – they were inevitable given the tension between an imamist ideology that held its rulers to be infallible and the fact that some caliphs were underage or incapable – the Fatimid court succumbed to bloody palace intrigue. In the prevailing insecurity army officers saw their chance and seized power. As we have seen, Saladin arrived with a force from Syria to bolster the tottering Fatimids, but instead ousted them in the year 1171. Al-ʿAdid died a mysterious death in captivity. Saladin banned Shiʿism and chased its adherents into prison or exile. He opened the palaces of al-Qahira and sold off the fabled treasure of the Fatimids, including a 2,400 carat ruby, an emerald four fingers in length, and the caliph's splendid library, to pay his Turkish troops. He replaced the Fatimids' elaborate bureaucracy with a feudal system that gave his officers direct control over all Egypt's rich agricultural land.

Such wealth enabled Saladin to stride from success to success in Palestine. At the Battle of Hattin in 1187 he dealt the crusader kingdoms a blow from which they never recovered. Thousands of Christian prisoners were marched the 400 miles back to Cairo. The captives went to work extending the city's fortifications, uniting al-Qahira and Fustat inside a single great enclosure wall. A colossal new fortress rose atop a spur of the Muqattam cliffs on the city's eastern rim. The Citadel was a fitting monument to this martial age. The biggest castle in the Middle East, it loomed high over Cairo as a testament to the arrogance of arms.

Saladin's heirs, the Ayyubid dynasty, ruled from the fortress for eighty years before they too were toppled by their army. The elite cavalry corps of Mamluks took power, so institutionalizing the harsh rule of a foreign military caste. They proved their worth on battleground after battleground, destroying the Mongol hordes that had swept in from the east in 1260 and crushing the last of the crusader states in 1291.

Unlike the courtly Fatimids and Ayyubids, however, the Mamluks were both ruthless and cynical. Baybars, the first great Mamluk sultan, paid bards to extoll his virtues as a champion of Islam, yet he died after over-indulging in his favourite brew, fermented mare's milk. He appeared to bolster the faith by appointing four chief judges – one for each doctrine of Sunni law – instead of relying on the Shafi'ite judge alone. In fact this innovation allowed the Mamluks to divide and rule the religious establishment. Baybars' court gave refuge to the Abbasid family, the titular leaders of Sunni Islam, when they fled Baghdad before the Mongols in 1258. The line of Abbasid caliphs continued at Cairo, but Baybars and his successors maintained them as toothless props to their own legitimacy, hauling them out of pampered seclusion only for show.

Through cunning and tireless energy, Baybars forged a state that mobilized all resources for his army. He and his twenty-four chief amirs spent lavishly on importing, training and equipping new ranks of Mamluk soldiers. He was a formidable foe. One crusader commander described him as more brilliant than Caesar, but nastier than Nero. His character emerges in a taunting letter he wrote to Bohemond VI, ruler of the crusader principality of Antioch, in the spring of 1268. In elegant rhyming prose, Baybars compliments the prince on his demotion to the title of count. It is a pity, he continues, that Bohemond was absent at the time of Antioch's fall:

> Hadst thou but seen thy knights trodden under horses' hooves, thy palaces invaded and ransacked for booty, thy ladies bought and sold at four to the dinar of thine own money! Hadst thou seen thy churches demolished, the crosses sawn in sunder, thy garbled gospels hawked about before the sun, the tombs of thy nobles cast to the ground ... Then thou wouldst have said, 'Would God that I were dust!' ... This letter holds happy tidings. It tells thee that God watches over thee to prolong thy days, insomuch as thou wert not in Antioch!

When the tally of two centuries of war was counted, Cairo had reason to sound triumphant. All its trading rivals had been eliminated: Baghdad and Damascus had been sacked by the Mongols; Christian Antioch, Tyre and Acre by the Muslims; Constantinople by crusaders who had double-crossed their erstwhile Christian ally, the Byzantine emperor. Cairo was the capital of the strongest military power of the age. Not only did its Turkish-speaking rulers control the holy cities of Mecca, Medina and Jerusalem, they also held personal title to all the rich agricultural land of Egypt. For two and a half centuries their revolving fiefdoms siphoned all the wealth of the country into the capital.

In the brief half-century respite before the great plague struck in 1347, the city flourished as never before. Its area nearly doubled during the reign of Sultan al-Nasir Muhammad ibn Qalawun (which, with two brief interruptions, lasted from 1293 to 1341, making him the longest-ruling Mamluk sultan). A building boom transformed the vast open ground between the Citadel and Bab Zuwayla into a densely peopled quarter. In the western and southern suburbs Mamluk officers built palaces; in the city centre mosques and colleges; in the cemeteries magnificent tombs.

Yet, for all its splendour, victorious Cairo had ultimately lost out. The two centuries of non-stop warfare sparked by the crusades had caused inevitable change. Merchants had lost their prestige to soldiers. Tolerance and a cosmopolitan outlook had given way to narrow-mindedness. The nature of government had turned predatory. The Mamluk lords who now owned Egypt had no attachments to its future or to its past: no loyalty except to their own class. The country was simply there to be exploited.

In Europe, by contrast, the ruling nobility retained their link to the land. When it prospered, they prospered. The political divisions that kept them weak also fostered keen competition in trade and industry and technology. Moreover, Europe had just received a healthy injection of new ideas. The crusaders may have been booted out of Palestine, but they gained immeasurably from contact with the civilized East. Europe learned from the Arabs the arts of papermaking, of navigation by compass, of the use of watermills, of glass and crystal manufacture, of ceramics and dyes, of the uses of soap and perfume. A trader from Pisa by the name of Leonardo Fibonacci introduced Arabic numerals to Italy after a visit to Egypt in the twelfth century. Architects from Amalfi copied the pointed vaults and arches they had seen in Fatimid Cairo; the Gothic style they inspired took Europe by storm. Others brought back the principles of Greek medicine and chemistry which Europe had forgotten, but which the Arabs had translated, practised and improved upon.

From Muslim armies Europe picked up the trappings of advanced warfare: the stirrup, the crossbow and the recurved composite bow, the mangonel, the combustible missile, and the pomp of kettledrums and tournaments, uniforms and heraldic signs like the fleur-de-lis, the double-headed eagle and Baybars' own seal of the lion rampant ('Baybars' meaning 'Lord Lion' in Turkish.) They adopted the Mamluk pastime of playing cards, transforming the hierarchical symbolism of the sultan's court: the mallet of the *jukandār* or polo-master was shortened and rounded into clover-shaped clubs; the napkin of the *ustadar* or chief steward was preserved as diamonds; the *nai'b* or deputy became the knave. The Europeans learned to train homing pigeons, a sport which the Fatimids had so perfected that when the Caliph al-Aziz

(AD 975–96) had expressed a wish to eat cherries, which did not grow in Egypt, his wazir could present him with a full bowl the following morning: informed of the command by pigeon post, the governor of Lebanon had clusters of the berries tied to the feet of flocks of doves, who flew their sweet cargo by relays the whole 400 miles to Cairo.

From consumers of luxuries the Europeans grew to be producers. By the fifteenth century the balance of Mediterranean trade had shifted firmly in their favour. Europe still imported spices, dyes, precious stones and other primary goods, enriching Cairo's merchant classes and the state that taxed them. But the best manufactures were now made on the northern shore of the sea. The soap of Marseilles, the paper of Fabriano, the glass of Murano outclassed and undersold their Arab models. Renaissance inventiveness perfected technologies like the watermill and the treadle loom, then guarded its advances with secrecy and patents. Meanwhile Egypt's main industry, textiles, sank into decline. During the lifetime of al-Maqrizi – the historian died in 1442 – Cairenes were to switch from wearing fine Egyptian linen to cheap European cloth. Imports affected other industries in the same way. The number of sugar mills at Fustat, for instance, dropped from sixty-six in 1325 to nineteen in 1400.

In many ways it was the very success of the Mamluk sultanate that pushed Europe to overtake it. In the fourteenth and fifteenth centuries Cairo exercised a near monopoly of trade to the Indies. Its rulers, ever fearful of palace intrigue, ever pressed for money to buy and maintain new generations of slave soldiers, clamped increasingly crippling duties on commerce. By one sultan's decree in the 1430s, for instance, the price to European traders for a load of pepper – bought in India for two dinars and exchanged at Mecca for ten – was to be no less than eighty dinars. 'Because this city is situated where she is,' complained one Venetian of Cairo, 'merchants cannot do else than come there and allow themselves to be devoured as the Soldan and his officials wish.'

In time, Europeans found they could do otherwise. Aside from beginning to manufacture their own goods, they sought new trade routes. By the end of the fifteenth century Iberian sailors – having improved the performance of their square-riggers by adding lateen sails copied from the Arabs – had discovered the New World and rounded the Cape of Good Hope. Portuguese marauders harried traffic even in the Red Sea, which Cairo's rulers of the past 500 years had seen as an Egyptian lake. These upstart challengers, moreover, were armed with guns – heavy weapons that the proud Mamluk horsemen could not wield from the saddle and refused to lug around on foot.

EVEN AS THE Mamluk amirs of the fourteenth and fifteenth centuries competed to embellish their capital, its spirit had changed. War, disease and the state's short-sighted manipulations hardened attitudes. It was the martially minded Mamluks who herded their womenfolk into harems and insisted on the veil. It was the slave soldiers who built Cairo's notorious twin prisons, the Sweater and the Peeler, (so named, presumably, for the unpleasant symptoms that incarceration in them induced). The Mamluks devised such ghastly forms of public execution as crucifixion on crosses strapped to camels' backs – followed by a parade of the naked victim through the city – and bisection at the waist, and impalement on a greased pole. Under their rule Jewish and Christian ghettos developed for the first time: to keep the masses under heel, the Mamluks encouraged and abetted religious bigotry.

In 1442, for instance, a Cairo mob marched to the foot of the Citadel. Someone had reported that a plank in the wooden pulpit of a synagogue was inscribed with the name of Muhammad. To appease the rabble, the sultan had three rabbis tortured to confess who among them had profaned the Prophet by treading on his name. Two of them died, and the third converted to Islam.

Touchiness about such matters had earlier been raised by the sultan al-Mu'ayyad Sheikh. Towards the end of his reign (which lasted from 1412 to 1421) he decreed that Muslim preachers should descend one step on their pulpits before mentioning the ruler's name, so as to ensure it would not be uttered on the same level as God's. The pious gesture greatly boosted al-Mu'ayyad's popularity. He needed the plaudits, because it was widely known that his drinking habit had led to severe bouts of gout. (Al-Mu'ayyad had, moreover, a scandalous taste for handsome young Mamluks. He was said to have raged on hearing that one of his amirs had paid 1,000 dinars to spend time in the company of a particularly delectable royal cupbearer. But he forgave the dalliance when the amir joked that if the boy had not been al-Mu'ayyad's own property, the sultan himself would have paid 10,000. The amir was lucky: al-Mu'ayyad had some eighty of his amirs executed for other slights.)

Mamluk rule was generally harder on Coptic Christians than on Cairo's small Jewish minority. When al-Mu'ayyad banned Copts from government service, he was not the first sultan to do so. Earlier prohibitions had always weakened, however, given the need for the Copts' famed financial acumen. Al-Mu'ayyad's enforcement was unsubtle: he had his highest-ranking Coptic scribe stripped naked and paraded through the streets. So ended common spectacles that the contemporary historian Ibn Taghribirdi described as unseemly, such as Muslims being obliged to stand before a seated Christian official, or to walk beside a mounted Christian. No longer would supplicants have to kiss the hem of some powerful Nazarene's garment. From now on, the Christians 'decreased the size of their turbans and the width of their sleeves'. Our witness found this greatly to the sultan's credit. 'Perhaps God will forgive all of al-Mu'ayyad's sins, for it was one of the greatest measures for the supremacy of Islam,' was Ibn Taghribirdi's approving comment.

It was strange that al-Mu'ayyad should have felt any need to suppress the Copts. The previous century had already seen the definitive eclipse of Christianity in Egypt. Until then this had been the religion professed by most of the country's people, especially outside the capital. Starting in 1293, however, repeated riots led to waves of conversions. In 1301 a dignitary visiting from Morocco, where resentment at the ongoing Christian reconquest of Spain was intense, expressed outrage at the liberties allowed to infidels in Cairo. Ashamed, the Mamluk governor of the city enforced the long-forgotten dress code. Any Christian or Jew who did not wear a blue or yellow identifying turban, he declared, could be lawfully plundered by the Muslims. In 1321 eleven churches in Cairo were burned to the ground, and in 1354 four more. The sultan confiscated Church property, banned even Christian converts to Islam from state employment, and had soldiers destroy the most famous relic of Fustat, a Christian martyr's preserved finger that was annually dipped in the Nile to provoke the flood. 'When the Christians' afflictions grew great and their income small, they decided to embrace Islam,' wrote al-Maqrizi. 'It was a momentous event in Egyptian history. From that time on, lineages became mixed.' In other words, the Copts were reduced to their present proportion of under a tenth of the population.

The change was profound. By the end of the Mamluk sultanate no upright Muslim, not even an aristocratic man of letters like the historian Ibn Taghribirdi, would have thought fit to engage in philosphical debate with an infidel. A great horseman and a famed wit, Ibn Taghribirdi was also one of Cairo's most distinguished literati, an authority on court etiquette and a talented translator of Turkish and Persian poetry. Yet not only did he positively gloat over persecution of the infidel, in his time the very word 'philosophy' was a term of abuse. To philosophize, in fifteenth-century Cairo, meant to engage in prattle.

By contrast, a gentleman of the twelfth century such as Abd al-Latif of Baghdad would have taken pleasure in discussing Plato with the chief rabbi of Cairo. Indeed, the doctor described Maimonides as a scholar of very superior merit. By some contemporary accounts, his original purpose in travelling to Cairo was to have the pleasure of hearing the Jewish sage lecture.

A century before that encounter, the Fatimid court physician Ibn Ridwan had respectfully dedicated several of his hundred-odd scientific works to a Jewish colleague, Yahuda ibn Saʿada. Ibn Ridwan personified the upward mobility that learning conferred in that liberal age. Born the son of a humble Giza baker, he had financed his studies by selling horoscopes. Having prospered as a doctor, he delighted in scouring the book markets of Fustat and Cairo. By his own account Ibn Ridwan's private library contained all but twelve of the fifty-five known works of Hippocrates, as well as Dioscorides' *Book of Herbs* and the books of Rufus of Ephesus, Oribasius and Paul of Aegina, as well as the *Comprehensive Book* of the ninth-century Arab physician Abu Bakr al-Razi, who asserted the primacy of human reason in all affairs. Ibn Ridwan owned scientific texts such as the *Almagest* and the *Quadripartia* of Ptolemy, as well as the philosophical works of Plato, Aristotle, Alexander of Aphrodisias, Themistius, and Muhammad al-Farabi, a fellow Muslim who daringly hinted that religion merely served those who needed its symbols to grasp the truths revealed by philosophers.

Ibn Ridwan would have had access to the imperial library established by the Fatimid wazir Ibn Killis, a converted Jew whose organizational genius laid the foundations of the Fatimid state. Among 100,000 books, the library was said to contain 18,000 manuscripts on the sciences of antiquity. Even the Fatimid caliph al-Hakim (996–1021), who was widely thought to be insane, patronized learning. He endowed Cairo with an astronomical observatory and a scientific institute known as the House of Wisdom. There polymaths like Ibn Haytham, whose treatise on optics was the first to describe the camera obscura, and scientists like Ammar ibn Ali, who devised novel treatments for eye diseases, received state grants for their research. (Ibn Haytham, however, was obliged to feign madness for several years because his capricious patron blamed him for failing to come up with a scheme to dam the Nile.)

Intellectuals of the Fatimid era held impassioned debates. Ibn Haytham exchanged theories on the nature of the Milky Way with Ibn Ridwan, who himself was locked in a fierce, decade-long scientific dispute with a Christian physician named Ibn Butlan. The latter mercilessly taunted his colleague over his supposed arrogance and ugliness. This little verse he penned drew titters in all the salons of Fatimid Cairo and Fustat:

When they saw his face
The midwives swooned.
Alas! They moaned,
Had we but left him in the womb.

Seven centuries separated Ibn Ridwan from the arrival of Napoleon in 1798. Curious as to how Cairene intellectuals diverted themselves, an Arabist in the French expedition compiled an inventory of one Azharite scholar's library. The list spoke volumes about the decline in intellectual standards. The only non-religious works he owned were a treatise on love, an anthology of songs and poems, a book of historical curiosities, a sex manual, formulas for marriage and divorce contracts, and models of epistolary style. There were no printed works. Although Arabs had practised wood-block printing as early as the ninth century – 600 years before Gutenberg – the science had died out. And even though they knew of Europe's advance to movable type, Cairo's literate class had shunned the invention for fear its use might challenge their practical monopoly of the written word.*

*The ulema felt that they were defending their profession, the whole purpose of which was to interpret the intent of an author's words. Steeped in the art of Koranic exegesis and the art of calligraphy, they believed the value and meaning of a text was not inherent but had to be re-created by correct reading and writing. Printing, it was

LATER ARABS LIONIZED Saladin for defeating the crusaders and uprooting what was regarded as Shi'ite heresy. Yet if his introduction of theological schools did succeed in reimposing Sunnism, it was at the cost of restricting free inquiry. When it came about that the only education Cairo had to offer was religious, intellectual life withered. Plato was forgotten. The hereafter came to outweigh the here and now. Those scholars who did not succumb to Sufi mysticism sought perfection of form, of comportment, not perfection of the mind. Debate about the correct Islamic manner of washing, or eating, or over questions like whether a woman need perform ritual ablutions after a visitation by jinns, replaced philosophical conjecture and scientific invention.

Not even a sage like Abd al-Rahman Ibn Khaldun, the brightest star of Islam's fading intellectual firmament, dared to challenge the religious conventions of his age. Before his arrival in Cairo at the end of the fourteenth century this man's extraordinary career had already taken him into distinguished service at the courts of the Arab West. Fate had sent him into the dungeons of Fez and dispatched him as ambassador from King Muhammad V of Granada to Dom Pedro the Cruel of Seville. That Christian monarch had been so charmed that he offered to return Ibn Khaldun's long-lost family estates in Spain. But the scholar had tired of politics, and instead retreated with his books to the mountain redoubt of an Algerian Berber tribe. During this four-year private hejira he composed his magisterial *Prolegomena,* a penetrating inquiry into the nature of history that described the efflorescence and decay of civilizations in terms of inevitable

believed, would multiply not knowledge but the errors of the ignorant. It was this logic, along with the need to control information for political ends, that in 1516 led the Ottoman sultan Selim I to ban printing on pain of death. Non-Muslims were exempted: a Hebrew printing press operated at Cairo from the sixteenth century.

cycles. The scope and sophistication of this work made Machiavelli's *The Prince,* written a hundred years later, appear shallow and amateurish by comparison.

Ibn Khaldun set out on the Pilgrimage in 1382. Shortly after landing at Cairo he learned that his wife and daughter, who were to follow him to Mecca, had drowned in a storm off Alexandria. Grief-stricken, he opted to stay in the Mamluk capital. Here he lived for the last quarter-century of his life. When in favour with the sultan he served as a stern and respected judge: such was the ease of access to position that a learned man enjoyed in medieval Islam. He also lectured at some of Cairo's most prestigious colleges: at al-Azhar, at the Qamhiyya *madrasa* founded by Saladin, at the *madrasa* of the amir Sarghatmish, and at the dervish monastery of the amir Baybars al-Gashnakir.

He was a gifted teacher. His novel theories on the psychology of power – on its rise through the strength of tribal solidarity and its decline through decadence – and on economics, metaphysics and pedagogy deeply impressed his students. One of these was al-Maqrizi. Cairo's pre-eminent chronicler considered Ibn Khaldun's *Prolegomena* to be the cream of all knowledge. Of its style, he said it was 'more brilliant than a perfect pearl and finer than water fanned by a zephyr'. Later judges were equally impressed. The British historian Arnold Toynbee reckoned the *Prolegomena* the greatest work of its kind ever created in any time or place.

Ibn Khaldun was no anticlerical radical. A sometime Sufi and an authority on the sayings of the Prophet, he went so far as to condemn philosophers for relying too much on reason. The highest state of human perfection, he believed, was pure mystical faith achieved by 'tearing the veil of the senses'. Yet his teachings still offended the prickly orthodox – perhaps because he hinted that human action guided history as much as did the will of Allah, or maybe because he thought faith could not be achieved through reason. Whatever the case, al-Azhar, Cairo's pre-eminent college and the world's oldest university, banned his *Prolegomena* from its curriculum. The ban lasted 500 years – until the 1920s.

As Europe evolved from Renaissance to Reformation to Enlightenment, Cairo wove itself an Islamic cocoon. Poetry – an art so prized by the Ayyubids that one sultan had his favourite bards sleep in his own bedchamber – was replaced in esteem by calligraphy: in Mamluk Cairo a single illuminated Koran was often more valuable than the sumptuous mosque that housed it. Interest in human medicine – a science so perfected that the Cairene physician Ibn al-Nafis (1213–88) was describing the circulation of blood 350 years before its 'discovery' by William Harvey – waned in favour of the veterinary science required by the horse-mad Mamluks. Cairo's fifteenth-century artisans created intricate geometric patterns in wood and marble marquetry. Their productions were superbly elegant, but they were also sterile.

The Arabs may have invented algebra and elaborated trigonometry, but when an eighteenth-century governor challenged all seventy of al-Azhar's professors to solve an unchallenging mathematical puzzle only one of them could come up with an answer. It was hardly surprising. Since the time of Saladin, the only use al-Azhar had found for mathematics was for calculating divisions of inheritance by Islamic law. In the early twentieth century al-Azhar was still relying on a mathematical text written by Ibn Haytham, the Fatimid scientist, a thousand years before.

Of course Ibn Khaldun saw things differently. The stature of Cairo as the greatest centre of learning in his time, he said, was due to Saladin and his Mamluk successors. The Turkish chieftains of Egypt, he wrote, feared the sultan's rapacity so much that they endowed schools and other foundations to employ their children. 'The result of this is that endowments have multiplied so as to attract men of learning from as far as Iraq and Morocco.' But a mere century later, at the end of the Mamluk era, Leo Africanus was to offer a more critical report. The inhabitants of Cairo were 'very kindly people and merry fellows', he said. 'Yet, though they excel at fine speech, they do very little ... Many give themselves to the study of laws, but very few to letters. Whereas their colleges are always full of students, very few gain profit from this.'

The 'rapacity' noted by Ibn Khaldun was, moreover, to exact its inevitable toll. The Mamluk system was destined to follow the cycle of decline which the scholar's own theory so brilliantly predicted. His student al-Maqrizi catalogued a litany of fifteenth-century ills due to Mamluk venality: inflation and debasement of the coinage, the degradation of high offices of state, the institution of monopolies and the forced sale of merchandise, corruption, and 'the eagerness of officials to hunt down the rich so as to relieve them of their fortunes'.

Finally, the lawlessness of the Mamluk soldiery itself accelerated decline. Over time the rigid discipline and loyalty of these uprooted northerners had deteriorated. By the late fifteenth century they had become a parasite class who claimed their outrageous privileges as rights and treated the common people with contempt. An example: at one time prankish Mamluks decreed a tax on baldness, and proceeded to ride about the city knocking off turbans to assess the levy. These splendid archers and riders chafed at the urban confines of Cairo. They became, said al-Maqrizi, more promiscuous than monkeys, more larcenous than mice, and more destructive than wolves. He decried their riotous behaviour with the fiercest words he could summon: 'They broke into bathhouses and abducted women by force. They carried themselves to excesses that even the Franks, had they been masters of the country, would not have committed.'

On 18 May 1516 the entire Mamluk army mustered in the hippodrome at the foot of the Citadel, kicking up a pall of dust that obscured their sultan's great castle. Each of the twenty-four chief amirs took charge of his own slave troops, some with a

thousand fully equipped cavalrymen, others with a hundred, or forty or fewer. The Sultani Mamluks, an elite corps clothed in white linen robes and armed with bows, lances and both short swords and long, were 5,000 strong. The whole great clanking, shuffling army lined up in ranks, until at length Sultan Qansuh al-Ghuri himself descended from the palace. A grey-bearded dilettante of seventy-five whose passions were perfume and flowers, al-Ghuri now gave the signal for the procession to begin.

The soldiers marched through the heart of the city in file after file. The blare of the royal trumpeters and the drill of the kettledrummers, the trample of hooves and the spine-tingling ululations of the women of Cairo echoed down the length of the Qasaba, clattering off the stone walls of Sultan Hasan's gigantic mosque and thundering under the high arch of Bab Zuwayla. Three gorgeously caparisoned, silent-footed elephants ambled in the lead. The Mamluk cavalry, resplendent in the battle uniforms of their various houses, stretched thereafter for a continuous mile. The captains of the guard followed in their tall felt hats, succeeded by the drum-masters with their forty kettledrummers; then the supreme judges of the four schools of law, the chiefs of the dervish orders with their multicoloured turbans, the sheikh of the mendicants, and the headman of the *ḥarafish* – the organized rabble of the city. And now a great sympathetic cheer greeted the lone figure of Caliph al-Mutawakkil, the last of the Abbasid line but by this time a mere mascot, whose sole duty was to confirm the sultan in office. As the fashion-conscious chronicler Ibn Iyas records, he wore a tasseled Baghdad-style turban and a Baalbek coat with black silk embroidery.

The sultan's high-stepping led-horses came next, the first pair with tall headdresses shaped like sugar loaves, saddle covers of the royal yellow silk, and side drums; the succeeding pair with gold-edged saddles and gold-embroidered coverings; and the last with saddles of crystal inlaid with gold and studded with agate set in silver. Then came the foot-guards, armed with halberds; the sultan's baggage train, including forty huge illuminated Korans, their cases draped in yellow silk; and incense bearers. The sultan himself followed through the scented smoke, mounted on a spirited bay with gilded saddle and cloth. He wore a simple campaign bonnet (not his usual six-corned turban of state) and a white riding coat embroidered with a wide band of gold on black silk which was said to weigh 500 *mithqals*. On his fingers were rings of ruby, turquoise, emerald and diamond.

Through the gate the procession marched, and on up the Qasaba past the tombs of previous sultans of Cairo: al-Mu'ayyad, al-Salih Ayyub, al-Mansur Qalawun and his son al-Nasir Muhammad, and al-Zahir Barquq. It passed al-Ghuri's own lavish and sparkling new funerary complex, between the green-tiled dome of the tomb chamber and the minaret of his mosque across the street. Along the whole route to Bab al-Futuh – the Gate of Conquest – shopkeepers called out prayers for success, while the ladies trilled from upstairs windows.

But in the backstreets there were mutterings. The people of Cairo had been taxed to the hilt to pay this army. Even the dung gatherers had been gouged without mercy. Not long since a raging mob had murdered the chief tax collector. And even so it was said that the army of a generation before had been twice as large; that the campaign bonus paid to each amir had been five times greater. Sultan al-Ghuri himself looked haggard. The Mamluks had not won a significant victory since their conquest of Cyprus eighty years before. For all their martial skill and finery, their equipment had changed little in two centuries.

By contrast, the army of Ottoman Turks which they were to meet had blasted its way with guns and artillery from triumph to triumph since capturing Constantinople in 1453. Selim I, the Ottoman sultan, had earned the epithet 'Selim the Grim' by murdering as many of his male relations as he could lay hands on, for the purpose of assuring his succession. He was known to be fresh and confident after his latest victory over the Persians (whose shah, provocatively, kept a pet pig called Selim).

A few in the Qasaba crowd may even have heard that the Ottomans had rebuffed al-Ghuri's peaceful overtures. The Turks had recently overrun a buffer kingdom in eastern Anatolia that was friendly to the Mamluks. Selim the Grim's envoy had been welcomed in the Citadel nevertheless – only to hurl before al-Ghuri the severed head of his fallen ally. Indeed, the Ottoman sultan's provocations knew no bounds. He had humiliated Cairo's latest ambassador, stripping him naked and forcing him to carry a bucket of manure on his bare head. Among those who knew of such things, there were rumours that al-Ghuri's newfangled cannon, on which so much had been spent, had proved immobile and failed to work. Worse, there were whisperings of treachery.

THREE MONTHS LATER the awful news arrived from northern Syria. The Ottoman army had routed the Mamluks. Selim the Grim's light field artillery had panicked their horses. His plodding infantry, armed with the harquebus that the Mamluk mounted archers disdained as unmanly, had decimated their thundering cavalry charges. One of al-Ghuri's commanders had betrayed the Mamluk sultan, pulling the whole left flank of his army out of the battle. The Ottomans had captured the caliph himself, along with the sultan's Korans, the emblems of the Mamluk state and the fifty camels laden with gold which the sultan had chosen not to leave behind in the Citadel for fear the treasure would be purloined. As for the great Qansuh al-Ghuri, he had fallen from his charger and died of apoplexy. His body was lost.

To complete the army's shame, Bedouin marauders attacked the remnants which fled back to Cairo. The stragglers arrived in the city, as the chronicler Ibn Iyas wrote, 'in the most pitiful state of nakedness, hunger and weakness, with their garments opened at the neck ... It was a time to turn an infant's hair white, and to melt iron in its fury.'

By February 1517 Selim the Grim was at the northern gates of Cairo. Again, his artillery smashed the last stand of the Mamluk cavalry. His drunken, beardless troops charged into the city, and for four days they ran amok in rape and pillage. They captured some 800 Mamluks, beheaded them, threw their bodies in the Nile, and spiked their heads on lances to decorate Selim's camp. When, some weeks later, the last of the Mamluk generals was betrayed to the invader, Selim had him hung from Bab Zuwayla.

Then began the organized plunder of the city. 'The scum and scoundrels of Egypt', as Ibn Iyas describes them, 'would inform the Ottomans of the resources of princesses and ladies, and their costly clothing was carried off. In short, the treasure houses of the land fell into the hands of the Turks ... with clothing and weapons, horses and mules, male and female slaves, and everything of value.' The Ottoman soldiery rounded up passers-by, 'regardless of rank', and forced them with whips to haul the spoils to the docks. Selim himself divested the palaces of the Citadel of all their furnishings, not sparing priceless manuscripts or carpets, porphyry columns or marble floors, or holy relics like hairs from the Prophet's beard and his famed sword Zulfiqar. He ordered the rounding up of all the leading citizens. Nearly 2,000 of the wealthiest merchants, the finest craftsmen and the most scholarly jurists were then shipped off to Constantinople as hostages. When Selim himself had gone, the Ottoman viceroy he left behind fired the staff of the Citadel palaces – the eunuchs, the cooks, the porters and grooms and cupbearers. 'In short,' lamented Ibn Iyas, 'he abolished the entire old system of the Citadel, and introduced the order of the Ottomans, which is the most evil of all orders.'

Caliph al-Mutawakkil, captive in Constantinople and pining for Cairo, surrendered his title as spiritual leader of Sunnite Islam. In exchange, the last Abbasid – fifty-fourth in his line, the descendant of the Prophet's uncle and of the fabled caliph Harun al-Rashid – was granted a modest stipend and allowed to return to his beloved city by the Nile. Here he died in obscurity.

Cairo's medieval glory was over. From being the proud seat of a great empire, the fountainhead of Islam and the market place of the Mediterranean, the city tumbled into mediocrity. It became an Ottoman garrison town, a place of lesser significance within a vast empire whose army and fleet marauded from the Danube to the Tigris to the Gulf of Lyons. During 300 years of Ottoman rule, not a single monument was raised that could compete in originality or splendour with the great mosques and colleges and tombs of the Mamluk era.

YET IT WAS not so dire as all that. Cairo did indeed stagnate under the Ottomans. The empire's distant capital on the Bosporus did draw away talent and tribute. The seafaring skill of the Dutch and Portuguese did choke off transit trade from the Indies. But Cairo remained a large and generally prosperous city, second only to Constantinople in the Ottoman realm. Decline did not set in for real until the empire as a whole began to fall apart.

The Ottomans, quickly satiated by the sacking of Cairo, reformed Egypt's administration. Fiefdoms were abolished and replaced by a more structured system of tax farming. Personal wealth and inheritance were respected once more, and not so tightly monopolized by the military class. For a time a new commodity – the coffee of Yemen – replaced Indian spices as a source of rich profits. Private individuals built sumptuous town houses and endowed the city with the dozens of public drinking fountains that still dot the Old City. Impressive mosques were raised – such as those of Sinan at Bulaq, of Sulayman Pasha in the Citadel, or of Malika Safiyya off Muhammad Ali Street – although these were mere copies of grander structures in Constantinople. The pleasure quarters around the seasonal lakes at Azbakiyya and Birkat al-Fil expanded; minstrels plied their waters in elegant caiques while parties of ladies picnicked in the surrounding orchards.

As for the undeniable decline in traditional crafts, the lack of royal patronage from the Citadel was not the only reason. It was equally due to the proliferation of guilds that rigidified taste: to enter any of the 300 organized trades in Ottoman Cairo – including those of bath attendant and night-soil carrier – a novice had to ascend a strict hierarchy from apprentice to partner to master craftsman. The system guaranteed job security, even for thieves, who maintained their own guild (the master of which could occasionally be paid to return stolen goods). But it stifled creativity.

If some change was positive, much of what did not change was negative. The overriding concern of Ottoman governors was to ensure the supply of Egyptian grain and the annual cash tribute to Constantinople. How these were obtained was of little concern. The existence of the Mamluks – not as rulers but as a self-perpetuating, largely Turkish-speaking warrior class that was eager to keep native Egyptians under heel – suited the Ottomans well. Indeed, in 1521, only a few years after the conquest, the governor had to call in Mamluk irregulars to restore order when his own troops rioted – they were angry because their favourite opium dealer had been executed for pushing his wares during the holy month of Ramadan. The old grandees of Cairo were allowed to continue recruiting fresh Mamluks. Their choice was, however, less discriminating than in the past. Germans, Hungarians, Sudanese and Maltese now washed up in Cairo as mercenaries or slave soldiers. Even the sons of Mamluk freedmen, who had traditionally been banned from joining the warrior class, bolstered the households of the leading beys (the term 'amir' having vanished with the Mamluk sultanate).

With time, the strength of the Ottoman garrison declined. Its officers grew less interested in the business of governing than in the business of making money. By the seventeenth century

Mamluk beys had come to control every important office in Egypt, and, as Constantinople's hold loosened, their depredations increased to the point that Ottoman governors relinquished any pretence at authority. With the capital enmeshed in court intrigue and war in the Balkans, the best its agents in Cairo could do was to play off the powerful beys against each other. The city split into two Mamluk-led factions that fought vicious, decades-long turf wars for control of tax-collecting privileges, customs duties and protection rackets. The introduction of carbines and pistols made their feuding far bloodier than it ever had been. Rival houses now sought to anihilate each other by ambush and assassination. Nothing was sacred in these gangland wars: even the tomb of Sultan Hasan served as a platform for rebel artillery when shelling the governor's residence in the Citadel. The Ottoman garrison itself – underpaid and far from home – tended to join in the hunt for spoils.

Between 1688 and 1755 the Mamluk beys, with their allies in the Ottoman garrison and among Bedouin bandits, deposed no fewer than thirty-four governors. They even instituted a salaried post for an official whose sole task was to deliver the command '*Anzil!*' – 'Step down!' – to the Ottoman sultan's cringing envoy, whose palace in the Citadel had crumbled into disrepair. By the mid eighteenth century Cairo was independent of Constantinople in all but name; the annual tribute it sent had fallen from 800,000 ducats at the conquest to a mere 400,000 sequins at a fraction of the value.

In the countryside the Mamluks' tax collection degenerated into outright banditry. Not even the capital was safe. Bedouin horsemen raided the city's cemeteries, kidnapping mourners and carrying them off into the desert. City folk rioted with increasing frequency. They had plenty to complain about: famines, plagues, inflation and tyranny. Neighbourhoods turned into gated fortresses whose inhabitants bolted themselves in at night. The town houses of the rich became castles with high, forbidding walls, baffled entrances, and treasures secreted under their floors. But no place was immune from violence, not even al-Azhar: in 1689 ten students died in a squabble over the university rectorship.

Along with trade and crafts, learning declined. By the eighteenth century only twenty *madrasas* still functioned in Cairo, down from the seventy-five in al-Maqrizi's day. 'The hands of greed reached into the *waqf* endowments, and their supervisors neglected to spend on students and teachers' is how the Egyptian polymath and historian Ali Pasha Mubarak described this period a century later. 'This increased year by year until teaching stopped and the books were sold. The schools became barns and animal pens.' While Napoleon's doctors reckoned infant mortality at 60 per cent, the only local method of learning medicine they observed in 1800 was for students to memorize long-obsolete texts by copying them over and over.

Superstition went unchecked. Visions of doom took hold of the people. They were so strong that on at least three recorded occasions in the troubled eighteenth century half the citizenry fled to surrounding fields and desert when rumours spread that the end of the world was at hand. Their fear was not surprising: hunger, poverty, disease and strife had reduced the city's population to under a quarter of a million by 1800.

Europeans who ventured to Cairo now recoiled at its medieval squalor. They were appalled to see the rag-clad rabble cowering at the sight of their mongrel Turco-Mamluk overlords, splendidly dressed thugs who would, as a French visitor said, 'shed the blood of a man as they would that of cattle'. The common people were backward and fanatical. Widespread ignorance had left them with what Carsten Niebuhr called 'a relish for very insipid diversions'.

The once great trading city exported no manufactures. It imported rice from the Carolinas, and even spices were now procured from European merchants. The grand stone-built institutions of the old Mamluk sultanate had cracked, buckled and collapsed. The newer buildings were mostly poor affairs, cheaply built of wattle and mud. The city's arteries had sclerosed; most were twisted alleyways, wrote Niebuhr in 1761, 'which terminate not in any principal street, so that those who live at the bottom of them can converse from the back of their houses, yet must walk a quarter of a league before they can meet'. Outside the decaying city walls were vast untended mounds of garbage and whole quarters of derelict houses. Egypt, visitors reported, was oppressed, underpopulated and ripe for picking by some ambitious European power. Her capital, the beautiful Mother of the World, had mouldered into an unsightly old age.

CHAPTER SIX

The Phoenix Caged

In a few more months the European streets will have cut right through the old dumb dusty city which now crumbles peacefully upon the fellahin who live in it. It is the quarter of the Franks, the town of Italians, Provençals and Maltese – the future emporium of British India – which is flourishing, glittering and growing.

Gérard de Nerval, *Voyage en Orient,* 1843

The vanquished always seek to imitate their conquerors in their dress, insignia, beliefs, and other customs and usages . . .

Ibn Khaldun, *Prolegomena, c.* 1380

IT IS THE spring of 1889. Carriages clip-clop down neat, wide avenues lined with orange trees in blossom. The patter of bare feet – the feet of liveried Nubian runners – accompanies the rumble of the grander private broughams. But most of the vehicles are hired calashes, with their hoods tucked back to allow passengers a view of the Ismailia Quarter and its parade of new villas behind cast-iron fences, as well as the occasional picturesque diversion of a native going about his labours.

Several of these conveyances converge on one address, the headquarters of the Khedivial Geographical Society. One by one they drop their fezzed and top-hatted charges at the premises of the learned society. Representing Science are Dottore Commendatore Onofrio Abbate Pasha, former head of public health and now physician to his highness the khedive; Falaki Pasha, director of the Khedivial Observatory; and Herr Doktor Vollers of the Khedivial Library. Fakhry Pasha, the minister of justice, is present, along with his *chef de bureau* Gaillardot Bey and the lawyers Figari and Bonola Bey and Borelli Bey, the latter freshly returned from three years' adventures among the savage Galla of Abyssinia. Mr Gibson, commissioner of state domains, and his compatriots Colonel Wingate and the explorer Mason Bey represent Great Britain, whose Army of Occupation has been noisily installed at the nearby Qasr al-Nil barracks for seven years. Count Zaluski of the Public Debt Commission represents Finance. Commerce and Trade are in attendance, too: Herr Timmermann, administrator of the railways, and Mr Andre Bircher, a Swiss trader in watches, ivory and ostrich feathers, can vouch for their interest in the progress of knowledge. Among other guests are several titled Europeans who have wintered in Cairo. On this occasion there are no ladies to enliven the proceedings.

Dr Abbate opens the meeting with correspondence. A fellow member has sent a letter from the Upper Congo, where he has been busy exploring the jungle lands of the Bangala tribe. It confirms at first hand the news already brought by telegraph of Mr Henry M. Stanley's latest sensational exploit. The American explorer, journalist and self-promoter has just 'rescued' Emin Pasha, the governor of Egypt's Equatoria province. For four years, ever since the Mahdist revolt in the Sudan and the grisly murder of Egypt's governor at Khartoum, Charles Gordon, Emin has been stranded 3,000 miles from Cairo – from civilization itself – at the furthest limit of Egypt's African empire by the source of the White Nile.

The Congolese epistle rouses a polite rustle of satisfaction.*

*A year later, the society will host Stanley himself in Cairo and hear of how, at the

Then, at Dr Abbate's invitation, a certain Monsieur Piperno conducts into the room a strange figure, a middle-aged man of modest stature wearing a frock coat and cravat. The man graciously bows to the company. He would be unexceptional, except that his face is entirely enveloped in long, silky hair of light auburn colour, such that only his faintly Oriental eyes peek forth – like those of the soon-to-be-invented Teddy bear. A murmur of interest ripples through the room.

This specimen, Monsieur Piperno explains, is none other than Moung Phoset, a member from the fourth generation of a family brought in 1801 out of the forests of northern Laos to the court of the king of Burma. In those forests there exists, he says, an entire tribe of aboriginals presenting the same remarkably hirsute appearance. Like Mr Phoset, they are to be distinguished not only by this feature, but also by their singular lack of molar teeth in the dental apparatus. Monsieur Piperno concludes by inviting the assembled gentlemen to examine the *Homo hirsutus,* assuring them that Mr Phoset is gentle and speaks excellent English.

His distinguished colleagues having examined Mr Phoset's dentary anomaly, Dr Abbate again takes the podium, pinches on his pince-nez, and shuffles his notes. The learned address he now delivers touches on the disciplines of anthropology and physiology and the controversial work of Mr Darwin. Following a discourse on the discovery of the *Homo hirsutus* – the distinguished medic suggests that a more apt nomenclature would be *Homo capillaris* – he cites the pioneering studies of Mayer and Kaathoven in showing the links between teeth and the cutaneous surfaces of mammals such as whales and armadillos. In short, Dr Abbate argues that this fascinating specimen is not a mere freak of nature, but rather a natural product of racial evolution. Mr Phoset, he

---

end of his gruelling 1,000-mile march to the safety of the coast, Emin Pasha (a Viennese Jewish convert to Islam) toppled accidentally to his death from a balcony just after toasting the kaiser at a celebratory banquet thrown by the *Kommandant* of German East Africa.

asserts, represents a small but obscure branch of humanity, *une variété de race,* as he calls it in his Sicilian-accented French.

Polite applause. Several members volunteer comments. Notably, Count Zaluski remarks that the similarly hairy aboriginals of northern Japan, the Ainu, are believed by their countrymen to be descended from the intermingled blood of man and wild bears.

A CENTURY BEFORE the enactment of this quaint scene, with its polyglot cast of sedately curious pashas and beys, no Cairo native had ever seen such a thing as a horse-drawn carriage. The city's streets were simply too narrow to contain them. No one had ever heard of Burma. No one even knew, or found especially intriguing, where the source of their own Nile was, aside from the fact that it lay far off, deep in the lands where African slaves came from. Of what use would such knowledge be? Other than the rare eccentric traveller, the sole Europeans in the city were a handful of traders. Intrepid Provençals and Italians, mostly, they dressed in mufti – turbans and kaftans and slippers – so as not to be openly laughed at by common folk, or insulted. Even so, they risked being flogged by a Mamluk if they got in his way.

It was this kind of maltreatment – in point of fact no different from that meted out to native Copts or Jews or even ordinary Muslims of the lower orders – that gave Napoleon Bonaparte an excuse to invade Egypt in the late spring of 1798. Of course there were other, more practical, reasons: the economic potential of Egypt and the weakness of its Ottoman masters; Napoleon's megalomania and his romantic visions of the East; his wish to threaten Britain's hold on India; the desire of rivals in Paris to send the obstreperous twenty-eight-year-old general as far away as possible. All this went unmentioned in the propaganda leaflets Napoleon's half-breed translators composed while bound for Egypt aboard his flagship *L'Orient.* The Great Sultan Bunabart, these tracts simply declared, had come as the servant of Allah and of the Ottoman sultan. His mission was to punish the wicked Mamluks and rescue Egypt from their grasp.

When copies of the leaflet reached Cairo, along with ominous news that a vast infidel army had taken Alexandria, its rigid, inelegant script excited as much comment as the contents. No wonder: the science of printing had practically vanished from Egypt. Learned men like Abd al-Rahman al-Jabarti, scion of a family of Azharite sheikhs and the sardonic chronicler of his unhappy times, examined the text with puzzlement. Indeed, al-Jabarti's history, the twenty-seven-volume *Marvels of Deeds in Annals and Lives,* devoted far more space to a critique of Napoleon's grammar, spelling and style than to his meaning. The sheikh concluded this scholarly savaging with a wish that God should strike with dumbness the tongues of these infidels who have no religion but the rules of Reason. So much for the Great Sultan Bunabart's protestations.

On 17 July 1798 the Mamluk beys called for a general mobilization. The able-bodied men of Cairo grabbed staves and kitchen knives and rushed to the port of Bulaq, raising such a tumult that to a scornful al-Jabarti it seemed they were waging a war of noise. The main body of the Mamluk army, meanwhile, went out to meet the French. Its soldiers, says al-Jabarti, were 'at odds with each other, envious, fearful for their lives and their comforts, immersed in ignorance and self-delusion, arrogant and haughty in their attire and presumptuousness'.

When 25,000 French troops came in sight of the Pyramids at the village of Imbaba across the Nile from Cairo, the outnumbered Mamluk cavalry did not wait. Tall in the saddle, with what a French officer described as complexions of roses under their silk turbans, these superb horsemen gripped their reins in their teeth as they charged headlong across the fields of clover. At full gallop they fired first their carbines, then braces of pistols, which they tossed behind them for their servants to collect. Those Mamluks still in the saddle then launched their javelins, before drawing scimitars – they wielded one in each hand – to slash through the enemy at close quarters.

The technique had proved effective against Bedouin bandits and peasant tax-evaders, but the well-equipped French, grouped in neat squares, blew apart the Mamluks with canister-shot, grapeshot and controlled musket volleys. Few of the flamboyant warriors got close enough to do any damage. 'The dust thickened and the world became dark from the smoke of the gunpowder,' says al-Jabarti. 'Men became deafened from the constant firing, and it seemed to them the earth was shaking and the heavens falling.' After a mere three-quarters of an hour the Mamluk dead – a thousand in all – littered the ground. The remnants of their magnificent army sped off to the south. The French had lost twenty-nine men.

When the Egyptian army was put to flight, continues the chronicler,

> The Franks turned their muskets and guns on the eastern shore and fired on it. Having sufficient evidence of the rout, the grandees and the people made off and left all their baggage and tents as they were, not taking anything. The citizens made for the city and entered it in droves, all of them scared out of their wits and expecting destruction, crying out in lamentation, wailing and beseeching God to save them from this fateful day, while the women cried out from the houses at the tops of their voices.

The Mamluk beys having fled or gone into hiding, it fell to the only authority left, the native-born sheikhs of the great mosques, to surrender the city. On 24 July the Franks entered Cairo unarmed, laughing in the market places and paying outrageous prices. Napoleon took up residence in the eastern suburbs by the lake of Azbakiyya in the newly built palace of Alfi

Bey, a wealthy Mamluk. To the surprise of the common people, 'Bunabart' was not a devil with foot-long fingernails, as the beys had said.

The first few months of an occupation that was to last for three years passed peacefully enough. Cairenes were fascinated by such novelties as the cafés and restaurants that Italian entrepreneurs established. Crowds collected to watch the soldiers in their funny tight *banṭalūns* lounging in upright chairs at long, high tables, spearing their food with forks, imbibing intoxicating liquors, and having their purchases totted up on itemized bills. Aside from the French habit of apparently never removing their boots, even in sleep, what most struck al-Jabarti was their subservience to women. A few hundred camp followers had sailed with the army from France, and these ladies roamed about unveiled. 'They rode through the streets at a gallop, laughing and joking with people of the lowest class. This indecent freedom appealed to those women in Cairo who had not been well brought up; and since the French prided themselves on their slavery to women and showered them with gifts, the native women began to enter into relations with them.'*

The French amused Cairenes by declaring that they would launch a device which could fly through the heavens and carry people to distant lands. When their tricoloured hot-air balloon collapsed after a short flight, observers like al-Jabarti were relieved to find that the claim was in jest. 'It turned out to be like the kites which household servants build for festivals,' he sniffed. A far more practical innovation was an instrument the French used for their work in demolishing the gates of the city's separate quarters and in building fortifications. It was a sort of cart with two handles at one end and a wheel at the other, in which the scrawniest labourer could carry the equivalent of five basket-loads

*To this day, peasant women of the Nile Delta wear dresses cut in the fashion of late-eighteenth-century France.

with the greatest ease. (Later, under the influence of another occupying army, this thing would come to be known as a *barawīl*.)

Most impressive of all, however, was the French devotion to learning. Obsessed with putting his stamp on history, Napoleon had insisted that a team of distinguished scientists accompany his expedition. Considering the fate his army would meet, the move proved prescient. These hundred-odd *savants* – astronomers, linguists, antiquarians, botanists, engineers and so on – attacked their subject with a diligence that Egyptians found astonishing. Three years of frantic research went into the making of a twenty-four-volume encyclopedia. The *Description de l'Égypte* filled gaping holes in Europe's knowledge of the country, its people, its crafts, its flora and fauna, and its ancient monuments.

To al-Jabarti's surprise, the *savants* welcomed native visitors to the institute they had established in another confiscated Mamluk mansion. More amazing still, considering that barely one in a hundred of his own people was literate, al-Jabarti found its library crowded with French soldiers reading in silence. In the institute's laboratory the sheikh was shown chemistry experiments that changed liquids into solids. He was given a jolt by a strange force called electricity. He admired the precision and fine workmanship of the infidels' scientific instruments. He marvelled at the skill of their artists, who minutely recorded not only Egypt's flowers and insects, but also its pagan antiquities and even its leading personalities with portraits so lifelike they seemed about to speak.

Yet there was something perplexing to al-Jabarti – disturbing even – in all this industry. The Azharite approved of a fellow sheikh who commented, after a French ornithologist had explained his work, that this classifying of animal species was a waste of effort. Had not the Prophet declared conclusively that there were 10,000 kinds of beasts above the water and 20,000 of fishes in the sea? Another sheikh asked whether French science could permit a man to be in two places at once. When told that it could not, he dismissed their magic as impotent. Even to al-Jabarti that was silly, but still the French laughter hurt. In between his lines lurked a nagging fear that, to the French, his city and all its proud traditions, and maybe even he himself were nothing but a freakish exhibition. To be observed as a 'specimen' was disconcerting. One can just picture the bearded sheikh, in his solemn dark kaftan and red clerical cap, struggling for dignity when the smirking French scientist zapped him with an electric shock. For the Cairene then, as now, there was no torment worse than being laughed at.

From an initial wary respect, relations between occupier and occupied soon deteriorated. The Ottoman sultan, Egypt's nominal suzerain, not only denied complicity with the Franks but dispatched armies to chase them off his turf. Napoleon trounced the Turks on land, but fared less well against the British Navy. Within two weeks of France's victory at the Battle of the Pyramids, Admiral Nelson had sunk most of the French fleet, stranding the grand Army of the Orient in Egypt. Cut off from supplies, reinforcements and, most importantly, cash, Napoleon resorted to desperate means to raise funds. It was this, more than the shame of being subjected to rule by the infidel, more than the urgings of the Mamluk beys conducting a guerrilla war in the south, that provoked uprisings in Cairo.

The first of these broke out within six months of the conquest. When the French decreed a range of summary taxes on property in October 1798, rabble-rousing clerics – 'those lacking foresight', in al-Jabarti's words – preached holy war. Mobs shouted for the victory of Islam and attacked the invaders with whatever weapons came to hand. The French suffered 300 casualties in two days of rioting. Their response was to shell the city continually for an entire afternoon, concentrating on the Mosque of al-Azhar. At night they stormed into the shell-shocked streets and, to the horror of the sheikhs, charged into the ancient mosque on horseback and sacked it. 'When morning unsheathed the sword of dawn and the black raven of darkness flew from its perch,' says al-Jabarti, the foreigners were again in charge of the city. Some 3,000 Cairenes had perished.

France's Army of the Orient endured two more years. Disease and a futile campaign against the Turks in Palestine sapped its numbers. Napoleon ratted out, leaving his army to fend for itself in Egypt while he himself sneaked back to Paris to pursue his career. Rather than embrace *fraternité,* Cairo again rose in revolt in 1801. This time the French lost control for five full weeks, and only clawed their way back with a bombardment that flattened whole districts. When the guns stopped firing the port of Bulaq, the pleasure quarter of Azbakiyya and the working-class neighbourhood of Husayniyya were smashed into rubble.*

In the end it was not the people of Cairo and not the tired old Ottoman sultanate that chased away the infidel. A British force landed at Alexandria. Too exhausted to put up much fight against its technological equal, the Army of the Orient came to terms. It was allowed to withdraw peacefully. On 15 July 1801 the last French troops marched away from Cairo. They left the city morally as well as physically battered. They had shaken Cairo's complacency; punctured its self-esteem.

IN THE WINTER of 1841 a Frenchman by the name of Gérard Labrunie arrived at Cairo. The illegitimate son of a Napoleonic officer, he was a man of melancholic disposition and fervid imagination. To readers in France he would be better known as a romantic poet, and by his pen-name: Gérard de Nerval.

Nerval was in mourning. His mistress, a *demi-mondaine* of the Paris stage, had just died of consumption. His career as a

*This was not the only destruction wrought by the French. They had already damaged the remaining palaces in the Citadel so as to improve its utility as a fortress. 'They disfigured its beauties,' lamented al-Jabarti. 'They demolished the palace of Salah al-Din and the council halls of kings and sultans which had high supports and tall pillars, as well as mosques and chapels and shrines.'

pamphleteer was adrift. The exotic air of Cairo, he thought, would cure his spleen. The lonely Parisian also pined for Oriental romance, it seems, because he endured slaps and rebuffs from quite a few veiled women of Cairo. One day he courted danger by trailing a giggling pair of hooded ladies halfway across the city. With a last coy glance they vanished into a doorway. The foiled voyeur shrugged. But then a manservant appeared in the door, signalling with downward flicks of his hand for Nerval to enter. The Frenchman nearly swooned in anticipation of a scene from the Porter's Tale in *The Thousand and One Nights,* a story in which a humble delivery boy is inveigled by a lady client into a night of erotic revelry.

But nothing here was quite what it seemed. The veiled houris, it transpired, were themselves French, and had set out on purpose to tease their countryman. They offered nothing more than a polite tea.

Nerval was obliged to resort to the slave market. To his delight, the salesmen proved accommodating. They undressed their wares, opened their mouths to show off their teeth, made them prance up and down, and took particular care in showing off the elasticity of their breasts. For twenty-five pounds Nerval purchased an eighteen-year-old Javanese girl who he was told had been captured by Indian Ocean corsairs and sold at Mecca. Her thrilled new owner hired a donkey to transport the prize to his rented lodgings. The romance ended there. Far from being a pliant concubine, the girl proved a terrible burden. Bored, pouting and petulant, she refused to cook or clean.

Nerval draws a veil of discretion over their more intimate affairs. What he does concede is that he was soon plotting to get rid of her. But at the merest hint of being set free she stamped her foot down. 'Free?' she scoffed – and one wonders in what language that Nerval understood – 'And what do you expect me to do? And where am I to go?'

Given such frustrations it was hardly surprising that her

master should pronounce the city of *The Thousand and One Nights* a disappointment. 'Cairo lies beneath ashes and dust,' he wrote; 'the spirit and the progress of the modern age have triumphed over it like death.' Only the growing colony of Europeans seemed to Nerval to show signs of liveliness. Indeed, the foreign shopkeepers whose welfare had so concerned Napoleon were doing very nicely. A bustling Frankish quarter had sprung up west of the Old City, rising from the ruins of bomb-damaged Azbakiyya. Aside from Castagnol's pharmacy and an English tavern selling madeira, port and ale, rows of glass-fronted shops displayed the manufactures of Manchester and Mannheim at prices that were bankrupting local industries. Cairo even boasted a European theatre where the ladies appeared unveiled. But most appalling of all, in the eyes of the thwarted romantic, were the bizarre apparitions now commonly seen trotting through the native city.

Picture, writes Nerval, a gentleman mounted on a donkey, with long legs trailing to the ground. His round headdress, 'which is half a mattress and half a hat', is adorned with a thick quilting of white cotton piqué to fend off the sun. Under his green dust-proof veil he wears two pairs of tinted goggles framed in blue steel. His India-rubber outer garment is coated with waxed linen – a safeguard against the plague and the chance touch of the passer-by. 'In his gloved hand he clutches a long stick to swat away any suspicious Arab, and as a rule he never goes out without having his own groom on one side and his dragoman on the other.'

This creature, the tourist, is suddenly ubiquitous. To Europeans far less adventurous than Gérard de Nerval, Cairo has become as routine a destination as Baden-Baden. Steam packets ply the Nile. Memsahibs on their way 'out' to India enjoy the starched bedlinen of Mr Shepheard's English Hotel until the semaphore signal from Suez announces the arrival of the regular Bombay steamer. Then their well-sprung coach will follow a trail of soda-water corks across the desert to the Red Sea port – corks left, no doubt, by those heeding one British guidebook's tip that travellers should ease the overnight journey with 'two dozen bottles each of sherry, brandy and water'.

A few years before, visitors to the Pyramids had been obliged to hire guards to scare off Bedouin bandits. Now the ancient site was firmly policed; an enterprising compatriot of Nerval's had even turned a pharaonic tomb into a fancy restaurant. An alarmed Yankee described arriving at the Sphinx in the 1840s, and being charged by tattered villagers wielding clubs; but the clubs were for beating off competitors – the other hawkers of mummy beads and jars of water for the tourists whose strange passion it was to scramble heavenwards and plant their conquering feet on the summit of Cheops's sepulchre. When Nerval himself was hoisted and propelled by a team of four native jockeys to the top of the Great Pyramid, he found there, among the multiplying graffiti rudely scratched in the ancient limestone, 'some merchant of Piccadilly's advertisement for improved patented boot-black'.

WHAT HAD HAPPENED was this: shortly after France's Army of the Orient bailed out, Cairo had been commandeered by a renegade Ottoman officer called Muhammad Ali. Captaining a band of Albanian mercenaries sent to resecure Egypt for the sultan, Muhammad Ali had instead intrigued to toss the freshly installed Ottoman governor out of the Citadel. He knew full well that the sultan in far-off Constantinople was too deeply entangled in domestic woes and wars with Russia to care. Having little choice but to accept the coup, the sultan recognized this impetuous vassal as his viceroy in Egypt.

In 1807 Muhammad Ali's Albanians fought off an ill-planned British invasion, and celebrated famously by spiking several hundred *Inglīz* heads around Cairo. Soon after, and with gangland panache, the viceroy finished off the last potential threat to his hold. He invited all the remaining Mamluk grandees of Egypt to a banquet in the Citadel. Having eaten their fill, the twenty-four chieftains and their 400 armed and mounted slave retainers descended in single file down the steep, narrow passage to the fortress's lower gate. The Albanians slammed the doors shut and drilled the trapped horsemen with bullets. Cairene myth has it that one bey escaped by leaping over the ramparts on his charger. The tale does not explain whether he survived the subsequent extermination of 3,000 more Mamluks who were hunted down in the streets of the city.

With his position now unchallengeable, Muhammad Ali executed one of the greatest land grabs in history. He confiscated the feudal farms of the Mamluk grandees, and soon afterwards stripped Cairo's religious institutions of their 600,000 prime acres of *waqf* landholdings. Accustomed to financial security and high social standing, the great mosques and law colleges of the city – including al-Azhar itself – found themselves scrounging for sustenance along with the stray cats whose thirteenth-century endowment would now no longer provide a daily meal in front of the residence of the chief cadi.

At a stroke Muhammad Ali had decapitated Cairo's medieval order. The stifling power of both the beys and the clerics was finished. Egypt had become the viceroy's private plantation; and this new master, unlike his predecessors, was a man of vision as well as ambition. Born in Thrace in 1769, Muhammad Ali had grown up in the polyglot and increasingly westward-looking city of Salonica. Experience in soldiering had made him fully aware of the Ottoman Empire's relative backwardness. And so, with roughshod disregard for niceties or precedent, he set out to remodel Egypt in the shape of the disciplined European armies he so admired.

With the help of French advisers – many of them former officers in Napoleon's army – Muhammad Ali made wrenching changes. He ordered wide-scale planting of a new strain of cotton which was to be the cash crop that would fuel economic revival.

He broke with 2,000 years of tradition by forcibly drafting native Egyptians both for his army and for vast public-works projects. He reorganized the government into bureaux staffed with salaried officials who were promoted on the basis of merit. He instituted the first secular schools in Cairo, and began to send Egyptians abroad to learn European languages and sciences.

The building of canals brought a million new acres under cultivation and speeded the export of cotton. The cotton made Egypt – or rather its master – rich, and thrust the country into the gears of global trade and finance. The French-trained army brought advances of another kind. On behalf of the Ottoman sultan it defeated a fundamentalist insurgency in Arabia and an insurrection in Greece.* On Muhammad Ali's personal account it conquered the Sudan, and then, to the impotent sultan's discomfort, began to chip away at the Ottomans' own domains. By the 1830s the viceroy of Egypt's realm was more extensive than the fifteenth-century Mamluk sultanate: the provinces of Sudan, Hijaz (including the Holy Cities of Mecca and Medina), Syria, Palestine and even – briefly – half the Turkish homelands of Anatolia had fallen under Muhammad Ali's control. His son Ibrahim led a brilliant campaign that brought the model Egyptian army to within a few hundred miles of Constantinople. The upstart was challenging the very existence of the Ottoman Empire.

Muhammad Ali had become a major player. His mistake was to table his cards too soon for the rough and novel game of geopolitics. Fearing that Russia would exploit the weakness of the Ottomans to make a lunge at the Mediterranean, Britain and

* The insurgents were a puritan anti-Sufi sect known as the Wahhabis. A century later their champions, the al-Saud family, captured Mecca and conquered most of Arabia. Saudi Arabia still adheres to strict Wahhabi Islam. The Greek insurrection (1824–5) was the first round of Greece's War of Independence. Muhammad Ali's success in crushing it roused European sympathy for the Greeks, which helped them win independence from the Ottomans in 1829.

France intervened with their fleets. With his army now in danger of being cut off in Syria, the viceroy bowed to European strength. He agreed to pull back. In exchange the Ottoman sultan granted Muhammad Ali what he really wanted: a permanent title to the viceroyalty for his descendants.

Nominally, Egypt remained a province of the Ottoman Empire. But Cairo was once again a capital city, the seat of a dynasty.

GÉRARD DE NERVAL may have been a fine poet, but he was also a terrible Jeremiah, of course. (Ten years after returning to France he went mad and hanged himself.) Cairo had not yet changed as drastically as he said. Leaving aside the Frankish frills of the Azbakiyya quarter and a modest clutch of factory chimneys by the port of Bulaq – and ignoring the bulbous new mock-Ottoman mosque atop the Citadel, where Muhammad Ali Pasha was buried – at the viceroy's death in 1849 the city looked little different from half a century before. True, it had been tidied and made secure from bandits. Streets had been labelled, numbered and cleared of obstructions. The mountainous piles of accumulated rubbish outside the walls had mostly been levelled. Yet a very different Cairo from Nerval's emerges from the writings of his English near-contemporary, Edward Lane.

Lane had given up a career as an engraver in order to study Arabic. He arrived in Cairo in 1825, and for twenty-four years he studied the city, its language and traditions with passionate single-mindedness. His encyclopedic *Account of the Manners and Customs of the Modern Egyptians* was a pioneering work in social anthropology. It still stands out as a uniquely thorough and objective portrayal of an essentially medieval city – down to the details of such things as child-rearing practices, magic, music, dress and table manners. In Lane's view the impact of change had reached no further than the ruling elite. 'Some Egyptians who had studied for a few years in France declared to me that they could not instil any of the notions which they had there acquired even into the minds of their most intimate friends,' he wrote. 'European customs have not yet begun to spread among the Egyptians themselves; but they probably will ere long; and in the expectation that this will soon be the case, I have been most anxious to become well acquainted ... with the state of society which has existed ... for many centuries, and which many persons have deemed almost immutable.'

Like Lane, other Europeans were driven to capture what they knew was a world that was bound to vanish. Artists like the Frenchman Prisse d'Avennes, the Scot David Roberts and the Englishman Robert Hay found Cairo an incomparable source of the exotic. Writing to his daughter in the winter of 1839, Roberts painted this picture of his labours: 'The narrow, crowded streets make it difficult to do drawings, for in addition to the curiosity of the Arabs, you run the risk of being squeezed to a mummy by the loaded camels, who, although they are picturesque in appearance, are ugly customers to jostle.' His grand architectural views of the city, widely reproduced in lithographs, were largely responsible for the popularization of Orientalism in Western art – a movement that would not fade entirely until Hollywood's Sindbad films of the 1940s.

Cairo was still a place where the European imagination could wander unrestrained by the conventions of the times. Gustave Flaubert, a more famous man of letters than Nerval, was thrilled by the city's charms. Never mind if the viceroy had banished all the whores of the Bab al-Luq quarter, he wrote to friends in Paris: the rest of the town was an open-air *bal masqué*. The visitor could wind up his turban, frolic in fancy Moorish robes, recline with his hookah on a divan, and drink in the sounds of the Orient. 'The little bells on the dromedaries are tinkling in your ears, and great flocks of black goats are making their way along the street, bleating at the horses, the donkeys and the merchants,' he lyricized in the winter of 1850. 'There is jostling, there is argument, there are blows, there is rolling about, there is swearing of all kinds, there is shouting in a dozen languages. The raucous Semitic syllables clatter in the air like the sound of a whiplash ... it is delightful.'

Flaubert devoured this rich meal with gusto. He wandered the bazaars, had himself massaged in the Turkish baths, and sailed up the Nile to the great temples of Upper Egypt. There he dallied at last with a certain Kuchuk Hanem, a dancer exiled from Cairo. It may have been she who gave him the syphilis that shortened his life.

Yet Nerval was not entirely wrong. At mid century Cairo had indeed changed. It was just that the deeper shifts were subtle ones. European attitudes had begun to impress themselves. Whereas a visitor in 1820 had been struck by the clash between the 'squalid wretchedness' of the Egyptians and the 'external splendour' of the ruling class of Turks, now a new breed of native Cairene had begun to flourish. Teachers, bureaucrats and engineers – these *effendis,* as they were known – had been trained by foreign instructors in the secular schools Muhammad Ali had established. They had read the scientific texts translated at his Institute of Languages and printed at his press. Some had studied, at the viceroy's expense, in the distant capitals of Europe. The effendis not only worked behind desks in nameplated offices, they not only ate with knives and forks, they also wore coats and trousers, and occasionally tinted glasses against the sun too. A few even drank alcohol. They scorned superstition and frowned on such practices as slavery. What was exotic to Flaubert was backwardness to them. They dreamed the European dream of Progress.

Under their influence the pace of change began to accelerate. Telegraph and railway networks spread. Regular train services linked Cairo to the Mediterranean in 1854, before such countries as Sweden and Japan had even begun to lay tracks. The poll tax on non-Muslims, which had lapsed in 1815, was officially abolished. Christian missionaries were allowed to practise. With the legal privileges for their nationals which the European powers extorted from the supine court in Constantinople,* these openings made Cairo a magnet for foreign fortune hunters. Carpet-baggers flocked from all over the Mediterranean: Levantine Christians and Jews fleeing persecution; Greek and Italian tradesmen, merchants and moneylenders.

The city also attracted distinguished European professionals. The French physician Clot Bey founded Cairo's first modern hospital and medical school in the 1820s, and instituted basic public-health services which were considered a model of their kind – including a nationwide network of trained midwives. It was at Clot Bey's hospital that the German scientist Dr Theodor Bilharz discovered the life cycle of schistosomiasis, a debilitating disease endemic to Egypt, in 1853. The Palermo-born Onofrio Abbate arrived in Cairo in 1846 and stayed on for sixty years – excepting a return to Sicily in 1860 to join the victorious Giuseppe Garibaldi's red shirts on their march to unify Italy. (Abbate was a staunch republican – he even named his son Washington.). Aside from being chief physician to Egypt's rulers, Abbate published research into such variegated topics as the anaesthetic properties of cocaine and the transmission of rabies among street dogs. He accumulated state decorations from Brazil, Hawaii and Bavaria as well as Turkey and Egypt. The French archaeologist Auguste Mariette not only founded the Egyptian Museum, but was one of the first antiquarians to introduce

*Known as the Capitulations, the privileges included preferential trading terms, tax-free status for foreign residents, and exemption from local laws. Here is Rudyard Kipling's explanation: 'Everyone in Cairo has the privilege of appealing to his own consul on every conceivable subject from the disposal of a garbage-can to that of a corpse. As almost everyone with claims to respectability, and certainly everyone without any, keeps a consul, it follows that there is one consul per superficial meter, arshin or cubit of Ezekiel within the city.' Onerous to Egyptians, the Capitulations remained in effect until 1947, albeit in diminishing form.

scientific methods of excavation. In 1854 his compatriot Ferdinand de Lesseps inspired the viceroy with the vision of a Cairo that would once again control the greatest trading route in the world: work began on a sea canal across the Isthmus of Suez.

Along with the effendis, these *khawagāt** began to impress their needs. Together they formed a prospering ruling class that demanded plate-glass windows and balconies instead of wooden screens, carriages instead of donkeys, staged artifice rather than bazaar storytellers, servants not slaves. It required modern laws and means of communication, running water and paved streets. Under the constant gaze of these people who saw the old city as a picturesque anachronism, Cairo grew uncomfortable in its skin.

WHILE THE CIVIL War raged in the United States, momentous events overtook Egypt. An Englishman named John Hanning Speke discovered the source of the White Nile in 1862. A new viceroy assumed the throne at Cairo. The value of Egypt's cotton sales quadrupled in a single year when the Yankee fleet blockaded Confederate harbours. The effect of the windfall was to delude the new ruler, Muhammad Ali's French-educated grandson Ismail, that he was rich enough to turn Egypt into France, Cairo into Paris, and his court into Versailles. Egged on by European bankers who stampeded to offer credit, Ismail spent and spent.

The khedive – for this was the grand title Ismail acquired by means of a hefty bribe to Constantinople – was in a hurry. He was planning the biggest party the world had ever seen. For the opening of the Suez Canal he was determined that his capital

*The term, derived from a Persian word meaning 'lord', referred in Egypt originally to Greek and Italian merchants, particularly slavers. By the twentieth century it embraced all Europeans, and had come to have a mildly pejorative sense akin to the Mexicans' *gringo*. The singular is *khawāga*.

should be a showcase, a seat fit for royal European guests. It required open squares adorned with heroic statues, and gaslit avenues lined with palaces and villas. It needed parks with grottos and Chinese pavilions and pleasure lakes rippled by pedal boats. It simply had to have a comedy theatre and an opera house, a museum and library, and learned institutes like the Khedivial Geographical Society.

And so, until the debts were called in, the great one-by-two mile tract of land between Cairo and the Nile became a vast building site. Roads with sidewalks were laid. Plots were given to any person who would spend not less than £2,000 on a villa and finish it within eighteen months. Concessions were granted – to a certain Charles Le Bon – for municipal gas and water. Monsieur Barillet-Deschamps, the chief landscaper for the city of Paris, whom Ismail had met at the 1867 Exposition Universelle, was hired to landscape the Azbakiyya district into a municipal park on the model of the French capital's Bois de Boulogne.

As for the city's medieval core, it was simply ignored except for two cannonshot-straight carriageways driven through its core. It might have suffered worse: Ali Pasha Mubarak, Ismail's energetic minister of public works, was all for tearing down the great funerary mosques. To him they were simply painful reminders of Mamluk oppression. 'We no longer want to preserve such memories,' Mubarak declared, 'We want to destroy them as the French did the Bastille.' He actually said this later, in 1881, but the intent was there. He was stopped by yet another modernizing innovation: the conservationist lobby.

The canal's inauguration in 1869 was a triumph for Ismail. Europe's nobs and nabobs migrated to Cairo en masse for the occasion. The Crown Prince of Prussia, Prince Louis of Hesse, Henry of the Netherlands and a trail of other luminaries trundled through the new streets in a flotilla of sumptuous landaus. The khedive, being a great ladies' man, was conspicuously attentive to

Empress Eugénie of France.* The residential and guest palaces, the cast-iron bridge over the Nile flanked by bronze lions, the Opera House and landscaped parks were in place. So 'civilized' was Cairo that it had actually become the centre of Egypt's own vast colonial empire. In his bid to compete with the Great Powers, Ismail had hired ex-Confederate American officers – then the most experienced military professionals available – to lead his army deep into Africa. The slice of territory they had carved out by 1870 was half the size of the United States, making Egypt's empire the largest in Africa at the time. The European explorers sponsored by Ismail had mapped and described the whole of the Nile basin, which for the first time in history had fallen almost entirely under Egyptian rule.

Long after the festival flags came down, Ismail's Cairo enjoyed many a splendid occasion. The khedive was keen to surround himself with sparkling company. With an official salary double Queen Victoria's, he could afford to lavish stipends on assorted down-at-heel royalty. One such was the Contessa della Sala, who was to remain a fixture of Cairo society for thirty years. She had married a dour Russian nobleman, whom fortuitously her lover, a handsome Austrian count, killed in a duel at Saqqara. She was famed for her wit: when a performing Indian fakir's loincloth slipped at one party, she broke the embarrassed silence by chirrupping, '*Ne vous inquietez pas. Ce ne sont que des bronzes!*'† In later years the contessa liked to regale friends with tales of the khedive's Trimalchian extravagance, such as the production of *Aida* at his opera house in which genuine Ethiopian slaves numbered among the 3,000 performers.‡ The effigies of ancient gods required for

*The khedive was rumoured to have presented Eugénie with a solid-gold chamberpot, in the bowl of which glittered an emerald set in an eye: Ismail, too, had green eyes.

† 'Don't be alarmed. They're only bronze!'

‡ Ismail had commissioned Giuseppe Verdi to produce an Egyptian-themed opera for the Suez Canal inauguration. The Italian composer failed to complete *Aida* on

the opera's grand processional march were real ones, purloined for the occasion from Mariette's museum. At the banquet afterwards in Ismail's new 500-room, 24-acre Italianate palace at ʿAbdin, six of the sultriest dancing girls were borne into the dining hall on gold platters, garnished with custard. Or so the contessa claimed.

Ismail's energy was not all wasted on fun. Under his rule 5,000 schools opened, giving Egypt a better state education system than, say, tsarist Russia had at the time. The country's networks of railways and irrigation canals expanded by leaps and bounds. Ismail created a parliament and codified laws on the Napoleonic model: in the view of the effendis, Islamic sharia was simply too cumbersome to deal with the modern world of affairs. The khedive welcomed immigrants, allowing them to own land and creating a special foreigners' court to replace the tangle of consular jurisdictions bequeathed by the Capitulations. Some newcomers were to have a lasting influence. Syrian Christians, such as the Takla brothers who founded the daily newspaper *Al-Ahram* in 1876, were to pioneer Arab journalism.* The fortunes of Egypt's native minorities also improved. Reforms greatly increased the amount of land in private ownership, and for the first time in a millennium Egypt's landed aristocracy was to include a large number of Coptic Christians. Non-Muslims were well served indeed by Ismail: in 1872 no fewer than 486 retailers of wine and spirits competed for custom in Cairo.

The khedive also abolished the slave trade. Admittedly, the move was half-hearted: Ismail's own favourite concubine, a Circassian by the name of Nesedil who owned her own magnificent palace outside the city, was allowed to keep her staff of eighty Caucasian and Abyssinian slaves. Ownership of eunuchs

---

time, so Cairo's Opera House opened with a performance of *Rigoletto* – perhaps a more appropriate work anyway, considering what was to befall Ismail.

*Incidentally, many of these modernizers had fled their native Beirut because the American missionaries there denounced them as Darwinists.

remained a status symbol for the upper classes into the early twentieth century. Yet Cairo's slave population – estimated at some 12,000 in the 1850s – did dwindle away. Sadly, what Gérard de Nerval's Javanese purchase had probably feared came true: most freed slave girls ended up as prostitutes, joining a growing class of Cairenes that found their station diminished by the breakdown of the old social order.

Ismail's liberality bore other dreadful costs. When his lavish spending overtook revenues from cotton, his creditors sealed their grip on Egypt's future. Even as peasants were taxed to destitution, the khedive's Paris and London bankers bided their time, cranking the interest on successive loans to outrageous heights. In 1878 Egypt's debt stood – by their sleight-of-hand accounting – at a whopping £100 million, an amount then equivalent to ten years of cotton exports and far surpassing, in relative terms, the debt burden of any developing country in the late twentieth century. Having mortgaged his own properties – not even Cairo's Opera House was spared – Ismail was obliged to sell the family silver. Egypt's share in the Suez Canal was knocked down to Britain for a paltry £4 million, a sum which the waterway was soon earning in annual revenues.

Still the creditors pressed. When the khedive refused to surrender his finances to foreign controllers they called in their chips. The Ottoman sultan, a debtor himself to the same gang of usurers, was arm-twisted into firing off a telegram addressed to 'the ex-khedive of Egypt'. Despised by his overtaxed subjects, Ismail sailed obediently into exile in 1879. He left the throne to his milksop son Tawfiq, who happily abandoned the hot potato of Egypt's finances to a cabal of foreign accountants. From now on, half of Egypt's revenue was to be siphoned into European banks.

Cairo boiled with indignation – not for love of Ismail, but out of wounded pride. Effendis joined with clerics and soldiers to protest against European interference and privilege. Orators expounded terms never heard before in Arabic: Liberty, Tyranny, the Egyptian People, Nationalism. The weak new khedive seesawed. One day he supported the nationalist army officers, who were led for the first time not by a Turk but by a native Egyptian colonel, Ahmad Urabi. The next day he cravenly pleaded for European intervention. As Cairo grew more impassioned, the foreign powers blustered and sent their fleets to Alexandria. Events began to spin out of control. Native xenophobes rioted in the port city. European newspapers howled at their 'Oriental savagery'. Soon after, British ships destroyed Alexandria with a bombardment of astounding ferocity. Colonel Urabi became a national hero overnight. Khedive Tawfiq sped offshore to the safety of the Royal Navy.

To European powers at the starting line of their race to colonize the world it was unthinkable that so rich a prize as Egypt – straddling as it now did the world's most vital waterway – be left to a rabble-rousing dictator. Intervention was inevitable; the only question was who was to intervene. At the last minute France balked, so it was a solely British force that marched to fight Urabi. At Tel al-Kabir, fifty miles north-east of Cairo, its Gatling guns cut the Egyptian army to pieces. Tawfiq returned to his capital under British escort. On 30 October 1882 – by which date some 30,000 'rebels' were interned in desert camps – the second European army in less than a century paraded through the stunned city.

CHAPTER SEVEN

WHERE WORLDS COLLIDE

With the polo, the balls, the racing and the riding, Cairo begins to impress itself upon you as an English town in which any quantity of Oriental sights are kept for the aesthetic satisfaction of the inhabitants, much as the proprietor of a country place keeps a game preserve or deer park for his amusement.

William Morton Fullerton, *In Cairo*, 1891

To be French-speaking in Cairo before the 1952 Revolution was to belong to a group of people who felt themselves deeply rooted in Cairo as a place, and probably believed that their lives would be spent in that city until death disseminated them to their various cemeteries, distinguished only by religion or rite ... It was to think of Cairo as home, but to believe that Paris was the navel of the world.

Magdi Wahba, 'Cairo Memories', 1978

OCCUPIED CAIRO WAS a city of veils and mirrors. Britain exercised power from behind a screen of niceties, downplaying its role as first among equals of the controlling powers. The khedive stayed on his throne and sustained his nominal allegiance to the Ottomans. Britain's consul-general merely 'advised' him as to who his ministers and what their policies should be. Like the khedive himself, these morning-coated, tarboosh-capped officials were shadow puppets: European under-secretaries made sure they jigged to London's tune. 'The British are easy to deceive,' joked Nubar Pasha Nubarian, a French-educated Armenian who was three times prime minister of Egypt, both before and after the occupation. 'But just when you think you have tricked them, you suddenly get a tremendous kick on your backside.'

Up in the Citadel, homesick soldiers scratched bad English verse over the fading French and Turkish and Arabic graffiti. Down below, the Old City lost its glamour. It crumbled just as Gérard de Nerval had predicted. Whole streets of traditional houses vanished, and were it not for the last-ditch efforts of a few conservationists the great mosques and schools would have too. Rich Cairenes aspired to a different style now. Finding the old winding alleyways claustrophobic, they moved to Italian-style villas along the broad carriage streets of the new quarters. The traditional guilds disbanded. Their trades collapsed in the face of European manufactures – all except for the crafts sold in the tourist bazaar.

Across town, foreign businesses prospered, their position bolstered by British arms and by a legal system skewed in their favour. By the turn of the century the *khawagāt* owned 96 per cent of the capital on the growing stock exchange; they owned the banks, the hotels, the luxury shops and the factories working flat out to supply the construction boom that was rapidly realizing Khedive Ismail's ambition of a Paris by the Nile. Along the Ismailia Quarter's avenues, said a visitor in 1908, there was nothing to be seen that could be said to be native, 'except it be a Sudanese porter seated on a bench outside a sumptuous mansion, half hidden by palms and tropical shrubs'.

German, Austro-Hungarian, French and Italian architects had given much of this new city a *belle époque* veneer, with a twist here and there of Islamic decor to maintain the Oriental atmosphere. A sort of French municipal dream progressed staidly from Opera Square to nearby ʿAtaba Square, the hub of Cairo's rapidly expanding tramway network. An equestrian statue of Ismail's father Ibrahim Pasha, (from the Paris studio of the sculptor Cordier) faced west in front of the Opera House itself. To his right were the Azbakiyya Gardens, with their winding paths and fountains, their banyan trees and bandstand, and the Italianate quarters of the Khedivial Fencing Club. Behind Ibrahim and to his left stood the domed main post office and the fire department, with its shiny red engines pulled by thirteen specially imported English carthorses. Foreigners saw justice done at the imposing Mixed Courts building across the street, in the middle of ʿAtaba Square. (The Native Tribunal was tucked away in a back alley.) Behind the square's arcaded shopfronts there rose the wrought-iron-and-glass roof of the new Marché Central. The facility, with its numbered aisles of vendors, its strict opening times and sanitary inspectors, seemed to challenge the ways of the Old City that spread out from here to the east. Nearby, a designer named Oscar Horowitz had capped the five-storeyed department store of Victor Tiring et Frères with a glass globe illuminated from inside and held aloft by four cast-iron strongmen. Native ladies giggled at their nakedness. (A hundred years later, black loincloths would be painted over the offending parts.)

Two civilizations overlapped at ʿAtaba Square. To the British authors of an Egyptian yearbook published in 1909, their meeting was like a scene of battle:

> What with the raucous shouting of the pedlars, the rattling of the water-carriers' tiny brass trays, the blowing of motor-car trumpets and the ringing of tram bells, the grinding of wheels and the clanging of iron-shod hoofs against the cobbles – the uproar heightened by the voices of men and women in passionate controversy – it is as though an Oriental Bedlam had been let loose ... Here East meets West, and the struggle between the two elements still rages at its greatest height ... To the West lies Europe, to the East the Orient. Gradually the former is encroaching upon the latter, so much so that in the

Mousky, a Levantine thoroughfare interlaced by Arab lanes, the huge signboard of a well-known whisky firm tops a wakf or religious establishment.

By 1910 an eighth of the city's 700,000 people were foreign-born. West of ʿAtaba Square they outnumbered Egyptians three to one. The *khawagāt* had their own coiffeurs, their haberdashers and bootmakers, their hospitals and clubs and schools. The other Cairo became to them a mere backdrop, a place to venture for occasional thrills or for sketching picturesque views. Increasingly, the foreign way of seeing became the way the city saw itself: by 1925 a third of Cairo's pupils were enrolled in foreign schools, taught in a score of religious persuasions and half a dozen languages. To ambitious Egyptians the acquisition of technical English or diplomatic French became a prerequisite for advancement.

The *khawagāt* constructed not just attitudes and whole new districts that soon dwarfed the old town, but also a social order whose very complexity reinforced their sense of security. Down near the bottom – but still several notches above native day labourers – were the Maltese, south-Italian and Greek artisans: master masons, plasterers and ironmongers, and also the waiters and petty criminals and the prostitutes whose trade flourished under consular protection. Their privileged position outraged Egyptians like Amin Boktor, an American-educated professor. Under the banner of the Capitulations, he wrote, Cairo had become a haven for the outcasts of Europe: 'the Athenian vendor of adulterated drinks, the Monte Carlo keeper of a gambling den, the Parisian matron of a house of prostitution, the Neapolitan receiver of stolen goods, the Viennese apothecary who sells narcotics under the guise of patent medicine, and white slave traffickers, smugglers, murderers and pugilists of all sorts'.

Next up the social scale came a clerical class of francophone effendis, Armenian tram conductors, Bosnian salesgirls and Bulgarian secretaries. Cairo's pharmacists and physicians, its engineers and its caterers and fancy jewellers came from further north. The best photographers were German, the swankiest bespoke tailors English, the finest confectioners Swiss-Italian. The French and their speech dominated intellectual life. Jews from throughout the Diaspora took prominence in finance; Syro-Lebanese in trade. Behind the foil of the khedive and his cabinetfuls of landowning pashas, 2,000 British and several hundred French bureaucrats managed affairs of state. The foreigners' salaries were so comfortable that when one Italian judicial adviser returned to his former post in Italy he found he was earning less than his secretary in Cairo.

Tongues and races mingled amid the tight ranks of tenements in Cairo's new working-class districts – Shubra, Abbasiyya, Bulaq. They mixed happily on the whole, even if the influence was mostly one-way, and even if marriage across religions remained rare. Middle-class Syrian Christians and Sephardic Jews, then native Copts and finally many Muslims adopted Mediterranean dress, manners and phrasing. Copts named their children Marie and George instead of their Arabic equivalents, Maryam and Girgis. Courting Levantine couples whispered, '*Je t'aime*'; to say the same thing in Arabic came to seem a touch vulgar. By the Bulaq railyards, Italian anarchists roused native workers to strike. Under the ceiling fans of cafés called Rex and Excelsior, Trieste-born retailers in spats and Borsalinos experimented with water pipes while turbaned Upper Egyptian wholesalers struck deals over their first glasses of whisky. Drink was the least of the vices foreigners brought: by the 1920s cocaine and heroin were supplanting hashish and opium as the drugs of choice.

North of the Azbakiyya Gardens, Cairo's two pleasure quarters sat snugly back to back. At one end *khawāga* pimps with switchblades watched over pale Smyrna tarts with medical certificates. At the other brooded darker-complexioned *baladi* professionals, the king of whose roost (in 1916) was a hugely fat transvestite Nubian. In a mockery of Muslim prudery he would sit enthroned in his alley, veiled in white, patchouli-scented, encumbered with gold bangles and anklets, extending a bejewelled hand to be kissed by some passing minion. Eventually the British-officered police hauled him off to prison.

Divisions grew starker in the higher ranks of society. Upper-class Egyptians admired European achievements, but chafed at the privileges seized by their uninvited guests. The outsiders, meanwhile, viewed their hosts with undiluted disdain. Writing her memoirs in 1935, an English resident said that during fifty years in Cairo she could not recall any intimacy between Europeans and Egyptians. What Mabel Caillard remembered was the mutual discomfort of forced social occasions: foreign ladies wincing at a palace buffet when the less sophisticated of the khedive's courtiers took their fingers to the food and 'noisily ejected such morsels as were not to their taste', even as these same gentlemen scowled at the obscenity of 'their shamelessly *décolletées* neighbours'.

Although a sprinkling of Egyptian pashas were Francophile or Anglophone enough to meet with the approval of the *haute khawagerie,* most were reckoned to fail in their attempts. 'They dance with foreign ladies, wear Frankish clothes, smoke cigarettes, enjoy French plays and, but for their Eastern habits of tyranny, peculation, insincerity and corruption, they might for all the world be Europeans' was the archly back-handed judgement of the British historian Stanley Lane-Poole in 1892. The colonial arrogance was even fiercer in private. At an English official's sumptuous villa on Opera Square in the 1880s, the gloomy hostess gave Caillard the impression that, 'if anyone so high-born could have feelings at all, hers were concentrated on her detestation of the country in which she was forced to reside, of the native servants, of the climate...' The poet Robert Graves, who taught at Cairo University in the 1920s, met an English cotton manufacturer who defended the conditions in his factory on the grounds that pulmonary consumption was one of the few checks on Egypt's unhealthy population growth.

At least the British were even-handedly aloof. While the French patronized the Continental, the Savoy and the Semiramis, the British stuck strictly to Shepheard's Hotel. Their Turf Club and Gezira Sporting Club were exclusive. One snooty Brit dismissed the rival Khedivial Club as being the resort of 'foreigners and gyppos'. The corseted matrons who taught at an English school in Cairo, recalled a former student, 'regarded the French as wogs and the Egyptians as a cut above camels'.

Of course everyone else exacted quiet revenge: the prices in Cairo shops, notes another memoir, varied according to whether the customer spoke Arabic, French or English. English speakers always got skinned.

IT WAS MONEY that sealed the peace. The British ran Egypt as a business whose simple object was to pay the debt dividend and generate wealth on top with which to buy British goods. To this end – and over the protests of Egyptian nationalists – the school system founded by Khedive Ismail was largely dismantled. The British downgraded the Ministry of Public Instruction into a department of the Ministry of Public Works, and reduced its share of the government budget to under 1 per cent. (The department's reputation sank so low that wags claimed a British employee implored an old school friend he had met by chance not to let on that he was working in Education, since he had told everyone 'at home' that he played piano in a brothel.) The health and housing needs of the poor were ignored. Investment was channelled instead into the maintenance of order and the expansion of infrastructure: into telephones and tramways, dams and canals and roads.

The formula worked – at least to the advantage of the

occupiers and the native elite. The momentum of that Western notion, Progress, seemed to be sustained. Great fortunes grew out of real estate, cotton, tourism and, beginning in the 1920s, large-scale industries like sugar and textiles. Egypt was still an overwhelmingly poor country, but its per capita income in 1913 was two-thirds of Italy's – and much higher among the growing urban middle class. The capitalization of the Cairo Stock Exchange soared from £7 million in 1890 to £100 million in 1910. Oval Egyptian cigarettes, rolled by barefoot girls in the dim-lit manufactories of Cairo and sold under the gold-embossed name of Coutarelli or Simon Arzt, became the world standard of smoking elegance. Land prices spiralled wildly upward. Despite the hiccup of a crash in 1907, the value of lots in one suburb soared in the twenty years before the First World War by a heady 1,000 per cent.

A storm of property development transformed Cairo. With the completion in 1902 of the first dam at Aswan – built by the British firm John Aird & Co. with Egyptian labour and money – the banks of the Nile became stable enough for construction. Garden City, an enclave of grand town houses by the river, was laid out in sweeping French curves. A Swiss hotel magnate developed the island of Gezira. French interests plotted the suburb of Qubba Gardens. The Belgian industrialist Baron Édouard Empain bustled into Cairo, fresh from business successes in the Congo and in building the Paris Métro. Armed with plenty of money and a visionary's enthusiasm, he persuaded the government to grant him a huge tract of desert land north-east of the city. Here he resurrected the ancient town of Heliopolis as a modern satellite city of neo-Moorish villas and apartments. Connected to Cairo by high-speed tram lines, his desert oasis boasted a racetrack, a Luna Park fairground, a sumptuous hotel*

*The Heliopolis Palace Hotel was later nationalized, renamed the Uruba Palace, and remodelled into the offices of republican Egypt's head of state.

and 25,000 well-heeled inhabitants by 1925. Baron Empain's own villa was modelled on a Hindu temple, complete with naughty gargoyles and sugar-loaf domes. The centrepiece of the new Heliopolis was, as in the ancient one, a house of worship. But this time it was to be a neo-Byzantine basilica. The obligatory mosque was far more modest, and set amid the third-class housing of Heliopolis's 'servants' quarter'.

Fifteen miles south of Cairo, facing the ruins of Memphis across the Nile, an ancient sulphur spring had been developed into a chic spa. Aside from healing baths and luxury accommodation, Helwan-les-Bains was equipped with a Japanese garden fitted with pagodas and plaster Buddhas. The fresh air of the nearby desert made it an ideal place for pony rides and picnics.

Beginning in the 1890s a group of closely intermarried Sephardi entrepreneurs quietly bought up fields along the railway that linked Cairo to Helwan. By 1904 they had amassed enough land to incorporate the venture. Landscapers were brought in, and building codes were laid down. Maadi, as the village was called, had grown by the 1930s into a smug and exclusive suburb peopled by Egyptian patricians as well as *khawāga* bankers and brokers. Alpine chalets abutted pillared and porticoed neo-classical mansions. Bougainvillea hedges separated Raj-style bungalows from steep-roofed manor houses that could have graced Surrey or Scarsdale. Garden competitions, Boy Scout and Brownie troops, a sporting club with a golf course and a yacht club on the Nile, churches, mosques and a thriving synagogue completed this suburban dream.

By 1910 even the first of Cairo's modern districts had succumbed to progress. Apartment blocks and office buildings had supplanted the original villas of Khedive Ismail's model city. The city centre had shifted westward, away from ʿAtaba Square and towards the Nile. What was now downtown Cairo had become a dense zone of shops and offices that looked little different from Milan or Barcelona. Mabel Caillard, returning in

1912 after five years' absence, was dismayed by the speed of change. 'The spaciousness, the dignity and quietude of the old residential quarters were utterly gone; the old mansions had yielded to rows of buildings and garish shops ... Even Gezira, that green isle of recreation, had on its fringes *houses*.' And again, another Briton returning after the Great War: 'All the glorious avenues of trees are cut down, great gardens swallowed up by enormous European buildings, and the beauty is gone.'

As Cairo sweated out the summer heatwave of 1914 – thermometers bubbled at 117 in the shade – Europe went to war. When the Ottoman sultan stopped equivocating and backed Germany, his Egyptian province found itself in the absurd position of being formally a part of one power while physically under occupation by its enemy. This was an anomaly that not even the muddle-loving British could stand, and so they quickly ripped away the veil that had shrouded their rule. They replaced the khedive with his more pliable uncle Husayn Kamil, proclaimed him sultan, declared the country a British protectorate, and clamped it under martial law. Turks, Germans and Austro-Hungarians were tossed into internment camps. Armenian refugees flooded in (and later Ionian Greeks and White Russians). The leading Egyptian nationalists, meanwhile, were deported to Malta.

Fresh troops swelled Cairo's token British garrison, as well as the pockets of the city's whores and hawkers. Australians drilled by the Pyramids and rioted in the sleazy dives behind the Azbakiyya. One in eight picked up venereal disease from the red light district's 3,000 registered prostitutes. But Cairo was still a lot safer than Gallipoli, where half the 500,000 soldiers sent to beat Johnny Turk were killed or wounded. Cairo's hospitals bulged with Gallipoli evacuees, and when the doomed campaign was at last called off some 200 generals were said to have checked into Shepheard's Hotel. They were not idle for long. In 1917

British forces pushed out of Egypt by the overland route, capturing the Ottoman provinces of Syria and Palestine.

The real war touched Cairo only once, when a German Zeppelin dropped a bomb that killed a lady walking her dog in front of the Eastern Telegraph Company headquarters. Meanwhile, the rich profited. The poor suffered – starved even – as food shortages doubled wartime prices. The British army not only requisitioned thousands of horses, but commandeered 20,000 peasants into work battalions where a quarter perished from disease.

The high-handedness stoked Egypt's long-smouldering nationalism. Within months of the Armistice in November 1918 it had burst alight. The spark came when Britain banned an Egyptian delegation from the Versailles peace conference, and instead jailed or exiled its leaders, chief among them a stern, straight-backed pasha by the name of Saad Zaghloul. In the spring of 1919 strikes and riots paralysed the country. Cairo crowds, joined by all classes and even – a key precedent – by women, clamoured for the release of the nationalist heroes. Mobs taunted and sometimes attacked British soldiers, who occasionally shot back. Railway, telegraph and electricity lines were sabotaged. British goods were boycotted. After three years of unrest, Britain relented. Egypt regained both its pride and its independence in 1922. A landslide election brought in Zaghloul as prime minister.

The wildly popular nationalist was also a realist. In the interest of maintaining order, Zaghloul agreed to lingering British influence. Foreign advisers stayed on until retirement age. Consular privileges remained. British troops controlled the Suez Canal, and in Cairo they continued to occupy the Citadel and their Nileside barracks by the Egyptian Museum. Husayn Kamil having died, the new monarch was given wide powers and a grander title. The Italian-educated twelfth son of Khedive Ismail, King Fouad I was dapper and dour. He was also rapacious, authoritarian and contemptuous of his Egyptian subjects, whose language he could speak only haltingly. ('*Ces crétins*' was his habitual slur.) While his personal fortune expanded – his son Farouk inherited 75,000 acres of the world's richest farmland – Fouad saw to it that his parliament's nationalist leanings were contained. The legislature was in any case stacked in favour of those who could buy peasant votes – which is to say cotton-planting pashas whose ultimate interest lay in defending their vast estates.

With money gushing in from the postwar boom, the native and foreign elites began to mingle more freely. Pashas summered on the Riviera, browsed the bookstalls by the Seine, and occasionally – like the American millionaires of the time – picked up Impressionist artworks to take home to Cairo.* Their sons, educated by Jesuits or Franciscans, maintained the habits of the *khawāga* administrators they replaced. The rich Cairene wore his tarboosh with pride, observed a visiting New Yorker in the 1920s, yet he lived 'like a Parisian' and had a club which in cuisine and luxurious appointments was 'second to none in London'. As Egyptians took up tennis and golf, poker and bridge, even the Gezira Sporting Club began to admit a token few smart-set natives. (Famously, Gezira's squash pro would allow his British trainees to get far ahead, then declare 'My game' and proceed to ace every volley.) Patrician ladies began to discard their veils like autumn leaves. Department stores like Cicurel, Hannaux, Orosdi-Back and Sednaoui catered to the new tastes with the latest fashions from Paris and the catalogues of Christophle, Louis Vuitton and Mappin & Webb. Even middle-class Egyptians now sported jackets and ties, hung *tableaux romantiques* on their walls, and stuffed their salons with all the Louis XVI fakery that Signor Pontremoli's fancy downtown furniture showroom flaunted.

* Such gleanings can be seen today at the Mahmud Khalil Museum in Giza, whose collection includes originals by Pisarro and Monet as well as Ingres, Courbet and Millet.

The visitor from New York claimed he had seen no town outside America where so many 'large and rich-looking houses' were being built:

> They are not all beautiful, but they are undoubtedly very costly. It is costly to build an imitation Gothic cathedral as your private dwelling; it is costly to put in Moorish ceilings, and Arabesque marble floors, to have huge and lofty rooms, and loggias with marble balconies ... The roads are broad; luxurious motorcars abound; and there is a dazzle of expensive finery which is not the less alluring because the face of the wearer is half-veiled ...

The streets of the city centre, with their rusticated and cupolaed apartment houses, traffic lights and café awnings, re-created the life of European boulevards down to the last detail. A stroll down ʿImad al-Din Street would take one past such establishments as Tonazakis' Patisserie, Claridge's Restaurant-Bar (Prop. Georges Boucherot) and Joseph Glaser, frame-maker, next to the Empire Cinema. The nearby American Cosmograph played silent greats to the strains of an orchestra conducted by maestro M. Poliakov. Occasionally the cinema hosted gala events, such as the charity ball for the Cairo Jewish Hospital on 15 February 1928 reported by the weekly *Étoile Égyptienne*:

> Towards midnight, amid general animation and with the champagne flowing freely, it was time for distribution of cotillions and prizes, to sustained applause. Then Kiku's jazz band struck up, and young and old danced into the early hours.

The leading hotels of Cairo were top-rate, according to the 1929 *Baedeker*: 'At most of them evening dress is *de rigueur* at dinner.' The opera, which still maintained gauze-screened boxes for veiled ladies, kept busy with a polyglot round of performances. Its 1929–30 season offered three amateur productions in English and one in Turkish, 22 plays and comedies in Arabic, 25 operettas in French and 55 operas in Italian. The news-stands at Mengozzi's bookshop on King Fouad Avenue sagged under sheaves of local foreign-language journals: *Le Progrès, La Bourse Égyptienne, Le Journal du Caire, La Liberté, La Patrie, Le Reveil* and four other dailies in French; a handful in Greek, Italian and Armenian, as well as the English-language *Egyptian Gazette*, founded in 1881 (and still going in 1998). Francophone scientific and literary reviews proudly displayed Cairene inventiveness. It was on their pages that Cairo-born poets Ahmed Rasim and Edmond Jabes and the novelist Albert Cossery began literary careers that would carry them to later fame in Paris.

Important social occasions brought together all the city's tongues and confessions and persuasions. On 15 May 1928, for instance, Cairo's high and mighty gathered at the plush, Babylonian-style temple of Shar Hashamaim on Maghraby Street for the wedding of the daughter of His Eminence Senator Chaim Nahum Effendi, member of the Egyptian Academy and grand rabbi of Cairo. Among the guests were the ministers of war and of public instruction (both Muslims), the minister of foreign affairs (who was a Copt) and a former minister of finance (who was Jewish). King Fouad graciously delegated his master of ceremonies to attend. The governor of Cairo made an appearance, too, along with assorted ambassadors and bank chairmen and the gorgeously bearded delegates of the Greek Orthodox, Greek Catholic, Coptic Orthodox, Coptic Catholic and Armenian Orthodox Churches, as well as scions of such prominent Jewish families as the Cattaouis, Mosseris and de Menasces (the latter three being French-speaking but by origin respectively Egyptian, Italian and Turkish).

Cairo no longer aspired to be cosmopolitan; it already was. According to the 1927 census a fifth of its people belonged to minorities: there were 95,000 Copts, 35,000 Jews, 20,000 Greeks, 19,000 Italians, 11,000 British, 9,000 French, and uncounted numbers of White Russians, Parsees, Montenegrins and other exotica. (By contrast, all colonial India in 1930 was home to just 115,000 people classified as 'whites'.) The city's population surged past a million in the 1930s as landless peasants began to arrive in significant numbers, along with a rich clutter of Europeans fleeing Hitler. Thirty thousand cars jammed streets where sleek apartment buildings pushed ever higher. Billboards touted a range of Cairo-made goods: 'Shelltox – The Insect Executioner', '*Exigez les Eaux Gazeuses N. Spathis!*'; Dr Boustani's Cigarettes, Bata shoes, and movies shot in Cairo studios such as *Layla, Girl of the Desert*, a costume drama starring Bahiga Hafiz.

Foreigners still dominated business. A single European bank, the Banque Belge et Internationale, owned all of Heliopolis in addition to Cairo's entire tramway and electricity networks. Sixteen out of seventeen subcontractors for the sheerly modernist Immobilia Building, an eighteen-storey, 218-unit downtown apartment complex completed in 1940, were *khawagāt*. The chief of the Central Bank in that year was still a Sir Edward Cook; Isaac Levy was the head of the Federation of Industries. But, under a treaty Egypt had signed with Britain in 1936, foreigners' legal privileges were to be phased out within ten years. Already Cairo produced its own skilled engineers and architects and financiers. By 1948 Egyptians owned 40 per cent of shares on the Cairo Stock Exchange, and four-fifths of shares in companies formed since 1933. The richest tycoon in the city (aside from the king) was a pure Egyptian: Abboud Pasha, sugar magnate, proprietor of textile mills, chemical plants and shipping lines – and owner of the Immobilia Building.

The city was cruel as well as sophisticated. In the 1940s half its children were dying of diarrhoea and malnutrition before the age of five. While literacy among foreigners pushed 90 per cent, only one in seven Egyptians could read. Away from the spacious streets and grand villas of the new quarters, the vast majority of

Cairenes made do without running water or electricity. They could only dream of a day when they could buy a bicycle or even a pair of decent shoes.

EUROPE AGAIN RUMBLED into war, and Europe's troubles again reverberated in Cairo. Pressed to stretch its treaty with Britain to the fullest, Egypt granted the Allies use of its bases, ports and railways. With Italy attacking from its colony in neighbouring Libya, and Germany advancing down the Balkans to Greece, Cairo again fell under martial law. Censorship was imposed, and this time thousands of Italian-Egyptians joined Germans, Hungarians, Rumanians and others in prison camps.* In a typical wartime tragicomedy, quite a few Austrian or German Jews were Catch-22ed into the same prison barracks as diehard Nazis.

By 1941, 140,000 Commonwealth troops were stationed at Cairo. Officers accustomed to London's Blitz languished in the city's swank hotels, joking that if all else failed, the sleepy service at Shepheards' famous Long Bar was sure to defeat the German advance. (Revelling in his reputation, the Swiss barman, Joe, fixed a house poison called The Suffering Bastard.) Here those well-born few who had wangled commissions in the more romantic units – in espionage, counter-espionage or sabotage – traded tales of raids in the desert and of parachute drops to Balkan partisans. But in this class-ridden army the better bars were off-limits to the troops, most of whom were billeted in flea-ridden suburban camps. On leave in the city they did what soldiers always do, and misbehaved. A favourite Tommy pastime – reminiscent of prankish Mamluks – was to knock the fezzes off as many Worthy Oriental Gentlemen as they could. Another was to sing along as

*Most Italian-Egyptians were ardent Fascists: in a junk shop I came across a snapshot of a blackshirt rally on some Cairo street, complete with Duce salutes and bemused native bystanders.

the Egyptian national anthem was played at Cairo's movie houses, but with obscene lyrics that began:

King Farouk, King Farouk
'Ang 'is bollocks on an 'ook

The more artistically minded among the occupiers toured mosques and dabbled in poetry, but even this latter conceit betrayed antipathies. A certain Private Broome penned this unlovely verse about Cairo, and had it published in one of the city's several wartime literary reviews:

Howling hell of every breed
Every colour, every creed
Indigo Nubian
Swarthy Greek
Overall that garlic reek

Shouting vendors seeking trade
Beggars sleeping in the shade
Clanging tram
Raucous horn
'Backsheesh!' from the newly born

The loathing was more than mutual. Egypt was fed up with the *Inglīz*. Most Cairenes longed to see them lose.

King Farouk, a rapscallion of sixteen when he ascended to the throne in 1936, hated the limits Britain imposed on his freedom. In particular he bridled at the heavy-handed nudgings of London's ambassador, Sir Miles Lampson. The six foot five diplomat, who in not-so-private referred to Farouk as 'The Boy', felt Egypt should have a more convincingly anti-Axis government. On 4 February 1942 Lampson rolled tanks up to the gates of ʿAbdin Palace. The King was ordered at gunpoint to name Whitehall's choice, Mustafa Pasha al-Nahas, as prime minister. Farouk was still relatively slim, relatively chaste and overwhelmingly popular.

His humiliation was felt by every Egyptian, and even more acutely by the Egyptian army that swore personal allegiance to their king.

Cairo swallowed its pride for the time being. The occupying army's overwhelming presence made active resistance unwise. Besides, the spectacle of *khawagāt* at war proved diverting. Enjoying their front-row seats, the city's café punters wagered on Hitler's moustache or Churchill's cigar. Meanwhile exotic extras swaggered across the stage, among them the toppled emperor of Ethiopia and the exiled kings of Albania and Greece (the latter inseparable from his English mistress), Prince Paul and Princess Olga of Yugoslavia, and plotfuls of hangers-on and pretenders. At the Mena House Hotel by the foot of the Pyramids, Winston Churchill, Franklin Roosevelt and Chiang Kai-shek conferred in November 1943. Owners of nearby villas that were to house the great men's entourages hiked up the rents outrageously. Back in the city a cast of refugees worthy of the set of *Casablanca* – that one-horse town at the wrong end of the Sahara – mooned about gin joints and lobbies, getting fleeced by bazaar hustlers and entwined in black markets.

Indeed, moneymaking on a colossal scale smoothed Egypt's feathers better than anything. Leaving aside the untold marginals who prospered as shoeshiners, grifters and so on, the British army directly employed 200,000 Egyptians. Local industries flourished as imports dwindled. Between 1940 and 1943 bank deposits, the dividends of the Egyptian Hotels Company and the stakes at the Gezira racetrack tripled. The number of millionaires rose from fifty to 400. At the war's end Britain owed Egypt £500 million.

There was much drama to be relished before the finale. In the summer of 1942 Field Marshal Erwin Rommel's Afrika Korps pushed to within an afternoon's drive of the Egyptian capital. At Cairo Station it was mayhem as thousands fought for space on trains to Palestine. Ambassador Lampson tried to calm nerves by having his servants repaint the cast-iron fence at the Residence, the palatial Victorian mansion by the Nile which still serves

British ambassadors. But the starched upper lip wilted for all to see when the British HQ in Garden City incinerated its archives to keep them out of Nazi hands. Egyptian nationalists looked on gleefully as charred imperial secrets gusted through the streets.

Paper trails of another kind led British spycatchers on a desperate hunt across the city, from the Turf Club bar to the Kit Kat Casino and at last to a luxury houseboat moored on the Giza shore. They were in luck. The Nazi agent they caught had been woefully indiscreet. Addicted to high living, the dashing German-Egyptian had spread a tell-tale chain of forged banknotes through half the city's nightclubs.* Still, the fact that he had sneaked into Cairo at all, crossing 2,000 miles of desert from Libya to skirt the front lines, gave the Allies a scare. They were also impressed by the cleverness of the German cipher, which was based on Daphne du Maurier's best-selling spine-chiller *Rebecca*.

Far more helpful to Rommel than his spy's barside gleanings, in fact, was the American military attaché. With innocent diligence he reported every detail of Britain's desert campaign, beaming messages to Washington in a code that the Italians had long since cracked. The loophole was only just plugged in time for Britain's last-ditch offensive at El Alamein, fifty miles west of Alexandria. The October 1942 battle was to be the turning point of the Desert War.

Rommel, starved of supplies because of Hitler's suicidal assault on Stalingrad, retreated helter-skelter towards Tunisia. By 1943 the war had receded from Cairo for good – just in time, because the champagne had finally run out. Water pipes burbled now to intrigues that were closer to home. Muslim radicals began to agitate for guerrilla action against the British. Much to the

* The spy also ushered a key player into the limelight: convinced that his radio was on the blink, he had called in an Egyptian signals officer named Anwar al-Sadat. Like many Egyptian nationalists, Sadat had been impressed by German might, and was eager to help the enemies of his own British enemy. Exposed, Sadat spent the rest of the war in jail.

embarrassment of Cairo's Anglophile Jewish aristocracy, Zionist extremists murdered Lord Moyne, the British colonial secretary, as he left his house by the Gezira Sporting Club in November 1944. A month later a nationalist lawyer smuggled a pistol into the Egyptian parliament, which had just, belatedly, declared war on Germany. Firing point blank, the assassin shot dead the new prime minister, Ahmed Pasha Maher.

As Berlin fell and thousands of Egyptians lost their wartime livelihoods, censorship was lifted. Scandal after scandal shook the city. Nepotism, graft, stock-market fixing; no tool, apparently, had escaped the grasp of governments held unnaturally in place by British arms. Corruption continued unabated into the late 1940s, but the most titillating rumours were of another kind, and all focused on one man: King Farouk.

THE KING IS playing poker at the Royal Automobile Club on Qasr al-Nil Street. His opponent calls, tabling three aces. Farouk twirls his moustache. He has three kings. His pudgy fingers flick down the cards one by one. 'King of hearts,' he says. 'King of spades. King of clubs.' He pauses for effect, then thumps both palms on the table top: 'And the King of Egypt!' With a great belly laugh Farouk scoops the pot. His henchmen cackle.

The tale is apocryphal, of course, but utterly in character.

By the time he was deposed at the age of thirty-two, Farouk had become a byword for rottenness. But a mere dozen years before his demise the boy king had thrilled Egyptians as a latter-day Tutankhamun. When he married seventeen-year-old, sweet and chaste-looking Farida Zulfikar* in 1938, Cairo crowds went so wild that half a dozen people were trampled to death in the

* The Queen dropped her own name, Safinaz, to adopt the royal name of Farida. A fortune-teller was said to have told King Fouad the letter F was lucky. Farouk's sisters were named Faika, Fawzia, Fathia and Faiza.

crush. At least the well-wishers' wallets were safe: so fervent was the patriotic mood that the Cairo pickpockets' guild had advertised a moratorium on liftings for the royal wedding.

Farouk was the embodiment of all the youthful pride which colonized Egypt desperately needed. The first of his dynasty to speak decent Arabic, the young king was tall, good-looking and ostentatiously pious. After an assassin's pot-shot missed, courtiers fanned the tale that the bullet had lodged in the Koran which he never failed to carry in his breast pocket. For a time Farouk sported a holy man's beard. He even hired a genealogist to prove that his great-grandfather Muhammad Ali was descended from the Prophet. Such appeals to Muslim feeling helped ensure that when his cronies rigged the 1939 elections, bringing in a government of boot-licking royalists, few dared to complain. Farouk was no fool. Right to the end his political meddling was oiled with bribes, threats, blackmail and the slickest publicity.

At heart, though, the king was an amiable joker. A typical Faroukish tease: he booby-trapped the ʿAbdin Palace reception rooms with a giant tiger skin, placed just on the exit route where bowing, backward-walking supplicants were bound to trip over it. Farouk had Cairo's most notorious Fagin sprung from jail to teach him the pickpocket's trade. Bored by protocol, he tested his legerdemain at an official dinner with Winston Churchill. As the whisky-soaked prime minister patted his pockets – his missing watch was a prized heirloom, having been a gift from Queen Anne to Churchill's ancestor the Duke of Marlborough – Ambassador Lampson purpled with apoplexy. The grinning Boy let the diplomat stew, then clapped his hands. A footman produced the trophy with a flourish.

Farouk owned four main palaces, innumerable rest houses and hunting lodges, a private train and two splendid yachts. But his favourite toys – at least before he discovered buxom ladies – were cars. Farouk loved to drive himself, at high speed, and so kept 200 automobiles, including a Mercedes sent as a gift by Hitler.

All were red – in fact no cars but the palace's were allowed to be red. Setting a fashion that persists among Cairo's latter-day klaxomaniacs, he fitted some with trick horns. One Packard faked the yelping of a dog, which made for laughs when other motorists swerved, thinking they must have struck some poor cur.

Cosseted by yes-men, unbounded by money or appetite, fun-loving Farouk was doomed to decay. His humiliation by British tanks was compounded by Queen Farida's inability to produce a son and heir (and, rumour had it, by her taunts about his impotence). The foiled monarch bloated and balded. He became a predator. He could not be refused. When Farouk crashed parties, hostesses rushed to hide antique baubles and virgin daughters. Ten years into his reign, students at Cairo University hissed at their king. The message was clear. Farouk had somehow to retrieve his popularity.

He chose to play a reckless King's Gambit. Posing as leader of the Arabs, he donned his Supreme Commander uniform, mounted a white charger, and reviewed his troops. Then he sent this untested army of peasant conscripts to Palestine, where the nascent United Nations had just decreed a Jewish state. Ibn Khaldun could have predicted the outcome. New nations, the Arab sage had theorized, were made by nomadic peoples inspired and united by a sense of mission. Old states crumbled when their dynasties and great cities grew pompous and effete. The Palestine War of 1948 pitted two such opponents. Egypt fought in half-hearted defence of its Palestinian neighbours' rights, with an eye to profiting from an inflamed Arab nationalism. Israel's citizen army fought for a millennial dream; it battled against its own burning nightmare of racial extermination.

The Egyptians were trounced. The ragtag Israelis overran their UN-decreed borders, hounding half a million Palestinians into permanent exile. Israeli speedboats sank the Egyptian navy's lumbering flagship, the *Prince Farouk*. Egyptian soldiers complained that their guns had literally backfired. They were right: arms-dealing buddies of the king had sold his army dud Second World War leftovers. While at an isolated Egyptian outpost a valiant major named Gamal Abd al-Nasser withstood a month-long Israeli siege, Farouk played poker and cavorted with *khawāga* girls in palace bubble baths. Muslim and Zionist bigots united in fury: both his current mistress and his poker pals were Jewish.

In the middle of it all – with bombs exploding in Cairo cinemas and Jewish-owned department stores; as prisons filled with Israeli spies, Communists and fundamentalists; as yet another cholera epidemic raged – the now corpulent Farouk capped his *annus horribilis* by divorcing Farida. From then on his fortunes tailspinned. Members of the Muslim Brotherhood assassinated first the Cairo police chief and then another prime minister, Mahmud Pasha Nuqrashi, who had made the fatal error of banning the shadowy organization. Palace thugs retaliated swiftly, gunning down Hasan al-Banna, the Brotherhood's founder and Supreme Guide, on the steps of the Young Men's Muslim Association.

Not even Farouk's own mother, Queen Nazli, left him in peace. Knowing her wild ways, his father, King Fouad, had locked her in purdah. Released by her son, the widow twirled through a string of affairs that culminated in a Continental *menage à trois* with her youngest daughter and a junior Egyptian diplomat who was half the Queen Mother's age (and a Copt into the bargain). When the trio steamed off to the United States in a fireworks of flashbulbs, Farouk was outraged. And when his mother told the San Francisco papers that her daughter was marrying this Christian commoner, he disowned them.

Humiliated by the war, disgusted by family and politics, Farouk sailed to Europe. The summer of 1950 was to be a season of epic debauch. His entourage of Albanian bodyguards, secret police, tasters, doctors, aides and cronies (among them a former palace electrician, Antonio Pulli, now a procurer of lady companions) filled eleven fresh black Cadillacs. This king's fleet cleaved a wake of scandal from Marseilles to Deauville to Biarritz and San Sebastian and back to the Riviera. Farouk was on a roll. One night he cleared $60,000; the next $40,000 – which was heady takings in 1950. Finally, at Cannes, the king's luck bombed. To his credit he lost to a pro – 'Lucky Mickey' Hyman. But just as the winner reached for his $80,000 pile of chips, a heart attack dropped Lucky Mickey dead.

Cairo smouldered. Unemployment soared. The gulf between rich and poor overspilled with grotesquerie. Two thousand pashas and beys kept a third of all fertile land in vast estates. The royal family alone owned 600,000 acres. Four million peasants shared all the rest, or worked the big plantations at a wage of ten cents a day. While the chefs of the Carlton Hotel at Cannes slaved to satiate Farouk's bottomless stomach for lobster thermidor and dozen-egg omelettes, the typical Cairo family rarely ate meat or fruit, even while haemorrhaging half its income on food. The stock market tumbled. Flight capital drained from the country. Cabinets revolved and fell. While *khawagāt* complained of being spat at by patriotic hotheads, one visitor was appalled to see an Egyptian officer upbraid a soldier by slapping him, then opening his mouth and spitting into it

Politicians tried to ride popular anger. Foreigners, unprotected now by the exhausted European powers, made an easy target. New legislation rolled back their privileges. Arabic became the sole legal language. Quotas squeezed foreign ownership and employment. Italians and others released from internment found it hard to reclaim their confiscated property. The upper crust of Cairo's Jewish community began to slip away – to Paris, mostly, rather than the Promised Land: the lights of Tel Aviv looked pretty dim from Cairo.

Then, as if his summer binge were not enough to keep tongues clucking, Farouk had the bad taste to marry a plump sixteen-year-old named Nariman Sadeq. (He had seen her with her fiancé in a jewellery shop, and split the couple with an offer they couldn't refuse.) The palace publicity boilers were by now unrestrained by modesty. Among the lashings of kitsch they cooked up: a wedding gown for Nariman studded with 20,000 diamonds, a song on the radio titled 'Glory for the Reign of King Farouk', electric victory arches that flashed the initials N and F, hundreds of fatted calves slaughtered for charity.

On one night of his thirteen-week European honeymoon, at a single marathon baccarat game, Farouk blew a record $150,000. Back in Cairo the next winter Nariman bore him a son. Farouk made the delivering doctor a pasha on the spot. The following Saturday – 26 January 1952 – as the Egyptian army's top brass toasted the baby crown prince at a palace banquet, Cairo burst into flames.

THE CHIEF BUFFOON of Egyptian folklore is a fellow called Goha. No one is as maddening as Goha. His naivety is so preposterous that it amounts to cunning.

Goha sells his house. The new owners have hardly settled down when the buffoon barges in like he still owns the place. Saying nothing, Goha crosses to a wall, hangs his cloak on a nail, and leaves. The next morning he returns to retrieve his cloak. At night he hangs it up again, and so on for several days. At last, driven to despair, the occupants demand to know by what right he keeps intruding. Goha shrugs. 'I sold you the house,' he says, 'but I did not sell you that nail.'

To Egyptian eyes the colonial endgame Britain played was just like Goha and his nail. Egypt had got its house back: in 1947, after shooting dead thirty demonstrators outside their Qasr al-Nil barracks in the centre of Cairo, British troops withdrew from the capital. The star-and-crescent flag was raised over the Citadel for the first time in sixty-four years. But Britain, like Goha, kept a thorn in Egypt's side. Eighty thousand British soldiers remained in control of the Suez Canal. In Cairo, British officers on leave still tippled on the Shepheard's Hotel terrace. The Turf Club and the Gezira Sporting Club remained their preserve.

As Britain refused to budge from the canal and unrest in Cairo matured into strikes and rioting, orators upped the nationalist ante into pure demagoguery. In October 1951 Prime Minister Mustafa al-Nahas abrogated the treaty granting Britain bases on the canal. His minister of the interior, Fouad Serageddin, openly urged the Muslim Brothers to mount guerrilla attacks. Britain clamped curfews and roadblocks on the Canal Zone. In response, Serageddin ranted on Cairo radio that the *Inglīz* were unleashing dogs to savage bound female captives. A Cairo daily offered a £100 reward for the murder of any British officer. All Britons in government employment, including university lecturers, were sent packing – some after lifelong careers in Egypt. King Farouk himself decreed that the boards of all clubs be Egyptianized.

Then disaster struck. Seeking a scapegoat to blame for guerrilla attacks, Britain's commanding general sent troops to disarm an Egyptian police barracks in the canal city of Ismailia. Fouad Serageddin ordered his men to resist, and so the British blasted the barracks with tank fire, killing fifty police conscripts.

As news of the massacre reached Cairo next morning, angry crowds gathered. At Opera Square they milled outside the open-air terrace of Madame Badia's cabaret. Someone spotted a police officer drinking whisky. The crowd taunted him for getting drunk while the British were murdering his brothers. A brawl started. A match was struck. When fire engines arrived the crowd slashed the hoses. Some said the police themselves joined in. From the collapsing roof of Madame Badia's establishment flames licked across the movie hoardings next door, where the Cinema Opera was playing *When Worlds Collide.*

As it became clear that the police were not going to intervene, the mood turned menacingly festive. Bands of arsonists – many blamed the Muslim Brothers, others claimed they were right-wing hooligans or Communists or even secret police – fanned out through the European Quarter. They jemmied open hastily shuttered shops and torched them. They drenched cinemas with gasoline and set them alight; the Rivoli (*Spy Hunt*), the Cairo Palace and the Metro (*The Valley of Decision*, with Greer Garson and Gregory Peck) were all gutted. They stormed the Turf Club; ten *khawagāt* were burned alive. As the Cairene novelist Naguib Mahfouz described the scene, the din was unbearable:

> It was as though all earth's atoms were screaming at once. Flames swept everywhere, dancing in windows, crackling on rooftops, flickering at walls, and lunging up into the smoke that hung where the sky should have been. The burning stank hellishly, a combustion of wood, clothing and oil ... Repressed anger, stifled despair, pent-up tension, all that had been brewing inside the people burst forth, erupting like a whirlwind of demons.

At two p.m. the mob crashed into Shepheard's Hotel, where the service buttons in the vast bedrooms with their Persian carpets and fifteen-foot ceilings were marked 'Native'. The vandals stacked the lobby furniture and cheered as the whole grand Victorian pile burned to the ground in twenty minutes flat. Miss Christina Caroll, an American soprano who was to play Desdemona at the Cairo Opera that night, threw a sable coat over her negligee and escaped with other guests into the hotel garden. An anonymous call-girl was less lucky. She plunged to her death from a fourth-floor balcony.

The incendiarists then set off in trucks, burning bars and nightclubs across town and right along the Pyramids Road. Not even King Farouk's favourite casino was spared; 'Paris at Night', a revue starring Annie Charlier and Serge Lancy, would not be staged at the Auberge des Pyramides that Saturday. At last, as opportunists looted the scorched merchandise of chic stores like

Ben Zion, Gattegno and Davies Bryan, the army moved in. Shots echoed, and the streets cleared under curfew.

What people who saw Black Saturday all remember – and they differ about nearly everything else – is the smoke. An inky, ash-flecked pall swallowed the whole of downtown Cairo. At nightfall the sky glowed a sickly pink. When morning dawned with a sodden, carbonized stench, even those who had set the fires were astounded by the damage. Nearly every symbol of cosmopolitan Cairo lay in ruins. Some 700 shops and buildings, whole avenues of smart premises – banks, bookshops, stationers, car dealers, travel agencies and every single liquor outlet – were wrecked. Aside from the hundred dead, 12,000 were made homeless and 15,000 jobless – including the Shepheard's Hotel's Swiss head porters, Italian head waiter and German head housekeeper.

Unable to pull out Goha's nail, Cairo's malingerers had burned the house down.

Six months later, while Farouk frolicked at his seaside castle in Alexandria, armoured cars rumbled through the heat of the Cairo night. Without firing a shot, the army occupied the ministries and parliament and palaces. On state radio a young officer broadcast a statement. A secret society of Free Officers, said Anwar al-Sadat, had assumed power to restore stability.

THE COUP OF 23 July 1952 sealed the fate of Cairo's cosmopolitan elite. Farouk and family were dispatched into exile. His court and cronies were tried and packed off to prison. They shared cells with a roster of public enemies that grew to include Freemasons and Rotarians as well as leftists and fundamentalists. Pashas lost their titles: they were now called feudalists. Their country estates were sifted into peasant-sized morsels.

The rise of Egyptian nationalist passion brought particular unease to members of the venerable Jewish community. Their alienation from the Egyptian mainstream – by class, as many were rich, and by language and outlook, as many had adopted French speech and European manners – was compounded by their inevitable association with Israel. Despite assurances of protection from Gamal Abd al-Nasser, who took over the leadership of Egypt's revolutionary government in 1954, Jewish anxiety was to deepen further. In that same year, police caught fourteen Israeli agents who had tried to sabotage Egypt's foreign relations with a bombing campaign aimed at targets like Cairo's American Cultural Centre and British Council offices. Several of the saboteurs were Egyptian-born Jews. In February 1955, Israeli paratroopers ambushed an Egyptian army convoy in Gaza, killing thirty-eight soldiers. As Egypt's border with the Jewish State subsequently heated up, so did popular antipathy to all that was Jewish.

Cairo may have swiftly rebuilt its European-looking façade after Black Saturday's fire, but to most of the city's Europeans it was now just that: a façade. They could feel their place in the country's future shrinking by the day. At the Hellenic Club, the Circolo Italiano and the Alliance Israelite the talk was of timetables, of cousins in Montreal and – *sotto voce* – of false-bottomed suitcases. Fortunes began to filter out of Cairo – so many that a Swiss banker I was to meet forty years later smiled at the memory: 'Ah, the early fifties. Now *that* was a golden age,' he sighed.

The furtive trickle overseas was soon to burst into flood. Denied Western finance to build a new and mightier dam on the Nile, Nasser nationalized the Suez Canal in July 1956. Britain, France and Israel invaded Egypt in response. International outrage forced the aggressors out, but the damage had been done. In Cairo – whose outskirts British jets had bombed – xenophobia scaled new heights. All British and French nationals were deported, their property seized. The many Cairene Jews who had secured French citizenship in the advantageous days of the Capitulations were sent packing too, along with unlucky colonials like the British-passport-holding Maltese. Other aliens took the hint, which was given added edge by new laws that banned foreigners from owning property while making Egyptian nationality all but unobtainable.

The deportees were to have one consolation. They escaped the staggered calamities of the early 1960s, when the military regime systematically ruined what remained of Cairo's pre-revolutionary elite – native Copts and Muslims included – confiscating hundreds of companies, homes and farms in the name of The People. By the end of that decade the foreign community had dwindled into insignificance. All of Cairo's Jewish schools, its Jewish hospital and orphanage, and all but two of the city's twenty-nine synagogues had closed for lack of custom. In the 1970s stone merchants and squatters began to take over the untended Jewish cemeteries. On a visit in the 1980s I found a young couple with four children cosily installed in a particularly splendid neo-pharaonic vault. The tomb dwellers had unsealed the columbarium inside, finding it made convenient built-in shelving for clothes, cooking pots and a colour TV set.

Other alienated Cairenes fared less badly. The Greek and Italian contingents faded slowly, not so much because Cairo had lost its gloss as because their booming old countries drew away the youth. Those fixtures of Cairo for a century – the Greek grocer and the Italian workshop foreman – were reduced to a tiny few. Among those who stayed was my mechanic Beppo, a fourth generation Calabrian-Egyptian – but his children went to Italy. The Syro-Lebanese mostly held out and intermarried, growing more Egyptianized and less Francophone with each generation. The Armenians thrived; their 2,000-strong community kept up its schools, clubs and charities (and certainly did better than those who accepted an invitation from Stalin to settle in the Soviet Republic of Armenia in 1949: on arrival in their homeland they were stripped of all possessions and packed off to Siberia).

In the new, Egyptianized Cairo some of the old *khawāga* habits and institutions survived. The best private schools continued to teach in French, English, German and Italian. Evening dress was still required at the opera, where even Arabic orchestras continued to wear dark jackets and bow ties. Cairo's elite stayed in fashion sync with the West, adopting blue jeans and disco dancing; aspiring to instal fitted kitchens and to take the kids to Disneyworld.

Quietly, inexorably, the bland new style of global commerce has replaced the old home-grown cosmopolitanism. Instead of the musty but charming Shepheard's and Continental-Savoy, Cairo's flagship hotels are now high-rise Hiltons and Sheratons. (One chain has redeveloped the old palace where Empress Eugénie stayed for the Suez Canal opening, and calls its bar Eugénie's Lounge.) Downtown restaurants like Caroll and Estoril still serve *escalope pannée, macaronis au four* and *artichauts à la Grecque*. But the old establishments have begun to feel like relics. Trendier venues have proliferated. Cutting-edge Cairene taste now runs to Tex-Mex vegetarian, drive-in Big Macs, sushi and satay and Milanese modern. The patrons of such fare are mostly native Cairenes, but see themselves as citizens of the world. They are watchers of satellite TV, browsers of the Internet, and consumers of multinational-brand detergents that fight out turf wars on the local airwaves.

CHAPTER EIGHT

CONFLICT AND FUSION

In order to escape from the West they had to learn from the West. Must they abdicate their personality, then, to survive?

Jacques Berque, *Egypt: Imperialism and Revolution*, 1967

THE OLD CLUBHOUSE terrace at the Gezira Sporting Club makes a fitting stage for deposed royalty. It is a brick and plaster replica of an ocean liner's lido deck. Where the ship's funnel should be stands a chimney inscribed with the year 1935. Perched up there, cawing black crows take the place of seagulls. Down below, outside the shade of the faded awning, beyond the swimming pool and the curve of the rail where the ship's broad wake should churn under the setting sun, mongrel kittens scamper over ragged flower beds.

Most afternoons the prince sits alone here, primly aloof from adjacent tables of garrulous retired generals and gossiping divorcees. Small, pale and baby-shaped, he wears an immaculate grey suit of 1940s cut. His expression hints that an invisible pomander is floating somewhere near his noble nose. His mother may have been, as some say, a Spanish dancer, but the prince is still every inch a royal. He is a descendant of Muhammad Ali Pasha and a cousin of King Farouk – and the only prince to have stayed on after the 1952 revolution. A big fish in an evaporating pond, so to speak, he drifts daily in Garbo-like solitude from the peeling elegance of the Automobile Club dining room (where his cousin played poker) to the dowdy old Gezira (where British Hussars and Lancers sparred at polo).

The prince reminisces over iced lemonade, speaking softly in clipped tones that betray prolonged immersion in the cold showers of an English public school. The army officers' coup took him utterly by surprise, he says. He had been a young innocent at the time, a lover of music and the arts with a horror of politics. (In a 1951 *Egyptian Gazette* I find a paparazzo's snap of a box at the Cairo Opera. The little prince stares whimsically askew, a shy cherub in a white tie, dwarfed by his long-necked, diamond-chokered mother.) The cruellest thing was seeing his family's property scattered. He speaks of how he followed the post-revolutionary auctioning of royal belongings, of how he watched everything in his own small chambers at the ʿAbdin Palace lotted and sold along with the jewels and Sèvres china and Cousin Farouk's vast stashes of rare coins, guns and girlie pin-ups.

'Such a magpie for trinkets, poor chap. But what he really liked was ladies' *bosoms!*' An expression of distaste flickers.

Strangely, though, neither his own small collection of first editions nor his few pieces of antique furniture and not even the pictures – his prized possessions, the prince being an accomplished amateur painter – were ever mentioned in the public sale catalogues. For twenty years he assumed the stuff had all vanished, or been purloined like so much else by some cheeky army officer.

At this point the prince glances archly at our neighbours, looking more than ever like Winnie the Pooh's maudlin friend Eeyore. 'Ew,' he sniffs, 'I do hope they aren't listening. I've had quite enough trouble with generals.'

All those years, while the dictatorship of Colonel Nasser lurched further leftward, the prince lived hand to mouth on a penurious state pension, forbidden to travel and fearing arrest any minute on some laughable charge of a royalist plot. In his small

Garden City apartment every valuable, from teaspoons to chaises longues, was labelled and regularly inventoried by zealously uncouth inspectors, just in case he might presume to try to scrape up some extra cash by flogging what was now considered state property. He never dared ask what had happened to his things in the palace.

But then sometime in the 1970s – by which date the vindictive fervour of the revolution had at last subsided – an acquaintance told him that in some flyblown alley in the slums behind ʿAbdin there was a man who was said to be selling palace loot.

I could just picture the prince politely enquiring of an astonished grease monkey in one of the ʿAbdin district's car repair shops as to the whereabouts of a certain junk shop. And then finding the *galabiyya*-clad proprietor slumped unshaven in a lopsided cane-bottomed chair on the shady side of a dank alley, facing the two holes in the wall opposite that constituted his showroom. The crafty junk dealer would have appraised this rare customer in a single blink.

'And the extraordinary thing', the prince continues, 'was that in his horrid little cave the man did have treasures from the palace. How he acquired them I haven't a clue. Nothing really valuable, of course, but he had my things.'

The prince was able to buy back a few of his own possessions – the first editions at least, and two of the paintings, and one favourite gilt chair.

'It was my own small *coup* against the *état*,' he titters. 'I do so like gold, too, don't you? It's so . . . *cosy*.'

The prince now grows serious. Leaning back in his chair, he squints wistfully into the sunset. After a long pause he speaks.

'That was the positive thing, I suppose. Before the revolution I had never met a real Egyptian. They are marvellous people, you know.'

THE FIRST HALF of Cairo's twentieth century saw the West overwhelm the East. High heels and two-tones clattered up marble stairs; camelskin babouches rustled down. The century's second half saw the reverse: silken slippers shuffling down, bare peasant feet and army boots stomping up. To the cosmopolitans their fall was a tragedy, an end to Cairo's golden age. To the vast majority of the city's people – those faceless folk whom Cairo's last prince had never met – it was a hard-won triumph.

The roots of that triumph ran deep.

Egyptian national consciousness had its first stirrings in the Urabist revolt of the 1880s. Then, sheikhs and soldiers, pasha landowners and urban effendis had united in the struggle against foreign domination. But that brief Cairo Spring, and with it the notion of independence, was soon crushed under the combined weight of British arms, debt and the momentum towards modernization generated by European immigrants and their money. The gravity of it flattened Egypt's self-confidence. In 1907, when the peasants of a Delta village beat off a troop of British soldiers who had come to shoot their domestic pigeons for sport, it was Egyptian, not British, judges who sentenced four of the fellahin to hang. Even a nationalist firebrand like Mustafa Kamil, a French-trained lawyer whose speeches electrified Cairo in the brief decade before his premature death in 1908, was too timid to call for outright independence. He compromised his platform by pleading for support from Paris and Constantinople.

Rather than challenge the British head on, cooler minds turned instead to laying the groundwork for a national revival. The early decades of the twentieth century saw the founding in Cairo of Egypt's first secular university, its first trade unions and professional syndicates, and its first bank with all-Egyptian capital. Literary and scientific salons proliferated, exposing Cairo's intelligentsia to every issue of the modern day, from Darwinism to Lombroso's theory of criminality to the twists of the Dreyfus case. Amateur troupes staged Arabic versions of Molière and

Racine as well as the first plays by Egyptian writers. Cairo's press and publishing industry grew, stimulated by contact with the West and by a relative freedom that attracted intellectuals from across the waning Ottoman Empire. The whole vocabulary of Progress – terms like enlightenment, democracy, empiricism, social consciousness and class struggle – were brought into Arabic usage here. In the realm of ideas, Cairo was on the move.

By way of example, as early as 1898 a judge by the name of Qasim Amin had published a treatise that put into accessible, logically argued language what European critics had long suggested. Egypt's backwardness, said Amin, was due to the low status of its women. The key to progress was female education. In a second volume he went further and demanded that women abandon the veil and that they be granted equal rights, including the right to vote. The response was heated. A thirty-book barrage of criticism blasted Amin as a closet atheist, an effeminate, a panderer to colonialism, a traitor to Islam. Yet history was on his side. Amin had set its machinery in motion. Egyptian women did leave the home and enter the world. When nationalist demonstrations broke out in 1919 women were in the vanguard – albeit still in veils.

This was soon to change. In 1923 a pasha's daughter named Hoda Shaarawi scandalized Cairo by stepping off a first-class railway carriage and brazenly tossing back her veil. The bitter experience of being raised under the tutelage of eunuchs in a harem and married off against her will had turned her into a passionate feminist. Immersion in French literature – she had taught herself the language – helped her to articulate her feelings. With her immaculate social credentials and personal daring, Shaarawi was in a position to inspire others. Only five years after the shocking incident at Cairo Station, the city's illustrated magazines revealed that all but a few of the high-born ladies paying condolences to the wife of the great nationalist hero Saad Zaghloul went unveiled. A decade later the veil was seldom seen at all among the upper classes. It had come to be regarded as a brand of backwardness.

If Qasim Amin's ideas generated acrimony at first, his goal was shared by every Egyptian. The questions he asked were the very questions that were to frame intellectual debate in Cairo for the rest of the century. What were the secrets to Europe's success? How could Egypt duplicate Western achievements without surrendering its Eastern identity? How could Cairo, a city starkly divided between haves and have-nots, pulled partly towards Paris and partly to Mecca, regain its sense of wholeness?

Some said the decline of the East was due to the ossification of Islam. Muslim reformers like Sheikh Muhammad Abdu (1847–1905) called for purging the faith of useless accretions. There was no reason, believed Abdu, why reason should conflict with revelation. Couldn't Muslims embrace useful Western ideas and still keep their identity? Again, though many disagreed, history seemed to go Abdu's way. Subtle reforms did occur in the teaching of Islam, for instance the reintroduction of Ibn Khaldun to the curriculum of al-Azhar – where Abdu briefly served as rector. Practices like the charging of interest, which traditionalists denounced as sinful usury, came to be widely accepted. Islamic sharia continued to define rules of marriage and inheritance, but civil, criminal and commercial codes modelled on European law grew to dominate legal thinking.

Some intellectuals demanded iconoclasm, not reform. Islam, they argued, should be separated from public affairs. Egypt was above all a Mediterranean country, they said. Indeed, Ancient Egypt was the fountainhead of European civilization. It was only natural that the current of influence should flow back again, that Egypt should assimilate European progress and grasp what was best: Bismarckian discipline, Cartesian logic, the social ethics of Bentham and Mill. In time, the liberals were confident, democracy and secular universal education would replace religious principles with civic ones.

Others said that nationalism – passionate and even irrational – was the source of Western power. Egyptian schoolchildren, too, could learn to sing anthems and salute the flag. They could be made to feel Egyptian first, not Muslim or Christian, rich or poor. This was to be the strongest trend of all, subsuming and absorbing the work of feminists and reformers, liberals and traditionalists in the fight against foreign dominance. Nationalism was one theme around which all could unite, and they did so to great effect: uninterrupted strikes, demonstrations and a consumer boycott against the British broke out in 1919. Passions ran so high that a Coptic priest was said to have marched into the Mosque of al-Azhar at the height of the unrest. When he shouted that the British had got their pink cheeks from sucking the blood of Egyptians, the Azharite students hoisted him onto their shoulders and carried him to the mosque pulpit to deliver a speech. In the face of such united emotion, Britain was forced to back down. Egypt won its independence in 1922.

In the 1920s and 30s Cairo emerged as the forward-looking capital of a young nation, a confident city graced with institutions of democratic government, of learning and the arts. In these years Egyptians rediscovered their ancient past. Spectacular archaeological finds – most dramatically the unearthing in 1922 of the boy pharaoh Tutankhamun's intact, gold-stuffed tomb in Luxor's Valley of the Kings – inspired a flurry of building in neo-pharaonic style. Saad Zaghloul was himself laid to rest under the outstretched wings of Horus in a magnificent, temple-like mausoleum. Mahoud Mukhtar (1891–1934), a brilliant, Paris-trained sculptor, reworked ancient themes in the granite monument he designed for the entrance to Cairo's flourishing new university. *The Renaissance of Egypt*, as it was called, showed a peasant girl casting back her veil with one hand and rousing a sleeping sphinx with the other.

The city's medieval architectural heritage was also revived. New mosques shunned the later Ottoman forms and reverted to the older, purely Cairene style of the high Mamluk era. A few notable buildings fused Islamic designs with art deco – a blend whose remarkable success owed much to the fact that European decorative arts, from William Morris to Matisse to the sets in Hollywood's *Thief of Baghdad*, had drawn strongly from encounters with the Arab East. In a sort of celebration of Cairo's diversity, one pasha's 1920s villa incorporated three vast reception rooms: one in the French style, one Arabesque – with geometric-inlay fountains, carpets and low divans – and one decorated with pharaonic motifs, including brass door handles cast in the shape of eyes of Horus.*

Cairo produced its first generation of modern writers. Dropping the poetical, alliterative language of the past, they tackled themes like the clash between town and country, between freedom and the constraints of tradition. Their introduction of new forms – the novel, dramatic realism, free verse – revitalized Arabic literature after centuries of stagnation. While its press experimented with biting satire and fierce polemic, the city held up a mirror to itself in theatre, too. Music halls and playhouses sprouted in the vicinity of Opera Square; these were venues for pioneers of the Arabic stage like Yusuf Wahbi and George Abyad. The first Egyptian feature film, *In the Land of Tutankhamun*, was screened in 1923. Cairo produced its first talkie in 1932, by which time the city could already boast a major film industry, complete with cigar-chomping moguls and preening starlets. Naguib al-Rihani was Egypt's own, and highly original Charlie Chaplin. Muhammad Abd al-Wahab, son of a muezzin in the Bab al-Shaʿriyya district, was a crooning composer – a sort of Bing Crosby rolled into Irving Berlin. He was pulling in £20,000 a picture by the 1940s. Leila Murad, the daughter of a cantor in the old Jewish Quarter, was Egypt's screen sweetheart, the nice

*Bahieddin Pasha Barakat's villa by the Nile in Giza was torn down, like so much of genteel Cairo, in the late 1980s to make way for a luxury high-rise.

girl next door who was always falling into trouble and singing her way out of it.

Cairo began to project itself, and its free-spirited urbanity struck other Arabs as a revelation. Baghdad and Beirut hummed to the tunes cut at Sono Cairo studios and devoured glossy Cairene magazines, marvelling at their daring cartoons and commentary and their ads for motor cars, elevators, refrigerators and dance revues. Egypt's capital became a magnet for Arab talent. Its lights drew a generation of performers who rebroadcast the city's rhythm and dialect to their own countries.

BUT THE IMAGE was not quite real. In the movies, slick city reason triumphed over crusty country manners. The poor boy's hard-won education paid off. He earned his promotion and won the heart of the rich girl, whose stern pasha father inevitably turned out to have a heart of gold.

The facts were different, and kept bumbling on to the set. In the reality of Cairo in the 1930s and '40s, the boy whose family sacrificed all to pay for his schooling most likely remained poor. He scorned the rich girl because, with her mascara and Paris gowns, she was too 'Western'. And the rich girl was bound to marry her rich cousin anyway, in accordance with Egyptian tradition. The stern pasha was in all probability a greedy capitalist and a buyer of votes in rigged elections. He lived in luxury in Cairo, while the serfs who worked his cotton plantation shared their mud huts with chickens and goats. The city slickers were not benign. They were sharpsters who, according to the joke of the day, swindled their country cousins by selling them Cairo tramcars. In return, rural newcomers disdained to use city sidewalks and grazed their sheep in public parks.

The triumph of modernism, of urban manners, was far from assured. Conundrums which were to become typical of the post-colonial world were at work: as education spread, so did discontent; as public health improved, population growth erupted. Freed from British tutelage, the government did indeed raise spending on education, from 1 per cent of the budget in 1920 to 12 per cent in 1940. But in that year three-quarters of Cairenes remained illiterate. The new schools produced a surfeit of bureaucrats, but not enough doctors or engineers. Beginning in 1930, Cairo began to grow so fast that it lost control of its own sprawling slums, let alone its ability to 'civilize' the hinterland. Outside the city, the amount of cultivable land per farmer had dwindled by a third in the first three decades of the century. Landless peasants flocked to the capital, bringing with them a deeply traditional outlook. As fast as the city could urbanize, the country was ruralizing the city. Away from the boulevards, new working-class quarters without sewage, running water or electricity re-created the scale and habits of country villages. The old solidarities, however, were gone. In the press of urban living, families split. Jobs in factories and offices were insecure. Child labour and sixteen-hour working days were common.

The veil may have been dropped as a form of dress, but the range of traditional mores it represented remained. In Coptic churches, for example, women were no longer segregated behind a wooden screen. Yet, although they sat in full view now, modesty required that they should be separated from men by the centre aisle. The ways of the modern city and its cosmopolitan elite were attractive, but they remained beyond the financial grasp or cultural inclinations of the impoverished majority. The sense of privilege that still surrounded the *khawagāt* was seen as corrupting and demeaning. The ineradicable misery of the poor belied the veneer of progress.

This process was at work on other levels, too. In politics, lingering British influence subverted the triumph of independence. Palace meddling eroded the achievement of democracy. Within a decade of its proclamation, King Fouad had suspended the liberal 1923 constitution no less than four times. The press law of 1933 clamped a muzzle on dissent. Democracy came back, but the tampering had weakened it beyond repair. Politics turned dirty. Parties in power used the police to frame opponents, made alliances in pure opportunism, and bribed voters with impunity. The nationalist front splintered into opposing and increasingly violent factions.

The cracks in the intellectual world also widened. As literacy spread, those who had been left behind, who still lived in the traditionalist world of the village and Cairo's backstreets, found a voice. While translations of Marx and Bertrand Russell trickled off the bookstalls lining the Azbakiyya Gardens, what sold like hot cakes were hagiographies of the Prophet and the four Rightly Guided Caliphs, and the pamphlets that the Muslim Brotherhood began to produce promoting Islam as a modern Utopia. The liberal vanguard discovered that their foreign ideas had propelled them out of acceptable bounds. They awoke with a shock to find themselves isolated from their own society.

Bitter feuds broke out between secularists and traditionalists. Al-Azhar expelled a professor in 1923 after he claimed that Islam did not prescribe a specific form of government: that, in effect, there was no such thing as an Islamic state. A similar fate befell Taha Husayn, a blind scholar and pioneering historian who in 1926 published his research on the seemingly innocuous subject of Arabic poetry of the pre-Islamic period. Husayn, a poor village boy who had trained at both al-Azhar and the Sorbonne in Paris, argued that nearly all this poetry had been misdated. Since it was probably written after the revelation of Islam, he claimed, its vocabulary was useless for understanding the Koran. At a stroke he demolished centuries of Koranic exegesis. Worse, in explaining his methods, Husayn stated that historians should set aside accepted belief and rely strictly on evidence. The Koran may have mentioned Abraham and Ishmael, he noted, but this was not enough to establish their physical existence.

From al-Azhar came howls of protest and charges of blasphemy. The matter was taken to court in a blaze of publicity that echoed trials over the teaching of evolution in the United States and that presaged future furores such as Salman Rushdie's *Satanic Verses* sparked sixty years later. A liberal judge dismissed the case, arguing that Husayn's intent was not deliberately hostile to Islam. Nevertheless the scholar was fired from his post at Cairo University. Subsequent editions of his book excluded any mention of the prophets.

The liberal climate of pre-revolutionary Cairo ensured that Taha Husayn was to fare better than his disciples would a few generations later. The university reinstated him. In fact he rose to become first a dean, and later rector of the university, before becoming Minister of Education in 1950. Yet the movement which secularists hailed as Egypt's Enlightenment had begun to lose momentum. Obscurantist litigators had laid their mines. Certain subjects were to remain taboo. From now on, intellectuals who were bold enough to assert the primacy of reason over revelation knew they were doing so at their own peril.

BETWEEN 1930 AND 1950 Cairo's population doubled to 2 million. At mid-century, as antibiotics reduced the toll of disease, it was growing at a rate of 3.7 per cent a year. The Second World War, which had brought foreign armies and great events to Cairo's doorstep, had shaken up the new generation. The disastrous 1948 war with Israel had embittered it. Its members could not be content with the paternalistic ways of the past any more. They wanted action. The revolving cabinets of the late 1940s tried to cope. But their liberal legislative agenda – freeing labour unions, expanding public health, housing and education, promoting national industry, and limiting foreign domination of business – could not keep pace with demand for change.

Cacophony reigned in this city that produced 11 Arabic daily newspapers, 190 magazines, 60 feature films a year, and scandal and strikes every day of the week. Tolerance succumbed to violence as Fascists and religious extremists rallied to radical visions of an Egypt 'purified' of alien influence. The populist sheikh Muhammad al-Ghazali captured this feverish mood, warning in 1950 of the dangers of Western cultural imperialism and its supposed agents: 'The West surely seeks to humiliate us, to occupy our land, and to destroy Islam by annulling its laws and abolishing its traditions ... The faction which works for the separation of Egypt from Islam is really a shameless, pernicious and perverse group of puppets and slaves of Europeans.'

Trade unionists, Communists* and Muslim Brothers – the Brotherhood, though banned in 1948, boasted half a million members in the late 1940s – played cat and mouse with King Farouk's secret police. Each claimed an exclusive right to the masses; each claimed a monopoly on the future. But Cairo in its confusion longed not for slogans but for a saviour.

Coming just six months after the great Cairo fire on Black Saturday, the silent coup of 23 July 1952 brought a sense of tremendous relief. Cairenes were only too willing to surrender their troubles and to project their hopes on the army, which at the time seemed the only uncorrupted institution left. Crowds cheered the self-effacing new *rayyis* or president, General Muhammad Naguib, so trim and modest compared to the elephantine Farouk. The youthful officers surrounding Naguib – earnest, articulate soldiers untainted with foreign affectation – seemed the ideal of a new kind of Egyptian man. They looked confident, and this was the quality Cairo yearned for.

For most the enchantment endured. For some – and not only for Cairo's cosmopolitan elite – it was soon cut short. Police shot dead eight striking workers within a month of the coup, putting

*Nearly all the key leaders of Egypt's Communist movement were Jewish. Several converted to Islam in the late 1940s, to quash charges of Communism being a Zionist conspiracy.

paid to notions that Egypt's new leaders were sympathetic to the powerful Communist movement. Rather than hold elections as promised, the regime abolished political parties. Hapless politicians were rounded up, tried and imprisoned. In 1954 the handsome, broad-shouldered leader of the younger officers shunted aside General Naguib and declared himself *rayyis*. Gamal Abd al-Nasser was soft spoken and bookish. His favourite tune was Rimsky-Korsakov's Orientalist fantasia *Scheherazade*; his favourite writer was Voltaire. But this army colonel was no lily-livered Candide. His security forces squashed critics with unprecedented zeal, dispatching some 3,000 of them by 1955 to prison camps where many endured torture. Charged with plotting Nasser's assassination, the Muslim Brotherhood was crushed. As six of its leaders were led to the scaffold, one of them cried out a curse on the revolution.

To its detractors the revolution was a cruel joke. The old order had been torn down only to be replaced by a regime that harked back to Mamluk rule. Trusting no one, Nasser handed out fiefdoms to his officer friends: governorships of the provinces, directorships of nationalized companies, editorships of newspapers. Like a jealous sultan of old, he chiselled away the memory of his predecessors. Street names changed: Ismailia Square, the hub of the modern city, became Tahrir (or Liberation) Square. King Fouad Avenue was now called 26 July Avenue, after the date of Farouk's departure into exile. The new government claimed all the achievements of the past as its own. Free public education, progressive labour laws, public health and housing, the Arab League;* all these things were expanded under the new regime, which neglected to mention that they had been initiated by the old. With the school curriculum sanitized, a whole generation grew up ignorant of its own past, believing that Egypt

*Founded in 1945, the Arab League embodied hopes for Arab unity. It has never lived up to them.

before the revolution had been a sorry place of oppressed peasants lorded over by imperialist lackeys and wicked feudalists.

Cairo forgot itself. Privately funded institutions mouldered in disuse: the Geographical Society, the Institut d'Égypte, the Agricultural and Ethnographic and Railway and European Art museums that celebrated Victorian ideals of Progress. The monuments of the Old City were again allowed to decay; the private charity that had restored and preserved them was subsumed, like nearly all voluntary organizations, into the state bureaucracy.* Farouk's palaces, which had at first been thrown open to the public as exhibits of royal decadence, were closed and converted to offices for the army, the police and the presidency. A single, soft voice poured from the radio, drowning the old cacophony of debate, reducing the old quandaries to idle café chatter.

To the chagrin of Nasser's victims, it was a voice that touched the masses. The *rayyis* was a masterly orator. Egyptians thrilled to hear a leader speak in words they could understand, proclaiming a vision they had only dreamed of. Forget democracy, forget Islam; it was Nasser who embodied the aspirations of the real people. He was Rob Roy and Robin Hood: see the *rayyis* in the newsreels passing title deeds to sharecroppers, busting up the great estates. See him biting the tail of the British lion, nationalizing the Suez Canal. See him champion the cause of the little man, opening schools, granting diplomas, working for Arab independence and unity, hobnobbing with those other Great Liberators Tito and Nehru and Kwame Nkrumah.

The hero leaped from one seeming success to another, and Cairo basked in his glory. The city took on a new, serious, look. The swelling number of police exchanged the quaint tarboosh for the beret (those police in uniform, that is: the number of secret

*In the 1960s the annual maintenance budget for all the 600-odd registered medieval monuments in the city was £600.

police grew disproportionately). Bureaucrats wore military-style safari suits instead of the pinstripes favoured by pashas – whose titles were now abolished anyway. Belly dancers were required to cover their midriffs. Prostitutes and beggars were shooed off the streets. Stark, functional angularity ruled in the new monuments rising along the Nile – the river itself having been tamed by the massive Soviet-funded and -designed High Dam at Aswan. The Cairo Tower, a 600-foot high lotus blossom in concrete mesh capped with a revolving restaurant, rocketed skywards near the Gezira Sporting Club in 1955.* Symbols of the new age replaced the old British army barracks at Qasr al-Nil. In their place rose the headquarters of the Arab League, a Hilton hotel and a low-budget copy of the UN's Manhattan offices which was to house Nasser's monolithic political party, the Arab Socialist Union. The radio and television tower, a thirty-storey rectangle planted in a massive round base, beamed Cairo's revolutionary ideals across the Arab world and beyond. South of the city, the shady spa of Helwan-les-Bains was transformed into an industrial complex complete with steel mills, cement factories and assembly plants for cars, electronics and armaments. Here, proclaimed Nasser, Egypt would manufacture everything from needles to rockets – note the virile imagery.

After a decade in office Nasser announced a social revolution to complete his political coup. In the new Egypt, the paternal state would take care of everything. Along with finance and heavy industry, the press, cinema, theatre and publishing were nationalized. From now on the Ministry of Industry would make things, while the Ministry of National Guidance and the Ministry of Culture would channel thoughts and their expression. Just as in the early years of the Soviet Union, the arts did indeed flower at

*In his memoirs, former agent Miles Copeland revealed it was CIA money that funded the tower. Nasser had diverted a $3 million cash bribe to this frivolous purpose as a slap in the face to Yankee meddling.

first in the enthusiasm of change. In the three years following 1962 Cairo theatre audiences grew sixfold and became acquainted with Brecht, O'Neill and Chekhov as well as a maturing dazzle of local talents. The city gained a symphony orchestra and a classical ballet troupe. Realism touched with a stylized hint of folklore set the visual tone. Muralists glorified the new institutions with neo-pharaonic warriors piloting MIG fighter planes instead of chariots; with muscle-bound, tractor-driving peasants and wrench-wielding proletarians. Studios toned down the soft focus of romance and tuned up cleancut images of peasants rising against feudal overlords and of Omar Sharif on the waterfront, fighting for the rights of the working man.

One summer morning in 1961, many an ex-pasha was to spill his Turkish coffee on reading the headlines in *Al-Ahram*. To finance the march to socialism, the government had just made it practically illegal to own assets worth more than £10,000. Anything in excess of this amount, whether it be a Garden City villa or a stake in the Cairo Electric Tramways Company, was to be seized. Four thousand of Egypt's richest families were ruined. The Syro-Maltese, Greco-Armenian and other polyglot titans of industry found their desks occupied overnight by bureaucrats and army officers. The change of command had a peculiar historical resonance; just as in Mamluk days, the 'depredations of the Soldan' were again to suffocate private enterprise.

As the state took over, it took on responsibility for housing even as Cairo's population doubled again to 4 million by 1960. Ranks of slab-concrete tenements sprouted, and whole new districts were laid out to absorb both the urban poor and the new bourgeois cadres created by the regime. The City of Engineers, the City of Journalists and Victory City promised vistas of neat, modernist cubes marching into fields and desert. The fact that the dwellings were cramped, hot and shoddy; that the neat street plans often dead-ended in sand dunes or farming villages, was of no account. The important thing was the dream.

The vision seemed so real that Egyptians were by and large willing to forgive the imprisonments, the dispossessions, the cronyism and the atmosphere of fear. The cosmopolitans were leaving; the sons of the soil would be in charge. Until the flood of university graduates became so huge that their degrees were debased, Nasser's education policies seemed a triumph. (The ratio of teachers to students at Cairo University went from 1:6 in 1950 to 1:60 in 1962.) Until buildings decayed and collapsed for lack of maintenance, his 1961 decree fixing rents at the level of 1944 seemed an act of mighty magnanimity to the poor. Until it became clear that they were madly overstaffed and lost money, state industries were seen as the engine that would drive Egypt to a prosperous future.

The Egyptians were not alone. To all the nations that were, like Egypt, just recovering from European colonization, Nasser's Cairo seemed a vanguard city. Half the liberation movements of the 1960s set up offices here. From Radio Cairo, the African National Congress broadcast encouragement in Zulu and Xhosa to its oppressed brothers in South Africa. At Cairo University Yasir Arafat stirred exiled Palestinians to fight for their rights. It was to Cairo that the youthful Saddam Hussein fled after his first murder – he had gunned down an Iraqi politician in the streets of Baghdad in 1962. Here the future dictator skulked in university corridors, drank in ideology and studied, of all things, law. Nasserism was infectious: by the end of Nasser's term most Arabs lived under totalitarianisms inspired by his. Their political language was Cairo's; from Algiers to Aden they spoke of the inevitability of socialism, of Arab unity and Afro-Asian solidarity, of freedom from Western hegemony.

IN JUST ONE day the mighty edifice of the New Egypt collapsed. On 8 June 1967 Radio Cairo declared that the sneak attack launched by Israel three days before had collapsed. Egyptian forces had shot down 200 enemy warplanes. Its triumphant army would soon be marching down Dizengoff Street in Tel Aviv. On 9 June Gamal Abd al-Nasser addressed the nation. His voice trembling, the *rayyis* confessed that his country and its allies had just suffered the most humiliating defeat since the fall of France in 1940. The enemy had not only wiped out three-quarters of the air force in one morning's surprise attacks, not only lopped off the whole Sinai Peninsula – and with it Egypt's richest oilfields – not only killed 12,000 Egyptians, captured 60,000 and entrenched itself behind the impregnable barrier of the now sealed Suez Canal, it had also occupied the Holy City of Jerusalem. The disgrace was so complete, Nasser concluded, that he had no recourse but to resign.*

A wail of pain and anger rose up from the defeated city. The millions who had spent a week glued to radios, chain-smoking through the night-time blackouts and air-raid sirens, now poured out of houses and offices. It was a kind of spontaneous mass enactment of an operatic finale. The Hero was wounded, but the People would carry him to a dignified end. 'Gamal, Gamal,' the crowds shouted, and even many who detested Nasser joined in, enthused by the moment, refusing to let him quit. And so the saviour was resurrected.

In following years Cairo paid the price of Nasser's folly in full.† It was a sombre period. Queues for rationed food curled around corners. Brick anti-blast walls obstructed building entrances. Windows and headlamps were painted over in blackout

*Nasser's resignation speech did not in fact reveal the full scale of Egypt's losses in the Six Day War. This dawned only later.

†Nasser's mistakes were multiple. In response to other Arab leaders' taunts that he was a coward, he dismissed UN peacekeepers and blocked Israel-bound shipping. He believed his generals when they assured him that his forces were fully prepared to withstand any Israeli military response. He naively expected Israel to believe him when he said he had no intention of attacking it. And he allowed his people to be grossly misled about what was happening.

blue. Soldiers' boots thundered on the roofs of trains. Israeli warplanes screeched arrogantly overhead, dropping the occasional bomb on schools and factories. Imagined spies lurked everywhere. Loiterers were arrested as saboteurs; a woman of my acquaintance was picked up and hauled in for the crime of painting a picture of the University Bridge: had she not seen the sign that said 'No Photo'? All investment was halted in favour of rebuilding the army. Telephones, roads and sewers decayed. Toilet paper and light bulbs and scores of other necessities grew scarce. As Israeli guns wrecked the cities along the Suez Canal, half a million refugees swarmed into the already overburdened capital.

All the unspoken fears, the crushed dissents that had accumulated since the revolution burst into the open. The humour turned bitter. When Nasser went to Moscow to plead for aid, it was said, Leonid Brezhnev told him he was sorry but the Egyptians would have to tighten their belts. 'All right,' replied the *rayyis*, 'Send us belts!'

The old question returned with a new, accusatory, urgency. Who was to blame for Egypt's weakness? Generals were tried and jailed for criminal incompetence. Nasser's best friend from army days, minister of defence Abd al-Hakim Amir, committed 'suicide' while under house arrest. The regime itself split. The faint-hearted said socialism had sapped the country and carried it into the losing Cold War camp. Diehards said it had not been strictly enough applied; that the West – through its agent Israel – had cut Nasser down to size precisely because his success made him a threat. Students chanted in the streets for more justice and less oppression. They shouted for guns to fight the enemy. Imprisoned fundamentalists rattled their bars to say We Told You So.

Even the common people – Nasser's 'masses' – divided. For every illiterate street-sweeper who had proudly seen his school-smocked children learn to read, seen them gain the unimaginable distinctions of a college degree and a government salary, there was another whose son had died in the war or been beaten in jail.

Cairo tried to veil itself in the revolutionary image, to see nothing but the factories, the crowds of students and workers, the wide streets of the new quarters. But demoralizing tales kept stripping away the emperor's clothes.

Take the story of an architect friend whom I will call Iskandar. (One legacy of the Nasser period is a lingering fear of speaking out.) Like every able-bodied man Iskandar was drafted into the army after the Six Day War. One day his general summoned him in a panic. The *rayyis* was to inspect an airbase in the desert the following week. But there was a hitch. The base did not exist. The president could not inspect an empty patch of sand. Something had to be created, double quick, and Iskandar, being an architect after all, was the man to do it. My friend was given trucks and a squad of peasant conscripts. They slapped together prefab buildings. They hauled rocks into straight lines suggesting roads and runways, and for good measure painted them republican red, black and green. But Iskandar's master stroke was this: he trucked his men into Cairo at night and had them uproot dozens of roadside trees, carry them into the wasteland, and stick them in the sand. Within days the trees had wilted, and in fact Nasser never showed up to congratulate Iskandar's commanding officer on his green thumb.

THE REVOLUTION WAS by no means all farcical artifice. The changes, and many of the gains, were real. Nasser had opened the Cairo of aristocrats and cosmopolitans to the common people, much as Saladin had done seven centuries before with the court city of the Fatimid caliphs. The street that had divided the old quarters from the new – the former Shariᶜ Ibrahim Pasha, renamed Shariᶜ al-Gumhuriyya, or Republic Street, after the 1952 revolution – was no longer such a barrier between values. (Now, cynics said, the whole town decayed evenly.) The creation of a vast, centralized bureaucracy had raised Cairo's primacy in Egypt. The revolution had built a dominant new class of petits bourgeois, of commuters and managers. It had exposed new ranks of Egyptians to the ideals of social justice; given them the sense that they could be modern without selling out to the West. It had given Cairo a self-image as the unchallenged capital of a renascent Arab world, a light to the newly independent nations of Asia and Africa.

Nasser never went as far as radical Muslim reformers like Turkey's hard-drinking dictator Kemal Atatürk, who abolished the Arabic script, or Tunisia's secularizing president Habib Bourguiba, who banned polygamy. Still, to some traditionalists his revolution seemed, ironically, to serve the very colonialist goals it professed to oppose. It was Nasser who abolished the Christian, Jewish and Muslim religious tribunals that had governed family law until 1956. The breaking of the Muslim Brotherhood,* the suppression of Sufism and the absorption of al-Azhar into the state – along with nearly the entire educational Establishment – had the effect of muting religious reactionaries. Indeed, mosque sermons now proclaimed that Nasser's ideology of socialism had all along been inherent in Islam.

The Enlightenment project – though stripped of democracy – seemed poised to effect deeply rooted social change. The metropolis dispatched engineers, doctors and teachers to educate the countryside in new city ways. Government subsidies and professional unions brought a sense of importance to the many artists, writers and film-makers who joined their persuasive skill to the revolution's aims. Outside the capital, sweeping land reforms empowered fellahin for the first time in history. In the city, more marriages were now made more for love rather than to reinforce family alliances. Dating couples held hands as they strolled along the Nile embankment. A visitor in 1968 could remark that Cairo boasted more female dentists and physicians than most Western cities, with scarcely a veil in sight. The divorce

* Some 18,000 suspected Muslim Brothers were imprisoned in 1965 alone.

rate – whose extremely high level before the revolution had reflected women's low status – plummeted from one in three marriages to under one in ten. Women had won the right to vote, even if this could be exercised only in referendums that Nasser always won by a stupefying margin. (Which inspired this tale: the secret police were known to transmit the latest jokes to Nasser. Hurt by all the scorn, Nasser ordered them to bring to him a man reputed for his caustic wit. 'How can you say these things about me?' the *rayyis* whined. 'Everyone loves me. It's a proven fact: 99 per cent of them voted for me.' The joker raised his palms defensively. '*That* joke isn't one of mine,' he said.)

But perhaps the most enduring legacy of the revolution was unintended. Egyptians had always been characterized as the most home-loving of peoples. Now they began to emigrate en masse, voting with their feet. Largely it was an exodus of brawn as workers flew to the newly rich Arab oil states to make their fortunes. But educated Cairenes, too, left by the thousand, continuing the crippling brain drain that had begun with the loss of the city's Jews and Greeks and Italians.

In 1996, the *Wall Street Journal* could report that Egyptian-born Americans were the most highly educated of 110 immigrant groups identified in the United States: 60 per cent had university degrees, a quarter of them at postgraduate level. This erosion of talent was to have devastating effects on Cairo – in a process of aesthetic defoliation as the class that patronized arts and public gardens and fine buildings disappeared; in a diminution of civil society as private initiative was abandoned and bureaucratized; in a deterioration of quality – in everything from building standards to the crafting of laws – as pen-pushers and party cronies took over the skilled professions.

NASSER DIED ABRUPTLY in September 1970 – so abruptly that there were rumours of poison. Two million people trailed the fallen hero's coffin through the centre of Cairo. Like a latter-day Mamluk sultan, the *rayyis* was laid to rest in a giant funerary mosque – but one of reinforced concrete rather than stone, with picture windows and plaster filigree.

Anwar al-Sadat, an old and trusted colleague of Nasser's, made his entrance. Sadat was absolutely, vividly a man of his age, one of the inheritors of the cosmopolitan city that King Farouk left behind. Born in an obscure Delta village in 1919 – the year of Egypt's revolt against British rule – he was raised in Cairo, where his father worked as a minor bureaucrat. In 1938 – King Farouk's coronation year – Sadat entered the War College at Heliopolis. His family could barely afford the uniform. Boys of humble origin had only recently begun to be admitted to the academy, and poor cadets like Nasser and Sadat never forgave their subsequent humiliations. Unlike well-connected graduates who were posted to cushy jobs in Cairo, both future presidents were billeted to a dreary garrison in deepest Upper Egypt.

As a young, disillusioned officer, Sadat experimented with every political trend of the turbulent 1940s. For a time he dallied with the Muslim Brotherhood (as had Nasser). He also tried on the green shirts of the Fascist-inspired Young Egypt Party, and immersed himself in the pro-Axis, anti-British underground during the Second World War. Most of all, though, Sadat seemed to be struggling to forget his origins. After the disaster of the 1948 war against Israel he abandoned his officer's uniform. Having done time for his involvement in an assassination plot, he forsook politics and went into the transport business. Significantly, he divorced his first wife, a simple girl of lowly birth, in favour of a pale-skinned middle-class lady who was half Maltese.

With the revolution, Sadat found himself whisked to the pinnacle of power. He and his old officer chums were in charge, and free to remodel Egypt as they chose. But for the eighteen years of Nasser's rule Sadat stayed wisely in the background. He became a propagandist for the regime, sloganizing about Arabism, socialism and the glories of the Soviet Union. Playing the role of a journalist – wearing the revolution's trademark short-sleeved safari suit – he rode the tide that swept Egypt through nationalizations and mobilizations, that seemed to empower people like himself, to give them a modern identity.

Sadat's search for identity – incidentally, the phrase became the title of his autobiography – took a new twist after Nasser's death in 1970. Now, as president, he revealed what must have been long-repressed doubts about the course of the revolution. Sadat tossed out Soviet advisers and threw open Egypt's doors to capitalism. He abandoned Nasser's Arabism and trumpeted Egyptian uniqueness. He betrayed his Arab allies and made a separate peace with Israel. His wardrobe blossomed. One day he appeared in an admiral's starched whites wielding a baton, the next in a Paris-tailored suit gesturing with a briar pipe. When Cairo's sophisticates laughed at such antics, Sadat turned on them. Police rounded up left-wing cynics while the president counselled his 'children' to return to Islam. He rediscovered his long-discarded native village and proclaimed it a symbol of purity, of the true Egypt. There in the Delta – to the puzzlement of locals who better understood his father's impulse to escape to Cairo – Sadat would hold court, donning peasant robes and fingering worry beads, and ponder the state of the world with visiting *khawāga* dignitaries.

Sadat wanted desperately to be a man of the people. But which people? His profusion of muftis echoed Cairo's own confusion, its splintering among classes and generations and convictions. This unease, this nagging sense of incompleteness, was natural in a city that had mutated far faster than the human ability to grasp its meanings. The rocketing rate of Cairo's growth would alone have undone dreams of a stable world. But add to that the gyrations of its politics, the beating of war drums and the clash of symbols – Western and Eastern, urban and rural – and you begin to understand the Cairene's deep distrust of wrappings and institutions, his longing for ideals, his resort to humour and religion.

IN OCTOBER 1973 Sadat led his people into another war against Israel. As much as a battle to retrieve captured land, it was for Egyptians a fight to save lost honour and self-esteem. In these terms Egypt did well. Its army beat back the much-better-armed Israelis from the Suez Canal. Quickly resupplied by the United States, Israel counter-attacked. The October War ended with a shaky stalemate, but Egypt had regained much of its pride. In subsequent negotiations it was to win back all of its land as well.

The relief of peace allowed Sadat to depressurize the system. He released political prisoners, promised elections, and welcomed foreign aid and investment and tourism. A furious storm of change swept over the demobilized capital. Money came out of mattresses. Private construction boomed. The new chain hotels on the Corniche soon dwarfed adjacent Nasserist instutions. So many old villas were ripped down and replaced by apartments that an ex-pasha I know declared it was a good thing Nasser had stolen so much property, because at least the mansions he had converted into schools and police stations would be saved from speculators. Emigrant labourers sent home colour TVs and rials and dinars that were ploughed into acres of jerry-built, unplanned housing. The edges of the city bristled with antennas and iron reinforcing-bars. Brick tenements without power or plumbing sliced into lush green fields in a patchwork of land grabs.

Money began to undermine Nasser's pyramid of bureaucratic power. Inflation punished workers on fixed salaries while enriching tradesmen. Importers and contractors minted cash. Casting off wartime isolation, Cairo binged on conspicuous consumption. Lapels, ties and trouser bottoms flared absurdly. Heels and luxury apartment buildings elevated to dizzy heights. New boutiques contorted foreign names in blinking plastified neon. Painted floozies who catered to rich Arab visitors flounced out of shops called Up Pop and into nightclubs like the Parisiana, the Salt and Pepper and the After Eight. Shiny Chevrolets slipped from the showrooms of Shady Motors into snarled streets that swiftly became so clogged that concrete flyovers had to be tossed up with helter-skelter disregard for beauty. Meanwhile, huddles of peasants squatted numbly outside agencies touting cut-price fares to jobs in Libya, Iraq and the Persian Gulf.

The city rediscovered fun; it revelled in the joys of noise. As the great singer Umm Kulsoum and her generation of balladeers passed away, amplifiers squawked a new breed of ditzy Cairo pop. Admen reworked revolutionary hymns into jingles for deodorants and hairspray. Television ousted the last public storytellers from cafés. Billboards blotted out slums. In theatre and film, slapstick and frivolous romance came back. Night-time instincts, suppressed under Nasser's austerity, resurfaced. Hashish parlours thrived – on boats in the Nile, in the cemeteries, and even in salons overlooking the Gezira Sporting Club. The president himself was said to enjoy a good smoke. His own brother was rumoured to be a big-shot drug runner.

Eight million strong in 1980, Cairo seemed more than ever on the verge of chaos. Public services could not cope. Sewage seeped from manholes. Stretches of the ancient Qasaba looked like a shallower Venice: I once found tourists being gamely gondoliered on a donkey cart through the sludge outside the mausoleum of Sultan Qalawun. Buses sagged under their overload, while taps sputtered and died from lack of pressure. Rogue electricians made fortunes tapping high tension wires for domestic use. And the telephones! In 1975 you could finish the paper through to the obituaries while waiting for a dial tone. Once the auspicious signal sounded, theories abounded over successful means of dialling. The most popular was to hold the final digit and say *bismallah*.

Around this time a friend's doorbell rang. 'Congratulations', said the beaming herald on her doorstep, 'your phone has come through!' What phone, my friend wanted to know. The company official explained that it was the line her parents had applied for when she was born, twenty years before.

I recall another scene from this era. The pressure of people seemed to propel the city ever upward, and so the army had built an emergency footbridge to circle Tahrir Square. In the centre of this metal ring the Ministry of Information had erected a giant poster of a pharaonic Sadat in his admiral's whites. Circumambulating with the crowd one morning, I found a leather-faced peasant shouting at this graven image. '*Ya rayyis!*' he called out over the roar of traffic, rocking on his feet, raising his arms to heaven. 'Oh hero of war and peace! My water buffalo has died. My children are hungry!' Onlookers shrugged and grinned. A policeman came and took the disconsolate fellah by the hand.

It was in these years, too, that the state discovered it could no longer afford its revolutionary pledge to educate, heal, house, feed and employ the masses. Preoccupied with foreign affairs, Sadat shied from admitting the rupture of Nasser's social contract. It was easier to export the unemployed to the Gulf and to dream of new cities than to confront Cairo's reality. It was easier to proclaim democracy and rig its results than to abolish party and police controls. It was easier to speak grandly of an Open Door Economic Policy than to either upgrade or dismantle the swollen public sector whose needles rusted and whose rockets didn't work.

For lack of any policy state services began to privatize themselves. With schools working two or even three shifts a day, and classes averaging eighty students, teachers made up for dismal salaries by giving private lessons on the side. In government hospitals there were no bedclothes or syringes any more, let alone medicines: such things had to be procured by patients. Some unscrupulous private hospitals, meanwhile, were found to be buying kidneys off poor Cairenes to sell them to the rich. Every city bus listed to starboard under the weight of passengers jamming the doors; private jitney buses began to pick up those not fit enough to survive the scrum. Petty corruption grew rife. Nasser's guarantee of a government job for every college graduate became a fiasco. Bureaucrats showed up once a month to collect their paltry pay; their despairing bosses preferred it that way, because offices simply did not have enough chairs to seat them in. A peek in those days into rooms at the Mugammaʿ, the colossal state office building on Tahrir Square, would reveal secretaries diligently peeling potatoes, darning socks and knitting sweaters for their children. A survey showed that the typical government staffer put in a grand daily total of seven minutes' real working time. Another poll found that 85 per cent of university students hoped to emigrate on graduation, so pinched were jobs and wages at home.

Egypt was falling into population shock. Cairo alone was growing by a quarter of a million people a year. The cost of subsidizing staple foods rose and rose. Studies revealed not only that the average Egyptian consumed more wheat than anyone else (200 kg a year), but that bread was so cheap – compared to everything else – that farmers were feeding it to chickens. (They were also feeding them the free contraceptive pills provided by the United States – until, that is, rumours spread that these magic hormones which made chickens fat also caused human impotence.

In January 1977 Sadat doubled the price of bread from one to two piastres a loaf. Cairo simply boiled over. For three days enraged citizens charged through the city, smashing cars and shop windows and surprising themselves with their own fury. But no one was as astonished as Sadat. Like kings before him, he had lost touch. He had forgotten just how close to destitution his subjects were.

Soldiers quelled the rioting with curfews, tear gas and buckshot, leaving several dozen dead. The *rayyis* renounced the price rise. But he never quite regained his composure. It was now that Sadat's speeches lengthened into a disappointed father's marathon harangues. How could his children misbehave so? From the window of the helicopter Richard Nixon had given him, Cairo looked neat and prosperous, if a little dusty. A sparkling new elevated highway sliced through its centre. (It had bulldozed out of the way a last monument to British rule, the All Saints Cathedral behind the Egyptian Museum.) On the desert horizon, beyond the Pyramids, lamp-posts staked out a future satellite city where multinational corporations would build factories to employ happy workers freed from the crowded capital. Both the bridge and the town were named for 6 October 1973, the day when Sadat's army pushed Israel back from the Suez Canal. They were the *rayyis*'s gift to the October Generation, as he dubbed the new, proud Egyptians he envisaged as following him into an era of peace.

SHARIᶜ AL-GALAʾ is a busy tunnel of a street that smoulders noisily under the 6 October Bridge. The Arab world's two biggest-circulation dailies, the staid *Al-Ahram* and the racier *Al-Akhbar*, have their headquarters here, halfway down the bus route from Cairo Station to Tahrir Square. Tall buildings suggesting Clark Kent's *Daily Planet*, they add a touch of sobriety to Galaʾ Street's high-pitched bustle. From their soundproof windows Cairo's top editors look out over the expressway and across the city centre. The shutters on the other side of these buildings, however, are all closed. That is because they overlook an eyesore, a huge wind-blown lot that is empty except for junked and parked cars, and beyond which spreads the sprawling range of tenements, railway yards and sweatshops that is Shubra, Cairo's Bronx or East End.

In Sadat's time a warren of tin and mudbrick shacks jammed the now vacant lot. Here, in the space of four football fields, lived some 24,000 squatters – a density of population forty times that of New York City. At Sadat's command this whole community was razed. Its inhabitants found themselves shunted out of sight beyond the Shubra railway yards, shovelled into a grim housing project of stacked concrete matchboxes. The old slum may have been cramped, but it had worked out its own mechanisms of survival. In the new site there was not enough water, or power, or transport, or room in the schools, or space in general. Worse, the social cohesiveness of the old alleyways had been uprooted.

In the summer of 1981 militant Muslim youths attacked an unlicensed Coptic church being built near the project. Rioting erupted – ominously, because this was the first serious intercommunal strife Cairo had witnessed since the Middle Ages. Central Security, a black-clad force of conscripts with karate training that Sadat had created in the wake of the bread riots, stormed the district and clubbed it into an uneasy peace. To give an appearance of balance, the *rayyis* banished the Coptic pope to a desert monastery.

Three months later Sadat was shot down by his own soldiers at 6 October victory celebrations. As it transpired, several of those in the assassination plot had family or friends whose homes had been destroyed by the *rayyis*'s urban renewal plans. Others had been radicalized by the very Islamic groups that Sadat promoted as a foil against the leftists he mistakenly saw as a greater threat. Sadat himself had released his killers' guiding ideologues from Nasser's prisons, yet these people were not thankful. Years of torture and privation had embittered them. They preached that Egypt's rulers, and indeed society as a whole, had betrayed Islam. It was the true Muslim's duty to set things straight, they said. And if not by words, then by the sword.

CHAPTER NINE

KEEPING THE FAITH

The most advanced countries of the world have subjected their systems to practical experiments. After many trials they progress, and the more they progress, the closer they come to Islam.

Sheikh Muhammad Mitwalli Shaarawi, in *Al-Raai al-Aam* newspaper, 1 July 1994

All earthly matters must be judged in respect of the interests of the afterworld.

– Ibn Khaldun on the Muslim theory of governance, *Prolegomena*, c. 1380

IT IS CLOSE by at first, starting with the intimate *pock* of a microphone and a discreet cough or two. Somewhere in the sleeping city an answering cough stutters. And now, as the local muezzin shuts his eyes and cups a hand by his ear, that first sound takes sudden shape as syllables and words rising strong and clear. An echo follows from far off. Then another in the middle distance, quickly joined by a third, and then more and more and more voices until a mighty chorus is soaring in rounds, relaying the call to prayer clear across the valley from east to west with such amplified force that God would not need to be All-Hearing to hear it. An electric cloud of sound accumulates and holds, suspended over the city for a full minute by the loudspeakers of some 15,000 mosques, before dissolving piecemeal into the twitter of the waking birds.

In this age of fluorescent light and twenty-four-hour TV, many Cairenes stay up too late at night to heed the muezzin's advice that prayer at dawn is better than sleep. Yet nearly all those late risers will find some way to appease God for ignoring the dawn call. They may add an extra prostration to one of the four remaining prayers that day, say, or pass alms to a beggar, or perform some other small act of piety.

The Egyptians, said Herodotus, were 'religious to excess, beyond any other nation in the world'. The focus of Memphis was the Temple of Ptah, not some Roman-style forum or senate. Not only was there no separation of religion and state, the pharaoh himself was man's direct link with the gods.

Beliefs may have changed since Herodotus visited Memphis, but religion still permeates the life of Cairo as it does that of few other great cities. At the grand scale there are the 100,000-strong congregations that pray in public squares every year to mark the end of Ramadan. They, like the vast majority of Egyptians, will have fasted by day for the full lunar month. The common effort of devotion will have turned the rhythm of the city almost upside down, with shops and businesses staying open into the small hours and daytime work dragging almost to a halt, and with an expectant hush falling over the valley at dusk until the precise moment when a cannonshot from the Citadel declares the day is done and the feasting begins.

Each Friday at noon, most Muslim men will endure considerable discomfort, packed cross-legged on the mats that spill outside mosques and block streets and sidewalks, in order to absorb the sermon that follows the weekly congregational prayer. All year long, Radio Cairo's Voice of the Noble Koran will bring the word of God to housewives peeling potatoes and truckers hauling them alike: it is the most popular station here, just as the books of TV preachers like Sheikh Muhammad Mitwalli Shaarawi outsell most other literature.

At a narrowcast level, fathers will whisper the *Fātiḥa* – the opening verse of the Koran – into the ears of the newly born. Children will compensate for naughtiness by scribbling graffiti that says, 'There is no God but Allah and Muhammad is His Prophet'. Clerks and students and even police officers filing reports will inscribe 'In the Name of God, the Merciful, the Compassionate' at the top of every foolscap page. They will do so simply because the Prophet Muhammad, upon him be blessings and peace,* is recorded as saying that no task should be begun without mentioning the name of the deity.

When asked about their health, Cairenes will unfailingly reply, '*Al hamdu lillah*' – 'Praise be to God!' If asked whether the number 66 bus stops at al-Azhar, they are likely to say, '*Inn sha'Allah*' – 'If God so wills it'. In so doing they are simply respecting these words in sura 18, verse 23, of the Koran:

> *And say not of anything: Lo! I shall do that tomorrow,*
> *Except if Allah will.*

Similarly, everyday questions like how to keep clean, what to wear, or whether to divorce one's spouse will find their answer in scripture. Even unconscious habits are often rooted in the *Sunna* – the exemplary actions of the Prophet as recorded by his Companions. If the city boasts a surprising number of endearing stray cats, it is largely because people feed them out of respect for the Prophet, who is said to have cut a piece from his cloak so as not to disturb a cat sleeping in his lap. Dogs, meanwhile, are shunned as pets because Muhammad scorned keeping them for any purpose but guarding or hunting.

* Strictly speaking, Muslims should pronounce this formula of praise after any mention of Muhammad. It is so common that for convenience Arabic keyboards shrink both this phrase and the word 'Allah' to single keys.

Overt piety is nearly universal. Not just Muslims but the million Coptic Christians of Cairo are fervent believers by and large. Not content that their religion is stamped on their identity cards – and is also usually evident from their biblical names – many Copts tattoo crosses on their wrists as a brand of faith. Not just monks and sundry ascetics but also many dutiful laymen fast for nearly half the year. They shun animal products throughout Lent, of course, but also on Wednesdays and Fridays and for forty-three days before Christmas, for fifteen days before Ascension Day and so on in a complex calendar of devotion. Icons of saints and of Pope Shenouda III, the one-hundred-and-seventeenth patriarch of the Coptic Church, are ubiquitous in Christian homes. Services in the city's 500 churches are usually packed – even those in the 10,000-capacity Cathedral of St Simeon, a cavernous amphitheatre blasted out of the Muqattam cliffs during the 1990s. On Thursday nights a vast throng, bussed in from across the city, gathers here to belt out hymns to the accompaniment of synthesizers, electric guitars and a light show that projects the image of the crucified Saviour on to a giant screen.

The institutions of both faiths work hard to maintain their place. Nearly every Coptic church holds Bible lessons. Al-Azhar runs an entire education system in parallel to the state's, including hundreds of primary and secondary schools across the country. Its Islamic university has expanded far beyond the confines of the tenth-century mosque at its heart, branching from its academic roots in theology, grammar, rhetoric and Islamic law into modern disciplines like science and medicine. With 160,000 students in all – including 12,000 from abroad – it is Egypt's largest university. In state schools religious studies are compulsory. State television broadcasts forty-six hours a week of Islamic programming (but a mere two papal speeches a year – at Christmas and Easter – which is a sore point for Copts). A third of Cairo's 3,000 private charities are religious in nature. The richest literary prizes in Egypt are given not for works of fiction but to winners of an annual contest for memorizing and reciting the Koran which is sponsored by the Ministry of Religious Affairs.

Foreign laws and fashions have made inroads in the past two centuries, yet traditional religion is still the window through which most Cairenes view the world. The populist brand of socialism pursued under President Nasser never challenged the tenets of faith – so long as faith did not interfere with the regime's political control. Cairo's secular universities did produce large numbers of left-leaning intellectuals from the 1950s to the 1970s, but their ideas rarely penetrated beyond a small circle. This mild secularizing trend lost credit along with the rest of the Nasserist project, and then was further diluted from the late 1970s onwards as crowding began to transform universities into diploma factories rather than places of learning.

As a result religious discourse remains so dominant that few Cairenes question the teachings of Scripture. Such things as the theory of evolution are generally dismissed as absurd: that history begins with Adam and Eve is not a matter for argument. Cairenes are quick to frown on unorthodox religious practices, too. But even sophisticates resort to seers and healers and other holy men. Belief in miracles and heavenly signs runs deep.

For instance, in April 1968 – ten months after the disastrous Six Day War – a Muslim bus driver walking home late one night in the suburb of Zaytun, close to ancient Heliopolis, spotted what he thought was a woman about to throw herself off the roof of a church. He ran to wake up the priest, but when the two men rushed back outside and looked up, they understood that the ghostly female form they were seeing was not a suicide but an apparition of the Virgin Mary. The Virgin of Zaytun became the talk of Cairo. Night after night that spring, so many miracle-seekers thronged the square in front of the church that the government was obliged to rent out chairs. It was only two months later, after fifteen people were killed in a stampede when a similar reported sighting at the Church of the Archangel

Michael in Shubra brought 10,000 Cairenes rushing to witness the Virgin, that the fervour began to wane.

ISLAM IS A legalistic faith. Its messenger may not be deified like the Christian Messiah (whom Muslims also revere as a prophet), but Muhammad is a lawgiver as well as a teacher. His revelation assumes added force from the fact that the Koran is taken to be the literal word of God as spoken in Arabic. This makes the tone of Scripture imperative, not allegorical. When a mosque preacher cites the Koran he prefaces the quote with the phrase 'And God, may He be exalted and praised, said...'

The time before Islam is known to Muslims as the Age of Ignorance, in that man was ignorant of the commands of God. There is no longer any such excuse for such ignorance, nor has there been since Muhammad's revelation closed 1,400 years ago. To obey God is both a duty and a precaution against punishment in the hereafter. Given the level of detail in the divine instructions, it is not surprising that Cairo, the Muslim city par excellence, should bear their imprint in every walk of life.

If medieval Cairo lacked a single great congregational mosque such as every Muslim town of importance had, it was only because the city's size meant no mosque could possibly contain enough people. Instead, each neighbourhood had its own house of worship. The interiors of these mosques – quiet, cool and clean, with their precise ordering of space and geometric channelling of the imagination – exalted religion by counterpointing the random, wanton nature of the street outside. They suggested a realm of perfection, an ordained perfection attainable by correct guidance, by obedience and by common effort. Beyond their walls the rituals of devotion, the formulas of speech and the knowledge that the law of the land derived from the word of God Himself secured a comforting reassurance that, if all was not well in this world, it would be so in the next.

The fact that Islam posits a single, divine source for laws has tended to imbed opposition to change (which is why authorities have often expressed change in terms of a return to a purer, more authentic interpretation of God's will). Yet Islam has adapted to changing times. Tobacco, for example, was scorned by clerics when it arrived in Cairo 300 years ago. The vice soon grew too popular to resist – at least until 1997, when the grand mufti, who is chief religious adviser to the Egyptian judiciary, again ruled smoking sinful, on the grounds that a Muslim should not knowingly harm himself. The ʿulema of sixteenth-century Cairo also declared coffee unlawful. Sufi devotees, however, praised its use for prolonging their seances. Merchants found it so lucrative a commodity that Cairo became the major entrepôt of the international coffee trade. In the face of such pressures, pious opposition dissolved. Similarly, many clerics resisted the abolition of slavery in the 1870s by refusing to marry freed slaves without the written permission of their former masters. Yet by the turn of the century only the very grandest houses still kept their ageing African eunuchs as status symbols.

Schisms have developed in recent years over such diverse issues as contraception, the practice of female circumcision and the propriety of banking interest. In nearly every case, practical considerations have triumphed over rigid tradition. Recognizing the danger of unchecked population growth, al-Azhar sanctioned birth control in the 1940s. In the 1990s the grand mufti reiterated the ruling that fixed interest rates were not equivalent to usury, thereby silencing conservatives who claimed that modern banks infringed Islamic law. As for the cruel custom of female genital mutilation, the mufti declared it was a mere folk tradition without a firm textual basis in Islam.*

* Sadly, the vast majority of Egyptian women still submit to the ancient practice. Religious reactionaries – including His Eminence Sheikh Gadd al-Haqq, rector of al-Azhar until his death in 1996 – continue to support it.

Because God's commands are held to be unassailable, those who profess to interpret His words exercise tremendous power. Governments have always sought to control this power. Dissidents have always contested their claim. But by hook or by crook – by threatening or pampering the religious Establishment – temporal rulers have usually managed to make spiritual leaders toe the line.

Like today's governments, Cairo's medieval sultans mostly achieved their ends through control of appointments to lucrative posts like judgeships and the bursaries of prestigious endowments. Occasionally they resorted to subtler means. For instance, in 1469 a controversy broke out over whether the popular Sufi poet Omar ibn al-Farid (1181–1235) merited veneration as a *wāli.* Most clerics believed he did not. Ibn al-Khaldun himself issued a fatwa condemning the poet's verses as 'monist' and calling for their destruction. The keeper of Ibn al-Farid's rich *waqf,* however, happened to be a friend of Sultan al-Ashraf Qayt-bay. To settle the matter, the sultan wrote to a respected sheikh asking for his opinion. In requesting a fatwa Qayt-bay cast himself as a humble supplicant, but his note was couched in terms that made it bluntly clear what the sultan wanted: 'What do you say about those who claim that our lord and master, the sheikh, the gnostic of God, Omar ibn al-Farid, may God protect him with His mercy, is an infidel?' The veiled threat worked. Two hundred years on, the Turkish traveller Evliya Çelebi could claim that some 200,000 people celebrated Ibn al-Farid's annual *mawlid* at the foot of the Muqattam cliffs.*

Even Napoleon, the first non-Muslim to rule in Egypt after the coming of Islam, tried to make allies of Cairo's clerics. 'O ye ʿulema, sharifs and imams,' read one of his proclamations, 'tell your folk that he who stands against me acts in error, for verily he will find no refuge. Nor will he escape the Hand of God, for

* The *mawlid* of Ibn al-Farid faded out in the 1960s, only to be revived again in the 1980s.

he stands in opposition to the destiny decreed by God, may He be exalted and praised. The man of sense knows that our deeds are His will...'

Napoleon's ploy failed. It was the clerics of al-Azhar who led the Cairo uprisings against him. Yet his instincts were right. Throughout Cairo's history religion had been a channel of communication between rulers and the ruled. It had been the frame for both consent and dissent. The men of the sword in the Citadel knew that to lose favour with the men of the pen down below was to risk inciting the mob.

By the late 1980s Cairo had bulged into a megacity, complete with smog and skyscrapers nudging nearly to the paws of the Sphinx. Public services had come under immense strain. Municipal water pressure had dropped to the point where every building had to install its own pump. A hundred separate neighbourhoods lacked sewage altogether. A million cars clogged the streets. Pundits predicted a crisis, an explosion of popular anger.

But the *rayyis* who was now in charge was a man of good sense. At the fateful reviewing stand where his predecessor was assassinated on 6 October 1981, Hosni Mubarak had ducked out of harm's way when the killers opened fire. The new president was a stolid manager, not a visionary. He made few false promises. He shunned grandiose projects and focused instead on fixing Cairo's shoddy infrastructure. Traffic and sewage soon flowed more efficiently along new conduits and bypasses, as did gossip down the rewired telephone circuits. A tree-planting campaign reversed two decades of urban desertification. Even the riot-provoking problem of bread subsidies was solved: the government played the old candy-bar trick and simply reduced the size of loaves. Massive doses of foreign aid – a reward for Egypt's regional peacemaking – spruced up the city's main arteries. France built a metro line. Japan donated a grand opera house to replace the old one.* China contributed a world-class conference centre. While less than half of Cairene households had running water at the beginning of the 1980s, at the end of the decade three-quarters were linked to water mains. The proportion connected to the official electricity grid rose from one-third to 84 per cent.

Finding their city habitable again – or at any rate in a process of reclaiming itself for the middle class – large numbers of émigrés returned. A new kind of cosmopolitanism began to flourish. International chain stores, high-tech discos, theme restaurants and shopping centres appeared. They catered to growing numbers of tourists and a burgeoning stratum of Egyptians who were accustomed to – and had the money to pay for – slick packaging and the promise of reprieve from Cairo's suffocating gravity. Television aired Hollywood serials and ads for air-conditioning, air fresheners and fresh air in the form of condominiums on the Red Sea and Mediterranean coasts.

Outside the middle class, the picture was different. The unzoned margins of the city buzzed with discontent. As the redistributive function of Nasser-style socialism withered, half a generation of youths found they faced a grim future. The government had promised jobs for all university graduates, but by the mid-1980s its bloated bureaucracy had reached saturation point. It had promised housing, but its badly built, inconveniently sited projects could not keep pace with demand. Despite the fanfare about new cities in the desert, few of the poor could afford to escape Cairo's crowded and rapidly expanding slums.

Even sex was effectively denied many, since Egypt's strict conventions demanded marriage, and marriage required money for dowries and furnishings and apartments. A sociologist estimated the cost of a working-class marriage in the mid-1980s at

* The original Opera House, built for the opening of the Suez Canal, burned down in 1970, just before a scheduled inventory-taking. The multi-storey parking garage erected on its site reflected sadly on the priorities of the 1980s.

25,000 Egyptian pounds – a sum that would take the average worker ten years of piastre-pinching to save. Not surprisingly, the 1986 census showed that more than a quarter of Cairenes of marriageable age remained single. Not only was this a frighteningly high proportion for a deeply traditional society – and one that suggested widespread sexual frustration – the evidence showed the number was rising.

This was a generation that felt it had little to lose. Yet it responded to an unfair and confusing world not by breaking conventions but by clinging to them with ever greater tenacity. It tuned in less to television's commercial fluff than to the prime-time preachers who claimed materialism was a Western disease. Its role models were no longer academics or politicians, but simple people it knew directly – people who had bettered themselves by making money in the Gulf, then returned home with fancy cars and wristwatches and veiled wives. At Cairo Airport you could sense the moral impact of such arrivals. You could sense the respect felt by those who went out to greet planes coming in from Jedda and Riyadh, their admiration for the fact that the émigrés had made it in the modern world without compromising their traditional outlook. Rather, they had held on to it, even reinforced it with the ultra-conservative values they had found in Saudi Arabia – a country whose possession of the world's largest oil reserves did, after all, provide striking evidence of God's favour.

This was a generation that felt betrayed by the slogans of the past – by shrill nationalism and half-baked socialism and hollow democracy. Looking for a source of hope, Cairo's disappointed, left-behind youth found a simple message plastered now on walls all over the city. The message said, 'Islam is the Solution.'

ʿAYN SHAMS, CLOSE by the lone remaining obelisk of ancient On, was one of Cairo's raw new districts ten years ago, a place where street patterns frayed and knotted away from the few paved roads. Its people were mainly country immigrants or newly-weds who could not afford to live closer to the city centre than this hour-long bus commute. Yet on the broad scale of Cairene poverty ʿAyn Shams ranked as fairly prosperous. Telephone wires, a few painted signs for doctors and lawyers and the odd parked car cosied in a pyjama-striped dust jacket suggested a tenuous upward mobility. The meat hanging in butcher shops looked fresh.

When I went to ʿAyn Shams in the spring of 1989 to report on a rumpus that had cost a few injuries and arrests, locals told us that, yes, the police had come the day before. They directed us to a corner mosque where militant youths – nice, clean-minded boys, the butcher said – had been smoked out with tear gas. The youths had been holding a sit-in prayer meeting here, and had refused to budge when police megaphones told them they were surrounded. (The story in *Al-Ahram* was different of course. The state-controlled newspaper said that the police had busted a gang of armed extremists who had been terrorizing the neighbourhood.)

The mosque was a half-finished structure of unsurfaced brick. Only the outsized loudspeaker and hand-painted sign tacked to one façade distinguished it from neighbouring houses. According to the sign, the building's upper storeys were intended to house a charity clinic. Such 'Islamic' institutions were sprouting all over the city in a rebuke to the inadequacy of the state. Paid for by public donations, they promised a kind of respectability to areas like ʿAyn Shams. They provided venues for occasions like funerals and weddings; outlets for charity food distribution on Muslim feast days; space for classes in sewing or needlework or adult education. The cut-price clinic here would not only serve the local poor, it would give jobs to medical graduates who could not afford to open their own offices.

A cop lounged in a cane chair outside the padlocked front door of the mosque. An empty tea glass sat in the dust next to the butt of his rifle. He claimed to know nothing of any disturbance, and in fact in this quiet little alley it was hard to imagine the pop of Central Security's tear-gas grenades. The cop watched warily as we chatted with passers-by. Some said the police had hauled off dozens of people. Others declined to talk at all. One lady rushed up to us, brandishing a shopping bag. 'Where is my son?' she shouted. 'Where have they taken my son?'

Discouraged, we headed back to the main street. We had just turned the corner when a small boy touched my arm.

'Are you the foreign journalists?' he whispered.

I nodded.

'Come back at eight o'clock. Wait outside the butcher's shop.'

What for?

'To meet the Doctor.'

The boy was there at eight. He said nothing, just motioned us to follow. Soon we were skulking through narrow shafts between houses, with the alleys that slanted off on either side emitting wafts of frying onion and leaky plumbing smells. There were no street lights, but the fluorescence from occasional open windows kept the boy in view. After several turnings he vanished into a dark cul-de-sac.

When we had gathered together in the blackness and waited a minute, a new guide appeared. He was a tall youth, and his short white robe and skullcap were easy to follow as he led us deeper into the district. At length he stopped, glanced up and down the empty street, and slipped into a dimly lit stairwell. Then, having knocked a complicated knock on a door, he turned. A grin spread across his bushy first-growth beard. His eyes – the wide, glossy eyes of a Byzantine saint – sparkled with sudden complicity. This caricature of a fundamentalist, I realized, was having just as much fun as we were – so much more diverting than killing time in cafés, this playing cops and robbers in the backstreets of Cairo, dressing up in snow-white costume and hobnobbing with the devils of the Foreign Press.

The door cracked, then opened. Quickly, we were inside a tiny salon and our guide was introducing us to the Doctor. We shook hands with a stout, clean-shaven young man in civilian trousers – a necessary disguise, I guessed, since beards and *galabiyyas* provoked police suspicion. He looked anxious behind his heavy glasses, but he and his friends – more bearded youths crowded the doorway to check out their catch – had the good manners that come naturally to Cairenes. The Foreign Press was plumped on to a gilt couch and plied with soft drinks. It was begged to forgive its hosts for their precautions.

The interview began. The Doctor spoke earnestly, using formal, classical Arabic so as to give resonance to his words – and maybe to show that he had earned his PhD (in veterinary medicine, as it happened, which fitted what sociologists describe as the 'profile' of the new breed of Islamic radical: boys of poor background with a degree in sciences that had failed to translate into upward mobility). He told us his name was Dr Ala' Muhieddin, and explained that he was the spokesman of the Islamic League. The League, he said, was a society of youths seeking to return Egypt to the straight path of Islam. What did they do? They held meetings in mosques to discuss ways to help each other and spread their message. The brother who had led us here, for instance, had wanted to get married. He, the Doctor, had found him a wife, the sister of another brother.

It all sounded harmless. So why were the police after them?

Ah, said the Doctor with a smile. We are living in an age of ignorance. This government and its servants are unwitting allies of the enemies of Islam. They are continuing the plot launched by Imperialism, a plot to uproot faith from the hearts of Muslims. They, like you – his eyes now drilled the Foreign Press – are afraid of us, because we speak the truth. They do not want the people to hear our message. That is why yesterday they came and broke the door of our mosque; why they beat and arrested some of the brothers and sisters, and shot poison gases into the House of God.

But we have other mosques, he continued, hunching forward on his chair. And if the government prevents us from doing our duty by our words, we will use our hands.

SIX MONTHS LATER, on 11 September 1989, an unmarked Peugeot crept along a crowded market street in Giza, on the other side of the city. Two men got out, stepped up behind Dr Ala' Muhieddin, and shot him in the head. After this the Foreign Press began to receive faxed messages from the Islamic League. Since the government rejected dialogue, the messages said, the League would take revenge. It was then that the game of cops and robbers turned nasty.

The next few years were tough on Cairo. Unused to real tabloid gore, the city had suddenly to cope with crime pages splattered with bombings and shoot-outs. A layer of civility seemed to peel away. There had always been a lot of armed security people on the streets, but they and their guns had always looked wilted and untended. Now bayonets gleamed; bootlaces were tied. Plain-clothes men in leather jackets peered into car windows at random checkpoints. As the amplified pitch of some mosque sermons reached hysteria, friends unlucky enough to live next to police stations reported nail-on-slate screams late in the night. The battle between the state and its fundamentalist challengers degenerated into a slugfest, a vendetta just like the bloody family feuds of the Upper Egyptian hinterlands (which was in fact where many of the principals – both hard-headed cops and hot-headed robbers – hailed from.)

Both sides came off badly. The state damaged its legitimacy by twisting laws and limbs to break its opponents. The Islamists betrayed their own ideals by asserting a monopoly on religion – a monopoly that absolved them of guilt from murder or theft or intimidation. But the real victims were innocents: bystanders caught in the crossfire of police raids; tourists attacked for the sole purpose of embarrassing the state; even schoolchildren maimed in a botched bombing of the prime minister's motorcade.

Still, Cairo never quite succumbed to the seriousness of it all. It helped that the casualty toll remained a fraction of any American city's annual slaughter. The violence seemed so alien that many clutched eagerly at conspiracy theories. When hit men ambushed the Speaker of Parliament – machine-gunning him in front of the new Semiramis Hotel's dining room, no less – and sped clean away on motorcycles, the denizens of many a downtown bar showed relief. These terrorists *must* have been foreigners, the common wisdom went: no Egyptian could have been so ruthlessly efficient. Speculation mounted as to whether the killers had been Israelis or Iranians, or perhaps even the mighty CIA. Slowly it dawned, though, that the sure-footed assassins had got the wrong man. The one they wanted was the minister of the interior, a hard-nosed heavy whose motorcade routinely passed the Semiramis Hotel. Instead they got a lightweight, an unctuous politician who was quite expendable to the regime. So at last the bar props conceded that Cairo did indeed have home-grown terrorists. True cynics drank toasts to the assassins for recapturing Egypt's lost martial pride.

Then there was the loony sheikh who could be seen every morning marching heedlessly through traffic near the fortress-like American Embassy, muttering about the end of the world and the triumph of Islam. He jabbed at the sky with a finger, coiled around which was a green string – green being the colour of Islam. Tied to the other end of the string, dragging in the dust, was a laminated Stars and Stripes. Commuters loved this distraction; I saw one taxi driver hand the holy man a flower.

More often, though, it was the killjoy fanaticism of some fundamentalists that provoked laughs, and this ridicule probably damaged their cause more than police muscle. One preacher declared that courgettes should be outlawed because of their suggestive shape. Another fatwa from an Islamist gang appeared in the papers: 'The Cairo Tower is against religion and Islamic *shariʿa* law. It must be destroyed as its shape and construction amid greenery could excite Egyptian women.' (But after the outspoken secularist Farag Foda made fun of such nonsense in a debate at the Cairo Book Fair, he was assassinated.)

Yet somehow scorn did not translate into popular opposition. Many Cairenes sympathized with the goals if not the means of the radicals. Their pious anger struck a chord – particularly as it contrasted with a common perception of the ruling class as effete, Westernized and corrupt. There was, for instance, the joke about the fundamentalist who had been released on parole. In his first week the undercover cop tailing him declared progress: he had seen the suspect light up a cigarette. The next week was even more encouraging: the man had walked into a bar and ordered a drink. In the third week the agent filed a glowing report. 'I recommend that the suspect be enlisted to work for us,' he reported. 'He has taken up visiting a brothel.'

A wave of religious conservatism washed over the city. Self-declared Islamists took over student and professional unions. The crowds of faithful at Friday prayers outgrew mosques and spread on to sidewalks and streets. In my own building the tea boy in a lawyer's office took to chanting the noon call to prayer down the stairwell. As often as not now, phone callers would challenge their respondents with an almost theatrically Islamic '*Al-salāmu ʿAlaykum*' – 'Peace be upon you' – rather than the simple old '*Allo?*' More menacingly, many Muslims no longer responded if you addressed them with a straightforward 'Good Morning': the old greeting was now widely taken as being reserved for Christians. When a second passenger got into a taxi I had hired – the practice of picking up as many fares as possible being perfectly usual in those days – he bid the driver '*Salāmu ʿalaykum*', then turned to me and said, 'Good morning.' There was something profoundly disturbing in this casual drawing of distinctions between people – between a driver assumed to be a fellow Muslim and a passenger assumed to be a mere infidel.

Islamic decorative motifs came back into fashion. Banks that claimed to charge no interest, beach resorts and hairdressers with segregated facilities, and even a limestone quarry jumped on the bandwagon and advertised themselves as being somehow 'Islamic'. Not even Cairo's new metro was immune. To ensure propriety, it set aside the first car of its trains for women. Very nice and proper; but ladies who strayed into the other cars now felt exposed. All this show brought to mind how Edward Lane had concluded his remarks on Cairene religiosity 170 years before: that, while the people of the city held piety to be the greatest virtue, the desire to appear religious led many to 'hypocrisy and pharisaical ostentation'.

Discrimination against Copts, a mild but ever-present phenomenon, increased in severity. A sociologist reported that children in one Cairo slum were playing not cowboys and indians, but Copts and Muslims. Taking the roll-call at a university exam, a professor laughed when a student gave him the extravagantly Christian name of Boutros Bataris – Peter Peters. 'Just one Boutros is quite enough to get you failed,' he quipped. It was a good joke, but only because everyone knew it was close to the truth.

Liberal-minded Copts like my architect friend Iskandar (whose experience decorating desert army bases now served him well as a landscaper of gardens for the rich) complained not so much of persecution, but of the sickly conservatism that had taken over their own Church. Talk of miracles increased. A Coptic cab driver told me St George had saved his wife from cancer. A distinguished economist embarrassed friends by insisting that a wad of cotton wool he had preserved in a bottle of oil contained an image of the Virgin Mary. Bumper stickers saying 'Jesus Saves!' and pictures of the lushly bearded Pope Shenouda III proliferated in competition with Islamic auto decor. Reform-minded Copts pleaded vainly for greater democracy within the Church and a repeal of its almost total ban on divorce.

Ominous tales ruffled the city in those years. They seemed to erupt from the deepest recesses of its medieval unconscious. There was, for instance, a widely believed story that Coptic Christians were waging a secret campaign to spray crosses on to the clothing of unsuspecting Muslims. Why this should be, no one seemed troubled to ask. *Al-Ahram* published a letter from an outraged reader warning that packages of New Zealand lamb, specially imported for Ramadan and guaranteed as slaughtered according to Islamic rites, were stamped 'Christchurch'. It was said that the soles of Chinese running shoes in one Cairo market were imprinted with the sacred words 'There is no God but Allah'. Headlines in the gutter press screamed that Israel had dispatched AIDS-infected prostitutes to seduce innocent Egyptian youth.

It was not enough for the government to deny the stories. When have the people of Cairo ever had reason to believe their rulers? Concrete measures were needed. So armed police were stationed outside churches to guard them. They sealed off streets in the north-Cairo district of Shubra, where yet another sighting of the Virgin Mary had magnetized a nightly crowd of miracle-seekers. Drivers were ordered to remove stickers from their cars, so as to cool the sudden spurt in communal rivalry that had turned Cairo's motor fleet into a parade of religious imagery. Al-Azhar University, the voice of Muslim orthodoxy, passed a fatwa banning loose-leaf desk calendars decorated with Koranic verses, lest their discarded pages be profaned. A hospital guard shot dead an AIDS patient who tried to sneak out of his ward.

For bar-goers the most immediate menace was the Muslim radicals' intolerance of alcohol. There were whispers that terrorists planned to slip poison into the vats at the Stella Beer brewery in Giza. For a time Cairene drinkers even worried that the government would ban liquor as a sop to Islamist opinion.

The anxiety was not unfounded. The regime seemed more concerned with survival than with any defence of secular freedoms. It was clearly prepared to go with the conservative flow, and in the process to sacrifice the occasional writer or film director or university professor, to allow their works to be banned in the name of defending the faith. What the state hoped for was to capture the middle ground by appealing to a milder, more tolerant, Islam. Official visits to mosques were televised, and moderate preachers were given prime time slots even as the security offensive pushed militants to ever wilder radicalism.

But as the years went by police succeeded in flushing radical gangs out of Cairo's slums (including one which had come to be known as the Islamic Republic of Imbaba). Slowly but surely the Ministry of Religious Affairs took control of the thousands of private mosques that had mushroomed throughout the city. Fears began to calm.

The tide of violence had receded from the capital by the mid-1990s (although not from the remoter parts of Upper Egypt). It left behind a residue of bitterness, and some clear marks of change. Religion had reclaimed the absolute centrality to Egyptian identity that had been challenged for a hundred years. Secularists hunkered down, hoping their version of sense would, some time in the future, cease to be taboo. Booze and bawdiness no longer featured at wedding feasts in the popular quarters, as they always had. Most of Egypt's provinces went dry. Cairo's bars, however, stayed open.

I ONCE RENTED A room on one of the lesser Greek islands. It belonged to a widow. Although born and raised in Cairo, Madame Eleni had left in the 1960s after the Egyptian colonels had nationalized her husband's vinegar factory in Shubra. She was sad, mostly. Portraits of her husband loomed waxily above the heavy sideboard in her front room. But speak of Cairo, the Cairo of her youth, and she smiled.

'Ah, Cairo!' The long syllable would roll out like a sigh. 'The womens of Cairo is so much helegant. She is the most beautiful womens of the world. Always the clothis, the hats, the glovis she is from Paris.'

Then she would push away her coffee cup and ask, 'The womens, what she is wearing in Cairo now?'

In the Cairo Madame Eleni left behind, quite ordinary shoppers strolled Qasr al Nil Street in bright sleeveless frocks. Rich girls in Heliopolis flicked through *Paris-Match* and wondered if they could get away with this year's even shorter hemlines. Their mothers applied lipstick and clasped pearl chokers over plunging necklines for nights at the opera or the packed monthly concerts of Umm Kulsoum, Nightingale of the Nile, Planet of the East, who strutted the Cairo stage laden with ten-kiloton diamond earrings until her retirement in 1973.

But now, in the 1990s, Madame Eleni would be shocked. The dominant style is retro seventh century. The arbiters of fashion are stern sheikhs for whom the models of feminine virtue are the numerous purdahed wives of the Prophet. TV reruns of romances churned out by Cairo's studios during the 1940s and '50s, or panning shots of the audiences at Umm Kulsoum's concerts, reveal a lost age of daring: 'Shame on you,' tuts a masked lady in a sari to a line of long-legged chorus girls in one 1949 musical hit – and then she drops her disguise to reveal the leggiest legs and skimpiest two-piece of them all.

The Cairo gossip mags of today – like *al-Nugūm* and *Al-Kawākib* ('The Stars' and 'The Planets') – report that half the galaxy of old-time starlets have got religion now, repented their sins and journeyed to Mecca in atonement. Shams al-Barudi, who featured as a prostitute in the most sexually explicit Egyptian film ever made (*The Maltese Bathhouse,* released in 1973), has publicly renounced her past and donned the veil. According to persuasion, the short skirts and decolletés in old movies now provoke either nostalgia or an outrage akin to what the ancient Hebrews felt for the fleshpots of Egypt.

What would Madame Eleni make of today's Qasr al-Nil Street, where the plaster mannequins sometimes show not even their blue dolls' eyes? What they display is not so much fashion as Koranic exegesis. There is full defensive cladding for the seriously pious: dark, tent-like garments tipped with Minnie Mouse gloves so that not the tiniest speck of corrupting flesh is revealed. Glasses are worn over the translucent veil when necessary, and this admission of weak eyesight becomes the sole hint of the black ghost's intimate characteristics. Milder zealots can choose bonnets and turbans and jelly-mould caps in a rainbow of hues, and half-veils that expose the eyes. More common is the mid-length wimple that pins, nun-like, tight around the face and covers the hair and the arms to the wrist. Then there is the simple headscarf, worn in combination with anything you like from tracksuits to school uniforms to violet organza ballgowns.

Most of this headgear is in nylon or polyester, which makes fortunes in the Cairo summer for sellers of heat-rash powders. But ask an armoured damsel if she is hot and you get this spitting riposte: 'It's cooler than the fires of hell!'

There are those that still boldly, and often with elegant aplomb, defy the inferno. Many such ladies can be recognized as Copts by the tell-tale crucifixes they wear. Some are as Muslim as anyone, but despair of the clerics ever fixing on precise sartorial standards.* Others don't care if they do. But increasingly such

*While the ʿulema concur that Islam requires modesty of dress, the question of degree remains open to interpretation. Reformers say the Koranic verses in this regard refer only to the Prophet's own wives, and insist, moreover, that the seventh-century terminology of female coverings cannot be presumed to have twentieth-century

people feel like daredevils. On the streets, those who don't make a gesture to modesty risk stares and allusive comment. They challenge the power of conformity – a power that is peculiarly intense in an overwhelmingly poor society.

In the cramped confines of the neighbourhoods where the vast majority of Cairenes live and struggle for self-esteem, it is a given that what you may lack on the material scale can be made up for on the moral register. For many, the cheap veil solves a closetful of problems. As a public declaration of modesty it appeals to prospective mothers-in-law – arguably the most powerful force in Cairene society.* With privacy at a premium, the veil provides a private space of sorts. It is even a liberator, in that in-your-face piety lets women venture where they might not feel comfortable otherwise, such as onto public transport and into jobs and politics. Indeed, apologists for the veil claim that by neutralizing femininity it neatly abrogates the whole question of gender. And it is true that only with the reintroduction of the veil have a brave few Cairene women taken to the streets as taxi drivers – who are, by the way, just as aggressive and fare-gouging as their toughest male competitors.

The extraordinary range of female attire is a mirror to Cairo's complexity. It reflects a compartmented society, a society where one person's divine duty may be another's perverse masochism. The fact is that for a century Cairenes have felt torn between Paris and Mecca. They have tried on many costumes, struggling to feel comfortable, seeking a middle way but seeing, in their images, extremes as saints or sinners.

---

equivalents. Some Islamists suggest that men, too, should be forced to dress with prescribed modesty.

*According to a 1995 survey, 72 per cent of marriages in Cairo were arranged by families; 40 per cent of married women had never been alone with their husbands before their wedding day; 12 per cent were married to maternal cousins.

ISLAM IS AMBIVALENT about many habits, including drink. Its clerics curse the vice in varying degrees, and have done so ever since the Prophet commanded that a drunkard who was brought before him should be pummelled with shoes and sticks. But alcohol – the very word is Arabic in origin – has always been the muse of Muslim poets.

In Cairo, drink is spiked with a tincture of sin. Local bars have the feel of speakeasies. Late every night beer-bellied shopkeepers, two-bit lawyers, pamphleteering intellectuals and petty gangsters pack downtown dives like the Cap d'Or and the Tout Va Bien. Hawkers ply the zinc-topped tables through smoke pungent with guffaws and beer-spill. By closing time Cleopatra butts and lupin shells muffle the floor tiles.

At the Anglo-Egyptian on Sharif Street the one-eyed barman used to offer a range of sticky local potions, among them Tony Toker Red Label, Chiras Renal and Goldon's London Dry Din (the latter in a recycled Gordon's Gin bottle, with a tame-looking German Shepherd replacing the boar's head on the authentic label). But these outrageous etiquettes were not the Anglo's greatest attraction. Its draw was that Sabri and Shawqi, two jaded old souses with wicked tongues, held court there. This was their club. Anyone who could entertain them was welcome, and, as the gut-rot brandy-and-soda lost its bubble in the late hours, anyone who could stomach their rheumy reminiscing was welcome too.

Sabri was paunchy, rumpled and unshaven. Shawqi was tall, stooped and never failed to wear neckties that gave an impression of neatness but could have been profitably distilled into Dry Din. Both were classic public-sector types – bright boys from poor families raised to position, self-respect and a progressive outlook by Nasser's socialism. They had sailed the optimism of the 1950s and '60s, then crashed into despair with Egypt's shattering defeat in the 1967 war. Like countless other public servants, they had seen their prestige dwindle ever since, and then plummet when Sadat replaced the old hierarchy of power with a new hierarchy of money – a commodity which both men were far too honest and decent to acquire by the usual bureaucratic means. Now they were balding, pickled in self-pity and shellacked with cynicism.

By day – which meant the couple of hours he spent at his office – Shawqi was the boss of the neon-signs department at a state-owned advertising agency. (To him Tahrir Square owed such glaring delights as Vitrac jam's multicoloured fruit display, Milkyland's blinking cow and Coca-Cola's endlessly pouring and fizzing red neon soda.) By night Shawqi was a dreamy raconteur. He subsisted on a diet of bar food: turnips soaked in brine, lettuce, peanuts and lupins. At one o'clock every morning he tottered home to the flat he shared with his mother – except during Ramadan. Into this month of fasting Shawqi crammed an honest year's worth of devotions: during the last week he even camped in religious retreat at his neighbourhood mosque. The effort was heroic, but on the other hand – as Sabri would gleefully observe – the Anglo closed for the duration of Ramadan anyway.

Sabri made a living as an editor at *Youth and Sports* magazine, an organ of the Ministry of Information's Radio and TV Union. He was better known – though not well known – as a poet. Some nights Sabri would bring a transistor radio to the Anglo. At ten o'clock he would command silence for the poetry programme. As the intro of classical lute music faded and the voice of Farid Reesha oozed on to the air – the mellifluous Reesha having oiled his way to fame by composing saccharine odes to Motherhood and Fatherland – Sabri would open his commentary with a profane broadside. 'Son of a whore,' he would hiss, and for the next half-hour he would punctuate every one of Reesha's pregnant pauses, every tremolo swoon and heaving emphasis, with enough vitriol to vaporize the radio.

Sabri's virtuoso tongue-lashings revealed generations of unnatural habits among the Reeshas. But for all his contempt Sabri was, like most of Cairo's disgruntled intellectuals, beholden to the same state control of teaching and publishing and broadcasting that had made Reesha's moist eyes and diction synonymous, to the mind of bourgeois Cairo, with poetry. The sad fact was that Sabri suffered a nagging fear that his own work – much influenced, he said, by Shakespeare's sonnets – got published only because he himself was part of the publishing bureaucracy.

While they agreed that the present was the worst of times, Sabri and Shawqi held opposite opinions on most subjects. The golden age, Sabri believed, had been the rule of President Gamal Abd al-Nasser, when Egypt closed itself to the outside world and searched for its soul. For Shawqi it was the presidency of Anwar al-Sadat, when the country reopened its doors.

Shawqi was something of an Anglophile. He fondly remembered playing soccer as a barefoot boy with British soldiers in front of their barracks by the Egyptian Museum. Whisky, he always used to say, was the queen of drinks. It was what made the British Empire great, he would say. He would glare at me for a while, as if the exorbitant price of decent Scotch was my fault, then add, 'You know how Winston Churchill beat the Germans? He drank one bottle of whisky every night!'

It was this repeated assertion of Shawqi's that made another version particularly pungent when I heard it some time later.

Near the ruins of Fustat, in a district where cemeteries merge with tanneries and slaughterhouses, a joyous crowd gathers on Saturday nights by the shrine of the Prophet Muhammad's great-grandson Zayn al-ʿAbdin. In no time at all they transform the dirt-floored courtyard outside the tomb into an open-air dance hall. The songs that set them into swaying motion are Sufi odes – love songs in remembrance of God and his Prophet. A beaming sheikh, seated on a stage above the fray, belts the words into a microphone, backed up by the beat of a tabla and the whine of reed flutes and two-stringed fiddles. The dance is open to all comers, so long as the mood catches them. Each defines their own step, their own arc of swinging or twirling. A wide-eyed peasant youth thrashes his torso back and forth, miraculously never colliding with the ageing spinster who wheels like a top through the throng. A policeman in white summer uniform hops up and down in a trance, his boots unlaced, grunting to the rhythm. All around, boys and old men and barefoot girls shuffle and twist.

Last time I was there, the modest café to one side of the impromptu show was doing a raging trade. Revellers who fell out of the dance in exhaustion would revive themselves here with a hot, sweet infusion of ginger or cinnamon, then bound back into the mêlée for an encore. I was sitting with friends as temporary guests of a gang of boisterous neighbourhood toughs. They barraged us with questions, and in good-natured mischief encouraged us to join in the dance. Had we not heard about Tahra, the American lady who danced here every week? She was highly spiritual, they nodded. Her name itself meant Purity. Perhaps, if we waited, we would have a chance to see her.

And indeed after some time a pale face bobbed its way in our direction. It could only be Tahra the Pure. She wore a filmy green shawl over a long black robe. She had Birkenstock sandals, bangles on her arms, and a Mexican-Bedouin headdress of beads and coins.

'Hi, guys,' she called out, and collapsed into the chair next to mine. Her mascara was leaking.

'Oh Christ,' she said, clapping a hand to her beaded forehead. 'I've got *such* a hangover.'

Her name was actually Tara, and she was from Marin County, California.

'Isn't this great?'

With that she leaped up and hurled herself into the dance.

A short distance away, amid the dark courts and cenotaphs behind Zayn al-ʿAbdin's tomb, we found a large tent of canvas draped over a tall wooden frame. A gas lamp lit the interior, the rush matted floor of which was filled with cross-legged fellahin.

One of them rose and beckoned us in. His eyes bulged as if he had seen an afreet.

The Sufi disciples silently made way, shifting their weathered feet and sinewy calves, directing us to a red curtain at the back of the tent. It parted, and we were ushered through wafts of frankincense into a smaller space where a dozen black-cowled women sat in a circle around their sheikh. His beard was dyed with henna; his Rasputin eyes were rimmed with kohl. He motioned us graciously to sit on his right, and continued his labours.

The sheikh held a small square of paper in the palm of one hand. He closed his eyes and muttered a while, then scribbled letters and forms on the paper. He folded it carefully into a tight triangle, kissed it, touched it to his forehead and passed it to the woman nearest him. The spell disappeared into her bosom, and like a conjuror's trick re-emerged as a five-pound note. The sheikh's client pressed this into his hand. He in turn passed it to a little blind boy I hadn't noticed who sat just behind him.

Tea appeared as the sheikh turned to us. He questioned gently. What was our religion? From which land had we come? Then he spoke for us, and everyone listened.

'There was a great fighter before you were born, and he was the *rayyis* of the *Inglīz*. This man was not a believer, but he was a wise man and a strong man. The *Inglīz* in his times were fighting a war with the *Almān*, whose *rayyis* was Hitler. It was a very long war, which cost many lives. It was such a big war that they called it the World War. The *rayyis* of the *Inglīz* – his name was Winston Churchill – won the big war. And after he won he wrote a book. And in this book, he told of his secret power. And his secret power was this: every night before sleeping, Churchill would read one chapter from the Koran!'

It is not the Cairene way to challenge such beliefs, even if you know them to be untrue. And so I let it pass.

CHAPTER TEN

HIGH LIFE, LOW LIFE

Delhi is a great place – most bazaar storytellers in India make their villain hail from there; but when the agony and intrigue are piled highest and the tale halts till the very last breathless sprinkle of cowries has ceased to fall on his mat, why then, with wagging head and hooked forefinger, the storyteller goes on: 'But there was a man from Cairo, an Egyptian of the Egyptians, who' – and all the crowd knows that a bit of real metropolitan devilry is coming.

Rudyard Kipling, *Letters of Travel,* 1908

ONLY ONE CAIRO institution is more common than the mosque: the *qahwa* or coffee house. Statistics are less accurate now than when Napoleon's army counted 1,350 coffee houses in the City of a Thousand Minarets, but the ratio of 200 citizens per café has not declined much. By this reckoning the cafés of modern Cairo must number well over 30,000 – surely no exaggeration if you take into account the range in scale and grandeur of the city's *qahwas,* from cavernous rooms and terraced casinos by the river to makeshift teastalls in the City of the Dead, and if you consider that most men will spend some time in one every day, and probably have to look no further than the nearest street corner to find it.* These all-male preserves are Cairo's main resorts of business and pleasure. They combine what in Western cities would be the functions of park benches, news-stands, shoeshine parlours, local bars, Masonic lodges and company cafeterias.

As befits a great market city, a place of highly specialized trades, every Cairene *qahwa* fills a particular niche. At the Deaf and Dumb Café off Tawfiqiyya Square silence reigns, because this is where the city's hearing-impaired meet to trade jokes in rapid-fire sign language. When movie producers need stuntmen and beefy extras – what the French call *comparses* – they head straight for the rowdy Qahwat al-Kumbars on Alfi Street. The numerous sidewalk cafés of Muhammad Ali Street serve as agencies for nightclub musicians and belly dancers. The Zahrat al-Bustan Café thinks itself highly intellectual, while Qahwat al-Shisha in Bab al-Luq attracts connoisseurs of the water pipe. Others offer the finest of hot infusions and cold drinks: hibiscus, ginger, fenugreek and cinnamon teas in winter; tamarind, almond and lemon juices in summer.

The peculiarity of the Café of the Sick is harder to discern. Its tall, low-silled windows overlook a narrow, village-scale street near the ʿAyn Shams University Faculty of Medicine. A few customers sit alone indoors at its dozen rickety tables, caressing their water pipes to a rhythmic purr. But most prefer company to solitude. They huddle in groups to talk politics, clatter dice across boards, or slap down cards in mock-aggression. The single waiter bustles like a bumblebee, joking and hollering orders to the back of the room, where the tea boy rinses glasses, stokes charcoal for water pipes and, when free, stares at a TV set perched high in the corner.

It is the picture of a typical Cairo café. Yet something is

* The 1996 census shows about 15,000 cafés in Greater Cairo – but it counts only those which pay taxes.

wrong. Definitely wrong. To start with, important pieces are missing: here a customer's limb, there an ear or an eye. Then, odd additions have accumulated, too. Protuberances bulge under robes. A turban becomes, on closer inspection, a disturbingly bulbous bandage.

The mood is relaxed in the Café of the Sick, but there is an alertness to the way chairs are angled, to the way eyes sweep the doorway. These are professional, appraising glances. If the newcomer happens to be an unknown sick person, or one whose ailment duplicates a regular's, the looks will tell him this turf is claimed. When the man in the doorway wears a white coat, though, all heads swivel and the card games stop, just as if the intruder packed silver spurs and a six-shooter.

'Good morning, Doctor,' shouts a man wheeling forward on a hand cycle. 'God preserve you.'

'Any service, Doctor?' chimes a one-eyed domino player.

The white-coated man is not a doctor. He is a lowly orderly from the nearby university hospital. No matter. He ignores the flattery, pulls a scrap of paper from his pocket, and reads in a commanding voice.

'One goitre. One chronic bilharzia. Two dermoid cysts. One right-sided heart failure.'

He stops, scans the room and addresses the hand-cyclist, who appears to have some kind of authority here.

'Where's Omar the Liver?'

'He's at Dr Hassaballah's lesson, *ya bey*. But he'll be free at four o'clock.'

'Good. Send him round then.'

Meanwhile several of the customers have left their chairs. With the amiable weariness of men going to work, they follow the orderly down the street and into an apartment building. There, in some small room rented by a doctor for this purpose, students will examine and question the patients.

The university up the road is ostensibly free, but it is so

crowded and ill-equipped that aspiring medics gladly pay handsome fees for such hands-on practice. Their professor pays his 'patients' in turn, and this is how the mildly but chronically damaged of the Café of the Sick make their daily bread. It is not a bad living, either, especially for those stars who boast multiple afflictions. (A friend relates that, during examination of a cyst on one old pro's knee, a student enquired about a peculiar lump on his temple. 'Sorry,' said the patient unflappably. 'That's off duty today.') Other lucky souls are present with rare and classic symptoms. Such is the case with Omar the Liver. His perfectly enlarged hepatic organ, waxy pallor and emaciation make him so ideal a case of advanced bilharzia that instructors find him indispensable. Since the disease is endemic to the Egyptian countryside, his services are in constant demand.

The professionally sick have the pride of professionals. They often learn their specialties better than the students. Even those who cannot read or write their own language can reel off chapterfuls of technical terms in English (which remains, controversially, the language of medical instruction in Egypt). This skill proves its worth at clinical-exam time, when students must diagnose diseases according to the symptoms they find. Unfortunates who fail to slip their test cases a five-pound note bomb the exams. Sound tipping, however, guarantees faultless diagnosis.

'Ask me if I drink a lot of liquids,' the patient might whisper while the proctors are not looking. 'Its typical of *diabetes insipidus*.'

'*Dry cough* not *productive cough*,' hints the victim of right-sided heart failure. 'And don't forget my *dyspnoea* or *hepatomegaly*.'

ON THE SURFACE Cairo's ways of coping seem hopelessly tangled and sclerotic. They can be maddening. They can even be cruel to those not armed with money or influence or a sense of humour. By and large, though, the city's mechanisms work. They employ the unemployable. They feed the hungry: many in Cairo are malnourished, but no one starves. Many are badly housed, but fewer are homeless than in most great Western capitals. Helped by the warm climate, by the handiness of washrooms in mosques and by the Muslim stigma against alcohol, Cairo's indigent rarely present as sad a spectacle.

In richer cities formal structures, rules and regulations channel a smooth flow of things. In Cairo informal structures predominate. It is these that fill the yawning gap between claims and facts; between, for instance, the nominal promise of free education right through medical school and the fact that without costly private lessons there is no hope of passing exams; or between the rule that drivers must pass a test before getting a licence and the reality that a modest bribe will do instead. In this gap there is enormous room for diddling, for finesse – in short, for enterprise. And foolish people who try to do things by the book, or imagine they can streamline the system, do so at their peril.

Garbage provides an instructive example. Visitors often wonder why Cairo is so dirty. Some say the length of Egypt's history has so wearied its people that they don't see the point in removing detritus when it will only reappear. Others say the experience of the Nile flood, which conveniently used to flush the country clean once a year, remains deeply ingrained – despite the fact that the High Dam, completed in 1971, stopped it a generation ago. For whatever reason, public cleanliness has not improved much since the citizens of Memphis discarded papyri and broken pots in their streets. (The pharaohs themselves were blasé about trash: excavations at Tel al-Amarna, an Eighteenth Dynasty capital 200 miles upstream from Cairo, show that royal cooks dumped their dross right on the doorstep of the palace kitchens.)

Despite recent government efforts – like a poster campaign preaching that 'Cleanliness is a Part of Faith' – the Egyptian capital remains gloriously grubby. Its trash-collection system is a scandal – if, that is, getting the stuff out of sight and mind is assumed to be its goal. Change the objective, however, and it becomes a model of efficiency. Cairo's waste-disposal industry converts most garbage into usable goods, while employing more people productively than that of any other major city.

Most of this is achieved without fanfare by a highly organized network of private collectors who trundle about in donkey carts and haul their loads back to the ragpickers' colonies ringing the city. The *zabbālīn*, as these people are called, may leave behind a lot.* Their children may spend more time sorting rubbish than at school. The *zabbālīn* may live surrounded by trash and be shunned because they smell bad, but they have self-respect and job security for generation on generation. They even earn a decent income. And they form a vital link in the city's economy, supplying thousands of little workshops with recycled raw materials for everything from plastic flip-flops to car parts to television antennae. Discarded clothes turn into multicoloured rag rugs. Biodegradable stuff feeds flocks of chickens and ducks and herds of goats and sheep. Even pigs grow fat on Cairo's waste – since most of this industry happens to be run by Coptic Christians – and produce very tasty pork indeed.

There was a moment when some minister decided that the *zabbālīn* were an eyesore. He persuaded the American government to fund a project that would put them out of business. Uncle Sam flew in teams of high-paid experts who devised a new system. Large bins were to be placed on street corners. Giant Mack trucks would patrol. Their pneumatic arms would snatch up the bins and shake their contents into the trucks, which would then drive the waste into the desert and out of sight. This was the civilized way of doing things.

Cairo trashed the plan in no time flat. To begin with, its

* Ten per cent of garbage never gets removed at all, according to a 1994 study. The *zabbālīn* dispose of 50 per cent and municipal services the rest.

garbage was not like the fluffy, styrofoam American kind. It was rich and wet and heavy; and so, one by one, as the bins soared up and tipped their loads, the axles of the costly imported trucks snapped beneath them. The trucks themselves became trash, and their charred skeletons now littered the spontaneously combusting dumps. The bins, too, were badly designed. Their wheels were too small to roll over Cairo's rough streets. The garbagemen couldn't manipulate them into reach of the trucks, so the bins overspilled and rusted on corners. They became scrabbling grounds for alley cats. In the end, when these receptacles grew so noxious as to be *mish maʿqūl*, teenage ragpickers came with palm-fibre baskets and cleaned them out.

THE SIGHT OF a grubby little girl heaving a basket of refuse between honking Mercedes fails to shock Cairenes. This is not to say the city's people are heartless. Far from it. Spontaneous generosity is not the exception here, but the rule. The Ramadan charity campaign of one children's hospital regularly raises a million Egyptian pounds a day. And on a city bus I once witnessed a bidding frenzy erupt after a lady found she had left her purse behind. 'But how will you get home?' asked a woman carrying a tray of eggs. 'What will you do if you get hungry,' asked a gentleman as he fished deep into his *galabiyya* for his wallet. The lady tried to explain that it was all right, she was just going to meet her husband, but the passengers would not hear of it. Half a dozen hands pressed varying sums of money on her so insistently that she backed off the bus in embarrassment some way short of her destination. But then a young man ran after her, slipped money in her bag, and skittered away before she could thank him.

No, Cairenes are far from unkind. Yet daily experience, backed up by history, has taught them that life is not generally very fair. There has always been a sharp divide between rich and poor here. Money has always swayed justice. People with power have always abused it.

Reliefs in a tomb chapel at Saqqara, for instance, record a case of legal knavery from 1300 BC that could have come straight from yesterday's proceedings at the South Cairo District Court. The scene depicts Mose, a treasury scribe at the Temple of Ptah, standing triumphant before the judges of Memphis. He has won the last of five court cases, ending years of bitter litigation over title to an estate south of the city. A generation before, the hieroglyphic text explains, Mose's conniving cousin Khay had swindled the land from Mose's mother by bribing an official at the Heliopolis records office to forge the deeds in his name. Mose must have considered his success rare indeed, or he would not have made it the high point of his tomb.

Legal devilry persisted in medieval times. The annals abound with tales of corrupt judges and paid witnesses, and of rulers who simply bypassed the *sharia* courts to dole out punishment by whim. In the fourteenth century Ibn Khaldun was repeatedly forced from his judgeship for trying to limit the pervasive influence of professional witnesses. 'He ignored the requests of high officials and refused to hear the appeals of the rich,' wrote the historian Ibn Taghribirdi, 'so they began to speak against him until the sultan dismissed him.'

Justice could be swift and pitiless. Thieves were hanged. Rebels were beheaded or flayed alive. Murderers were sliced in two at the waist – after which procedure, according to Leo Africanus, the victim's top half could survive for as long as twenty minutes still talking. Baybars al-Jashankir, a short-lived Mamluk sultan,* had 300 tongues cut out after hearing a popular rhyme

*Not to be confused with the great Baybars who founded the Mamluk state, this Baybars usurped the throne briefly from 1309 to 1310 before being overthrown and executed. His name al-Jashankir comes from the Persian word for his rank at court before his rise to power: chief taster to the sultan.

making fun of his name. The pious fourteenth-century amir Shaykhun, who endowed Cairo with the lavish mosque and dervish hostel that face each other on Saliba Street, also introduced a novel torture. He had henchmen bore holes in one rival's shaved head. Cockroaches were inserted in the holes. A brass cap was applied and slowly heated so that the insects would eat their way into the man's brain.

Perhaps that victim was guilty. Such was not always the case. Passing through Cairo in 1435, the Spanish traveller Pero Tafur was perplexed to see three merchants executed at Bab Zuwayla for the 'crime' of failing to prevent their neighbour, a money changer, from being robbed. 'There are very many of us, and God increases our number daily,' Tafur's translator explained. 'If we did not punish both the criminal and the spectator, we could not live.'

Noting that Cairo's main courthouse was always jammed with litigators in 1840, Sir Gardner Wilkinson commented that nowhere was justice so far from the reach of a poor man as in Egypt. His description of court officials remains apt:

> The most efficient recipe for stimulating the torpid clerks is bribery ... So impatient are they of neglect in this particular that the moment they think some attention to court etiquette ought to be paid, they put forth every difficulty as a delicate hint. Whenever the simpleminded applicant, trusting to the evident justice of his cause, appears before them, they are far too occupied with other papers of long standing to attend to him: a particular person, whose attendance is absolutely required, is not to be found, or some official excuse is invented to check the arrangements of the business, and he is put off from day to day ... On the appearance of these marked symptoms, a sweetener should, in doctorial language, be immediately exhibited in a sufficiently large dose to allay the symptoms; and it is surprising to observe how the gladdened face of the man-of-law expands on taking the welcome potion.

When the Post Office introduced a savings bank, observed the British archaeologist Flinders Petrie a century ago, Egyptians reacted with astonishment. Who would be so foolish as to entrust their money to the government?

Today's Cairo is, in theory at least, fully fitted with modern systems of law, finance and administration. Government is big here – unnaturally, inflatedly so. The range of ministries, agencies, authorities, councils and higher councils is so complex that no one really knows where their purviews begin or end. Layers of national government overlap provincial and municipal and local authorities. A bewildering array of security forces keeps public order: traffic police, emergency police, transport police, antiquities police, tourist police, morals police, secret police and the even more secret State Security Investigation Department. Police districts dovetail into parliamentary districts that imbricate with tax districts and school districts and forbidden military zones. The city as a whole spreads across three governorates, each with its own presidentially appointed governor. There is no elected mayor of Greater Cairo; instead, the governor of Giza manages the third of the city that lies on the west bank of the Nile, Cairo Governorate oversees most of the city proper, but many of the rapidly growing northern suburbs fall within the Qalyubiyya Governorate.

Not surprisingly, given this muddle, workmen digging the first line of the Cairo metro in the 1980s kept stumbling on water mains and electric cables that motley authorities had laid without regard to anyone else's plans. Tangled administration is also a chief reason for the decay of Cairo's historic core. The varied agencies in charge of building codes (the Municipality), water (the state-owned Cairo Water Company), sewage (the Ministry of Housing), traffic (the Ministry of the Interior) and the maintenance of ancient monuments (the Ministry of Culture and the Ministry of Religious Affairs) rarely cooperate. 'Every minister has a finger in this city,' complains Milad Hanna, a former chairman of the Housing Committee in Egypt's parliament. 'They build what they like. There is no overall plan.' Cairo is fated to be mismanaged, he believes, until such time as it can elect the people who run it. That has never happened in the city's history. It is unlikely to happen soon: given the importance of the capital, an elected mayor of Greater Cairo would inevitably challenge the power of whoever ruled Egypt.

At the national level everything centres on Cairo. If a farmer in Zifta wants to increase his share of irrigation water, the chances are he must apply to the Ministry of Irrigation in Cairo. If a flat-footed conscript from Kom Ombo wants exemption from the army, he must go to the draft office in Cairo. If a postman's widow in Wasta has a pension claim, it is to Cairo that she must travel. Some time in their lives, nearly every able-bodied Egyptian will shuttlecock through the Cairene bureaucracy's maze of dim-lit corridors and dusty offices; will duel with its yawning, grasping officials; will accumulate sheaves of grudgingly stamped documents and consider themselves lucky to escape with their dignity and sanity intact.

It is an ancient ritual, as a scrap of papyrus found on the floor of a temple at Saqqara proves. In this Sixth Dynasty document, the foreman of a quarry across the river from Memphis complains that he and his crew were summoned to the city to receive their wages, and were then left to wait while the official in charge dithered for six days.

The accumulation of such trials endows Cairenes with a wariness towards institutions that is hard to shake. It is one reason why million-dollar transactions are, by preference, still made in sackfuls of cash. It explains why redress for wrongs continues often to be exacted in kind: the overburdened courts are so clogged with litigation as to make their justice painfully slow.*

*In 1996 alone, Egypt's 5,000 judges dealt with an astonishing 11,688,000 cases involving 44 million people, according to the Ministry of Justice. They rendered judgements in only 9.5 million of these, which explains why there were nearly 20 million lawsuits pending, or one for every three Egyptians.

Mistrust generates an immense feeder industry. Informal fixers and expediters specialize in piloting clients through the bureaucracy's prickly shoals. Public scribes, sellers of fiscal stamps and forms, photographers and photocopiers crowd the streets around government offices like money changers on the steps of the Temple.

Perhaps because they are allowed so small a part in making it, Cairenes tend to fear rather than respect the law. They fear the law not so much because it is perceived as just or necessary, but because they worry where it will strike next. A certain Mr Tunsi of Shubra, for instance, writes to *Al-Ahram* to complain that when he lost his passport he was denied another on the grounds that his name is clearly not Egyptian but Tunisian. Mr Tunsi's case was settled only when his sister chanced to discover their great-grandfather's Ottoman-era birth certificate in her attic. Or take this scene I witness in Tahrir Square: the lead car of a ministerial motorcade strikes a stray pedestrian. He survives. Plain-clothes men swoop down, scrape him off the asphalt, and drag him away – not to hospital but for interrogation as a possible terrorist. Such tales are the stuff of casual conversation here: diverting, but absolutely par for the course.

Cairo is a place where people learn early about the hazards of arbitrary power. Martial drills, gruelling exams and the whack of the cane shape memories of time done in state schools. For most men, three years of military service follow school. Aside from enduring bad food and flea-bitten desert camps that bake in summer and freeze in winter, conscripts commonly find themselves enlisted as drivers, errand boys and household servants for their officers.

Women escape the army, but tradition burdens all but those who can afford hired help with a heavy sentence of family service. A mere generation ago traditional conceptions of 'honour' tied many women to their homes. That has changed. The proportion of women who enter the workforce has risen steadily since the days when Cairo's pre-eminent modern novelist, Naguib Mahfouz, invented Si Sayyid, a character who beat his wife if he suspected she had so much as peeped outside. Yet even today only a fifth of Cairene women work outside the home. The majority who don't are expected to cook and clean for parents and brothers until marriage, when they must cook and clean for husbands and children. Housewives in traditional quarters prefer not to venture out alone. Even if it is only to go shopping, it is better to bring a child or relative along. That way, nosy neighbours can have no doubts as to the lady's respectable intentions.

Islam's patriarchal code favours husbands over wives, especially when it comes to divorce and custody of children. Families try to even the score by making sure their daughters enter marriage as fully equipped as possible. By Egyptian custom it is the groom who must provide the conjugal apartment and most of its fittings. If prenuptial bargaining is almost always protracted, amazingly detailed – down to the number of teacups – and horrendously stressful for all concerned, it is because this is the prospective bride's window of opportunity, the moment when she has power to dictate her terms. Often the fiancées who stroll hand in hand beside the Nile are not mooning and flirting as lovers do everywhere, but negotiating issues like the size of their future refrigerator, bed and TV set. These things are important: even if her husband turns out no good, the bride will at least have a degree of security, and the respect of her peers.

Constraints like these, compounded by poverty, deal out a hard hand to most Cairenes. Take the case of Umm Ahmad, a fifty-two-year-old mother of four.* She was married at the age of sixteen and widowed at twenty-five. Swindled out of the property she had inherited because she couldn't read the sale

*Traditional Eyptians believe a woman's real name should be veiled from the public. To prevent intrusion on their privacy, working-class mothers adopt the names of their first-born: Umm Ahmad is Ahmad's Mother.

contract, she was forced to work as a housemaid. Umm Ahmad still supports three of her children – she earns more as a maid than her daughter can make as a qualified doctor in a government hospital. The two women share one bed, and her sons take turns in another. In a single week two of her neighbours died. One perished in a bus plunge off a Cairo bridge that killed forty-seven passengers. The other, an unmarried woman of twenty-four who was treated like a servant in the two-room flat she shared with her two brothers and their wives, was driven to such despair that she doused herself in kerosene and struck a match.

Her case was extreme, but not all that rare. A 1995 household survey found that over a quarter of married women in Cairo had been beaten at least once by their husbands. More shockingly, three-quarters believed husbands had a right to beat them, and half said that refusing sex was an adequate reason. Still, in such respects Cairo was far ahead of other parts of Egypt,* a fact which reflects the impact of better education in the city.

In 1996, 26 per cent of Cairenes were officially classified as poor – that is, their annual income per person was less than the £E1,323 ($390) which the government's statistical agency said was needed for basic sustenance. (But even among the better off 74 per cent annual spending per person averaged only £E2,820, or $830, which is poor by any Western standard.) Yet Cairo's disadvantaged seem strangely averse to mounting organized efforts to improve their lot. This is partly explained by the historical lack of democratic institutions – a lack which is currently reinforced by laws that make it difficult to organize political parties,

* The government's 1995 Demographic and Health Survey found that 92 per cent of married rural women thought husbands had a right to beat them. In the Upper Egyptian countryside, 83.4 per cent said husbands would be justified if their wives refused them sex. That said, it should be noted that the survey was criticized for the small size of its sample. Also, wife-beating is traditionally associated with pride and masculinity and protectiveness; women who said they approved of the practice may have been expressing how strong the ideal husband's passion for his wife should be.

independent trade unions and even social clubs. The laws are backed up by what is probably the largest police force in any city in the world.*

Its latent coercive power seldom needs to be put to use, however. Cairenes – rich and poor alike – may have little sense of civic duty, but they have a strong sense of moral duty. This means that, when a street fight breaks out, onlookers rush to separate the antagonists, pacify them, smooth their ruffled feathers. The crowd's reaction is so reliable that tempers can be allowed a healthy release in the full knowledge that no real damage will be allowed.

If official community organization is largely absent, and if even spontaneous mass action like rioting is rare, nevertheless Cairo's poor have developed unique ways of coping. Most housewives, for instance, join friends in a *gamaʿiyya* or savings pool. By chipping in with a small monthly payment – typically £E100 ($34) or less – they gain periodic access to a lump sum that may allow them to pay for, say, a washing machine. In poor quarters, most families supplement their income by raising animals at home. In a typical two-room walk-up in a north Cairo housing project, for instance, a social worker found a sheep on the balcony, chickens in pens in a corner of the kitchen, and pigeons – a delicacy in Egypt – under a bed.

In the spring of 1996, a single raid on the slum district of Dar al-Salam netted 800 cases where citizens had illegally tapped the government's electricity lines. It was a classic example of what Asef Bayat, a sociologist at the American University in Cairo, describes as 'quiet encroachment'. This strategy of acquiring by stealth what you cannot gain otherwise, he says, may represent the key

*The Ministry of the Interior is wary of releasing statistics, and estimating the number of police is difficult because of the variety of overlapping forces and branches. To hazard a guess, though, there are probably 50,000–100,000 policemen in Cairo, enough for the city to still deserve its medieval epithet *al-Qahira al-Mahrusa* – Cairo The Well-Guarded.

technique that Cairo's poor use for dealing with state authority. Residents of public housing projects, for instance, commonly convert public space to private use. Open areas between housing blocks serve as animal pens, plant nurseries and market places.

An estimated 200,000 ambulant vendors ply their trade in Cairo, selling everything from toy cellular phones to *fūl* – the slow-cooked fava beans that are Egypt's staple breakfast. 'Almonds!' is what the *fūl* seller on Muski Street calls out, to suggest how sweet and delicious are his beans. But at the warning cry of '*Al-ḥukūma!*' – 'The government!' – hundreds of fellow street hawkers scamper off the busy street into the adjacent alleyways with their unlicensed trays of lingerie or watches or other goods for sale.

Street vendors join the 45 per cent of the city workforce that a Cairo University study defines as 'informal', which is to say non-taxpaying. This vast pool of labour may account for as much as a third of the city's economic output, the study found. Its members include not just itinerants but also most workers in Cairo's thousands of one-room workshops. The average 'informal' industrial establishment was found to have just four employees, often including children. A separate study found that 34 per cent of the workforce in the city centre's aluminium industry were under fifteen. Twelve per cent were under nine years old.

In some respects, informal workers can count themselves lucky. Unlike many university graduates – who make up the majority of Cairo's unemployed, because they find it hard to get prestigious office work appropriate to their degrees – they have full-time jobs. In fact the Cairo University study found that the informal sector's tax-free wages averaged three times starting salaries in a government office. And even if they had to endure sixty-hour working weeks, in often dangerous conditions and with no social insurance, workshop labourers had the advantage of escaping government meddling. Survey respondents thought this an important plus: distrust of the state was so strong that when the Cairo University team began surveying around Maʿruf Street, a warren of car-repair shops in the city centre, foremen simply pulled down the metal shutters on their shops. Persuading locals that the researchers were academics, not government inspectors, took weeks of patient explanation.

Cairenes seem to regard resistance to power as an art form. In 1996, for example, police tried to abolish jaywalking in Ramses Square by imposing spot fines. With its convergence of metro, train and bus routes pouring out an endless stream of commuters, it was predictable that the square should produce no less than 2,500 fines a day. But even after a month of diligent effort police were still ticketing one wayward pedestrian every twenty-five seconds during business hours.

The common belief that driving codes can all be bypassed with a toot of a horn makes for deafening noise levels on Cairo's streets. (Which brings to mind the Mamluk-era law which allowed only nobles to have private bands. The permitted number of musicians rose with rank, so that the amount of noise you could make reflected social status.) The cacophony is, however, only the most blatant sign of a much more generalized flouting of rules. Cairo's bureaucracy is as hopelessly snarled as its traffic, for example, but there is always a fast track smoothed by the right connections or money in the right palm.

In a witty account of years spent in Egyptian government service at the beginning of this century, Lord Edward Cecil recalled that it was considered bad taste to remain as Minister of Religious Affairs for longer than six months, so lucrative were the possibilities of filching from Islamic *waqf* endowments. Official posts are still held like franchises – even at very high levels. The occasional corruption scandal makes it into the papers. There is an outcry, followed by a clampdown, followed by a relapse into old ways.

THE JOB OF *bawāb* – the keeper of the *bāb* or door – is one of the most ancient and enduring of Cairene professions. In medieval times it inspired a whole literary genre. Condemnation of the *bawāb* was a standard poetical form that allowed poets to sigh at being denied access to lovers. Much of the opprobrium fell on African eunuchs, who were the *bawābs* of choice in great households because they could be trusted to preserve the chastity of the harem.

Every respectable apartment building in Cairo still maintains a *bawāb*. The doormen still tend to be African – or rather Nubian, because the Egyptians' upstream neighbours, many of whom moved to Cairo after losing their country behind the High Dam, have a reputation for honesty. But the modern *bawāb* seldom wields power enough to inspire plaintive verse. In return for a room in the basement and a token wage supplemented by tips from residents, his job is to clean, guard and oversee basic maintenance.

Like most *bawābs*, Uncle Muhammad in my building has a family to support and few means to raise his meagre income. He excels at one method, however: flattery. Two pay days after I moved in he had already promoted me from *ustāz* to *bey*, which is to say from mister to sir. With his end-of-Ramadan bonus I graduated to an honorary *duktūr*-ship. Currently I seem to be a pasha.

Uncle Muhammad's exaggerated respect is a genial affectation, mostly. My pashalik, I know, is bestowed with a large dollop of innuendo. As is so often the case in Cairo, the subtext to his form of address is more potent than the literal message. 'If you want to be thought a pasha,' Muhammad is really saying as he mock-salutes and presents arms with his toothless broom, 'then reward me as a pasha would.' (Which reminds me of a story a friend tells of his grandfather, who was a real pasha. The pasha rode a carriage home one day, and paid the coachman two piastres. The coachman protested that the pasha's son always paid five. 'But I', shrugged the pasha, 'am not the son of a pasha.')

Half a century after Egypt's socialist revolution, Cairenes retain a need to categorize, to place people in their station. Poor folk still speak of their 'betters'. The rich, meanwhile, tend to think of their good fortune as a sign of heavenly favour. Deference is thus not only accepted but expected. Woe betide lowly students who neglect to address their professors as '*duktūr*': not to do so could be taken as an excuse to fail them. In one case I know, a teacher flunked a student for the unintended sin of showing disrespect by crossing his legs in the great man's presence.

In a society where seniority, not achievement, is still the chief qualification for advancement, students are not encouraged to ask questions. Preserving the hierarchy of authority is generally seen as more important than the pursuit of knowledge. At any of Cairo's universities it is not uncommon to see students trailing after their teachers carrying their briefcases, just as in medieval times they would have vied for the honour of carrying an Azharite sheikh's slippers.

Cairenes themselves often take a dim view of this kind of sycophancy. Even 600 years ago al-Maqrizi chided his fellow citizens for 'amusing themselves' with what he called cunning and deceit. 'They excel at smiles and flattery more than any other people, such that they have gained fame for these traits,' the historian lamented.*

* This was the least of al-Maqrizi's protests. Here is what he wrote of the morals of Cairenes: 'Most are marked by lewdness and abandonment to pleasure, by a preoccupation with trifles, by credulousness, by weakness of will and resolution. They are skilled at cunning and deceit ... and amuse themselves with it ... They are wanton and careless. Our sheikh, Master Abu Zayd Abd al-Rahman Ibn Khaldun, may God have mercy on him, told me the people of Egypt behave as if they were released from the Day of Judgement ... Ibn al-Arabiyya said they were the slaves of conquerors; the smartest of youths and the most ignorant of dotards.'

To people from more egalitarian societies – including most Arabs – Cairo's extremes of verbal obeisance verge on the ridiculous. Respects such as 'Your Presence', 'Your Ladyship' and 'Your Happiness' are common. It would be perfectly normal, say, for a *munādi* – one of the self-appointed parking 'valets' whose services are vital on the city's clogged streets – to speak to a client thus: 'O Your Happiness the Pasha, I am at Your Lordship's command. Does Your Presence's car wish to be washed?'

The language reflects a deeply ingrained sense of hierarchy. It is a sense that harks back to the days when each office of the Mamluk court had its own special headgear, and when the dress of ordinary citizens reflected their confession as well as their profession. Perhaps it goes back even further, to a time when the Pharaoh was the living link between man and the gods, and when proximity to earthly power meant closeness to eternity. 'I was more esteemed by the king than any other servant,' is the proudest boast that Ptahshepses, a Fourth Dynasty high priest of Ptah, thought fit to inscribe in his tomb at Saqqara. 'His Majesty permitted me to kiss his feet, for His Majesty did not wish that I should kiss the ground.'

Five thousand years later Cairo's social pyramid remains sprawling at the base and slender at the top. Those at the bottom assume, as they always have, that the only way to gain power is to associate themselves with the lucky few who actually wield control. Institutions are usually dominated by a single boss whose strength of character enforces results. Business empires tend to spread across a range of activities, because entrepreneurs know that the speediest route to fortune is not technical skill but skilful exploitation of personal contacts in government. In the non-commercial world – even inside political parties – democratic practice is rare, and so commonly manipulated as to inspire little respect.

Even the police force runs by reverse gravity. (It always has done – in ninth-century Fustat it was characterized by a few top officials and a mass of low-paid agents and spies.) I once protested when my taxi turned, Cairene-fashion, down a narrow street clearly marked 'No Entry'. The driver didn't flinch, not even on finding an entire troop of uniformed foot patrolmen marching towards us. He was right. The cops parted ranks to let us pass. There was not an officer among them, I realized, which meant they had no authority to do anything.

'How many policemen does it take to equal one officer?' I asked the driver.

He thought a while. 'An infinite number, I guess,' he said at last.

DESCRIBING A PERIOD of unrest at the end of the third millennium BC, a Heliopolitan priest by the name of Neferrehu evoked calamity with these words: 'The country spins like a potter's wheel. Thieves become masters. Ladies of high rank are thrust out of doors . . .'

Throughout history the people of this city have seen the breakdown of hierarchy as the worst sign of disorder. Yet the evidence is that Cairene society has never once stopped reconstituting itself. Classes here have always been porous, not impermeable like Indian castes. The simple fact of having money or power has usually been enough to assure upward mobility. Within a generation of the military coup in 1952, for instance, children of army officers had widely married into the old landed gentry. One of the wealthiest industrialists in the city today started off as a private exam coach. Prominent showbiz stars, property magnates and all four Presidents of the Egyptian Republic emerged from humble origins.

Their rags-to-riches stories are hardly original, to judge from one Mamluk-era example. In the mid fourteenth century the Bureau of Songsters, a government agency which also licensed prostitutes and taxed entertainments, payed twenty dinars for an

Abyssinian slave girl named Ittifaq – which means Agreement or, more elegantly, Concord. Ittifaq was, enthused the historian al-Maqrizi, 'Black of obsidian blackness, beautiful of voice and faultless at song.' She so impressed the sultan of the time, al-Salih Ismail, that he married her. At Ismail's early death – unusually for a Mamluk sultan, a result of illness, not violence – his brother al-Kamil Shaʿban wedded Ittifaq on the very day of his accession. She found greater favour and happiness than any woman of the age, wrote al-Maqrizi, such that Shaʿban built her a palace whose furnishings alone cost 95,000 dinars. 'She had forty gowns studded with jewels, and sixteen embroidered with gold, and eighty veils, among them some worth 1,000 dinars, and the least of them 200 ...'

Ittifaq's career was just beginning. When Shaʿban was deposed in favour of his fifteen-year-old brother Hajji (Shaʿban was later strangled), the new ruler also married her. Hajji abandoned himself to his infatuation. 'Ittifaq became his sole occupation, and she took possession of his heart,' wrote al-Maqrizi. Her power increased to the point that she arranged for her music teacher to be given an amir's fiefdom. But Ittifaq's success aroused the jealousy of the Mamluk nobles. They forced the boy sultan to expel her from the palace and strip her of all her possessions, including a jewelled diadem valued at 100,000 dinars. Hajji was killed soon after, but Ittifaq's fame ensured her a soft landing. She married the wealthy wazir Hibat Allah, and when he died she married again. Her fifth and last husband, with whom she ended her days, was the sultan of distant Morocco.

FEW CAIRENE FAMILIES, even among the ruling class, can trace their ancestry back more than four or five generations. This is because wealth here has usually been fleeting. Islamic rules of inheritance have exerted a centrifugal force on property by breaking estates into like-sized chunks. The city's snakes-and-ladders political history has constantly readjusted the class structure.

But even without these influences, Cairo's preference for consumption over saving tends to whittle away fortunes. Presenting a good face has always been considered a prime social duty. Understatement is not heard in Cairo. Loudness is. The oppressive closeness of poverty reinforces the need to flaunt when you can. Flashy clothes, cars and $100,000 weddings with caviar by the kilo and palm trees made out of shellfish are de rigueur for those who can afford them. Even those who cannot will go bankrupt rather than lose face. A casual invitation to lunch often translates into a sumptuous banquet where the hosts besiege guests with course after heaping course of rich country cooking. Cairenes pay for such excess in high levels of obesity and cholesterol, but they avoid the far worse stigma of stinginess.

The grand houses of the medieval city maintained distinct rooms for public show and for private living. This domestic arrangement persists even in the smaller scale of modern apartments. The large salon with the gilt furniture and silver knick-knacks remains, like the inner sanctums of pharaonic temples or Coptic churches, reserved for the initiate. It is unsealed only for display occasions like receiving condolences and negotiating with future in-laws that need to be impressed. All other activity is relegated to an informal living room made cosy with TV sets, children's toys and easy chairs.

Cairene punctilio in dress and speech results from the same distinctions. Eat to please yourself, but dress to please others, advises an Egyptian proverb. Think what you like, but do not blaspheme out loud, echoes Islamic law. Caught by a roving television interviewer, the typical Cairene waxes eloquent on the goodness of his government. Away from the camera his tune is likely to change to scouring sarcasm.

This is a society where shame is felt to be more of a burden than guilt. Perhaps that is why a sharp line divides public from private behaviour, why Cairenes prefer to suspend disbelief, to pay lip-service to what they may personally feel is wrong or untrue. All kinds of mischief, meanwhile, go on with a wink and a shrug.

'We are an As If society,' a physician at the Qasr al-ʿAyni Hospital once explained to me. 'We speak of rules *as if* we intend to follow them. Our government acts *as if* it were a democracy. Some of my colleagues got medical degrees by hook or by crook, but they behave *as if* they were learned practitioners, because they sat exams *as if* they had not bribed the examiners.'

EVEN THE CITY'S geography reflects this behavioural gap.

At the end of the nineteenth century Cairo had two distinct parts: an Old City of meandering lanes and a New City of straight carriageways. There was no physical barrier between the two, but, as one Egyptian memoir pungently recalls, the contrast between the smell of frying food on one side and the smell of Greek bakeries and Swiss patisseries on the other was as sharp as barbed wire.

At the end of the twentieth century the city has sewn itself a complex quilt of similar divisions. West of the river, for instance, the main railway line to Upper Egypt stitches a border between the neatly laid-out streets of Muhandisin and the higgledy-piggledy burrows of Bulaq al-Dakrur. Both districts have grown up in the last generation, but whereas the former is purpose-built to the scale of the motor car, the latter sprouted spontaneously in pedestrian proportions little different from those of the medieval town. Muhandisin has trendy chain outlets, supermarkets and air-conditioned offices; Bulaq al-Dakrur has corner stores and open-fronted workshops. Muhandisin has hospitals performing heart bypasses and cosmetic surgery; Bulaq has cut-price clinics, herbalists and midwives. Muhandisin boasts trees, some modest parks, and high-rises built of reinforced concrete. Bulaq has no public open areas to speak of, and tenements made of brick that cram Muhandisin's horizontal density of people into a fraction of the vertical space.

Districts like Muhandisin give the city a convincing façade of boulevards and modern buildings, of street lights and signs. Yet only a minority of Cairenes inhabits the 'formal' town, the one which is seen from tour buses and official limousines and therefore is recognized and properly serviced by government. At least two-thirds live in unzoned, unplanned 'Popular Quarters'. Perhaps more: one housing survey has found that 80 per cent of new construction is in the Popular Quarters. The term covers a range of habitats, from country villages engulfed by the city – such is the case of Bulaq al-Dakrur – to the pre-modern parts of Cairo proper, to squatter communities on the city's fringes that one day will become urban spaces as dense as the old quarters.

Life in the Popular Quarters can be hard. The absence of privacy, the confining of wives and unmarried daughters in tiny apartments, and the lack of playgrounds for children create conditions for explosive family quarrels. The causes are often petty: dirty water dripping on someone's washing line, arguments between children, neighbours who clutter communal stairs with their junk. The chief of police in Imbaba – a poor district just north of Muhandisin, tells interviewers from *Al-Ahram* that his station registers at least a hundred fights a day between neighbours. A typical scuffle, he says, broke out after a housewife spilled water on the stairs in her building and a neighbour's child slipped. Fifteen people were hospitalized after the ensuing brawl.

Yet the inhabitants of places like Imbaba seldom look on their neighbourhoods as slums. Sewage may be leaky or non-existent, electricity sporadic, but the Popular Quarters boast a congenial intimacy that is rarely tainted badly by urban blights like crime and juvenile delinquency. Considering the depth of poverty in some parts of the city, the overall level of public safety is remarkable. Perhaps this is because, despite Cairo's size, most of its people still live in village-scale compartments. They know their neighbours. They care for their family reputations. They look on their small world as real. The formal, planned living arrangements across the tracks may be enviable – particularly for the greater level of privacy they afford their inhabitants. For the majority of Cairenes, however, they are easier to dismiss as alien.

In the thirteenth century, the Granadan poet Ibn Saʿid wrote that Cairo was a city within the means of the poor man. This was due, he said, 'To the abundance and low price of bread, the existence of concerts and entertainments within and outside the city, and the easy fulfilment of his desires: he does as he pleases, dancing in the markets, going about naked, and getting drunk on hashish and other products.' At the end of the eighteenth century a renegade Turk accompanying Napoleon agreed that poorer Cairenes seemed to have more fun: 'Sellers, porters, donkeyboys, artisans, pimps and prostitutes – in brief, the dregs of the populace – were delighted with their occupations because of the freedom they allowed.' At that time, Napoleon's *savants* estimated, two-thirds of Cairo's artisan class were regular consumers of such things as opium and 'honeyed hashish balls'.

Working-class Cairenes still indulge more freely than their 'betters' in drug-taking, flirting, joke-making and general tomfoolery. While weddings in the Popular Quarters fill alleys with mini-carnivals packed with spontaneous revelry, the costly ballroom affairs of the rich are monotonously staid. Swooshing up to five-star hotels in their *zalamukkas, budras* and *fagras* – as different models of Mercedes are popularly known* – the rich

* The names mean Chicken's Arse (for the high rear end of one model), Powder (for the fact that only drug dealers can afford them) and Slut (for the wide, rounded eyes of the headlights). Earlier Mercedes models were known as the Crocodile and the Pig – all of which reveals a great deal about what ordinary folk think of those who drive them.

in all their duds are destined to sit for hours enduring an interminable sequence of crooners and belly dancers. They are too busy being respectable; too wary of their reputations to get up and dance.

PERHAPS IT IS also a comfort to Cairo's poor that time is probably on their side. One day, if history is destined to repeat itself, the spacious quarters of the rich will be theirs. The fact is that the city's multiple avatars have all been born as exclusive zones for the elite, but have ended their days in the hands of the people. If there is one trait that has always marked this city, it is this eternal restless shifting.

Archaeologists speculate that the reason why Memphis's remains are so scant is that the ancient capital was a sort of movable feast of a city. The pyramid-building pharaohs probably built palace complexes next to their tombs. The great house (or *per-raᶜ* in the ancient language – which is the root of the word 'pharaoh') would serve as the temporary capital of the country. It would attract a generation of servers and hangers-on, all of whom would have to move as soon as the succeeding pharaoh chose a new site for his tomb and court. But, rather than fall completely vacant, the disused royal buildings were often taken over by the poor. Excavations at the valley temple associated with the Pyramid of Mycerinus at Giza, for example, have revealed that squatters had built mud huts inside the temple courtyard soon after the pharaoh's departure. It became, in the words of the authoriative pyramidologist Mark Lehner, a kind of sacred slum.

Muslim rulers, too, repeatedly abandoned older quarters that had grown too dense for courtly luxury. In the eighth century, Egypt's Abbasid governors founded an administrative quarter at the north-east corner of Fustat. They called it al-ᶜAskar, or The Soldiers' Precinct. A mere hundred years later, the governor Ahmad Ibn Tulun found al-ᶜAskar too overgrown for his liking.

He built an even more ambitious compound further north. Al-Qataʿi – The Cantonments – was said to have housed 10,000 troops in comfort, as well as palaces and pleasure gardens complete with menageries and – so later legend assures us – a pool filled with quicksilver where the ruler floated on silken cushions towed to and fro by slave girls pulling on silver chains. Ibn Tulun grew powerful enough to declare independence from the Abbasids: he coined dinars in his own name. But his dynasty was to be short-lived. In AD 905, an Abbasid army reconquered Egypt and levelled al-Qataʿi – all except for the central mosque, which had been built to a scale grand enough to provide praying room for the renegade governor's entire army.*

But the clearest example of Cairo's elite trying to escape the crush of the city was the founding of al-Qahira, The Victorious, in AD 969. In an assertion of aloofness from mundane affairs, the Fatimid caliph al-Muʿizz li Din Allah followed his predecessors in walling off empty lands to the north-east of Fustat. But within three centuries the parade ground between his two palaces here had become the Qasaba, the donkey-trampled main thoroughfare of medieval Cairo.

In modern times, dizzying population growth has combined with disregard of building codes to render many 'formal' districts too dense to attract the middle class. The *nās*, or respectable folk, have moved out, and the *shaʿb*, or masses, have taken over. Even new districts like Muhandisin have succumbed to de-gentrification. Their streets are now so crammed with cars and shops that, for want of parking, rich Cairenes have begun to head for the desert hills. Breaking a millennial taboo, speculators have snapped up land east and west of the valley. At the end of the twentieth century they are busy mapping out new walled cities for the

*Ibn Tulun's mosque is still the largest in Cairo. The great double walls ringing its huge courtyard have protected the building from later misuse as a caravanserai and a madhouse, and have even held off the recent tide of intense urbanization.

privileged. *Bawābs* – modernized by security guard uniforms – now patrol suburban theme communities with names like Dreamland, Beverly Hills, Greenland, English Village and Golf City. TV spots and colour spreads in the papers advertise the new resorts' pillared and porticoed villas as a gracious alternative to urban squalor. 'Everyone dreams of living here,' gloats one advertising plug, 'but not everyone can afford to.'

In a case that is typical of Cairo's erratic planning, the developer of one such estate found that a low-income housing project abutted his planned acreage of ranch-style villas. To protect his clients' swimming pools from prying eyes, the clever fellow bought all the six-storeyed tenements overlooking his property. He plans to tear them down.

TWO DECADES OF breakneck growth have uglified much of modern Cairo. Small budgets, tremendous demand for housing, lax regulation, and a drain of architectural talent abroad have combined to give the city a rough-hewn, unfinished look. Grandiose marble entrances give way to dark, narrow corridors and low ceilings. Haphazard accretions scar façades: pipes and cables and air-conditioning units, signboards and antennas and satellite dishes.

The aesthetic defoliation reaches into older parts of the city, too. In once gracious garden districts like Maadi, Heliopolis and Zamalek, high-rises have supplanted villas as fast as sledgehammers and piledrivers can pound. In downtown Cairo – the old Ismailia Quarter – the air of pre-war Europe that lingered mustily even a decade ago in such establishments as Weinstein Stationery, the Café Riche or the Groppi Tea Rooms is slowly expiring. The sense of space has changed. Mosques, street vendors and parked cars have conquered sidewalks intended for strollers. Advertising and remade storefronts obscure neo-pharaonic mouldings, art-deco doorways and swirling art-nouveau railings in wrought iron.

The style and habits of the old 'native' quarters, mutated by the modern scourges of mass production, amplified sound and neon, have made such deep inroads here that the khedive Ismail's stately boulevards have more the feel of a bazaar than of the Paris they were designed to emulate: the eminent Cairene journalist Kamil Zuhayri recalls that Gadallah, the most elegant bootmaker on Qasr al-Nil Street in the 1950s, used to put a single beautifully crafted shoe in its window. Now, like all the others on the street, its display is crammed with enough footwear to shoe Cairo Stadium.

Nevertheless, the old boundary marked by Gumhuriyya Street is still tangible. The thoroughfare stretches north to south from Ramses Square to the former royal palace of ʿAbdin. Khedive Ismail's neo-Parisian boulevards extend west from Gumhuriyya Street. But to the east the imposed order of the 'Occidental' city, with its sidewalks and traffic lights, fades. The organic order of the 'Oriental' quarter takes over.

This one and a quarter by three mile zone is what remains of the town which grew up around the royal enclosure built by the Fatimid caliph al Muʿizz. At a mere thousand years of age, it is far from being the oldest part of Cairo; there had already been Memphis across the river, and Ancient Heliopolis to the north, and the early Muslim capitals to the south. But this Old City, which Egyptians call the Cairo of al-Muʿizz, is the largest pre-modern quarter to have endured, its street plan substantially intact, down to the present. It is also one of the most densely used and populated bits of the metropolis. Little workshops cram every alleyway, turning out everything from auto parts to stuffed toy camels for the tourist trade. Narrow storefronts pack every inch of street frontage, while vendors' stands and barrows and donkey carts clutter the roadways.

Six-hundred-odd listed medieval monuments have been propped up or properly restored amidst the bustle here, enough to make the Cairo of al-Muʿizz an open-air museum of Islamic architecture. Other ancient cities may boast relics of a single great dynasty, but here they range in style and age across the spectrum of Islamic history, from the ninth-century Mosque of Ibn Tulun to the nineteenth-century palaces and fountains of Muhammad Ali Pasha. The splendid mosques and schools of the Mamluk era with their spacious courts, exquisitely curving carved-stone domes and three-tiered minarets modelled on the vanished lighthouse of Alexandria; the public fountains and the baths and caravanserais of the Ottoman period; the mansions of great merchant families with their marble marquetry and intricate latticework screens: all these noble buildings still reflect the glorious time when Cairo was the most princely capital in the world. Striking in scale and austere elegance, their façades pack long stretches of the Qasaba, the former processional way that is the spine of the Old City.

THE GRAND MONUMENTS have largely lost their functions, however. The fountains, endowed to the city by the pious and once filled daily by water-carriers, are dry. Excepting al-Azhar, all the old colleges of Islamic law are defunct, replaced by the law faculties of modern universities. Having aged beyond utility, most of Cairo's old heart has gently crumbled. The destructive rumble of constant traffic and occasional earthquakes has been compounded by leaky plumbing that sends corrosive liquids to be sponged up into ancient walls of porous limestone, which then crack, flake and pop off decorative panels of polychrome marble at an alarming rate. Concrete apartment blocks peer down into adjacent lots of rubble from freshly collapsed houses. A double-stacked overpass loops around three sides of a fifteenth-century mosque. In the markets, plastic and aluminium have largely supplanted leather and brass.

The decay may be sad, but in compensation the place is alive. It is a city in progress, with nothing of the pickled, sterilized quality of many a European *Altstadt* or the resurrected cuteness of colonial Williamsburg, Virginia. The Old City prefers to entice and conceal rather than display. To the first-time visitor there is still a sense of discovery in stumbling across, say, the ruins of the colossal fourteenth-century palace of the Amir Yashbak, where bats lurk in the basement next to a Ford Model T that has somehow ended its days here; or in seeing, from the balcony of a minaret, the sun set among dusty domes and smoke-shrouded spires.

There remains a sensible antiquity to the rhythm of the Old City, to the worn texture of every surface and the intimate scale of public space. The narrow lanes away from the main streets may no longer be overhung by the traditional tiered upper floors that closed out the sky and brought welcome shade in the summer, but they are still no wider than the medievally prescribed breadth of two laden camels, and still they are largely pedestrian. Aside, that is, from the beasts of burden which have replaced the once ubiquitous donkeys, which is to say diminutive Suzuki trucks rigged with Taiwanese sirens that play the 'Lambada' tune. (No wonder the Prophet said that the most hideous of sounds is the braying donkey.)

Instead of downtown Cairo's gone-to-seed department stores, here there are closet-sized *dukkāns* massed in highly specialized market places, their goods stacked in tantalizing pyramids. There is a street of sewing machines and a street of television sets, an alley of clocks and watches, a cul-de-sac of buttons, a bazaar of hand tools, with passages of screws and nails running into a whole district devoted to plaster dolls and dishes and *bonbonnières* for lavish weddings. Towards the Nile at Wikalat al-Balah, what started as trade in Second World War army surplus has bequeathed a teeming market where used clothes rub worn elbows with parts scavenged from old cars. By the old eastern walls there was, until the narcotics squad cracked down a decade ago, a district of drug dealers where young toughs weighed out loaves of hashish on trestle tables, and shrivelled old men squatted in the alleys on Friday afternoons waiting for the young son of Hagg Mustafa Marzouk to deliver a charity ration of opium from his father's copious stores. There are also streets where a sort of unordained assembly line can unfold, like one which evolves from the wholesale wood market to sellers of stuffings and brocade and clamps, to shapers of frames and carvers, to the sudden shock of the completed goods: glorious gilt Louis XVI thrones and sofas in purple velvet that look almost obscene in their ripe smugness as they bask along the earthen pathway.

Above all, there is a feeling of age-old territoriality to the Old City – of neighbourhoods in miniature built around a particular trade, a mosque, a café, a grocer and the tomb of some sheikh. The unit here is no longer the *quartier* or the borough framed by some topographic feature or great boulevard, but the homely *ḥāra,* the alleyway extolled in the novels of Naguib Mahfouz.

Once upon a time each *ḥāra* was practically autonomous. At the second hour after dusk, right after evening prayers, the neighbourhood *bawāb* would close the *ḥāra* gate and seal its inhabitants from the troublesome world beyond. When Napoleon's army captured Cairo two centuries ago they found a honeycomb of fifty or more *ḥāras* separated by walls and gates. The first thing they did was to remove the barriers – a decision whose wisdom was proved when the people of Cairo rose against the invaders and had to be blasted into submission by artillery fire.

Ever since, the fabric of the Old City has frayed. The Greeks abandoned the *ḥāra* of the Greeks, the Jews the *ḥāra* of the Jews – though a smattering of churches and synagogues still moulder neglected on back streets. The rich moved to newer, more spacious quarters with electricity and decent plumbing (or so they thought), abandoning tall mansions that were air-conditioned by means of tree-filled courtyards and high wind-catchers and splashing fountains. Those great houses not rescued by conservationists were oozed into by country immigrants. The newcomers tethered goats to brass doorknobs. They washed their clothes in the fountains and defenestrated lattice-work panels for kindling. From being places where differing fortunes mingled, the old *ḥāras* became not quite slums but solidly, proudly working-class.

It has been said that whereas the rich create fashion, the poor maintain tradition. The Old City remains the repository of timeless Cairene habits. Folk dress – the full length *galabiyya* for men and the black, wrap-around *milāya* for women – is suddenly more in evidence. It is here that a dwindling few ambulant vendors of liquorice drink, wearing their traditional baggy trousers with satin cummerbunds, ply their trade. They clink their brass cups like castanets, puncturing sounds of scolding and laughter, and in the tinsmiths' street compete with a tinkling cacophony of hammers like a gamelan running amok. Incense burners wander from shop to shop, swirling their censers and muttering prayers in exchange for a few piastres' tip.

During the holy month of Ramadan, Cairenes, drawn by some atavistic need for the Old City's intimacy, flock to the cafés and food stalls around the Mosque of al-Husayn. After long nights of feasting and revelry, the public waker makes his rounds before dawn, tapping a drum, rousing the faithful so that they can have a last bite or sip or cigarette before the daylight hours of fasting. Boys raise pigeons on the rooftops. Teenage girls fill water jars at the corner standpipes and sway homewards, delineating their curves in complicity with the café loungers across the way.

THE ASFOUR WAS a classic Old City café. Straw-bottomed chairs and spindly brass-topped tables cluttered the tiled floors of its interior. A stern-looking *maʿallim* or boss in a pristine white *galabiyya* ruled here as proprietor, bouncer and referee of his clients' backgammon and card games. Outside, his proud grapevine shaded a row of wooden benches overlooking the street.

It was here that I met Ashraf. I was sitting propped against the wall of the Asfour, assuming the role of a local voyeur with the assistance of the water maidens across the way, and with an excellent hubble-bubble for an accessory. I hardly noticed the stocky gentleman next to me, except to appreciate that he left me alone with my thoughts – an unusual luxury in Cairo.

After a time I finished the first of a pair of clay pipes stuffed with *maʿassil*, that sticky concoction of chopped tobacco stewed in molasses which is one of Cairo's finer inventions. Pleasantly buzzed with nicotine, I pincered the hot coals one by one on to the water pipe's collar-like brass saucer, removed the old pipe, and twisted the new one into place. But before I could top it with coals my neighbour leaned across and pinched a dark sliver of something on to the mixture. He said nothing, just sat back and grinned encouragement. Our eyes met for a second. I had to smile back. To refuse this capricious intrusion would have been a betrayal, an affront to the mood of Cairo, to my own Orientalist fatalism and to this beaming Cheshire Cat of a stranger.

The stuff was rich and resinous, a chocolate gas.

As I was to discover, Ashraf always carried a shilling's weight of hashish tucked in the elastic of his sock. A discreet flick of the toecap could drop the piece to the ground should the need arise in the form of a nosy plain-clothes man. I was to find that for a son of Ashraf's *ḥāra* there was nothing unusual in this. If anything, to smoke hashish was a sign of manliness, of respectability. It was part of a gentlemanly parcel of attributes – unfailing neatness in dress, assiduousness at prayer and fasting, disdain for politics, courtliness and firm generosity, independence and modesty, strength (Ashraf was short but had immense shoulders) – which together brought Ashraf the respect due to a true *ibn balad* or son of the soil.

We saw each other often over several years. Sometimes it was at Ashraf's business, a closet of a workshop where he and an assistant and a child apprentice assembled electric sugar-cane juicers – roll presses like the mangles on early washing machines

– to the accompaniment of a transistor radio. At five o'clock all the workshops of the *ḥāra* – no, of the whole city – would tune to the same station, and you could float for miles on a single, hour-long ballad of longing sung by Cairo's great diva Umm Kulsoum. Later we would retire to Asfour Café, where Ashraf introduced me to his circle of friends: Rida, a great rowdy ox of a butcher, Hagg Ibrahim the goldsmith, Mansour the mechanic. And sometimes Ashraf would invite me back in the evenings, to the local *mawlid* or to a wedding like his brother Fouad's, where to my surprise the climactic entertainment was a porn video played on a machine in the centre of the *ḥāra,* whose housewives shouted louche witticisms from open windows above while the menfolk seated below watched in awed silence.

Ashraf gave me new eyes to see the city, and it became a very different place for a time. Back in his *ḥāra,* the world may have been circumscribed by poverty and tradition, but it was complete. Tastes were simple but refined. People took pride in eating the best *fūl,* in smoking the cleanest water pipes, in being the most generous and gallant companions. Their links with the past were unbroken. Life revolved to the rhythm of the five daily prayers, of fasting in Ramadan and feasting in the pilgrimage season, and of the neighbourhood *mawlids.* Duties rather than needs framed behaviour: you could not be disloyal to friends or family, you could not remain unmarried, which meant you could not relent in saving the capital to buy and furnish the conjugal flat; and then you could not remain childless. As for the city at large, it was almost irrelevant except when it intruded in the guise of bureaucrats and police. Local gossip was far more pertinent than the affairs of Cairo. The greater city was seen as a temptress – wicked and wanton and possessed by others.

When Ashraf came across town to my side he was never quite at ease. There was a stiffness to his movements in my realm of wide, impersonal streets, of elevators and armchairs, of books and alcohol, and of female acquaintances who were neither veiled nor related to me by family yet who seemed to think it normal to mingle casually with strangers. I inflicted inadvertent embarrassments, like asking Ashraf to write his address without realizing he couldn't write; like forgetting that my bathroom was inadequately equipped for pious Muslim use. (How uncouth is mere paper compared to the spritzes and sprayers required by Islamic toiletry!) My surroundings, I realized, lacked the gravity of convention. Where were the formulas of speech, the mention of God, the standard praises and condolences, the gestures of hospitality? Where was the display that should have accompanied my good fortune: the glass cases filled with knick-knacks, the gadgets and the gilt?

It was through Ashraf that I came to realize how wide the gap between the two worlds of Cairo remained.

Ashraf had a cousin – or rather his mother's sister's son, in the precision of Arabic – who was doing a degree in art history at Cairo University. There were books that the cousin had to understand in order to write an important essay, and they were in incomprehensible English. For some reason I cannot now recall, I took upon myself the task of helping Ashraf's cousin to translate these books.

Feeling like an impostor, I made the late-afternoon rendezvous at Ashraf's workshop. The cousin looked too carefully dressed. He was prone to giggling, which was not encouraging. You could tell that, unlike Ashraf, this was someone determined to escape from the *ḥāra,* and so filled with unease. His interest in the history of art, it transpired, was institutional, not intellectual. He confessed that he had wanted a useful degree – in commerce, for instance. But because a single nationwide exam determines what Egyptians can study at university (top scorers are slotted into medicine and engineering; the dross into law and the arts), Ashraf's cousin had to suffer being assigned to art history.

The books were at the cousin's house, so we set off together through the alleyways on his Vespa, weaving through foot traffic and slowing for potholes until we came to a stop before the open doorway of an old house. The cousin pushed the scooter into a narrow courtyard with a dirt floor. Upstairs, a lady who had been hanging out washing clapped her shutters closed. Chickens tousled a pile of refuse in a corner. A startled pye-dog scooted out between my legs.

My host led me into an oblong room off the yard which was just big enough to fit a bench and a grossly outsized TV, complete with VCR. This was the showpiece, and Ashraf's cousin hovered around it as if for protection from the surrounding squalor. Would I like to see a *film amerikani*? Sure, I said, and instantly regretted the politesse, because the movie was an utterly appalling splatter flick. As far as I could tell from the screams and thrashing over the next hour, it was about an axe that comes alive and lops off half the teenage limbs of Texas. Each time my eyeballs abandoned yogic efforts to escape the massacre, ketchup squelched against the screen.

To complete the horror, the cousin's subject turned out to be abstract expressionism. He flipped through a book about Jackson Pollock, frowning at the illustrations, then resigned the heathen text to me and waited for my exegesis. But how to squeeze even the stubborn oxymoron of abstract expressionism into my limited Arabic, let alone the wider contexts of Western painting or art or philosophy, about which, it soon became clear, my pupil hadn't a clue? And how to extract sense from the hyperbole about the artist's discovering that his drip technique 'sowed arcs and whorls of virile colour' and that 'this was freedom at last'. It was a cultural short circuit. The only thing I could get across was that a man in America randomly dribbled paint on large canvases, and that certain pilgrims then worshipped these objects at museums and paid colossal sums for them. Even to me it sounded as fanciful as flying carpets. I think he believed me though, if only because it was written in a book, and there were pictures, and perhaps because it tallied with a general notion of inexplicable Western excess.

Days later, when I had recovered from my headache, Ashraf's cousin sent me a present. It was a small wooden box encrusted with a geometric inlay of ivory and mother-of-pearl – or rather artful plastic imitations thereof. A certain Eastern, Old World reproach seemed to lurk in this useful and pleasing object. I still have it somewhere, though chips of inlay have come unglued.

And then after several years I heard that the cousin had joined that immense drain of degree-holding Egyptians to the oil shiekhdoms of the east, and was driving trucks in Saudi Arabia. The money he sent home financed the building of a six-storey tenement in the *ḥāra,* filling the site of a house that had collapsed. (No casualties: the only people there at the time were making love on the second floor, and by some bizarre fluke their old brass bed slid to safety clean out the window and on to the alleyway.)

As for Ashraf, we drifted apart, each back to his own world and into his own version of respectability. Perhaps I had become too Cairene. My friends were now of a different class. To them the old *ḥāras* of Cairo were nearly as alien as the East End of Dickens' London would have been.

NOT FAR FROM Ashraf's neighbourhood, behind the millennium-old Mosque of al-Azhar, stands a great fifteenth-century mansion known as the House of Zaynab Khatun.

Just a few years ago two brothers from the impoverished Egyptian south – men of the very stock that, subsisting on a diet of bread and onions, have built and demolished succeeding Cairos – were labouring at the restoration of this house. One day when the foreman wasn't watching they pulled up a flagstone, and lo and behold there flashed a chink of gold. The brothers scrabbled in the black earth. The cache was huge, its value inestimable: some long-forgotten inhabitant, fearful of marauding Mamluks perhaps, had stashed hundreds and hundreds of gold dinars in the ground.

The brothers divvied up the treasure, swearing an oath of secrecy. Cunningly, they continued to work as day labourers while selling off the coins and salting away the cash. But then one day their own folly, their own fiery Upper Egyptian temper, betrayed them. Suspecting that the goldsmith who was fencing his share was cheating, one of the brothers got into a heated argument and tried to strangle the tradesman. Police arrived, looked at the merchandise, and immediately clapped both men in irons. Most of the cache was subsequently retrieved and housed in the Islamic Museum. The Upper Egyptians were thrown in prison. But, saddest of all, the tale set off a craze for ripping up floors and bashing at walls all over the Old City, much to the despair of conservationists.

The house is now a museum. Its imposing shape fills a corner made by a wiggle in the street behind al-Azhar. In the medieval style of the city, its first storeys are in cut stone, the upper ones of brick. The exterior walls are bare so as to deter the taxman, except for protruding *mashrafiyyas* – high windows of patterned lattice-work from where Zaynab Khatun could watch the outside world unveiled and still preserve her honour. The entrance passes under a low arch, then zigzags through a vaulted passage for greater security before emerging in a courtyard paved with flagstones. This is what Cairenes of the time aspired to: ownership of their own piece of sky, with a raised porch facing north across the open space to catch the cool Delta breeze.

It was just here, under this very block of pharaonic granite which makes a princely threshold to the courtyard, that the treasure was found, so the grizzled workman I find sitting alone here tells me. He is suspicious at first. Who am I? A police informer? A foreign agent? Or perhaps I know something he doesn't. But as he retells the story, reserve turns to rage. He plucks at his ragged vest and drawers. His Adam's apple jerks up and down as he rants in thick Upper Egyptian dialect. 'A curse on the government! Look at me. I want to eat meat. I want shoes. A curse on my family! My own brother's sons, the greedy bastards, never let on about the gold. They kept it all for themselves! And now what? The government feeds them in jail, for no work. Their children eat meat at home. And me, what about me? I eat nothing but bread and onions. A curse on them all!'

MY TAXI CRUISES away from al-Azhar and the House of Zaynab Khatun, high over the cluttered brownness of the Old City, until the flyover drops us into Opera Square. The driver doesn't know it, but I am travelling not only through centuries of time but also in another of Cairo's broad dimensions, going from depths of poverty to heights of wealth.

(And what scope this dimension has, I am thinking, recalling a day when I spent the morning in a ragpicker's hut surrounded by pigpens constructed of corrugated iron, and the afternoon at the luxurious apartment of a distinguished heart surgeon. Sitting on the dirt floor of that tin shack, where a live rat really did run across my companion's hand, the pretty young householder told us of her heart murmur and how she could not afford the operation she needed, and how she worried about who would raise her three children when she died. And then that same day, before a spectacular view of the Nile with the ragpickers' village far off on the smoky horizon, I lunched with the man who, as chance had it, was just the man she needed. How to connect those worlds?)

The taxi plunges into the downtown crush of cars and pedestrians. Haltingly, we move past this week's hoarding at the Cinema Miami. The poster painter has lovingly stroked each ripple of a muscleman's three-storey-high torso in fire-engine red.

In the background a damsel in distress inflates her green negligee while floating in mid-air with a gun and a stretch limo with a Mercedes star.

My driver is complaining. I would too, if I had to grind through the gears of a vintage Russian-built Fiat, in this buffalo-stampede of traffic, for ten hours a day to pay for my six children's schooling. (In fact the professional drivers of Cairo preserve a truly admirable cool considering the odds. Puttering along the Nileside Corniche once in some even cheaper Communist Bloc jalopy, I thought it was all over when a thunderous crash and hideous scraping jerked the taxi to a halt. The driver sat stock still. Then his head drooped down to the steering wheel. 'Again!' he moaned. It was not the first time, apparently, that the engine had fallen out.) We pull briefly alongside a blue police truck. The suspects boxed inside – religious terrorists? – are thumping on the metal walls and chanting 'God is great! There is no God but Allah!' A motorcyclist trailing storm clouds of bitter two-stroke exhaust cuts in front of us, nicking the Fiat's fender. My driver screams a profane genealogy out the window, ending in 'Son of a whore!' Survival here takes spirit as well as fatalism.

Soon we have crossed the river to the Giza side. A solid wall of high-rises crenellated with satellite dishes lines the shore. Cranes tower over a site upriver. A new colossus is going up where the penthouse is for sale at a cool $20 million. I know this because just last week at a stud farm near the Pyramids I met one of the contractors. The Italian engineer's job was to install an underwater sound system for the building's indoor swimming pool. The cost? A hundred thousand dollars. The Italian shrugged, distracted by the magnificent Arabian prancing in the corral. 'What for I dunno. They wannit, I build it.'

A sleek saloon flashes its highbeams and overtakes us. The owner is chatting on the phone, happy in the knowledge that his car is worth more than the lifetime earnings of a whole squadron of traffic cops like the one who has just waved him through a red light. (And, by the way, these cops have the highest levels of lead in the blood ever measured among any one profession anywhere in the world.)

Soon after, in a vast lobby panelled in polished granite, a trio of well-packed bodyguards eyes me as I step into the elevator. Up on the twenty-fourth floor a servant in a neat satin kaftan opens the door. It is my landlady's butler, Vegetables. His name isn't really Vegetables, but that is what Zaza calls him, affectionately, behind his back. She has a way of putting a comic twist on everything: her maid's code name, also a playfully direct translation of a common Egyptian name, is Emotions; the driver Hamdi is My Gratitude.

I find Zaza pacing in the salon.

'You can't be serious, Tutu, *mish maʿqūl!*' she is saying into the cordless phone, rolling her kohl-rimmed eyes for my benefit. She caps the receiver for a second. Her nails match the emerald on one finger. It is the size of a pigeon's egg.

'Be a sweetie and make me the usual,' she stage-whispers, gesturing towards the bar in the corner.

By the time I stir up a pair of vodka-and-tonics Zaza is flicking off the phone. 'God, that woman's a bore,' she says with her most winsome flash of little teeth. Then, noticing her nails as she fits a cigarette to her holder, she winks: 'Isn't this colour absolutely hideous? I love it.'

My landlady is the daughter of one of the more eccentric pashas. The noble Turkish blood shows in her parchment-pale skin, jet-black hair and utter lack of artifice. Her French and English are flawless, the product of many youthful summers spent at Gstaad, the George V and the Dorchester. Her taste in clothes runs to the trendiest of Japanese designers. Twice married and twice divorced, she has never worked a day in her life, thank God, as she would say.

With an army of cousins in high places, Zaza is also the source of the juiciest society gossip. Tutu is one of these cousins,

I gather, and has been regaling Zaza with the story of another cousin's marriage to some nouveau-riche industrialist.

'Can you imagine,' my hostess purrs, settling onto a chaise longue, 'the wedding invitations were engraved silver trays! I mean the trays *were* the invitation cards. A thousand of them. And the buffet!' – she downs another gulp of vodka – 'You won't believe it. It was supposed to be on some kind of *Out of Africa* theme, you know – coconuts and grass-skirted waiters. And they served the *saumon fumé* – this bit just kills me – on the *bald heads* of soldiers!'

She pauses for effect before explaining.

'The groom's uncle is a general, you see.'

I still don't get it.

Zaza waves a trail of impatient green nails: 'He ordered a whole brigade or whatever to shave off their hair, and shipped them in for the evening. You know, they had them sitting under the table with their heads sticking out through holes in the top, and the guests peeled the smoked salmon off their sweaty bald pates.'

She giggles, ending with a wince.

'We never had anything so *tacky* before the revolution, even if Papa did have the servants bury the leftovers in the garden so the peasants wouldn't see them. It's enough to make me take the veil!'

There is little likelihood of that, I think.

'Of course,' Zaza adds, 'Tutu thought the wedding was absolutely *marvellous*.'

LATE IN THE night, a Sri Lankan servant clicks open another bottle of Black Label. We are in the drawing room of a high-society decorator. The room has been done in Orientalist Baroque: aspidistras in brass urns, Bedouin carpets, divans studded with mother-of-pearl and draped with rugs from Persia and the Caucasus. It is a costume party. But if the few dozen guests are in fancy dress, the mood is sombre. News is out that a religious extremist has stabbed and severely injured the doyen of Egyptian letters, the octogenarian Naguib Mahfouz.

Out on the terrace overlooking the Nile, a Lebanese heiress in full biker's leather is telling a silk turbaned maharajah – a titled Belgian diplomat in reality – that force is the only thing that these bloody terrorists understand. They should hang them all, she insists.

The doorbell chimes and the host, who is in outrageous drag as Edith Piaf, sweeps through the party, Scotch in hand. The door bursts open. Two bearded intruders in long white robes charge into the room, yelling '*Allahu Akbar!*' and spraying the guests with machine-gun fire from their toy Kalashnikovs. The stunt is a success. It is carried off to shrieks and peals of laughter, and everyone is taken with the irony that one of the fundamentalist gunmen is the cousin of a Coptic minister in the government. The ice is broken, and as the dawn call to prayer approaches unheeded the host is performing his famous spoof of that darling of Cairo's Roaring Forties, Tahiyya Carioca, the slinkiest, sexiest belly dancer of all time.

CHAPTER ELEVEN

THE VOICE OF CAIRO

City suspended on words.
The alleys vocal chords,
Silence the scapegoat.
Edmond Jabes, *Les Clefs de la Ville,* 1951

O what a tongue we have:
It would melt even steel.
Ahmed Fouad Negm, colloquial poet, *c.* 1970

'*NOT EVERY SCRIBBLER is a poet, nor every hummer of tunes a singer. Not every fellow with a turban on his head is a learned sheikh, nor any man on a horse a knight. And not everyone who listens understands.*'

The rhythmic chant lulled the audience from the first word. But that final phrase, delivered in a rising pitch with a sly glare that dared them to join in the spirit of the telling, was a challenge. These were the 1990s, and this was an audience more attuned to Mozart and Molière than to folk tales told by an adenoidal fellah in a *galabiyya* and country shawl. But Izzat al-Qinawi, one of the last master storytellers of Egypt, held the Cairo Opera House in his spell.

This evening's tale was a single episode in the life of Abu Zayd, the legendary hero of the Arab tribe of Bani Hilal. The full epic would take far more than these thirty nights of Ramadan to tell – to tell how Abu Zayd's father disowned his first-born because the baby boy was black; how the young Abu Zayd endured exile to grow into a fearsome warrior; how he fought and nearly killed his greatest foe without realizing the man was his father; how the two were reconciled and Abu Zayd then led the Bani Hilal to victory over the kings of Tunis. Izzat al-Qinawi rode the story as if it were a stallion, trotting briskly in prose, sallying wildly into verse, and then shuffling down to a complicitous whispering narrative. From time to time the storyteller would stop dead, scan the crowd, pick out one listener, and demand to know if he was following. Just as Homer lavished punctillious detail on describing the shield of his hero Achilles, so did this modern minstrel elaborate his picture of Abu Zayd's miraculous sword in a flourish of superlatives. And just as the blind bard of Ancient Greece would have accompanied his voice with a harp, Izzat al-Qinawi sawed a reedy tune from his two-stringed fiddle. A drummer kept the beat, and a rustic chorus echoed the catchiest phrases.

The story ended, of course, on a note of high suspense: would Abu Zayd slay his own father? Were this not the staid Opera, al-Qinawi could have commanded a tribute of coins to reveal what happened next. Instead he got a standing ovation, and reviews in the next day's papers that proudly contrasted his native art with with the crassness of that more current form of serial drama, the TV soap opera.

LIKE ALL GREAT folk epics, the legend of Abu Zayd al-Hilali is rooted in historical fact. The Bani Hilal were a nomadic tribe who migrated westwards out of Arabia sometime in the eleventh century. They threatened Cairo, but the Fatimid caliph al-Mustansir paid off the marauding tribesmen, dispatching them to wreak havoc far away in the rival state that is now Tunisia. The story of their raiding then passed down orally from master storyteller to apprentice, gathering mythic nuances and plot twists through centuries of Bedouin memory until long after the Bani Hilal had settled or dispersed.

The legend of Abu Zayd was a perennial favourite in medieval Cairo, where storytelling was a highly specialized art. But tastes in narrative eventually changed, and then radio and television chased the old-time minstrels from city coffee houses. If it were not for the astoundingly capacious memories of a dwindling handful of professionals in the remote Upper Egyptian province of Qina – who happen to belong to the gipsy-like remnants of the Bani Hilal tribe – the story of Abu Zayd would have vanished.

In the Cairo of 1830 Edward Lane counted fifty reciters of the epic of Bani Hilal alone. But the city's coffee houses offered a broad repertoire in those days, ranging from tales of the Prophet to bawdy fantasies from *The Thousand and One Nights.* With thirty devoted practitioners, according to Lane, the romance of the Mamluk sultan al-Zahir Baybars rated second to Abu Zayd's in popularity. Whereas Abu Zayd battled in distant deserts among forgotten tribes, Baybars's exploits largely took place in the streets of late-thirteenth-century Cairo. This epic's origins lay not in folk tradition but in official propaganda.

As the founder of the Mamluk state – a state that was both internally unstable and perpetually at war – Baybars sorely needed to ensure the loyalty of his subjects. With the idea of promoting a cult of personality, he commanded court scribes to compose heroic accounts of his life. The sultan probably paid reciters to broadcast these tales of his piety and valour – much like the Ministry of Information's newsreels, with their rousing martial music and adoration of official occasions, that prefaced showings in Cairo cinemas until a few years ago. But over time Baybars's biography warped out of all recognition. What filtered down to Lane's coffee-shop listeners had blossomed magnificently into fable.

The less flattering medieval chronicles describe Baybars as a Mamluk slave who cleaved his way to fortune through ruthless soldiering and cunning politics. The storytellers' version presents him differently – as the orphaned son of a king who swashbuckles to fame, overcoming enemies and their plots to arrive in Egypt's capital as a respected amir. But at this point the demands of the Cairene audience appear to take over; fact and fiction diverge completely. Baybars hires a native stable boy by the name of Osman, and this appealing rogue elbows his master out of the story. Baybars the great warrior, whom history would record as the defeater of Christian crusaders and the Mongol hordes, from now on takes a back seat to this sidekick invented by the storytellers' imagination.

Osman is a classic urban character. Sassy and streetwise, he talks in Arabic rhyming slang to fool plodding Turkish-speaking officials. His Cairo is far removed from the courtliness of romance. The city which he calls his 'milch cow' is infested with gangsters and blackmailers, thieves disguised as sheikhs, crooked judges and bent secret police. Up in the Citadel, the reigning sultan is a hopeless drunkard.

Osman becomes the amir Baybars's guide to the Cairene underworld. His master, the ostensible hero, comes to represent the silent force of the state and is reduced to the status of a masked executioner. When he speaks it is in the heavy cadences of classical Arabic. The real protagonist – the one who gets all the best lines – is Osman. By a combination of blundering detective work and leadership of a motley gang of beggars, the stable boy delivers criminals to the law. He exposes the head of the secret police and the chief judge as uncircumcised infidels. In the end Osman traps the godfather of Cairo's underworld, a nattily dressed pimp and racketeer named Muqallad. Baybars dispatches all these wicked Christian imposters with his sword.

Perhaps it was this very unmodern note of religious triumphalism that erased the romance of Baybars from the twentieth-century storytelling repertoire. (Unlike the epic of the Bani Hilal, it is preserved only in writing.) Yet the depiction of Christians as a dangerous fifth column reflects how the story adapted to medieval public demand. It evolved from an official hagiography into a comic strip, a tale laced with all the conspiratorial undertones of working-class Cairo. Its real world was not that of the Citadel and its public affairs, but that of the *ḥāras* and market places of the city below. Its heroes were the rabble, not their masters. The real language was not Baybars's wooden-tongued Batman-speak. It was Osman's Cairene chaff.

THAT SPLIT BETWEEN high and low voices persists in Cairo today. It begins with the Arabic language itself.

The English poet Robert Graves remarked in the 1920s that his students at Cairo University seemed to have two distinct minds. They switched casually, he said, between what he called 'the irresponsible hedonistic café and cinema mind, which tends towards the French, and the grave moralizing bureaucratic mind, which tends towards the English'. Graves did not speak Arabic. If he could have, he would have realized that his students' native language offered ample scope for both 'minds'.

Just as Arabic music's use of quarter-tones allows for a much greater range of subtlety than the Western scale, the Arabic language spans a uniquely immense breadth. Sanskrit has evolved into Hindi. Latin has centrifuged into a dozen tongues. Arabic, however, has kept its polyglossic unity. It has maintained the vertical link to its roots even while branching into myriad contemporary forms. Its scope contains everything from the 1,400-year-old heavenly speech of the Koran to the poetry of thirteenth-century mystics to the argot of Cairo street urchins. It is as if everyday English made use of both the original Greek and King James versions of the Bible along with gangsta-rap and Pentagon bureaucratese.

Classical Arabic, the language of the written word, is seen as both immutable and universal. Its purity is institutionally maintained. A full-time staff at al-Azhar University vets every letter of every new edition of the Koran to ensure flawless concordance with ancient models. Protecting the literal word of God is a serious task indeed: theoretically, under Egyptian law, a misplaced diacritic in the Holy Scripture can result in a jail term. Cairo's Arabic Language Academy, meanwhile, struggles to preserve classical usages by sifting musty texts to find pure Arabic terms for modern things such as computers and radios.

Like its French counterpart in Paris, the academy fights a mostly losing battle. Cairenes persist stubbornly in calling their gadgets *al-radyū* and *al-kumbyūtar*. Their spoken language has adapted inexorably to a millennium of outside influence. It has Arabized French and Italian terms for arts and mechanics; Turkish for ranks and professions; English for science and business. '*Rubabikiyaaa!*' is what any dealer in cast-offs will cry as he pushes his barrow through Cairo's streets, probably quite unaware that he is speaking recognizable Italian: *robe vecchie* = old clothes. '*Alle uno, alle due, alle tre!*' goes the countdown of a Cairene auctioneer as he disposes of an *iskritwār istīl ambīr* – an Empire-style *escritoire* or writing desk, or a *tableau romantique,* a petit-point tapestry showing a picnic in some glade of eighteenth-century Bavaria such as any self-respecting Cairene mother-in-law would kill for.

Whereas classical Arabic is used sparingly in common speech, colloquial Arabic is rarely written down – except when its punch is needed, as in cartoon captions, song lyrics or advertising. As opposed to classical Arabic's vertical integration in time, colloquial Arabic undergoes horizontal variations according to geography. A Moroccan and an Iraqi have little or no hope of understanding each other unless they resort to the literary language – or at very least to the lingua franca of the Cairene dialect, which through music and film and television has projected itself throughout the Arab world.

Because of its scriptural roots, the high end of Arabic embodies an implication of how things *should* be. It is the language of ideals, of religion and the state: the language of the hero Baybars, in the model of his romance. The low end of Arabic – the speech of the anti-hero Osman – tends to reflect how things really are. Mostly the two voices stay apart, adding yet another dimension to the division of consciousness Cairo exhibits in its geography and manners. Sometimes the two fuse. A politician, say, will spice his high-blown rhetoric with some pithy colloquial phrase to underline a point. Beggars commonly quote from the Koran – the text which is the inimitable pinnacle of classical perfection – in order to attract alms.

High Arabic is what is used for news reporting. This gives current events a serious cast that has gone missing in the hyped-up West. 'Summit Meeting Achieves Important Positive Results for Arab Solidarity and Bilateral Ties': so reads a typically soporific *Al-Ahram* headline. Even the most lurid crime stories undergo a classical bleaching: 'Thus I was obliged to deal the foul miscreant a mighty blow, so as to avenge my dear slain brother' is how the testimony of a vendetta murderer is likely to be rendered in print. The elegance of Arabic script adds weight to the simplest of meanings: the exquisite calligraphic medallions stencilled on the scuffed and dented sides of city buses say nothing more than 'Cairo Transport Authority'.

The written language imbues official pronouncements with a sense of lapidary permanence. With Cairo's broadcasting and its major newspapers in the hands of the state, their voice naturally assumes the role played by court biographers in Baybars's time. They present the official history, the stock version. They order news not according to its significance but in order of the rank of the newsmaker – rather as Ancient Egyptian artists always pictured the Pharaoh three times the size of mere mortals. Occasionally the tone rises to the level of panegyrics nearly as saccharine as in a text found at Saqqara, which describes how courtiers replied to the pharaoh Amenophis III when he asked for advice on whom to appoint as chief steward of the port of Memphis. 'Would we tell Ptah [the god of crafts] how to do a job?' the courtiers replied. 'Would we teach Thoth [the god of letters] how to speak?'

But unlike other 'Oriental' places – unlike Maoist Beijing or Saddamist Baghdad, for instance – worldly old Cairo is richly endowed with scepticism. Down-to-earth attitudes have always devalued the currency of rhetoric. And in the absence of practical application, the sloganeering of official pronouncements loses impact. In one famous incident after Egypt's crushing defeat in the Six Day war, a group of Cairene writers petitioned the government to drop the word 'battle' from its propaganda. No real battle was being fought to retrieve the land Egypt had lost, they complained, and overuse had drained the word of 'power, effectiveness and credibility'.*

Egypt's favourite story in ancient times – judging by how often scribes copied it as a writing exercise from the Twelfth Dynasty onwards – was the Tale of the Eloquent Peasant. It says much about the country's enduring qualities that this story of a poor, oppressed farmer who talks himself all the way to the royal court of Memphis has never faded from folk consciousness. The biblical tale of Joseph was probably influenced by it. It inspired some of the earliest plays and musicals in twentieth-century Cairo. Even now a long-running cartoon series in *Al-Akhbar* pictures a peasant who sits humbly at the foot of the prime minister, but

* In similar vein, historian Nadav Safran ascribes the failure of democracy in Egypt to the high-blown associations given to the word in Arabic: 'The exclusively idealistic understanding of democracy is one of the reasons for the strange phenomenon that was repeatedly observed in Egypt, of various politicians and movements singing the praise of democracy while at the same time suppressing or even destroying altogether the institutions and procedures needed to make it function.'

manages to expose government bumbling by masterful circumlocution in preposterously countrified speech.

The endurance of the tale reflects the fact that, in an ancient country where power has always been concentrated among a small elite in the capital, words have often been the only weapon in the hands of common people. While Cairo's kings in every age have showered sycophants with gold, the common people have never shied from heaping rulers with ridicule.

Al-Mutanabbi was the most irreverent, and most beloved, of medieval Arab poets. Born in poverty as the son of a water-bearer in the Iraqi city of Kufa, he quickly developed a talent for verse that allowed him to wander across the Arab East from one wealthy patron to the next. He made it eventually to Cairo – or Fustat as the city was still known in the tenth century. Here he earned his keep as a panegyrist at the court of Kafur al-Zimam.

This African eunuch – whose name incidentally meant Camphor, a typically cloying name for a household eunuch, but laughable for a sovereign ruler – had risen to control Egypt in the twilight years of the minor Ikhshidid dynasty, just before the arrival of the Fatimids. Kafur was partial to his court jesters. When, after the great earthquake of the year AD 954, one exclaimed that the tremor had been caused by the people dancing for joy because of their ruler's virtues, he was rewarded with a purse of 1,000 gold dinars. Al-Mutanabbi, too, did well from such largesse. But in time he soured on his master. He accused Kafur of living high on the hog while the city starved. Inevitably, the poet was obliged to flee Fustat. He took revenge by firing off this satirical blast:

Before meeting that eunuch, I seem to recall,
I thought thinking took place in the head.
Now I've scanned his wits, there's no doubt at all
That thinking is done in the balls.'

Such biting repartee surfaces over and over in the annals of the city. It was after Cairenes began to chant similar rhyming insults that the Mamluk sultan Baybars al-Jashankir had 300 tongues cut out. (He was soon overthrown.) A further small example: five centuries after al-Mutanabbi, the historian Ibn Taghribirdi wrote of a corrupt governor of Cairo that if a shoe were to smite the nape of his neck the shoe would protest, 'For what sin am I being struck?' Sir Richard Burton recognized the same scoffing tone while translating *The Thousand and One Nights*. That amalgam of tales, he said, betrayed its Cairene influence with 'a rollicking Rabelaisian humour underlaid by the caustic mother wit of Sancho Panza'.

To this day, nothing is so admired in Cairo as sharpness of wit. No trait is so despised as having what Egyptians call 'heavy blood', which is to say no sense of humour. The general hilarity can be grating: the jiving and joshing in any Cairo market street will strain the patience of anyone but a Cairene. But taken in the right spirit it is just plain fun – and certainly more so than the sullen mind-your-own-businessness typical of the West. A keen sense of the ridiculous commonly spices the simplest exchanges. Where else would a taxi driver leap out of his cab, kneel down on the asphalt, and kiss the white line at an intersection? This happened once in front of me. 'See, *ya bey*,' the cabbie shouted to the cop who was about to ticket him, 'the white line isn't angry any more.'

With the same ease that Roman strangers discuss fine points of cuisine or Londoners the weather, Cairenes break the ice by cracking jokes and coining puns. The whiplash of humour can be heard at any café, capped by a round of belly laughs rising into peals of sheer delight. The best of Cairo's casual comics can snap punchlines back and forth for hours on end until they exhaust themselves with laughter. Most often the butt of humour is the unfortunate *Ṣaʿīdi* or country bumpkin from Upper Egypt. A sample tale: an Alexandrian, a Cairene and a *Ṣaʿīdi* are stranded in the desert. A jinn appears and grants them each one wish. 'Stretch me on the beach at Maamoura surrounded by girls in bikinis,' says the Alexandrian, and vanishes. 'Put me on a prayer mat in the Mosque of al-Husayn,' says the Cairene, and vanishes. The *Ṣaʿīhdi* looks miserable. 'I'm so lonely,' he says at last. 'Can't you bring my friends back?'

Not just *Ṣaʿīdis* suffer; Cairene humour holds nothing sacred. Within hours of President Sadat's assassination in 1981 the city reverberated with the crackle of freshly minted jokes. Sadat, many had noticed shortly before his death, had developed a tell-tale 'raisin' – the patch of puckered skin on the forehead that is a mark of excessive ardour in prayer. Few regarded his piety as sincere. When street sweepers cleaned up the fatal reviewing stand, I recall one café jokester saying on the very evening of the *rayyis*'s assassination, they found the presidential 'raisin' on the floor.

The art of withering satire was once so highly developed that any matron of Cairo's back alleys could, if provoked, savage a rival with an extended diatribe in rhyming prose. This unique form of verbal abuse, known as *radḥ*, was initiated by a gesture of contemptuous abandon as the assailant spread her *milāya* on the ground. Her speech was then delivered swaggeringly, with one hand crooked on the hip and the other cocked at the eyebrow. The salvo might go something like this:

You lowest of the low,
No lower can you go.
You rusty needle.
You dirty doormat.
*You're cheaper than a picture from a photomat.**

CAIRENES MAY STILL be merciless jokers, but the ritual taunting of *radḥ* is more likely to be performed on television these days

* This verse is adapted from one recalled from childhood by Dr Afaf Lutfi al-Sayyid (See bibliography).

than live on the streets. On the small screen, the mud-slinging of alley housewives may be pictured as undignified and unfeminine or, more cuttingly, as a quaint custom from a bygone age.

Radio and television are powerful mass acculturators everywhere. Their homogenizing influence is particularly potent in a city like Cairo, where only a slim majority can read and write. It is especially strong when the forces that control programming see themselves as engaged in a civilizing mission, and when few families have either the money or the physical space at home for other forms of entertainment. Even Cairo's knack for resisting authority has not stopped it from succumbing to the media's conformist pressure. In today's city, attitudes and aspirations are increasingly framed by television's orthodoxies – by its presentation of mainstream religion and consumerism and by its particular reconstruction of Egypt's past. In this way the heavy tones of high Arabic are making steady inroads into the carefree realm of the vulgate.

Cairo's Establishment is used to imposing its own image on the rest of Egypt. The critic Lewis Awad neatly expressed the city intellectuals' attitude to commoners thirty years ago when he declared their duty to 'rescue' their fellows from what he called 'the hellish coarseness lurking around them like a ghoul waiting to ambush them and swallow them up'. What Awad had in mind was what he saw as the need to guide tradition-bound Egyptians to more modern, secular notions of citizenship. Yet his sense of mission – and his fear of the ignorant mob – reflected a sense of distance from the masses that was little different from that assumed by Memphite nobles or medieval Mamluks.

The government took its civilizing mission all too seriously after the 1952 revolution. It assumed a full monopoly of the press and the airwaves. Newspapers which had reflected party or financial interests, and later television, which began broadcasting in 1962, became mouthpieces for the government. Censors sterilized movies, plays and even songs with modernizing, socializing intent. They produced a list of sixty-four images which could never be filmed. Everyday sights like donkeys, street vendors and beggars were deemed too 'uncouth' for public viewing. Scenes like strikes and demonstrations were 'destabilizing'; in the celluloid version of Cairo such events simply did not happen.

The state has relinquished many controls since, particularly regarding the printed word. Today, opposition journals cram Cairene news-stands with views from extreme left to far right. But whereas 73 per cent of respondents in a 1997 survey said TV was their main source of news, only 8 per cent said they relied on opposition newspapers. And whereas 90 per cent of Cairo households own a television, barely a third of adults are high-school graduates.

Moreover, the government has kept its monopoly of the airwaves. The broadcasting industry it controls is huge in scale. Some 30,000 people work on thirty floors of studios and offices at the Ministry of Information's mammoth Nileside headquarters. From here Radio Cairo beams forth the Voice of the Arabs, the Voice of Palestine, the Voice of the Valley (aimed at Egypt's upstream neighbours in Sudan), the Voice of Cairo and short-wave broadcasts in tongues from Amharic to Zulu as well as local programmes in French, German, English, Italian, Greek and Armenian. State television carries three channels in Cairo alone in addition to a satellite channel. In-house production fills nine-tenths of TV airtime – a significant feat in a world increasingly dominated by Hollywood. One recent Ramadan – the fasting month being prime viewing season, since Egyptians tend to collapse in front of their TV sets after their sunset breakfast – the Ministry of Information launched no less that eighteen serials. They ranged from a kitsch costume-drama version of the now-fashionable epic of Bani Hilal to sitcoms to socio-political sagas.

Popular serials draw 20-million-strong audiences and stretch to over a hundred episodes. Some, like the 1993 series *Layali al-Hilmiyya,* which traced three generations in the life of one of the older quarters of the city, tackle social questions realistically. On the whole, though, Cairo's TV fare is stodgy and didactic. This is perhaps inevitable given the alliance between the government's propaganda needs and the superior class attitudes of most producers and directors. The prim tastes of the conservative Arab oil monarchies impose a further constraint, since these countries constitute the major export market for Egyptian TV drama. Morality guidelines in Saudi Arabia, for instance, forbid a female character from appearing alone in a room with a male character who is neither her husband nor a close relative.

The cooks in the Ministry of Information kitchens keep Cairo's information diet bland, but they are not the only *bawābs* of public taste. With the excuse of maintaining cultural standards in music, a body known as the Listeners' Committee must approve all songs broadcast on Cairo radio. The stuffy committee rarely approves of innovation, so relegating popular sounds to the bootleg-cassette circuit. The pop singer Ahmad Adawiyya, who sold millions of tapes during the 1980s, has never had a single one of his innuendo-laced hits broadcast, because the committee considers them too 'base'. (Faced with a similar ban, one performer printed his cassettes with the address and phone number of the state censor.) Theatre and cinema suffer restrictions too. Film directors must submit both screenplays and finished prints to the government's Bureau of Artistic Content. And, although they have cultivated ad-libbing into a fine art, Cairo's stage actors can still face prosecution for departing from approved scripts or otherwise offending 'public morality'.

Political censorship may be less heavy-handed today than in the 1960s, but the religious revival of recent years has squeezed the margins of free speech in similar ways. In 1985, for instance, police raided a bookshop near al-Azhar. Tipped off by the university's clerics, they seized 2,000 illustrated copies of a work that a subsequent court ruling described as 'violating the rules of decency and negating the morality of Egyptian society so as to invite youth into deviation and corruption'. The offending text was none other than that classic of world literature *The Thousand and One Nights*. The case was dismissed on appeal, on the grounds that the book was a necessary resource for research, but the very idea that a classic work could be banned in modern times cast a chill over intellectuals. Imagine the Vatican trying to suppress Chaucer's *Canterbury Tales* or Boccaccio's *Decameron*.

The chill was to grow colder. The clash between the city's bawdy, light-hearted 'café and cinema' mind and its dour, moralizing side was to grow ever more violent.

In 1991, for instance, censors banned a play because of a single prop in the set. One side of a revolving pedestal showed an image of the Kaaba at Mecca – the shrine housing the sacred Black Stone that is the focal point of Muslim prayer. Turned around, the prop became an oil barrel on to which a belly dancer leaped. This hint at the double standards of Saudi Arabia, whose citizens may be pious at home but whom Cairenes are more likely to see cavorting in the city's gambling casinos, was judged inimical to Egypt's relations with the oil-rich kingdom. Mosque sermons denounced the playwright, who died soon after of a heart attack, penniless, at the age of thirty.

In 1992 a conservative *Al-Ahram* columnist accused an obscure, self-published novelist named Ala' Hamed of blasphemy for poking fun at various and sundry prophets. Hamed's books were suppressed. The author was fired from his job as a tax inspector and charged with blasphemy. Shortly after testifying in Hamed's favour at his trial, the outspoken secularist Farag Foda was shot dead outside his office. Police placed Hamed under twenty-four-hour surveillance for his own safety. 'My only crime', the beleaguered author told me in the cramped three-room walk-up he shared with his wife and two daughters, 'is that I failed to understand the space of freedom in Egypt. It is like this.' He drew a narrow circle in the air. Hamed was eventually given a one-year jail term.

In 1995, a knife-wielding fanatic stabbed Naguib Mahfouz,

injuring the eighty-two-year-old Nobel laureate so seriously that he could no longer use his writing hand. The would-be assassin's excuse was than in the 1950s al-Azhar had banned Mahfouz's novel *Children of Gebelawi* on the grounds that this story set in a Cairo alley was an allegory of Koranic history. A year later, courts forbade the screening of a film by Yousef Chahine, one of Egypt's most influential directors. Because *The Emigrant* was based on the bibical and (and Koranic) story of Joseph, it was judged to contravene the Islamic injunction against portrayal of prophets.

Another ruling that year aroused an even greater furore. After a two-year legal battle, Egypt's highest court of appeal declared that Nasr Abu Zayd, a respected Arabic-literature scholar at Cairo University, was an apostate from Islam. As such, he could not remain married to his Muslim wife. His mistake was to have suggested that parts of the Koran should be understood metaphorically, not as literal fact. 'He denies the attributes of God in that He is a king with soldiers, angels and a throne,' thundered a report from the state prosecutor. Professor Abu Zayd's books were removed from sale. Having no intention of divorcing, and fearing for their lives at the hands of religious extremists, the couple abandoned Cairo for a European exile.

The tribulations of Professor Abu Zayd shocked Cairene liberals profoundly. Despite its flaws, the justice system has long been seen as an ally in their cause. Now, it seemed, even this bastion of freedom both from the state and from religious zealotry had fallen. Yet those who took a longer view saw the ruckus as simply a nastier replay of the apostasy trials of the 1920s. It was another episode in the contest that has forged Cairo's world-view in this century – a contest that has pitted those who favour an open society against those who don't.

The important thing, in the end, may be that the contest remains unresolved. Cairo's intellectuals have not taken Professor Abu Zayd's defeat lying down. They have counter-attacked. Films, plays and popular TV serials have portrayed religious radicals as misguided, violence-prone opportunists. Liberal publishers have reissued controversial classics from Egypt's brief Age of Enlightenment. Young writers still dare to challenge sexual and religious taboos.

Sadly for them, few Cairenes pay much notice. This city may produce three-fifths of all books published in Arabic, but then the whole Arabic-speaking world releases fewer new books every year than does tiny Belgium. In years of riding the metro here I have never once seen anyone reading anything other than a textbook, a newspaper or the Koran. Publishers consider a meagre 3,000 copies to be a generous print run for a well-reviewed novel. Even such a prolific writer as Naguib Mahfouz earns far more from translation rights than he does at home: his own daughters, he says, prefer to see his books in film versions rather than read them. What do sell in the tens of thousands are overblown political exposés, religious tracts and, increasingly, works of yellow journalism that promise – but seldom deliver – titillation galore. In 1996, seven out of ten Cairo best-sellers flaunted scantily clad women on their covers next to titles like *Sex and the Jinn, A Lady From Hell* or *Girls For Export.*

As much as government meddling or religious prudery, it is the fickleness of the Cairo audience that keeps artists from pushing themselves to their limits. It is always easier to play for laughs here, to serve up clichés rather than strive for refinement. The lack of audience resonance often consumes youthful talents. Such is the case, for example, with a promising film-maker like Khayri Bishara, whose output switched from highly sensitive dramas in the 1980s to sappy musicals in the 1990s. Cairenes, it seems, have changed little in the 600 years since al-Maqrizi accused them of exalting frivolity over substance.

IRONICALLY, THE APATHY of the wider public brings Cairo's fractious thinking elite together in a shared sense of alienation. Secularists feel alienated from the religious discourse that is still the mainstream of popular expression. Religious radicals feel alienated from the Western influence they see as steadily encroaching on their Islamic heritage. The one group is accused of aping the West; the other of trying to recreate the past. Between these two extremes, other kinds of tension surface: the struggle between the entrenched, father-knows-best generation and younger voices clamouring for the oxygen of free debate; the alienating forces of Cairo's perplexingly rapid growth and of its class divisions. Yet the poles of discord also produce a magnetic pull, a longing to fuse into a common culture the realms of high Arabic and low, of foreign style and local tradition.

Sadly, it is mostly the case that Cairo's contrary currents fail to fuse. In fact mutual misunderstanding often mounts to intolerable extremes.

This is what 140 upper-class teenagers found in 1997, when they were hauled from their homes at dawn by anti-terrorist squads and hurled into prison. The trouble was that a scaremongering press had taken their cultish fashion for black lipstick, skull and crossbones T-shirts, rave dances and heavy-metal music as clear signs of Satan-worship. The narrow-minded public, propelled by class envy and led by the religious establishment, were happy to ride the ensuing wave of witch-hunting hysteria. And even if the rich kids had never, as it turned out, engaged in the orgies and drinking of chickens' blood that the gutter press had claimed, the common thinking was that they deserved a reprimand for straying so far West of the Egyptian mainstream.

So the satisfaction at their arrest was general. Yet even conservatives gaped at the medieval mindset shown by the president of the Higher State Security Court, who wrote to *Al-Ahram* with the explanation that these wayward souls should not be blamed for their wickedness, because they were in fact literally children of devils. 'A devil may marry a woman and this is a fact without argument,' wrote Judge Ahmad Badur. Whenever a man slept with his wife when she was menstruating, or did so without the cover of a sheet, or without first invoking God's blessing: whenever he allowed lapses such as these, said the judge, why then the Devil would slip in. And so, he concluded, 'Devils' children from human women are the gays and sexual perverts ... and that is why it is neither strange nor surprising that they should lean towards their real father, the Devil...'

The predicament of Cairo's heavy-metal fans, and indeed of its Western-oriented elite as a whole, is aptly described by the Arab-American scholar Fouad Ajami: 'Societies at the periphery of the [Western] world desperately flaunt the trappings of modernity, because the cosmopolitan layers intuitively feel their own isolation. On some level they realize that bourgeois civilization as process eludes them.'

Small wonder, then, that many modern Cairenes feel divorced from their fellows. Yet there is nothing new to the prevailing sense of alienation. A generation ago, the novelist Waguih Ghali wrote that Cairo looked cosmopolitan not because so many foreigners lived here, but because many Egyptians felt and acted like strangers in their own land.

In fact alienation has been the central, linking theme in literature since Cairo's emergence as a modern city. It appears in one of the first attempts in Arabic to emulate the form of the European novel, *The Story of Isa bin Hisham* by Muhammad al-Muwaylihi (1858–1930). Published in the 1890s, this is a Rip Van Winkle tale* about a pasha who rises from the grave fifty years after his death. The pasha wanders from the al-Khalifa cemeteries into the great bustling capital, and finds it has altered beyond all recognition. He is shocked to see native Cairenes disporting themselves in bars, and to see them dominated by foreigners in business. In one scene the old boy calls a cheating

*Actually, al-Muwaylihi's inspiration is more likely to have been the Koranic story of the People of the Cave, which, like the Christian legend of the Seven Sleepers of Ephesus, describes a group of youths who fell asleep in a cave, only to wake up hundreds of years later.

donkey driver an insolent peasant. To his astonishment the boy rebukes him: 'We are in an age of liberty,' declares the upstart. 'There is no difference any more between a donkey driver and a prince.'

A generation on, the influential writer Muhammad Taymur (1892–1921) kept an almost anthropological distance between the observing author and his characters. In his short story 'The Train', a representative sample of Egyptians argue in a train compartment over the question of education. An old Turk and a village headman agree that the poor should not be educated, lest they learn to lose respect for their masters. They appeal for support to the wisdom of an Azharite sheikh. The turbanned cleric replies in classical Arabic, with the smug assurance that his hallowed dictum will seal the issue. 'Offer not learning to the sons of the lower orders,' he intones. While a young, Europeanized effendi laughs off the incident, the narrator is struck with despair. It is the despair felt by the educated Cairene whose sense of belonging to Egypt is cramped by the burden of tradition. Yet as the author alights from the compartment, his ears buzzing with anger, the train roars and whistles as a symbol of the inevitable triumph of the modern world.

The novella *Umm Hashim's Lantern*, published in 1943, explored similar themes. The author, Yahya Haqqi, was, however, inspired by a more romantic nationalism and sentimental Islam. He resolved his hero's alienation differently.

The Umm Hashim of the title is a popular name for the Prophet's granddaughter Sayyida Zaynab, around whose shrine in the south of the Old City the action revolves. The story tells of Ismail, a boy from the neighbourhood who travels to Europe, becomes a doctor, and returns to find his fiancée stricken with blindness. Ismail recoils in horror when his mother reveals she has been treating the ailment by dribbling holy oil from the lamp in Umm Hashim's tomb into the girl's eyes. The doctor hurls the phial of oil out the window and storms off, disgusted with the ignorance and superstition of his own family. But as he wanders for days alone through the city he is drawn inexorably to Sayyida Zaynab. At last he comes back to his roots. Ismail enters the shrine of the saint, begs its guardian for some oil, and vows to devote his life to curing his beloved – with his science now reinforced by faith in miracles.

Cairo's modern literati, having seen their national literature evolve from romanticism to realism, would find Ismail's resolution unconvincingly naive. Secularists, in particular, would see in it echoes of the same contradictions that mark present-day debate (and, indeed, that have characterized intellectual life here since the first Cairenes returned from studying in Paris nearly 200 years ago, only to find that their people rejected the materialistic world-view they had acquired abroad). Yet the attempt, like Ismail's to bring together heritage and intellect, heart and mind, remains the overriding challenge for Egyptian intellectuals.

This explains why many look back to the two decades before the disastrous 1967 war as a golden age. In those exciting years when Egypt overthrew its colonial masters and embarked on wrenching social reform, Cairo experimented daringly with cultural fusions. New idioms emerged in music, theatre, painting and film. The voice of Cairo became for a time the modern voice of the Arabs as a whole. If alienation was what it spoke of, the words still had resonance. In differing ways, every Arab country had suffered that split in consciousness which Western domination effected between outward-looking cities and inward-looking hinterlands. But it seemed to be only in Cairo that some kind of resolution was being forged, and articulated in a tremendous outpouring of talent.

THE LONG REIGN of Egypt's great twentieth-century diva Umm Kulsoum encapsulated modern Cairo's golden age. Rarely in history has one artist entranced so vast an audience for such a span of years. Umm Kulsoum was Edith Piaf and Maria Callas, Frank Sinatra and Luciano Pavarotti rolled into one. To 150 million Arabs she was the Star of the East, the Nightingale of the Nile, the Lady of Arabic Song. To Cairenes she was simply *al-Sitt* – The Lady.

For the thirty-seven years before her retirement in 1973, listeners across the Arab world tuned radios to Cairo on the first Thursday night of every month. This was when Umm Kulsoum broadcast live from the Cinema Qasr al-Nil, in marathon concerts that often stretched to six hours in length, ending at three or four in the morning. So devoted were her followers that when one fervent aficionado failed to take his usual front-row seat at a concert Umm Kulsoum sent the police to find him during the interval. It turned out that his father had just died. The fan attended the second half of the concert anyway. In the 1960s an admirer in Kuwait sent Umm Kulsoum a silver Cadillac Eldorado fitted with a fridge and a TV. A farmer in the Nile Delta sent her a cow and a water buffalo. When Umm Kulsoum went on international tour after the 1967 war she raised millions of pounds to re-equip the defeated Egyptian army. During her terminal illness Syrian radio kept an open telephone link to her hospital for spot reports on her health.

Her funeral in 1975 surpassed President Nasser's. It brought over 2 million mourners on to the streets of Cairo. The crowd kidnapped her body, carried it the full three miles from Tahrir Square to the Mosque of al-Husayn, and would have interred Umm Kulsoum next to the head of the Prophet's grandson if the imam of the mosque had not pleaded for them to take the body to its proper grave.

Two decades later Umm Kulsoum's tomb in the al-Khalifa cemetery remains a popularly visited shrine. A website on the Internet preserves her memory, as does the Umm Kulsoum troupe which still performs her classics on the first Thursday of every month throughout Cairo's winter concert season. The Umm

Kulsoum radio station broadcasts from five to ten p.m. daily. Half the city tunes to the opening hour, carrying The Lady's rich voice – slightly husky in her later years – across town from shop to taxi to factory floor and family kitchen. Rare is the Egyptian – or indeed the Arab – who does not know the lyrics to such emotion-charged ballads as *'Al Atlal'*, *'Inta ʿUmri'* or *'Fakkaruni'*.* Rarer still is one who does not know the story of Umm Kulsoum: of how she was born around the turn of the century into dirt-poverty in a Delta village, gained widening fame as a Koran chanter at country weddings, and then reached Cairo and enduring stardom.

Her rise mirrored the city's transformation from a sleepy Arab town to a cosmopolitan capital. By the end of the 1920s this daughter of a village sheikh was earning $80,000 a year – which would have been a fortune even in Hollywood in those times. Her repertoire had shifted from traditional religious odes to love songs, with lyrics by famous poets set to tunes by modern Egyptian composers. Her accompanists were no longer *galabiyya*-clad yokels but top-notch musicians in jackets and bow ties. This girl who used to roll up her sleeves and eat with her fingers, wrote a critic in the Cairo weekly *Rose al-Yusuf* in 1926, now ate with a knife and fork, asked you '*Comment ça va?*' and answered '*Très bien, merci.*'

Early training in Koran recitation gave Umm Kulsoum perfect command of pure Arabic diction. Rigorous self-discipline gave her unparalleled vocal range and control. Her powers of improvisation were so great that it was said she never sang a phrase the same way twice. Responding to the calls for encores that make Cairene concerts as much a party as a spectacle, she could repeat a verse fifty times in a row, subtly varying pitch and intonation every time and driving listeners to ever dizzier heights of ecstasy. Nor did Umm Kulsoum rely on talent alone. Her personality was so forceful that by the 1940s she chaired both the Listeners'

* 'The Ruins', 'You Are My Life', 'They Made Me Remember'.

Committee of Cairo Radio and the Egyptian Musicians' Syndicate. For twenty years she exercised a practical veto over what Egyptians listened to. When the career of a rival, the Syrian-born star Ismahan, was cut short by a fatal car crash in 1946, it was rumoured that Umm Kulsoum was responsible. (My *bawāb* still believes this was the case, just as he stubbornly insists that Umm Kulsoum herself was poisoned by President Sadat's wife because the latter was jealous of the singer's fame.)

Umm Kulsoum was more than a great diva. To her generation she became the embodiment of an Arab cultural renaissance. Fusing classical training and folk sensibility with Cairo's polished urban forms, she pulled together the strands of a common identity that had been torn apart by colonialism. With her haughty demeanour undercut by a razor wit, and with her long-sleeved, high-necked gowns and trademark handkerchief and dark glasses, Umm Kulsoum's persona suggested a blending of Western style with Eastern modesty. Illiterate listeners found they could respond to the classical poems she sang. Educated critics raved at the subtlety she could bring to simple, colloquial lyrics. In the 1940s her aching rendition of the words 'Mere wishes do not gain demands / The world is won by struggle alone' seemed to express the very soul of Egypt crying for an end to British domination. When, in the 1960s, her voice trembled at the phrase from '*Al-Atlal*' 'Give me my freedom / Let loose my hands', her emotion evoked a range of longings, from the Palestinian yearning for nationhood to the demands of Arab women for equal rights.

UMM KULSOUM WAS the brightest star in Cairo's musical firmament, but she was not the only one. Other talents added to the city's lustre: the innovative rhythms and orchestration of prolific singer-composer Muhammad Abd al-Wahab, the slick virtuosity of Syrian-born Farid al-Atrash, the honeyed smoothness of teen idol Abd al-Halim Hafez. Before 1970 there was quite simply no Arab entertainer who approached any of them in popularity.

In fact rivals could not hope to compete. No place but Cairo had the means to transform talent into legendary fame. In 1950 the rest of the Arab world had produced a total of ten feature films. This city alone had turned out over 300 – with many reaching technical standards that matched the best European productions. From the 1940s to the 1960s Cairo studios were rolling out fifty films a year. Their musicals and steamy romances, stark melodramas and slapstick comedies entranced audiences that were still largely immersed in folklore. Egyptian directors' treatment of subjects like adultery, misogyny and homosexuality reflected a confidence in the need to prod and entice their Arab cousins into modernity. The glamorous settings of Cairo's celluloid world, the sleek Buicks and Cadillacs cruising avenues tinselled with neon and spangled with movie stars, projected an urban polish that was both tantalizing and disturbing. Very disturbing to some: when the 1941 hit *Intisar al Shabab* ('The Triumph of Youth') was shown in southern Syria, Druze tribesmen fired their rifles at the screen. They were shocked to see the green-eyed star Ismahan, who happened to come from a noble Druze family, appear in make-up and nylon stockings.

The images of over 2,000 Cairo-produced films form a collective Arab vision of the city. The stock sets of its studios are more familiar even than the Main Streets and mean streets of Hollywood: the grand staircase in the pasha's mansion where heroines swoon; the *ḥāra* in the Old City where doe-eyed maidens lower shopping baskets from balconies; the Pyramids Road nightclub where sequined dancers gyrate between tables of drunken admirers. Cairo is a pervasive cultural reference point: in Tunis, someone jokingly told me a friend should be sent to La Mannouba. 'That's our Abbasiyya,' he explained, referring to the district – mentioned often in Egyptian movie farces – where Cairo's equivalent of Bedlam or Bellevue is located.

These days critics complain of a decline in quality, yet the city still turns out three times more films than all other Arab countries combined.* Two international satellite channels beam out Egyptian movies twenty-four hours a day. Cairo's stars continue to dominate gossip columns across the Arab world. In the remotest Yemeni village actors like the comic Adel Imam or the melodramatic heroine Faten Hamama are household names. And whereas competitors in Arab cinema can rarely export productions, because a Syrian, say, would be baffled by dialogue in Tunisian dialect, everyone picks up on even the latest Cairene slang. Factory workers in Algiers or Aleppo can quote line by line from popular productions like the hit comedy *Madrasat al Mushāghibīn* ('The School of Troublemakers') which ran for four years on the Cairo stage during the 1970s and is still broadcast regularly in television form.

YET IF CAIRO remains the cultural cockpit of the Arab World, it is largely because there is still little competition. Just as the region has no other nation state so firmly rooted in its history and identity as Egypt, it has no other true metropolis to match Cairo: no city so complete with trappings like traffic jams and jazz bands, world-class opera and a rich daily choice of lurid crime stories, ballet and belly dancers and a scintillating nightscape of lights reflecting in the Nile. Its closest rival is Beirut. But that city, whose freewheeling lifestyle once drew Arab artists and nightclubbers, has been sundered by civil war. Damascus, Baghdad and Tunis stifle under intolerant ideologies. Their citizens would gape in wonder at the abundance of opinion flaunted on any

*To the despair of Cario film-makers, income from sales has never matched production volume. State TV swindles producers by charging as much for a sixty-second ad as it pays to air a two-hour film. As for exports, poor copyright protection, video piracy and the ban on public movie showings in wealthy Saudi Arabia mean that Cairo's money share of the world movie market is a measly 0.1 per cent.

Cairo news-stand. As for the petro-monarchies of the Arabian Gulf, sparse populations and rigid religious orthodoxy limit their chance of developing a cosmopolitan culture. True, Saudi Arabia has tried to buff its image by buying up prestigious Arabic-language newspapers and satellite TV stations. But it is largely Cairene journalists and technicians that produce their content – just as graduates of Cairo's five main universities make up half the teaching staff in the Gulf.

The fact is, however, that Cairo has never quite regained the dominance it achieved before Egypt's defeat in the Six Day War.

Its star waned rapidly after the disaster. The deaths, in rapid succession, of President Nasser, Abd al-Halim Hafez, Farid al-Atrash and Umm Kulsoum left a tremendous vacuum. (At Abd al-Halim's premature death in 1974, half a dozen heartbroken fans hurled themselves from windows in Cairo.) Economic hardship compounded the shame of military defeat. It was made all the more humiliating by the sudden oil-rush of money into the Arabian Peninsula that followed. Cairenes had long regarded the pocket emirates of the Gulf as cultural backwaters – 'tribes with flags' is how a retired Egyptian diplomat dismissed them to me at the Cairo Yacht Club, with a wave of his cigar. Now, in the aftermath of defeat, the proud people of Cairo were forced to turn to their neighbours for jobs, finance and even charity.

Cairo's cultural wealth seemed suddenly exhausted. The collapse of Nasser's pan-Arabist and socialist ideals wrecked the city's self-confidence. It ushered in a period of questioning and self-disgust. 'The failure of Nasser's revolutionary project was a terrible disappointment,' says Ahmad Abd al-Muʿati Higazi, Cairo's most distinguished contemporary poet. 'Intellectuals had been swept up in it, had sacrificed their independence of thought in the belief that freedom for all should come before individual freedom, even for those who were particularly gifted ... This was how cultural life declined. Many of our best writers and artists emigrated.'

Through the 1970s and '80s Cairo stumbled. Its creative class, pampered under Nasser (when not imprisoned), was now held in contempt by an increasingly materialistic, and increasingly religion-bound, society. New generations of artists found themselves hemmed in by convention and encumbered with the legacy of former glory. They waxed nostalgic not just about the old films and songs, but about the whole cosy, coddled world which was fast disappearing. The city's great literary cafés died out. Fishawi in the Old City, with its huge gilt mirrors and stuffed crocodile and bustling profusion of hawkers, shoeshiners and fortune tellers, became a hang-out for the tourist sandal brigade. The Café Riche downtown, with its mix of leftist conspirators and the secret police who surveilled them, closed because of a dispute over inheritance. The monastically airy Cecil Bar in Tawfiqiyya was converted into a bank. Naguib Mahfouz, a famous café devotee, dropped his habit of holding court at the Urabi Café in his old neighbourhood, Abbasiyya – traffic jams had turned the weekly excursion into a tiresome chore.

The loss of morale seeped into the pores of the city. It showed even in the physical appearance of the streets. From the mid-1960s to the mid-1980s, Cairene architects produced few buildings of note. Instead, there were monuments to greed, corruption and declining aesthetic sensibility. At Tahrir Square a neo-Islamic palace was torn down to make way for a high-rise that was never built because the owners went belly-up in a banking fraud. Similar scams left ugly skyscrapers by the Nile and the Gezira Sporting Club to moulder incomplete. Riverside parks were sold to international hotel chains. Private clubs for bureaucrats, trade unions and the army walled off most of the Nile's banks – Cairo's only lung for fresh air – from the common people.

In literature, no figures of stature rose to take the place of literary lions like the short-story writer Yusuf Idris or the playwright Tawfiq al-Hakim. Serious writers turned from social realism to black farce and fantasy – a shift that alienated them further from their meagre readership. Most, however, sold out to commercialism. Cairene theatregoers now had to endure ham-actors clomping across the stage and occasionally tripping over their microphone cords. In music, the introduction of synthesizers and studio mixing made the city's new music tinny, repetitive and forgettable. It was all razzle-dazzle and unctuous crooning; all image and no content.

The same was true in cinema. Reliant now on finance from the Gulf, film-makers grew beholden to their paymasters' taste for lame farce and turgid romance. Their productions became stock vehicles for actors like Husayn Fahmy, Egypt's lacklustre Robert Redford, and pneumatically vacuous starlets like Nadia al-Gindi and Layla Elwi. The few films with realistic content – by struggling directors like Muhammad Khan, Asma al-Bakri, Dawud Abd al-Sayyid or Atif al-Tayyib – rarely so much as broke even. They portrayed Cairo accurately, but the vision was too harsh, the troubles of the characters too uniquely specific to Egypt's capital, to have much resonance beyond the country's borders. By the 1990s the cinema industry as a whole was in steep decline.

Lack of funding and ideological drift, made worse by the state's policy of stuffing its organs with underpaid staff, reduced many of the city's cultural institutions to rudderless bureaucracies. At the Dar al-Kutub – the National Library, which houses the world's largest collection of Arabic books – thousands of priceless medieval manuscripts were begrimed with the dust that gusted in through broken windows. While the city's chain hotels built theme restaurants evoking the street life of the Old City, the Old City's real ancient monuments, its real crafts and markets, decayed. Cairo's faculties of fine arts, its Modern Art Museum and Cinema Institute, its academies of ballet and classical music and Oriental music – all sacrificed quality to quantity. Imitation replaced experimentation. Dinosaurs from the Nasser era clung to power in the Writers' Union, the Press Syndicate, the Bar Association.

Arabs, and Cairenes themselves, began to look elsewhere for inspiration.

The words of Umm Kulsoum's 1964 classic *'Fakkaruni'* seemed to describe the state of the city's consciousness:

They spoke to me again of you, reminded me, reminded me...
They woke the fire of longing in my heart and in my eyes...
They took me back to the past,
With its ease, with its joys and its sweetness ... and its pain and harshness.
And I remembered how happy I was with you,
And O my soul I remember why we came apart...

TEN YEARS AGO the Grillon, a downtown beer-garden where Cairo's Left Bankish riff-raff schmooze late into the night, felt like a castle under siege. The smoke-laden talk swirled in a closed circle. Round and round it went, from grim tales of fresh battles lost to religious conservatives to charges of treachery within the walls. Indeed, the loudest voices were raised against the many fellow-travellers – leftists and secular nationalists all – who had gone over to the enemy: had taken jobs in the Gulf and embraced the religious trend, or had joined the government's patronage-dispensing National Democratic Party and scuttled off to visit Israel, that paramount pariah of Cairene intellectuals.

The talk was not just the rankling of boozy malcontents. Petty rivalries over small pickings aside, there was a real sense that the 'hellish coarseness' Lewis Awad had warned of twenty years before was indeed on the verge of snuffing out the sputtering torch of Enlightenment. Events in the wider world all pointed to looming dangers. The Iranian Revolution and civil war in Algeria, continuing Israeli colonization of the Occupied Territories, the Gulf War and the arrival of American troops on Arab land: all these developments bespoke the continuing failure of Nasser's pan-Arab dream. Closer at hand, the Grillon crowd perceived a range of barbarians massing at the gates. Rabble-rousing, book-burning Islamists were one form. Clammy-handed bureaucrats were another. In addition, there were the corrupting influences of Gulf money and of slick advertising and Hollywood soap operas on television. Cairo's avant-garde of intellectuals – as they saw themselves – seemed about to lose the battle for the hearts and minds of the Egyptian masses.

A decade later the Grillon's leftist chatterers still talk of a crisis in Arab culture. They still see religious obscurantism and American hegemony as creeping twin evils. But the mood at the Grillon is both more sober and more spirited than it was. Not only have many bastions of liberalism failed to fall, but there is a quickening sense that Cairo is on the verge of change. Or rather that the engines of cultural life are beginning to catch up with the city's own pace of change.

If the city is indeed groping its way to a new century there is one simple factor to be thanked: money. The rapid globalization of the world economy has forced the government to realize that, in order to compete, Egypt must be both open to the world and attractive to private enterprise. Privatization of industries has not only revived the long-moribund Cairo Stock Exchange, it has reawakened dormant creativity. Foreign investment and a boom in tourism have begun to generate the wealth needed to sustain the arts. New production companies are poised to pump money into the film industry. A resurgence of private patronage can be seen in the number of galleries opening and new publications launched. It shows in the appearance of a style of modern architecture that may not yet be beautiful, but whose pharaonic pomposity, angular lines and lavishness with costly marble and granite are all recognizably Cairene.

Of course, the leftist denizens of the Grillon would be right to say that Cairo's new rich are on the whole less interested in arts than in luxury goods. In recent years, showrooms for Rolls-Royce and Jaguar have opened for the first time since the 1952 revolution. The pages of *Al-Ahram* are peppered with ads for such quaint comforts as a $1,500 heated, electronically controlled, self-cleaning toilet seat (with 'optional' built-in blow-dryer). The bouncer at Tabasco, a trendy new bistro, has developed a lucrative sideline. He offers a valet answering service: customers park their cellphones with him, and he wades into the throng of gilded youths to alert them when they get calls.

But if Cairo supermarkets now stock imported caviar and smoked salmon, they also boast a proliferating range of locally made luxuries. Gezira Sporting Club socialites who used to return from Europe with bulging suitcases now find they can kit themselves out at home. As in eleventh-century Fustat, the city is again producing fine linens and brocades, hand-woven carpets and elegant tableware. Those who can afford to plonk down $70,000 can even buy Cairo-assembled BMW and Mercedes cars.

Such extravagance may be unseemly, but it does have a trickle-down effect. Rising expectations and incomes – and the introduction of payment by instalment – mean that one in seven families now owns a car or motorbike. Three-quarters have washing machines and refrigerators. Working-class Cairenes now demand quality in goods and services. More importantly, the attraction of decent salaries has begun to plug half a century of brain drain. In such upcoming fields as design, computer software and finance, Cairo has begun to draw back its own skilled émigrés.

Of course, none of this can disguise the monumental scale of the city's problems. The materialistic middle class may have grown, but so has the marginalization of the poor. The levelling hand of the state has been lifted, leaving a vacuum that is being filled only patchily by private charity. This means that the better medical treatment, housing and education which are now available are available only to the few who can afford them. The vast majority of the city's people still buy their clothes from pushcarts, flea markets and bargain sales. They squeeze on to lumbering, jam-packed buses or risk the manic driving of jitney cabs because they cannot dream of affording taxi fares which would be considered rock-bottom in most cities (about 50 US cents a mile), let alone the luxury of a private car. The price of bread and onions will frame the lives of all too many Cairenes for some time to come. In the new, competitive world, their handicap is all the greater.

Cairenes are also paying a price for their government's (qualified) success at combating religious extremism. If the state has indeed relinquished some assets through privatization, the challenge from Islamist radicals has kept it determined not to surrender its authoritarian ways. This is bad news for Cairo. A city of this scale, with this rate of growth, needs a responsive, flexible government, not a cranky administrative machine built on loyalty to a regime that can no longer claim to represent more than the status quo. The travails caused by traffic jams, pollution and bureaucratic obstinacy – to name only a few of the daily hurdles faced by Cairenes – are unlikely to lessen unless the people of the city are allowed to set their priorities for themselves. And, by sweeping the issue of religion's role in public life under the carpet, the government has only succeeded in muffling core debates in Egyptian society. Their outcome has been left to be determined by fate. That fate may prove to be kind, or it may be violent. What is sure is that waiting for fate to decide can only leave intellectual life in unhappy suspense.

Today's city of 12 million inhabitants is no longer an intimate place where everyone who is anyone knows everyone else. Cairo is now a tough, impatient town. 'Oh yes, the average person is certainly better off materially than before,' says Mustafa Darwiche, an impish film critic who was twice fired from his job as state censor for being too permissive. 'But the quality of life has definitely declined. We can't afford to be so carefree any more.'

The battle for space, money and self-respect is fierce. 'A *mawlid* without the saint' is how the singer Ahmad Adawiyya describes the Cairo melée in a hit song about crowds. It is difficult, dirty and nerve-racking, agrees Sonallah Ibrahim, a soft-spoken writer who has chronicled his city's modern transformation in novels that juxtapose the farcical trials of middle-class life with the state media's pompous sloganeering. 'I don't like it,' he continues. 'I have to live here. It's not a choice.' Yet at the same time, concedes Ibrahim, Cairo is a rich city – 'a place that lets you put distance between yourself and others', as he puts it.

There are other layers of richness, too. Despite the cultural stagnation of recent decades, Cairo has escaped provincialism. The city remains a great mirror to the world at large, and a stark interface between tradition and modernity. Its special mix of piquant wit and whimsicality still provides an incomparable source of stories. Its people's stubborn defiance is exasperating, but it also ensures that their city will never easily succumb to the forces of global monoculture. Amid the bewildering din, the anxious public pomp and the insouciant private squalor, Cairo continues to exude that air of imperturbable permanence which only a proud and ancient city can give. Whatever challenges it may face, Cairo will surely endure. By the grace of Allah, for another five thousand years.

WALKING IN THE late afternoon down a wide, dusty street in the City of the Dead, I am beckoned by an old man who sits outside the door of his tomb dwelling. 'Come in, come in,' he beams, 'My house is yours.' Amid the cenotaphs of his ancestors he bustles about, preparing tea on a primus stove.

'No, I have not lived here many years,' he says. 'All my life I lived in Abbasiyya; that is my quarter. But then my building collapsed. I had no choice but to move to the cemetery.' He smiles. 'But don't think I am not happy. Here it is peaceful. I'm not alone with my dead relatives. I share my house with my little friends. Come, I will show you.'

From under a tall brass bed he pulls a little dovecote made of split palm stalks. A parade of sleek pigeons struts out into the room in single file. They preen and coo, totter over to the bright doorway, and fly off.

Sitting on his doorstep, sipping his strong, sweet brew, we watch them swirl in widening hoops. Similar squadrons released from rooftops near and far make circles in silhouette against the sky. And now, as the sunset call to prayer is sounded, the old man's flock of friends flutters home, alighting one by one to have their throats chucked, and to waddle plumply back into their cage.

The old man speaks into the silence. 'Of course I am happy,' he says. 'I live in the greatest city in the world.'

Glossary

There is no standard method of transliterating Arabic. I have tried to keep it simple by rendering proper names as they are commonly written in English, and by giving words Cairene, rather than classical Arabic, pronunciation. Lines over vowels indicate that the vowels are long and take emphasis. All letters are pronounced as in English, except those which don't exist in English, namely:

ṣ, ṭ, ḥ	Extra-heavy versions of *s*, *t* and *h*.
q	The Arabic letter *qāf* – like a k vocalized far back in the throat. In speech, Cairenes usually replace it with a glottal stop.
gh, kh	The first is pronounced like a gargle or the Parisian *r*; the second like a German or Scottish *ch* but harder.
ʾ	The Arabic letter *hamza*, pronounced as a glottal stop.
ʿ	The Arabic letter ʿ*ayn*; According to the 1904 edition of the Rev. R. Sterling's *Arabic Grammar*, it should be pronounced as a 'strong guttural produced by quick and forcible closure of the windpipe with the emission of the breath'.

Abbasids	A Muslim dynasty founded by descendants of the Prophet's uncle Abbas. The Abbasid caliphs ruled from Baghdad from AD 750–1258, and were recognized by most Muslims as the rightful leaders of all Islam. By the second half of this era they had lost the ability to rule in more than name. Following the fall of Baghdad to the Mongols in 1258, an Abbasid caliph was kept as a puppet at the Mamluk sultan's court in Cairo until 1517.
afreet	Ghost or ghoul.
al-Ahram	Cairo's newspaper of record.
al-Akhbar	A slightly racier rival of *Al-Ahram.*
Almān	Germans.
amir (*amīr*)	Commander or prince; a military rank below sultan.
Ayyubid	A Muslim dynasty, founded by Salah al-Din al-Ayyubi, or Saladin, which ruled at Cairo from 1171 to 1260.
bāb	Gate or door.
baladi	'Country' or 'local', as opposed to foreign.
banṭalūn	Trousers – from the French *pantalon.*
barawīl	Wheelbarrow.
barīza	Ten piastres.
bawāb	Doorman, porter or gate-keeper.
Benben	The stone or mound where Ancient Egyptians believed Creation began.
bey	Ottoman rank beneath pasha; the equivalent of a Mamluk amir.
bismallah	In the name of God.
caliph	From the Arabic *khalīfa,* meaning a successor, the term referred to the supreme ruler of Muslims, i.e. the Prophet Muhammad's 'sucessor' on earth. In some periods members of different families or

	sects claimed the title at the same time, e.g. the Abbasids and the Fatimids.
dinar	An Islamic coin, typically gold (from the Latin *denarius*).
dīwān	Administrative bureau or council; also divan or reception hall.
dragoman	From the Arabic *targum*ān, meaning translator; dragomen were hired by nineteenth-century tourists as guides and fixers.
dukkān	Small shop.
effendi	Turkish title which came to be applied to educated, white-collar professionals.
Fatimids	A Shiʿite dynasty which ruled from Cairo from AD 969 to 1171.
fatwa	A religious ruling.
fellah	An Egyptian peasant; plural fellahin.
fūl	Fava beans; slow-cooked, they are Egypt's national dish.
Fustat, or Misr al-Fustat	The precursor to Cairo, founded by the Arab general Amr ibn al-ʿAs in AD 641.
galabiyya	Long, simple robe – the traditional dress for Egyptian men.
gamaʿiyya	Cooperative or revolving savings pool.
gambari	'*Gambari, istakūza hayya!*' is a street seller's cry for shrimp and live lobsters.
ḥāra	Lane or alley; a small neighbourhood in the traditional quarters.
Heliopolis	The Greek name for the ancient city of On; also a modern district of Cairo.
ibn balad	'Son of the country' – often used to refer to native-born Cairenes.
imam (*imām*)	A prayer leader in a mosque; a spiritual teacher or guide; or the divinely inspired leader of a Shiʿite sect.
Inglīz	The English.

jizya — Poll tax traditionally imposed on non-Muslims in Muslim societies. It fell out of use under Ottoman rule, and was officially abolished in the mid nineteenth century.

khawāga — Western foreigner – a title of wary respect tinged with ironical contempt; plural *khawagāt.*

maʿallim — Literally, teacher, but more commonly meaning foreman or boss.

maʿassil — Chopped tobacco stewed in molasses – what is usually smoked in a *shīsha.*

madrasa — A school. In medieval times it referred to a college of Islamic law.

Mamlūk — Literally, 'possessed'. In Cairo the term came to be applied to specially trained military slaves, and subsequently to the sultanate established by them, which lasted from 1260 to 1517.

mamnūʿ — Forbidden.

maqābir — Plural of *maqbara,* meaning a tomb.

mashrafiyya — Wooden lattice-work screening traditionally used in Cairene houses, (commonly misnamed *mashrabiyya*).

mawlid — Literally a birthday, but the term refers to the annual feast in memory of a saint or holy person.

Memphis — The first capital of Egypt; its ruins lie just south of Cairo.

Middle Kingdom — The period of the Eleventh and Twelfth Dynasties, 2050–1780 BC

milāya — A long black shawl traditionally worn over the head by working-class Egyptian women, and drawn across the face.

mish maʿqūl — Not conceivable – i.e. horrible.

Misr or Masr — Means Egypt, and is also the popular name for Cairo.

mithqāl — A measure of weight equal to 4.68 grams.

munshid	A singer of Sufi ballads and odes in praise of God and the Prophet.
nās	People – with the implication of 'respectable' people.
New Kingdom	The period of the Eighteenth to Twentieth Dynasties, 1560–1080 BC, which saw a great revival of Egypt under pharoahs such as Tutmosis I–III and Ramses I–XII.
Old Kingdom	The period of the Fourth to Eighth Dynasties, 2600–2180 BC. This was the period of the great pyramid builders, when Memphis served as Egypt's capital.
On	The earliest city on the site of Cairo. The world was created here, according to Ancient Egyptian tradition.
Ottoman	The dynasty founded by the Turkish chieftain Osman. The Ottomans captured Constantinople in 1453 and Cairo in 1517, and the Ottoman sultans were Egypt's nominal rulers until 1914.
Pasha	An Ottoman title – a rank above *bey*. When Egypt became a kingdom in 1922, the title was widely bestowed on prominent politicians, businessmen and the like; it was abolished after the 1952 revolution. (In Arabic there is no letter *p* so the word is pronounced *basha;* plural *bashawāt.*)
Piastre	One-hundredth of an Egyptian pound. Equivalent to five US cents in 1945; one-third of a cent in 1995.
Ptolemies	The rulers of Egypt from 323 to 30 BC. Greek-speaking descendants of one of Alexander the Great's generals, they chose Alexandria as their capital. Cleopatra was the last of the Ptolemaic line.
al-Qahira	The Victorious – the name (referring to the planet Mars) given to the imperial city founded north of Fustat by the Fatimids in AD 969.

qahwa — Café.

radḥ — Rhyming abuse; mud-slinging.

rayyis — Chief or president.

rial (*riyāl*) — In medieval times equal to one-twentieth of a dinar; now it means twenty piastres.

Ṣaʿīdi — An upper Egyptian.

shaʿb — The people; the masses.

shāriʿ — Street.

sharia (*sharīʿa*) — Islamic law.

sharīf — Descendant of the Prophet.

shīsha — Waterpipe.

Shiʿite — Minority branch of Islam, distinguished by a belief in the right to rule of the Prophet's descendants through his son-in-law Ali.

shillin — Five piastres: a shilling.

Sufi — Disciple of Sufism, which is a form of Islamic mysticism. As an adjective, pertaining to Sufism.

sultan — Secular title meaning ruler or king.

Sunna — Exemplary actions of the Prophet.

Sunni — The mainstream, orthodox, branch of Islam as opposed to the Shiʿi or Shiʿite branch; those who follow the *Sunna* or customs recorded of the Prophet Muhammad.

tarboosh — A fez

ulema (*ʿulama*) — The men of *ʿilm* or science – i.e. scholars of Islamic religion, law and tradition.

wāli — A 'friend' of God – a person believed to be favoured by God and therefore respected as a saint.

waqf — A 'hold' on property: a form of Islamic endowment trust.

wazir (*wazīr*) — Chief minister or vizier.

zabbālīn — Ragpickers.

Bibliography

It was agreed with the editors from the beginning that there were to be no endnotes for this book. To make it easier for readers to trace sources, I have divided this list into chronological sections. Works that overlap historical periods will be found under the heading 'General'. So too will a few works of fiction, which deserve listing for their historical setting in Cairo as well as their excellence.

This is not intended to be an exhaustive bibliography on the subject of Cairo: only works which have actually been used in the making of this book are included.

General

Abu Lughod, Janet. *Cairo: 1001 Years of The City Victorious.* Princeton, NJ: Princeton University Press, 1971.

Aldridge, James. *Cairo.* London: Macmillan, 1969.

Ali, Maulana Muhammad. *The Religion of Islam: A Comprehensive Discussion of its Sources, Principles and Practices.* Lahore: The Ahmadiyya Anjuman Ishaat Islam, 1950.

Ameer Ali, Syed. *A Short History of the Saracens.* Delhi: Kitab Bhavan, 1926.

Amin, Ahmad. *Qāmūs al-ʿĀdāt wal-Taqālīd wal-Taʿābīr al-Miṣriyya.* Cairo: Dar al-Kitab al-Masri, 1981.

Berchet, Jean-Claude (ed.). *Le Voyage en Orient: Anthologie des voyageurs français dans le Levant.* Paris: Robert Laffont, 1985.

Bohas, Georges, and Guillaume, Jean-Patrick (ed. and trans.). *Le Roman de Baibars.*4 vols. Paris: Editions Sindbad, 1985–9.

Burton, Richard F. *The Book of the Thousand Nights and a Night.* London: The Burton Club, 1886.

Carré, J. M. *Voyageurs et écrivains français en Égypte.* 2 vols. Cairo: Institut Français d'Archéologie Orientale, 1956.

Clerget, Marcel. *Le Caire: Étude de géographie urbaine et d'histoire économique.* 2 vols. Cairo: Imprimerie Schindler, 1934.

The Encyclopedia of Islam, new edition. Leiden: E. J. Brill, 1995.

Farag, Fouad. *Al-Qāhira.* 3 vols. Cairo: Dar al-Maʿarif, 1946.

Fargeon, Maurice. *Les Juifs en Égypte depuis les origines jusqu'à ce jour.* Cairo: Maurice Sananès, Editeur, 1938.

Ghali, Waguih. *Beer in the Snooker Club.* London: André Deutsch, 1964.

Ghallab, Muhammad. *Les Survivances de l'Égypte Antique dans le folklore égyptien moderne.* Paris: Librairie Orientaliste, 1929.

al-Ghitani, Gamal. *Malāmiḥ al-Qāhira fī Alf Sana.* Cairo: Dar Nahdat Misr, 1997.

Ghosh, Amitav. *In an Antique Land.* New York: Alfred Knopf, 1993.

Glassé, Cyril. *The Concise Encyclopedia of Islam.* London: Stacey International, 1989.

Hakim, Besim S. *Arabic-Islamic Cities: Building and Planning Principles.* London: Kegan Paul International, 1986.

Hamdan, Gamal. *al-Qāhira.* Cairo: Kitab al-Hilal, 1993.

—*Shakhsiyat Misr.* Cairo: Dar al-Kutub, 1970.

Heyworth-Dunn, Gamaleddine. *Select Bibliography on Egypt.* Cairo, 1952.

Hourani, Albert. *A History of the Arab Peoples.* London: Faber and Faber, 1991.

Huart, Clement. *A History of Arabic Literature.* Beirut: Khayats, 1966.

Lane, Edward William. *Account of the Manners and Customs of the Modern Egyptians.* London: 1836.

Lane-Poole, Stanley. *Cairo: Sketches of its History, Monuments and Social Life.* London: J. S. Virtue, 1892.

Lyster, William. *The Citadel of Cairo: A History and Guide.* Cairo: Palm Press, 1993.

McPherson, J. W. *The Moulids of Egypt.* Cairo, 1941.

Mahfouz, Naguib. *Autumn Quail,* tran. Roger Allen. Cairo: American University in Cairo Press, 1985.

Manley, Deborah. *The Nile: A Traveller's Anthology.* London: Cassell, 1991.

Meinardus, Otto. *Christian Egypt Ancient and Modern.* Cairo: Institut Français d'Archéologie Orientale, 1965.

Pick, Christopher. *Egypt: A Traveller's Anthology.* London: John Murray, 1991.

Pickthall, Muhammad M. (trans.). *The Meaning of the Glorious Qur'an.* Mecca: Muslim World League, 1977.

Raymond, André. *Le Caire.* Paris: Fayard, 1993.

Rodenbeck, John, et al. *Cairo* (Insight City Guides series). Singapore: APA Publications, 1992.

Rodenbeck, J., Yousef, H., et al. *Egypt.* (Insight Guides). Singapore: APA Publications, 1988.

Ruthven, Malise, and the Editors of Time-Life. *Cairo.* Amsterdam: Life Books, 1980.

Sayyid, Ayman Fuad. *at-Tatawwur al-ʿUmrāni fi Madīnat al-Qāhira.* Cairo: Dar al-Misriyya al-Lubnaniyya, 1997.

Seton-Williams, V. and Stocks, P. *Egypt* (Blue Guide). London: A. & C. Black, 1993.

Solé, Robert. *Le Tarbouche.* Paris: Seuil, 1992.

Soueif, Ahdaf. *In the Eye of the Sun.* London: Bloomsbury, 1992.

al-Tarabili, Abaas. *Shawārīʿ Laha Tārīkh.* Cairo: Dar al-Misriyya al-Lubnaniyya, 1997.

Taylor, Walt. *Arabic Words in English.* (SPE Tract XXXVIII). Oxford: Clarendon Press, 1933.

Wiet, Gaston. *Cairo, City of Art and Commerce,* trans. Seymour Feiler. Norman; University of Oklahoma Press, 1964.

Zaki, Abd al-Rahman. *Hadhihi Hiya al-Qāhira.* Cairo: Dar al-Mustaqbal, 1943.

—*Al-Qāhira.* Cairo: Dar al-Mustaqbal, 1943.

FROM PREHISTORY TO THE MUSLIM CONQUEST (AD 640)

Baikie, James. *Egyptian Papyri and Papyrus-Hunting.* London: Religious Tract Society, 1925.

Ball, John. *Contributions to the Geography of Egypt.* Cairo: Government Press, 1939.

Bilolo, Mubabinge. *Les Cosmo-Théologies philosophiques d'Heliopolis et d'Hermopolis.* Kinshasa: UNESCO, 1986.

—*Le Créateur et la Création dans la pensée Memphite et Amarnienne.* Kinshasa: UNESCO, 1986.

Breasted, J. H. *Ancient Records of Egypt.* Chicago: University of Chicago Press, 1906.

—*A History of Egypt.* New York: Scribners, 1909.

Butler, A. J. *Babylon of Egypt.* Oxford: Oxford University Press, 1913.

Dimick, Marion. *Memphis, the City of the White Wall.* Philadelphia: University of Pennsylvania Press, 1956.

Doxiadis, Euphrosyne. *The Mysterious Fayoum Portraits: Faces from Ancient Egypt.* London: Thames and Hudson, 1995.

Dunand, F., and Lichtenberg, R. *Mummies: A Journey Through Eternity.* London: Thames and Hudson, 1991.

Edwards, I. E. S. *The Pyramids of Egypt.* London: Penguin, 1947.

Emery, Walter B. *Archaic Egypt.* London: Penguin, 1961.

Gaballa, G. A. *The Memphite Tomb-Chapel of Mose.* Warminster: Aris & Phillips, 1977.

Gardiner, Alan H. *Ancient Egyptian Onomastica.* Oxford: Oxford University Press, 1947.

Habachi, Labib. 'The Destruction of Temples in Egypt'. *Medieval and Middle Eastern Studies in Honor of A. S. Attiya,* ed. Sami Hanna. Leiden: E. J. Brill, 1972.

—*The Obelisks of Egypt.* Cairo: American University in Cairo Press, 1984.

Helck, W., and Otto, F. (eds). *Lexikon der Ägyptologie.* Wiesbaden: Harassowitz, 1980.

Herodotus. *The Histories,* trans. Aubrey de Selincourt. London: Penguin, 1954.

Hornblower, G. D. 'Further Notes on Phallism in Ancient Egypt' *Man* XXVII (1927).

Hume, W. F. *The Geology of Egypt.* Cairo: Government Press, 1937.

Jeffreys, D. G. *The Survey of Memphis.* London: Egypt Exploration Society, 1985.

Jones, Angela Milward. *The Pyramids and Sphinx at Giza.* Cairo: Palm Press, 1993.

Kees, Herman. *Ancient Egypt: A Cultural Topography,* trans. Ian Morrow. Chicago: University of Chicago Press, 1978.

Kitchen, K. A. *Pharaoh Triumphant: The Life and Times of Ramses II.* Warminster: Aris & Phillips, 1982.

Krupp, E. C. *In Search of Ancient Astronomers.* New York: Doubleday, 1977.

Lauer, Jean-Philippe. *The Pyramids of Sakkara.* Cairo: Institut Français d'Archéologie Orientale, 1991.

Lehner, Mark. *The Complete Pyramids.* London: Thames and Hudson, 1997.

Lewis, Naphthali. *The Greeks in Ptolemaic Egypt.* New York: Oxford University Press, 1986.

Malek, Jaromir, and Baines, John. *Atlas of Ancient Egypt.* Oxford: Andromeda, 1980.

Martin, G. T. *The Hidden Tombs of Memphis.* London: Thames and Hudson, 1991.

Mercer, Samuel. *The Religion of Ancient Egypt.* London: Luzac, 1949.

Morenz, Siegfried. *Egyptian Religion.* London: Methuen, 1973.

Moret, Alexandre. *Le Nile et la civilisation égyptienne.* Paris: Renaissance du Livre, 1926.

Plutarch. *De Iside et Osiride,* ed. J. G. Griffiths. Cardiff: University of Wales Press, 1970.

Porter, Beth, and Moss, Rosalind. *Topographical Bibliography of Ancient Egyptian Hieroglyphic Texts.* Oxford: Clarendon Press, 1934.

Saad, Zaki. *Excavations at Helwan.* Norman: University of Oklahoma Press, 1969.

Saleh, Abdel-Aziz. *Excavations at Heliopolis.* Cairo: Cairo University Press, 1981.

Siculus, Diodorus. *The Antiquities of Egypt,* trans. Edwin Murphy. London: Transaction Publishers, 1990.

Smith, H. S. *A Visit to Ancient Egypt: Life at Memphis and Saqqara c. 500–30 BC.* Warminster: Aris & Phillips, 1974.

Strabo. *The Geography of Strabo,* trans. and ed. H. C. Hamilton. London: Bohn's Classical Library 1857.

Thompson, Dorothy J. *Memphis Under the Ptolemies.* Princeton, NJ: Princeton University Press, 1988.

Trigger, Bruce. *Early Civilizations: Ancient Egypt in Context.* Cairo: American University in Cairo Press, 1993.

Velde, Hermante, *Seth, God of Confusion.* Leiden: E. J. Brill, 1967.

FROM THE MUSLIM CONQUEST TO NAPOLEON (AD 640–1798)

Abd al-Raziq, Ahmad. *La Femme au temps des Mamlouks en égypte.* Cairo: Institut Français d'Archéologie Orientale, 1973.

Abdel Hamid, Saad Zaghloul (ed.) *Kitāb al Istibsār fi ʿAjāib al-*

Amṣār. (by anonymous twelfth-century Moroccan author). Alexandria: University of Alexandria, 1958.

Abu Saleh the Armenian. *The Churches and Monasteries of Egypt*, trans. B. T. A. Evetts. Oxford: Clarendon Press, 1895.

Abu Sayf, S., al-Bandari, M., Qasim, M., and Wahbi, Y. *Mawsū ʿat al-Aflām al-ʿArabiyya*. Cairo: Bayt al Maʿarifa, 1994.

Adler, Elkan N. (ed.). *Jewish Travellers*. London, Routledge, 1930.

Africanus, Leo. *Description de l'Afrique*. Paris: Librairie d'Amérique et d'Orient, 1956.

Ali, Arafa Abdu. *Raḥla fi Zamān al-Qāhira*. Cairo: Madbouli, 1990.

Ali, Mustafa. *Mustafa Ali's Description of Cairo of 1599*, trans. Andreas Tietz. Vienna: Österreichischen Akademie der Wissenschaften, 1975.

Amitai, Reuven. 'The Rise and Fall of the Mamluk Institution'. *Studies in Honor of Professor David Ayalon*, ed. M. Sharon, Jerusalem: Cana, 1986.

al-Ansari, Umar Ibn Ibrahim. *A Muslim Manual of War*, trans. G. T. Scanlon. Cairo: American University in Cairo Press, 1961.

Ashtor, Eliyahu. 'The Karimi Merchants'. *Journal of the Royal Asiatic Society* XXXII (1956).

—*Levant Trade in the Later Middle Ages*. Princeton, NJ: Princeton University Press, 1983.

Ayalon, David. *Gunpowder and Firearms in the Mamluk Kingdom*. London: Valentine Mitchell, 1956.

—*Islam and the Abode of War*. London: Variorum Reprints, 1994.

—'The Eunuchs in the Mamluk Sultanate'. *Studies in Memory of Gaston Wiet*, ed. Myriam Rosen-Ayalon. Jerusalem: Hebrew University Press, 1977.

—'Mamluk Military Aristocracy during the First Years of the Ottoman Occupation'. *The Islamic World: Studies in Honor of Bernard Lewis*, ed. C. E. Bosworth et al. Princeton, NJ: Darwin Press, 1989.

—*The Mamluk Military Society*. London: Variorum Reprints, 1979.

—'Studies in al-Jabarti'. *Journal of the Economic and Social History of the Orient* III (1960).

—*Studies on the Mamluks of Egypt.* London: Variorum Reprints, 1977.

al-Baghdadi, Abd al-Latif. *The Eastern Key: Kitab al-Ifādah wal-Iʿtibār of Abd al-Latif al-Baghdadi,* (trans. K. A. Zand and John and Ivy Videan. London: Allen & Unwin, 1965.

Baybars al-Mansuri. *Mukhtār al Akhbār,* ed. A. S. Hamdan. Cairo: Dar al-Misriyya al-Lubnaniyya, 1993.

Behrens Abu Seif, Doris. *Azbakiyya and Its Environs, from Azbak to Ismail.* Cairo: Institut Français d'Archéologie Orientale, 1985.

—*Islamic Architecture in Cairo.* Leiden: E. J. Brill, 1989.

Berkey, Jonathan. *The Transmission of Knowledge in Medieval Cairo: A Social History of Islamic Education.* Princeton, NJ: Princeton University Press, 1992.

Blanc, B. et al. 'À propos de la carte du Caire de Matheo Pagani'. *Annales Islamologiques* XVII (1981).

Bleser, Paul. 'Le Pèlerinage du Chevalier Arnold Von Harff'. *Zum Bild Ägyptens im Mittelalter und in der Renaissance,* ed. Erik Hornung. Freiburg: Universitätsverlag, 1990.

Bovill, E. W. *The Golden Trade of the Moors.* London: Oxford University Press, 1958.

Brinner, W. M. 'The Harafish and Their Sultan'. *Journal of the Economic and Social History of the Orient* VI (1963).

Broadhurst, R. J. C. *A History of the Ayyubid Sultans of Egypt.* Boston: Twayne Publishers, 1980.

Butler, A. J. *The Arab Conquest of Egypt.* Oxford: Oxford University Press, 1902.

Chen, Mark. 'Jews in the Mamluk Environment: The Crisis of 1442'. *Bulletin of the School of Oriental and African Studies* XLVIII (1984).

Crecelius, Daniel, and Abd al-Wahab, Bakr (trans.) *Al-Damurdashi's Chronicle of Egypt, 1688–1755.* Leiden: E. J. Brill, 1991.

Creswell, K. A. C. *The Muslim Architecture of Egypt*. London: Oxford University Press, 1952.

Darrag, Ahmad. *l'Égypte sous le règne de Barsbay (1422–1430)*. Beirut: Institut Français de Damas, 1961.

Denoix, Sylvie. *Decrire le Caire: Fustat-Misr d'aprés Duqmaq et Maqrizi.* Cairo, Institut Français d'Archéologie Orientale, 1992.

Devonshire, R. L. *Some Cairo Mosques and Their Founders*. London: Constable, 1921.

Dodge, Bayard. *Al-Azhar: A Millennium of Muslim Learning*. Washington DC: Middle East Institute, 1974.

—'The Fatimid Legal Code'. *The Muslim World* L, I (1960).

Dols, Michael. *The Black Death in the Middle East*, Princeton, NJ: Princeton University Press, 1977.

—*Medieval Islamic Medicine: Ibn Radwan's Treatise 'On the Bodily Ills of Egypt'*. Berkeley: University of California Press, 1984.

—'The Second Plague Pandemic and its Recurrences in the Middle East: 1347–1894'. *Journal of the Economic and Social History of the Orient* XXVI (1983).

Dopp, P. H. 'Le Caire vu par les voyageurs occidentaux du Moyen Age'. *Bulletin de la Société Royale de Géographie de l'Égypte* XXIII– XXVII (1951).

Ehrenkreutz, Andrew. 'Saladdin's Coup d'État in Egypt'. *Medieval and Middle Eastern Studies in Honor of A. S. Attiya*, ed. Sami Hanna. Leiden: E. J. Brill, 1972.

Fischel, Walter. *Ibn Khaldoun in Egypt.* Berkeley: University of California Press, 1967.

Gayraud, Roland-Pierre 'Istabl ʿAntar (Fostat): Rapport de Fouilles 1984–5'. *Annales Islamologiques* XXII (1986); see also *A. I.* XXIII, XXV, XXVIII.

Ghistele, Joos van. *Le Voyage en Égypte 1482–83*, trans. Renée Bauwens-Préaux. Cairo: Institut Français d'Archéologie Orientale, 1979.

Glubb, John Bagot. *Soldiers of Fortune: The Story of the Mamlukes.* London: Hodder & Stoughton, 1973.

Goitein, D. S. *A Mediterranean Society: The Jewish Communities of the Arab World as Portrayed in the Cairo Geniza.* 5 vols. Berkeley: University of California Press, 1972–1988.

—'Slaves and Slavegirls'. *Arabica* IX (1962).

Grunebaum, Gustav von. 'The Nature of the Fatimid Achievement'. *Colloque International sur l'histoire du Caire,* ed. André Raymond, Michael Rogers and Magdi Wahba. Cairo: Ministry of Culture, 1969.

Haarmann, Ulrich. 'Regional Sentiment in Medieval Islamic Egypt'. *Bulletin of the School of Oriental and African Studies* XLIII (1980).

Hanna, Nelly. *Habiter au Caire: La Maison moyenne et ses habitants aux XVIIe et XVIIIe siècles.* Cairo: Institut Français D'Archéologie Orientale, 1991.

Hassan, Zaky Mohamed. *Les Tulunides.* Paris: Établissements Busson, 1933.

Hayes, John (ed.). *The Genius of Arab Civilisation: Source of the Renaissance.* London: Eurabia Publishing, 1983.

Heck, W. M. *Cairo or Baghdad: A Critical Re-examination of the Role of Egypt in the Fatimid Dynasty's Imperial Design.* Ann Arbor: University Microfilms, 1986.

Hitti, Philip. *Capital Cities of Arab Islam.* Minneapolis: University of Minnesota Press, 1973.

Holt, P. M. *The Age of the Crusades: The Near East from the Eleventh Century to 1517.* London: Longman, 1986.

—'Some Observations on the Abbasid Caliphate in Cairo'. *Bulletin of the School of Oriental and African Studies* XLVII (1984)

Homerin, Th. Emil *From Arab Poet to Modern Saint: Ibn Farid, his Verse and his Shrine.* Columbus: University of South Carolina Press, 1994.

Humphreys, R. S. 'The Expressive Intent of the Mamluk Architecture of Cairo'. *Studia Islamica* XXXV (1972).

Ibn Battuta, Muhammad. *Travels,* trans. Sir Hamilton Gibb. London: Hakluyt Society, 1958.

Ibn Iyas, Muhammad ibn Ahmad. *An Account of the Ottoman Conquest of Egypt*, trans. W. H. Salmon. London: Royal Asiatic Society, 1921.

—*Journal d'un Bourgeois du Caire*, trans. Gaston Wiet. Paris: Armand Collin, 1960.

Ibn Jobair. *Voyages*, trans. M. Gaudefroy-Demombynes. Paris: Guethner, 1949.

Ibn Khaldun, Abd al-Rahman Muhammad. *An Arab Philosophy of History: Selections From the Prolegomena*, trans. Charles Issawi. Princeton, Darwin Press, 1987.

—*Muqaddimat Ibn Khaldun*. Tunis: Dar al-Maarif, 1991.

Ibn al-Ma'mūn. *La Chronique de l'Égypte d'Ibn al-Ma'mūn*. ed. Ayman F. Sayyid. Cairo: Institut Français d'Archéologie Orientale, 1983.

Ibn Muyassar. *La Chronique de l'Égypte d'Ibn Muyassar*, ed. Ayman F. Sayyid. Cairo: Institut Français d'Archéologie Orientale, 1981.

Ibn Taghribirdi, Abul Mahasin. *History of Egypt 1382–1469*, trans. William Popper. Berkeley: University of California Press, 1954.

Idrisi, Abu Abdallah Muhammad: *Description de l'Afrique et de l'Espagne*, trans. Reinhardt Dozy. Amsterdam: Oriental Press, 1969 (reprint).

al-Imad, Leila. *The Fatimid Vizierate*. Berlin: Klaus Schwarz, 1990.

Irwin, Robert. *The Arabian Nights: A Companion*. London: Penguin, 1994.

—*The Middle East in the Middle Ages: The Early Mamluk Sultanate 1250–1382*. Carbondale: Southern Illinois University Press, 1986.

Issawi, Charles. 'The Decline of Middle Eastern Trade'. *Islam and the Trade of India*, ed. D. S. Richards. Oxford: Oxford University Press, 1970.

Kennedy, Hugh. *The Prophet and the Age of the Caliphates*. London: Longman, 1986.

Khan, Geoffrey (ed.) *Arabic Legal and Administrative Documents from the*

Cambridge Geniza Collection. Cambridge: Cambridge University Press, 1993.

Khattab, Aleya. *Das Ägyptenbild in den Deutschsprachigen Reisebeschreibungen der Zeit von 1285–1500.* Frankfurt: Peter Lang, 1982.

Khusrau, Nasir. *The Safarname of the Persian Nasir Khusrau,* ed. and trans. Mandana Nakhai. Ann Arbor: University Microfilms, 1980.

Knysh, Alexander. 'Orthodoxy' and 'Heresy' in Medieval Islam: An Essay in Reassessment.' *The Muslim World* LXXXIII, I (1993).

Kubiak, Wladyslaw. *Al-Fustat: Its Foundation and Early Urban Development.* Cairo: American University in Cairo Press, 1987.

Kubiak, Wladyslaw, and Scanlon, G. T. *Fustat Expedition Final Report.* 2 vols. Cairo: American Research Center in Egypt, 1989.

Lambert, Phyllis (ed.). *Fortifications and the Synagogue: The Fortress of Babylon and the Ben Ezra Synagogue, Cairo.* London: Weidenfeld & Nicolson, 1994.

Lane, Edward William. *Arabian Society in the Middle Ages: Studies from the Thousand and One Nights,* ed. Stanley Lane-Poole. London: Curzon Press, 1883.

Lane-Poole, Stanley. *A History of Egypt in the Middle Ages.* London: Methuen, 1901.

Lapidus, Ira. *Middle Eastern Cities.* Berkeley: University of California Press, 1969.

—*Muslim Cities in the Later Middle Ages.* Cambridge: Cambridge University Press, 1984.

Leaman, Oliver. *Moses Maimonides.* Cairo: American University in Cairo Press, 1990.

Lev, Yaakov. *State and Society in Fatimid Egypt.* Leiden: E. J. Brill, 1991.

Levtzion, N. 'Mamluk Egypt and Takrur'. *Studies in Honor of Professor David Ayalon,* ed. M. Sharon. Jerusalem: Cana, 1986.

Lézine, Alexandre *Trois palais de l'époque ottomane au Caire*. Cairo: Institut Français d'Archéologie Orientale, 1972.

Little, Donald P. 'Coptic Conversion to Islam under the Bahri Mamluks'. *Bulletin of the School of Oriental and African Studies* XXXIX (1976).

MacKenzie, Neil. *Ayyubid Cairo, A Topographical Study*. Cairo: American University in Cairo Press, 1992.

Maqrizi, Ahmad ibn Ali. *A History of the Ayyubid Sultans of Egypt*, trans. R. J. C. Broadhurst. Boston: G. K. Hall, 1980.

—*Kitāb al Khitat*. Cairo: Matbaʿat al-Nil, 1911.

—*Kitāb as-Sulūk li Maʿarifat Duwal al Mulūk*. Cairo: Lagnat al-Taʾlif, 1958.

Margoliouth, D. S. *Cairo, Jerusalem and Damascus*. London: Chatto & Windus, 1907.

Marmon, Shaun. *Eunuchs and Sacred Boundaries in Islamic Society*. Oxford: Oxford University Press, 1995.

Mayer, L. A. *Mamluk Costume*. Geneva: Albert Kundig, 1952.

Mehrez, Shahira. *The Ghawriya in the Urban Context*. Cairo: MA thesis, American University in Cairo, 1972.

Mignanelli, Bertrando de. 'Ascensus Barcoch', trans. Walter Fischel. *Arabica* VI (1959).

Muir, William. *The Mameluke or Slave Dynasty of Egypt*. Amsterdam: Oriental Press, 1968.

al-Mukaffaʾ, Sawiris ibn. *History of the Patriarchs of the Coptic Church*. Cairo: Société d'Archéologie Copte, 1948.

Musabihi. *La Chronique de l'Égypte de Musabihi*, ed. A. F. Sayyid and T. Bianquis. Cairo: Institut Français d'Archéologie Orientale, 1978.

Nasr, Sayed Hossein. *Ismaili Contributions to Islamic Culture*. Tehran: Imperial Iranian Academy of Philosophy, 1977.

Niebuhr, Carsten *Travels Through Arabia and Other Countries of the East*. Reading: Garnet, 1994 (reprint of 1792 Edinburgh edn).

Ohtoshi, Tetsuya. 'The Manners, Customs and Mentality of

Pilgrims to the Egyptian City of the Dead, 100–1500 AD'. *Orient* 29 (1993).

Petry, Carl F. *Protectors or Praetorians: The Last Mamluks and Egypt's Waning as a Great Power*. Albany, NY: SUNY Press, 1994.

Poliak, A. N. 'Les Revoltes populaires en Égypte à l'époque des Mamelouks'. *Revue des études Islamiques* III (1934).

—'Some Notes on the Feudal System of the Mamluks'. *Journal of the Royal Asiatic Society* XXIII (1937).

Popper, William. *Egypt and Syria under the Circassian Sultans*. Berkeley: University of California Press, 1957.

Raymond, André. *Artisans et commercants au Caire au XVIIIe siècle*. 2 vols. Damascus: Institut Français de Damas, 1973.

Raymond, André, and Wiet, Gaston. *Les Marches du Caire: traduction annotée du texte de Maqrizi*. Cairo: Institut Français d'Archéologie Orientale, 1979.

Revault, J., and Maury, B. *Palais et maisons du Caire du XIVme au XVIIIme siècle*. 3 vols. Cairo: Institut Français d'Archéologie Orientale, 1975–83.

Sadeque, Syedah Fatima. *Baybars I of Egypt*. Dacca: Oxford University Press, 1956.

Sanders, Paula A. *Court Ceremonial of the Fatimid Caliphate*. Ann Arbor: University Microfilms, 1984.

'From Court Ceremony to Urban Language: Ceremonial in Fatimid Cairo and Fustat'. *The Islamic World: Studies in Honor of Bernard Lewis*, ed. C. E. Bosworth, et. al. Princeton, NJ: Darwin Press, 1989.

Scanlon, George. 'Housing and Sanitation: Some Aspects of Medieval Public Services'. *The Islamic City*, eds A. H. Hourani and S. M. Stern, Oxford: Oxford University Press, 1970.

Sauneron, Serge. *Villes et légendes de l'Égypte*. Cairo: Institut Français d'Archéologie Orientale, 1983.

Shoshan, Boaz. *Popular Culture in Medieval Cairo*. Cambridge: Cambridge University Press, 1992.

Staffa, Susan. *Conquest and Fusion: The Social Evolution of Cairo* AD 642–1850. Leiden: E. J. Brill, 1977.

Stillman, N. A. 'The Merchant House of Ibn Awkal'. *Journal of the Economic and Social History of the Orient* XVI (1973).

Tafur, Pero. *Travels and Adventures, 1435–39.* London: Routledge, 1926.

Taylor, Chris. 'Sacred History and the Cult of Muslim Saints in Late Medieval Egypt'. *Muslim World* LXXX, 2 (1990).

Thevenot, Jean de. *Voyage du Levant,* ed. Stephane Yerasimos. Paris: Maspero, 1980.

Thorau, Peter. *The Lion of Egypt.* London: Longman, 1992.

Wiet, Gaston. *L'Égypte de Murtadi, fils du Gaphiphe.* Paris: Geuthner, 1953.

—*Les Marchands d'Épices sous les sultans mamlouks.* Cairo: Éditions des Cahiers d'Histoire Égyptienne, 1955.

—*Muhammad Ali et les Beaux Arts.* Cairo: Dar al-Maʿarif, 1949.

—'Personnes Déplacées'. *Revue des Études Islamiques* XXVII (1959).

—'Le Traite de famines de Maqrizi'. *Journal of the Economic and Social History of the Orient* V (1962).

Williams, Caroline. 'The Cult of the Alid Saints in the Fatimid Monuments of Cairo'. *Muqarnas* I (1983).

Winter, Michael. *Egyptian Society under Ottoman Rule.* London: Routledge, 1992.

Yellin, David, and Abraham, Israel. *Maimonides.* Philadelphia: Jewish Publication Society of America, 1903.

al-Zahiri, Khalil. *La Zubda Kachf al Mamalik.* Beirut: Institut Français de Damas, 1950.

FROM NAPOLEON TO THE PRESENT (1798–)

Adams, Charles. *Islam and Modernism in Egypt.* London: Oxford University Press, 1933.

al-Ahram Center for Strategic Studies. *Al Ḥāla ad-Dīniyya fi Miṣr.* Cairo: Al-Ahram, 1996.

Ajami, Fouad. *The Arab Predicament.* Cambridge: Cambridge University Press, 1981.

Amin, Samir. *l'Égypte Nasserienne.* Paris: Editions de Minuit, 1964.

Appleton, Thomas Gold. *A Nile Journal.* Boston: Roberts Brothers, 1876.

Armbrust, Walter. *Mass Culture and Modernism in Egypt.* Cambridge: Cambridge University Press, 1995.

Atiya, Naira. *Khul Khal: Five Egyptian Women Tell Their Stories.* Syracuse, NY: Syracuse University Press, 1982.

Awad, Louis. *The Literature of Ideas in Egypt.* Atlanta, Georgia: Scholars Press, 1986.

Baer, Gabriel. *Studies in the Social History of Modern Egypt.* Chicago: University of Chicago Press, 1969.

Balboni, L. A. *Gli Italiani nella Civilta Egiziana del Secolo XIX.* 3 vols. Alexandria: Societa Dante Alighieri, 1906.

Ballantine, James. *The Life of David Roberts, R.A.* Edinburgh: A. & C. Black, 1866.

Berger, Morroe. 'Cairo to the American Traveller of the Nineteenth Century'. *Colloque International sur l'histoire du Caire,* ed. André Raymond, Michael Rogers and Magdi Wahba. Cairo: Ministry of Culture, 1969.

Berque, Jacques. *Egypt: Imperialism and Revolution.* trans. Jean Stewart. London: Faber and Faber, 1972.

Bibliographic Guide to Contemporary Arab Cultural Values. Cairo: General Egyptian Book Organization, 1972.

Boktor, Amir. *School and Society in the Valley of the Nile.* Cairo: Elias' Modern Press, 1936.

Booth, Marilyn. 'Colloquial Arabic Poetry, Politics and the Press in Modern Egypt'. *International Journal of Middle Eastern Studies* XXIV (1981).

Brinton, J. Y. *The American Effort in Egypt.* Alexandria: Imprimerie du Commerce, 1972.

Caillard, Mabel. *A Lifetime in Egypt, 1876–1935*. London: Grant Richards, 1935.

Campo, Juan Eduardo. *The Other Side of Paradise: Explorations into the Religious Meanings of Domestic Space in Islam*. Columbus: University of South Carolina Press, 1991.

Cannon, Byron. *Politics of Law and the Courts in Nineteenth-Century Egypt*. Salt Lake City: University of Utah Press, 1988.

Cecil, Lord Edward. *The Leisure of an Egyptian Official*. London: Hodder & Stoughton, 1921.

Cooper, Artemis. *Cairo in the War*. London: Hamish Hamilton, 1989.

Copeland, Miles. *The Game of Nations*. London: Weidenfeld & Nicolson, 1969.

Cressaty, le Comte. *L'Égypte d'aujourd'hui*. Paris: Marcel Rivière, 1912.

Crouchley, A. E. *The Economic Development of Modern Egypt*. London: Longman, 1938.

Curzon, Robert. *Visits to the Monasteries in the Levant*. London: John Murray, 1849.

Danielson, Virginia. *The Voice of Egypt: Umm Kulthum, Arabic Song and Egyptian Society in the Twentieth Century*. Chicago: University of Chicago Press, 1997.

Description de l'Égypte. 20 vols. Paris: Imprimerie Imperiale, 1809.

Egypt, 1919. Alexandria: Whitehead Morris, 1925.

Egypt Human Development Report 1995. Cairo: Institute of National Planning, 1995.

Enkiri, Gabriel. *Ibrahim Pasha*. Cairo: Imprimerie Française, 1948.

Erlanger, Harry, Baron d'. *The Last Plague of Egypt*. London: Dickson & Thompson, 1936.

Fakhouri, Hani. 'An Ethnographic Survey of a Cairo Neighbourhood'. *Journal of the American Research Center in Egypt* XXII (1985).

Flaubert, Gustave, *see* Steegmuller and Wall.

Fullerton, Morton. *In Cairo*. London: Macmillan, 1891.

al-Gawhary, Mahmud. *Ex-Royal Palaces in Egypt*. Cairo: Government Printing Office, 1954.

Ghorbal, Shafiq. *The Beginnings of the Egyptian Question and the Rise of Muhammad Ali*. London: Routledge, 1928.

Gilsenan, Michael. *Saint and Sufi in Modern Egypt*. Oxford: Clarendon Press, 1973.

Graves, Robert. *Goodbye to All That*. London: Jonathan Cape, 1929.

Greener, Leslie. *The Discovery of Egypt*. New York: Dorset Press, 1966.

Herold, Christopher. *Bonaparte in Egypt*. London: Hamish Hamilton, 1962.

Holt, P. M. *Egypt and the Fertile Crescent 1516–1922*. Ithaca, NY: Cornell University Press, 1966.

—(ed.). *Political and Social Change in Modern Egypt*. London: Oxford University Press, 1968.

Hopkins, Nicholas (ed.). 'The Informal Sector in Egypt'. *Cairo Papers in Social Science* 14 (winter 1991).

Hopkins, Simon. 'The Discovery of the Cairo Geniza'. *Bibliophilia Africana* IV (1981).

Hopwood, Derek. *Egypt: Politics and Society 1945–81*. London: Allen & Unwin, 1982.

Tales of Empire: The British in the Middle East 1880–1952. London: I. B. Tauris, 1989.

Hourani, Albert, Khoury, Philip S., and Wilson, Mary C. (eds). *The Modern Middle East: A Reader*. Berkeley: University of California Press, 1993.

Ilbert, Robert. *Heliopolis: Le Caire 1905–1922: Genèse d'une ville*. Paris: Centre Nationale de la Recherche Scientifique, 1981.

Ismail, Muhammad Hussam al-Din. *Madīnat al-Qāhira min Wilāyat Muḥammad ʿAli ila Ismaʿil*. Cairo: Dar al-Afaq al-Arabiyya, 1997.

al-Jabarti, Abd al-Rahman. *ʿAjāʾib al-āthār fil-Tarājim wal Akhbār*. 4 vols. Cairo: Bulaq Press, 1882.

—*Chronicle of the First Seven Months of the French Occupation of Egypt*, trans. S. Moreh. Leiden: E. J. Brill, 1975.

Karnouk, Lilliane. *Modern Egyptian Art: The Emergence of a National Style*. Cairo: American University in Cairo Press, 1988.

Kinglake, Alexander. *Eothen*. London: Ollivier, 1844.

Kipling, Rudyard. *Letters of Travel, 1892–1913*. London: Macmillan, 1920.

Kishtainy, Khaled. *Arab Political Humour*. London: Quartet, 1985.

Kitroeff, Alexander. *The Greeks in Egypt, 1919–37*. London: Atlantic Highlands, 1988.

el-Koudsi, Mourad. *The Karaite Jews of Egypt, 1882–1986*. Lyons, NY: Wilprint Inc., 1987.

Krämer, Gudrun. *The Jews in Modern Egypt*. London: I. B. Tauris, 1989.

Kuhnke, La Verne. *Lives at Risk: Public Health in Nineteenth-Century Egypt*. Berkeley: University of California Press, 1990.

Lacouture, Jean and Simone. *Egypt in Transition*. New York: Criterion, 1958.

Lambert, Edwige, and Vinatier, Isabelle (eds). *Le Caire*. Paris: Autrement, 1985.

Landes, David. *Bankers and Pashas: International Finance and Economic Imperialism in Egypt*. Cambridge, Mass.: Harvard University Press, 1958.

Lane, Edward William. *Cairo Fifty Years Ago*, ed. Stanley Lane-Poole. London: John Murray, 1896.

Lane-Poole, Sophia. *The Englishwoman in Egypt*. 3 vols. London: Charles Knight, 1844–6.

Laskier, Michael. 'Egyptian Jewry under the Nasser Regime'. *Middle East Studies* XXXI (1995).

Loti, Pierre. *Egypt*, trans. W. P. Baines. London: T. Werner Laurie, 1909.

Lutfi al-Sayyid Marsot, Afaf. *Egypt in the Reign of Muhammad Ali*. Cambridge: Cambridge University Press, 1984.

—*Egypt's Liberal Experiment, 1922–37*. Berkeley: University of California Press, 1977.

—'Mud-Slinging Egyptian Style'. *Journal of the American Research Center in Egypt* XXX (1993).

Manning, Olivia, and St. Claire-McBride, Barrie. *Alamein and the Desert War*. London: Sphere Books, 1967.

Messiri, Sawsan. *Ibn al-Balad: A Concept of Egyptian Identity*. Leiden: E. J. Brill, 1978.

Mitchell, Timothy. *Colonizing Egypt*. Cambridge: Cambridge University Press, 1988.

Le Mondain Égyptien: The Egyptian Who's Who. Cairo: Imprimerie Lencioni, 1940.

Mostyn, Trevor. *Egypt's Belle Époque: Cairo 1869–1952*. London: Quartet, 1989.

Mubarak, Ali Pasha. *Al-Khitat al-Tawfiqiyya al-Jadīda*. 20 vols. Cairo: Bulaq Press, 1887–9.

Nerval, Gérard de. *The Women of Cairo* (trans. of *Voyage en Orient*). London: Routledge, 1929.

Nubarian, Nubar Pasha. *Mémoires*, ed. Mirrit Boutros Ghali. Beirut: Librairie du Liban, 1983.

Ostle, R. C. 'The City in Modern Arabic Literature'. *Bulletin of the School of Oriental and African Studies* XLIX (1986).

Pascal, Jacques. *Middle East Motion Picture Almanac*. Cairo: Société Oriental de Publicité, 1946.

Petrie, W. M. Flinders. *Ten Years Digging in Egypt*. London: The Religious Tract Society, 1900.

Philips, Thomas. *The Syrians in Egypt, 1725–1975*. Stuttgart: Franz Steiner, 1985.

Population Growth and Policies in Megacities. New York: United Nations Department of International Economic and Social Affairs, 1990.

Raafat, Samir. *Maadi 1904–1962: Society and History in a Cairo Suburb*. Cairo: Palm Press, 1994.

Rushdy, Rashad. *The Lure of Egypt For English Writers and Travellers in the Nineteenth Century*. Cairo: Anglo-Egyptian Bookshop, 1950.

Russell Pasha, Sir Thomas. *Egyptian Service 1902–46*. London: John Murray, 1949.

Sabet, Adel. *A King Betrayed: The Ill-Fated Reign of King Farouk*. London: Quartet, 1989.

Safran, Nadav. *Egypt in Search of Political Continuity (1804–1952)*. Cambridge, Mass.: Harvard University Press, 1981.

Sattin, Anthony. *Lifting the Veil: British Society in Egypt 1768–1956*. London: Dent, 1988.

Scharabi, Mohamed. *Kairo: Stadt und Architektur im Zeitalter des Europäischen Kolonialismus*. Tübingen: Ernest Wassmuth Verlag, 1989.

Searight, Sarah. *The British in the Middle East*. London: Weidenfeld & Nicolson, 1969.

Sessions, Stuart, et al. *Comparing Environmental Health Risks in Cairo, Egypt*. Washington DC: Agency for International Development, 1994

Shaarawi, Huda. *Harem Years: The Memoirs of an Egyptian Feminist*, trans. Margot Badran. London: Virago, 1986.

Singerman, Diane. *Avenues of Participation: Family, Politics and Networks in Urban Quarters of Cairo*. Princeton, NJ: Princeton University Press, 1995.

al-Siwi, Adel (ed.). *ʿAyn: Funūn Tashkīliyya*. Cairo: Adel al-Siwi, 1996.

Sladen, Douglas. *Oriental Cairo: City of the Arabian Nights*. London: Hurst & Blackett, 1911.

Société Khédiviale de Géographie. *Bulletin*, III, 5 (1890); VII, 4 (1909).

Soliman, Ahmed. 'Housing the Urban Poor in Egypt: A Critique of Present Policies'. *International Journal of Urban and Regional Research* XII, I (1988).

Stadiem, William. *Too Rich: The High Life and Tragic Death of King Farouk*. London: Robson Books, 1991.

Steegmuller, Francis. *Flaubert in Egypt*. Chicago: Academy, 1979.

Storrs, Ronald. *Orientations*. London: Nicholson & Watson, 1943.

Tekce, B., Oldham, L., Shorter, F., *A Place to Live: Families and Child Health in a Cairo Neighbourhood*. Cairo: American University in Cairo Press, 1994.

Thompson, Jason. '"Of the Osmanlees, Or Turks": An Unpublished Chapter From E. W. Lane's *Manners and Customs of the Modern Egyptians*'. *Turkish Studies Association Bulletin* XIX (1995).

Tignor, Robert L. *Egyptian Textiles and British Capital 1930–56*. Cairo: American University in Cairo Press, 1989.

Toledano, Ehud. *State and Society in Mid-Nineteenth-Century Egypt*. Cambridge: Cambridge University Press, 1990.

Van Nieuwkerk, Karin. *A Trade Like Any Other: Female Singers and Dancers in Egypt*. Austin: University of Texas Press, 1995.

Vatikiotis, P. J. *The History of Egypt From Muhammad Ali to Sadat*. London: Weidenfeld & Nicolson, 1980.

Vercoutter, Jean. *The Search for Ancient Egypt*. London: Thames and Hudson, 1992.

Volait, Mercedes. 'Architecture de la décennie pharaonique en Égypte (1922–32); *Images de l'Égypte*. Cairo: Centre d'Études et de Documentation Économiques, Juridiques et Sociales, 1991.

—*l'Architecture Moderne en Égypte et la revue al-Imara (1939–59)*. Cairo: Centre d'Études et de Documentation Économiques, Juridiques et Sociales, 1988.

Wahba, Magdi. 'Cairo Memories'. *Studies in Arab History*, ed. Derek Hopwood. London: I. B. Tauris, 1990.

Wall, Geoffrey. (trans.) 'Letter from Gustave Flaubert to Dr Jules Cloquet, a Family Friend, Cairo, January 15, 1850'. *New York Review of Books*, 10 August 1995.

Waterbury, John. *The Egypt of Nasser and Sadat*. Princeton, NJ: Princeton University Press, 1983.

Watson, Helen. *Women in the City of the Dead*. London: Hurst & Co., 1992.

Waugh, Earle H. *The Munshideen of Egypt: Their World and Their Song.* Colombus: University of South Carolina Press, 1988.

Wendell, Charles. *The Evolution of the Egyptian National Image.* Berkeley: University of California Press, 1972.

Wikan, Unni. *Life Among the Poor in Cairo.* London: Tavistock Publications, 1980.

Wilkinson, Sir Gardner. *Modern Egypt and Thebes.* London: John Murray, 1843.

World Health Organization and United Nations Environment Program. *Urban Air Pollution in the Megacities of the World.* Oxford: Blackwell, 1992.

Wright, Arnold (ed.). *Twentieth Century Impressions of Egypt.* London: Lloyds Greater Britain Publishing Co., 1909.

Zanaty, F., et al. *Egypt Demographic and Health Survey 1995.* Cairo: National Population Council, 1996.

Ziadeh, Farhat J. *Lawyers, the Rule of Law and Liberalism in Egypt.* Stanford, California: Stanford University Press, 1968.

Index

Abbas, uncle of the Prophet, 67
Abbasids, 66–7, 75, 126, 139, 142, 289–90
Abbasiyya district, 177, 332, 335, 341
Abbate, Onofrio, 149–50, 166
Abboud Pasha, 187
Abd al Latif of Baghdad, 38–9, 40, 51–2, 80–2, 132–3
Abd al-Hakim Amir, 223
Abd al-Halim Hafez, 331, 334
'Abdin district, 206
'Abdin palace, 170, 189, 205, 292
al-'Abdin, Zayn, tomb of, 260
Abdu, Sheikh Muhammad, 209
Abu Hanifa, 61
Abu Zayd al-Hilali, 308–10
Abu Zayd, Nasr, 323
Abyad, George, 211
Abydos, 22
Adawiyya, Ahmad, 321, 340
Al-'Adid, Caliph, 124, 125
Agricultural Museum, 218
Ahmose, pharaoh, 35
Aida (Verdi), 169–70&n
Ajami, Fouad, 326
Akhenaten, pharaoh, 45–6
Al-Ahram, 89, 170, 220, 233, 246, 253, 274, 287, 314, 315, 322, 325, 339
Al-Akhbar, 233
Al-Kamil al-Ayyubi, 69
Al-Kawākib, 255
al-Khalifa district, 26–8, 52–3, 57, 58–60
Albanian troops, 160–1
alcoholic drinks, 177, 253–4, 258, 260, *see also* wine
Aleppo, 85
Alexander the Great, in Memphis, 47, 55
Alexandria, 47, 49, 50, 77, 85, 125, 152, 172
Alfi Bey, 153–4
Algeria, civil war, 337
All Saints Cathedral, 233
alleys *see ḥārās*
Amalfi, 99, 128
Amenophis III, pharaoh, 315
America, 167, 337, 338
American Cultural Centre, bombed, 201
Amin, Qasim, 208–9

Ammar ibn Ali, 133–4
anarchists, 177
ancient monuments, plundered and reused, 36–44, 52
animals: markets, 26–7, 52–3, 58; veneration of, 53
ankh symbol, 50
Apis, sacred bulls, 40, 47, 48, 50, 53
al-Aqmar mosque, 124
Arab League, 217, 219
Arab Socialist Union, 219
Arab unity, 217n, 218, 221, 337
Arabic: Cairene culture and, 312–16; foreign influences, 313; sole legal language, 196
Arabic Language Academy, 313
Arafat, Yasir, 221
archaeology, 7, 28–9, 49, 53, 54, 121n, 167, 210, 289
architecture, xv, 14, 15, 128, 174–5; 20th century Egyptian, 210–11, 338; Egyptian architects, 187, 291, 335; Islamic, 210–11, 292–3, 335; tombs, 60, 76
art: ancient Egyptian, 10–11, 22–3, 314; and the French army, 155; galleries, 218, 336; Greco-Roman 41, 55; Impressionist, 184; Islamic, 252; Islamic, 252; Western orientalism, 164, 211
artillery, 140, 141, 142, 145, *see also* firearms
artisans, foreign, 176–7
Ashraf, 296–301
Assyrians, 22, 39, 44n
astronomy, 8, 133, 134, 149
Aswan, 9, 36
Aswan dam, 180
Aswan High Dam, 201, 219, 267, 280
'Ataba Square, 174–6, 181
Atatürk, Kemal, 225
al-Atrash, Farid, 331, 334
Atum, 4, 29
Augustus Caesar, 42, 49
Automobile Club, 192, 205
Avennes, Prisse d', 164
Awad, Lewis, 319, 337
'Ayn Shams district, 44n, 245–6
Ayyubids, 69, 72, 73, 126, 137
Azbakiyya: the Frankish Quarter, 159, 163; lakes and pleasure quarters, 117–18, 143–4, 153–4, 157, *see also* European Quarter; Ismailia Quarter
Abakiyya Gardens, xi, xii, 168, 175, 214
al-Azhar: college, 99, 136–7, 161, 209, 214–15, 225, 243, 293, 323 *see also* universities, al-Azhar; mosque, 83, 105, 122, 156, 161, 210, 301
Azharite sheikhs, 152, 281, 327
al-Aziz, Caliph, 128–9
Aziza the Beast, 113

Baal, temple at Memphis, 47
Bab al-Futuh, 38, 83, 102, 105, 123, 140

Bab al-Luq, 117, 164, 264
Bab al-Nasr, 105
Bab al-Sha'riyya district, 16, 211
Bab Zuwayla, 15, 83, 102, 105, 109, 113, 117, 119, 121, 142, 271
Babylon, Roman fort of, 49, 51, 92
Badur, Judge Ahmad, 325–6
Baghdad, 61, 75, 127, 212, 333; Abbasid caliphs of, 67, 73, 126
al-Bakri, Asma, 336
al-Bakri, Sheikh Ali, 70
ballet, 220, 333, 336
Balqish Jehan Raziya, Princess, 73n
Bani Hilal epic, 308–10, 320
banking, 95, 174, 187, 207, *see also* finance; interest charges
al-Banna, Hasan, 195
Barakat, Bahieddin Pasha, 211n
Barillet-Deschamps, M, 168
bars, 258, 337, *see also* taverns
Barsbay, Sultan, 76, 108–9
al-Barudi, Shams, 255–6
bathhouses, 110, 165, 293
al-Batniyya, hashish market, 122
bawābs, 280–1, 291, 295
Bayat, Asef, 277
Baybars al-Jashankir, Sultan, 270, 317
Baybars, Sultan al-Zahir, 126, 128, 310–11, 314
Bayn al-Qasrayn, 123
bazaars, xii, 15, 69n, 99, 174, *see also* markets; shops and shopping
Bedouin, 141, 145, 153, 160, 310
beggars, 219, 314, 320
Beirut, 212, 333
belly dancers, 19, 21–2, 219, 263, 289, 333
Benben, the, 4, 12, 44, 60
Ben Ezra, Synagogue of, *see* Geniza
Beth Shemesh, 44
Bilharz, Theodore, 166
Bircher, Andre, 149
Birkat al-Fil pleasure quarters, 117–18, 143–4
Bishara, Khayri, 324
Black Death, 82–4, 85, 103, 127
Black Saturday, Fire of Cairo, 1952, 197–200, 216
le Blanc, Vincent, 40–1
blood, circulation of, 137
Bohemond VI of Antioch, 126–7
Boktor, Amin, 176
Le Bon, Charles, 168
Bon Voyage port, 51, *see also* Peruw-Nefer port
Bonaparte, Napoleon *see* Napoleon Bonaparte
Bonola Bey, 149
Book of the Dead, 53–4
books: printed, 134, *see also* publishing
bookstalls, xi, xii, 214
Borelli Bey, 149
Bourguiba, Habib, 225
Brancacci, Felice, 107–9
Breasted, James Henry, 9
Brezhnev, Leonid, 223

bribery *see* corruption
Britain: presence in Egypt, 172–200; Suez Canal attack, 201; Suez Canal purchase, 171
British army, xvi, 149, 157, 260; at Tel al-Kabir, 172; defeat by Muhammad Ali, 160; Qasr al-Nil barracks, 149, 183, 197, 219; in World War I and after, 182–3; in World War II, 188–9, 190–1; withdrawal to the Canal Zone, 197–8
British Council, bombed, 201
broadcasting *see* Radio Cairo; television
building boom: under the khedives, 168, 174; under the Mamluks, 127; under Sadat, 229
Bulaq, 102, 143, 152, 157, 163, 177, 286–7
Bureau of Artistic Content, 321
Bureau of Songsters, 283
bureaucracy, 20, 219, 229, 244, 272–4, 279, 338, 340
burial customs: Christian, 55; Muslim, 56–9; pagan, 53–5
business: foreign control, 103, 151, 154, 159, 170, 174, 176–7, 187, 196, 202, 213, *see also* Europeans
Byzantium, 51

cafés, xi, 21, 154, 177, 263, 291, 296, 317, 335, *see also* coffee houses; restaurants
Caillard, Mabel, 178, 181–2
Cairenes: character of, 80, 89–90, 228–9, 269, 277, 280–3, 285–6, 297, 298, 315; cultural and social tensions, 18, 212–21, 319–28, 332–41; discontents and superstitions, 80, 140, 145–6; dress, 114–15, 139, 177, 255–7, 296, 307, 324; emigrés, 226, 230, 232, 245, 301, 334; Europeanization, 165, 176, 177, 184, 202–3; and French occupation forces, 154–6; intellectuals, 337–8; lifestyles, 296–307; living standards, 20, 212–13, 339–42; materialism, 338–41; middle class (*effendis*), 165, 167, 170, 171–2, 177, 180, 184, 244, 290, 339, 341; mobility of society, 283–6; religion and, 235–62, 321–3, 325, 340; revolts, 156, 157, 243, 295; savings pools, 277; sexual frustrations, 245; skills and abilities, 198; wit of, 316–18
Cairo: beginnings, 6–12; Ayyubid, 68–72, 125–6; city walls, 38, 45; Mamluk, 72–87, 107–9, 117, 126–30, 135–40, 143; Ottoman, 15, 87–8, 99, 109, 115, 119, 143–7; medieval city, xiv, 2–3, 15, 71, 95–122; French

occupation, 154–7, 295; 19th Century, 148–51, 161–72, 286; British occupation, 173–200; modern city, 12–14, 16, 184–203; modernizing pressures, 165–7, 176, 177, 184, 207–12; desert suburbs, 290–1; Old City, 92, 218, 286, 292–303, 336; orientalization, 292; administration of, 20, 272–4; ambience, x–xv; cleanliness of, 267–9; cosmopolitan nature of, x–xii, 176–7, 186–7, 201–2, 244, 254–5, 326; cultural influence of, 21–4, 210–12, 328, 332–4; intellectual revival, 207–12; intellectual stagnation, 334–7; decay, xii, xiii–xiv, 218, 293–4, 336; people of *see* Cairenes, *see also* Egypt; Fustat; individual districts by name; al-Qahira
Cairo Tower, 219, 251
Cairo Yacht Club, 334
calligraphy, 135n, 137, 314
Cambyses, 39–40
camera obscura, 133
canals: investment in, 179; irrigation, 162, 170; Ismail Pasha and, 167, 170; Muhammad Ali and, 162; Nile to Red Sea, 49, *see also* Suez Canal
cannabis *see* hashish
Capitulations, 166n, 170, 176, 201
caravanserais, 109, 290n, 293
Carioca, Tahiyya, 307
Caroll, Christina, 199
catacombs, of animals, 53
Catholic Church, 97, 101, *see also* Christians
cats: stray, 111, 161, 237; veneration of, 53
Cecil, Lord Edward, 279
Çelebi, Evliya, 241
cemeteries, 202, 230, *see also* catacombs; tombs; City of the Dead
Censorinus, 8
censorship, 319–24
Chahine, Yousef, 323
Champollion, Jean François, 42
Cheops, 12n, 32–3; Great Pyramid, 13, 23, 31–2, 34, 39, 42, 160
Chephren, pharaoh, 33, 39
Chiang Kai-shek, 190
children: early deaths, 187; homelessness, 17; labour, 18, 213, 278
Children of Gebelawi (Mahfouz), 323
China, aid to Egypt, 244
Christ *see* Jesus Christ
Christianity: missionaries, 166, 170n; representation in Baybars stories, 311–12; rise of, 50–1; Syrian Christians, 170, 177, *see also* Catholic Church; churches; Coptic Christians
churches, 100, 132, 181, 234,

238, 295; Church of the Archangel Michael, 239–40; police guards, 253
Churchill, Sir Winston S., 190, 193, 260, 262
cigarettes, 180
cinema *see* film industry
Cinema Institute, 336
cinemas, x, 21, 185, 303–4, 310, 329; bombed, 195; burnt down, 198–9
circumcision, female, 241
Citadel, 13, 243; of Saladin, 69, 101, 102, 125–6; building of, 35, 69, 125; under Mamluk sultans, 15, 78, 87, 107, 311, 312; under Ottoman rule, 142, 143, 145; damaged by the French, 156n; British occupation, 174, 183; Ibn Taymiyya and, 71; mosques, 143, 163; returned to Egyptians, 197, *see also* palaces
City of the Dead, 58, 88, 263, 341–2, *see also* cemeteries; tombs
Cleopatra, 42, 48–9
Clot Bey, 166
cocaine, 166, 177
coffee: Islam and, 241; trade, 99, 143, 241
coffee houses, 263–6, 296, 298, 310, *see also* cafés
colleges, 99, 110, 136–8, 161, 227, *see also* education; *madrasas*; universities
communists, 195, 200, 216–17
Companions of the Prophet: the *Sunna*, 237; tombs of, 57, 63
conservationists, 168, 174, 295, 302
Constantine, 51
Constantinople, 15n; sacked by Crusaders, 127; Ottoman rule, 140, 142, 144, 145, 162, *see also* Ottoman Empire
contraception, 232, 241
Cook, Sir Edward, 187
Copeland, Miles, 219n
Coptic Christians, 19; burial customs, 55; discrimination against, 252; fasts, 238; in Fatimid Fustat, 100; Ismail Pasha and, 170; miracles and, 239–40, 252–3; piety of, 238; Roman persecutions of, 51; and turbans, 115, 131, 132; under the Mamluks, 130–2; under Sadat, 234; women, 213, 256, *see also* Christianity
Corniche, the, x, 25, 229, 304
corruption, 192, 214, 232, 267, 270, 271, 279
Cossery, Albert, 186
cotton, 161–2, 167, 171, 180, 184
Crusaders, 35, 68, 72–3, 82, 101, 123–5, 128, 311
Culture, Ministry of, 219, 272
Cyril of Alexandria, 51

al-Dahr, Sayim, 39
Dahshur pyramids, 30–1, 39
Damascus, 85, 127, 333

Damietta, 125
dams, 179, 180, 201, 219, 267, 280
dance of the dead, 88–9
dancing, 288–9
Dar al-Kutub, 336, *see also* National Library
Dar al-Salam district, 277
Darwiche, Mustafa, 340
David (Maimonides's brother), 96
democracy, 231, 314n
dervishes, 65, 110, 136, 139, 271
Dhu'l-Nun al-Misri, 58
Diocletian, 51
Diodorus Siculus, 44–5, 46, 47, 49
Dioscorides, 133
disasters, natural, 79–82
discos, xi, 21, 244
diseases, 166, 183, 187, 215, *see also* health; plagues
dissent, suppression of, 213–14, 217, 221
divorce, 113, 225–6, 237, 253
Djedefre, pyramid of, 43
dogs, 166, 237
Dome of the Rock, 77–8
domes, 60, 75, 76, 77, 86, 175, 293
donkeys: for hire, 91, 120–1, 158; performing, 117–18; on television, 320
doorkeepers *see bawabs*
dragomans, xvi, 159
drama *see* film industry; television; theatre
drugs *see* cocaine; hashish; opium
dustheaps, 122–3, 147

economy: inflation, 229; unofficial, 276–9
education, 215, 217, 221, 231, 327, *see also* colleges; Public Instruction; schools; universities
Egypt: origin of the name, 11; Ancient, 6–12, 28–35; Arab (Muslim) conquest, 14–15, 51; army, 162, 190, 197, 200, 201, 229, 273, 274; colonial empire of, 162, 169; debt, 168, 171, 179, 207; foreign aid to, 243–4; gains from World War II, 190; identity and progress, 208–15, 225; independence of, 183, 210, 213; the social revolution, 219–21, 231, 334, *see also* Cairo
Egyptian Academy, 186
Egyptian Gazette, 186, 205
Egyptian Museum, 18, 22, 42, 43, 54, 55, 89, 166, 168, 170
Egyptian Musicians' Syndicate, 331
Egyptian nationalists, 172, 179, 182, 183, 184, 191, 192, 200–1, 207, 208, 210, 214
electricity, 155, 183, 187, 188, 213, 229, 230, 244, 287
Elwi, Layla, 336
Emigrant, The (film), 323
Emin Pasha, 149&n

Empain, Baron Édouard, 180–1
engineers, 177, 187, 225
Enlightenment project, 215, 225, 337
entertainments, 117–19, 180, 283, 288, *see also mawlids*
Epiphanes Eucharistus (Ptolemy V), 48
Ethnographic Museum, 218
Étoile Égyptienne, 185
Eudoxus, 11
Eugénie, Empress, 169, 203
eunuchs, 78, 107, 112, 170–1, 208, 241, 280, 316
Europe, 85, 99, 107–09, 128–30, *see also* Britain; France
European Art Museum, 218
European Quarter, xii, xv, 159, 199, *see also* Azbakiyya
Europeans: and Egyptians, 178–9, 184, 189, 190, 196, 202–3, 213; legal privileges, 166&n, 187, 196; needs of, 167; and Sadat, 228; social life, xvi–xvii, 176, 178, *see also* business, foreign control
exploration, 92, 167, 169

factories, 35, 174, *see also* industry
Fahmy, Husayn, 336
Fakhry Pasha, 149
Falaki, Pasha, 149
famine, 79–82, 89, 101
al-Farabi, Muhammad, 133
Farida, Queen, 192, 194, 195
Farouk, King: auction of possessions, 205–6; the British and, 189–90; exile of, 200; his gambling, 196, 197; inheritance, 184; life and loves, 192–7, 200, 205; tomb of, 89
fascists, 188n, 216, 227
fashion, 21, 229, 255–7, 305, 324
fasting, 114, 238, *see also* Ramadan
Fatima (Prophet's daughter), 67
Fatimid Empire, 67–8, 79, 96–9, 100–1, 123–5, 128–9, 133, *see also* Islam, Shi'ite
Fayoum Portraits, 41, 55
feasts *see* festivals and feasts
feminism *see* women, equal rights
fertility rituals, 60
festivals and feasts, 19, 45n, 64, 100, 115–16, *see also mawlids*
Fibonacci, Leonardo, 128
Figari Bey, 149
film industry, 187, 211–12, 215, 220, 225, 230, 254, 264, 321, 332–3, 336, 338
finance, 177, 187, 272, 338, *see also* banking
firearms, 130, 140, 145, *see also* military technology
Flaubert, Gustave, 164–5
Florence, 99, 107–9
Foda, Farag, 251, 322
food: cost of, 196, 232, 243, 288, 340; ready cooked, 104; subsidies, 232, 243
football clubs, 20

Fouad I, King of Egypt, 183–4, 186, 195, 213
fountains, public drinking, 143, 293
France: aid to Egypt, 243; French language, 177; scientists, 155–6; Suez Canal attack, 201; troops, 39n, 152–4, 156–7, *see also* Napoleon Bonaparte
Frankish quarter *see* Azbakiyya; European quarter
Franks, 73, 153
Frescobaldi, Leonardo, 102–3
Fulcher, Sir Geoffrey, 123–4
funeral processions, 59, 89
Fustat: Abbasid, 14–15, 51, 66, 92, 316; absence of ghettos, 100; air pollution, 119; al-Askar quarter, 289; Al-Qat'i cantonments, 290; cemeteries, 88; Christian relic, 132; cosmopolitan nature of, 95, 98–101; decline of, 101–2; famine, 81–2, 101; Fatimid, 67–8, 79, 69–9, 100–1, 123–5, 133; and Imam al-Shafi'i, 60; Jews of, 94, 97–8, 100–1; Saladin's wall, 125; sugar mills, 129; trade, 95–7, *see also* Cairo

Gaillardot Bey, 149
gambling, 21, 196, 197, 322
garbage *see* refuse; dustheaps
Garden City, 180
gardens, xi, xii, 117
gas supply, 168
al-Gashnakir, amir Baybars, 136
Geniza of Ben Ezra, documents, 93–6, 98, 100
Geographical Society, 148–51, 168, 218
Gezira, 180, 182
Gezira Sporting Club, xvi, 179, 184, 192, 198, 204–5, 219, 230, 335, 339
Ghali, Waguih, 326
al-Ghazali, Sheikh Muhammad, 216
ghettos, 100, 130
Ghistele, Joos van, 98, 104, 117
al-Ghuri, Sultan Qansuh, 139–41
Gibson, Mr (commissioner of state domains), 149
al-Gindi, Nadia, 336
Giza, 12, 13, 22, 23, 31–2, 37, 38–9, 43, 49, 54, 289
Giza Governorate, 272
Glaser, Joseph, 185
Goha's nail, 197, 200
Gordon, General Charles, 149
grand mufti, 241
Graves, Robert, 178, 312
Greece, independence struggle, 162&n
Greeks, 46–7, 176, 201, 202, 254–5
Groppi Tea Rooms, xi, 291
Guide to the Perplexed, The (Maimonides), 95
guidebooks, 57, 69, 92, 160, 185
guilds, 99, 144, 174, 193
Gulf States, 334, 336, 338

Gulf War, 337
Gumhuriyya Street, xv, 224, 292
guns *see* firearms

Hadrian, Roman Emperor, 50
Haj *see* Pilgrimage to Mecca
Hajji, Sultan, 284
al-Hakim, Caliph, 68, 124, 133
al-Hakim, Tawfiq, 335
Hamama, Faten, 333
Hamed, Ala', 322
Hananel Ben Samuel, 98
Hanna, Milad, 272–3
al-Haqq, Sheikh Gadd, 241
Haqqi, Yahya, 327–8
ḥāras, 118, 295–301, 312
harems, 78, 107, 113–14, 130
Harun al-Rashid, Caliph, 142–3
Harvey, William, 137
Hasan, Sultan, 85–7; mosque, *madrasa* & tomb of, 15, 86–7, 105, 145
hashish, 116, 122, 177, 230, 288, 294–5, 297
Hay, Robert, 164
health: public health, 166, 179, 213, 215, 217, 231, *see also* diseases; medicine
Hebrews in Egypt, 11, 33–4, 44, 315, 323, *see also* Jews
Heliopolis, xv, 11–12, 28, 29, 32, 35, 38, 40, 42, 44–5, 50, 270, *see also* On
Heliopolis district, 180–1, 187, 291
Heliopolis War College, 227
Helwan-les-Bains, 181, 219
Herodotus, 32–3, 40, 46, 54, 64, 236
heroin, 177
Hibat Allah, wazir, 284
hieroglyphs, 25, 36–7, 42, 48, 53–4
Higazi, Ahmad Abd al-Mu'ati, 334
al-Higaziyya, Tatar, tomb of, 112
Hijaz, 162
Holy Family, Flight Into Egypt, 50
homeless, the: children, 17; large numbers of, 104
Homer, xiii, 309
Horowitz, Oscar, 175
Horus, 5–6, 14, 50, 210
hospitals: 'Ayn Shams charity clinic, 246; Cairo Jewish Hospital, 185, 202; of Clot Bey, 166; free, 110; government, 231; Muhandisin, 286; of Sultan Qalawun, 77, 78, 110, *see also* health; medicine
hotels, xii, 174, 179, 180n, 185, 190, 203, 219, 229, 336, *see also* Shepheard's Hotel
House of Wisdom, 133–4
House of Zaynab Khatun, treasure, 301–2
houseboats, xv, 191, 230
housing, 215, 217, 220, 229, 230, 244, 272, 287, 290–1
hubble-bubble *see* water pipe
Hudud al Alam, 15

Hugh of Caesaria, Sir, 123–4
al-Husayn, Imam, 61–3
Husayn Kamil, Sultan, 182, 183
Husayn, Taha, 214–15
Husayniyya district, 157
Hussein, Saddam, 221
Hyman, Lucky Mickey, 196

Ibn al-Arabiyya, 281n
ibn al-'As, Amr, 51, 92
Ibn Battuta, Abu Abdallah Muhammad, 1–2, 56, 60
Ibn Butlan, 134
Ibn Daniyal, Muhammad, 118
Ibn al-Farid, Omar, 242
Ibn al-Hajj, 114
Ibn Hanbal, Ahmad, 61
Ibn Haytham, 133, 134, 137
Ibn Iyas, 74, 139, 141–2
Ibn Juzayy, 2
Ibn Khaldun, Abd al-Rahman, 135–8, 194, 209, 242, 270, 281n
Ibn Khaldun, Muhammad, 99
Ibn Killis, 133
Ibn al-Nafis, 137
Ibn al-Nahas, 79
Ibn Ridwan, 119, 133, 134
Ibn Sa'ada, Yahuda, 133
Ibn Sa'id, 120, 121, 288
Ibn Taghribirdi, 116, 131, 132, 270, 317
Ibn Taymiyya, 71
Ibn Thawb, Rida, 100–1
Ibn Tulun, Ahmad, ruler of Egypt, and Mosque of, 15, 289–90, 293
Ibrahim Pasha, 162, 175
Ibrahim, Sonallah, 341
icons, 238
Idris, prophet, 34
Idris, Yusuf, 335
al-Idrisi, Abu Abdallah Muhammad, 99
Ikhshidid dynasty, 316
Imam, Adel, 333
imams, infallibility of, 67, 124, 125
Imbaba district, 152, 254, 287
Imhotep, 29–30, 37, 48
Immobilia Building, 187
industry, 187, 219, 221, 338, *see also* factories
Industry, Ministry of, 219
Information, Ministry of, 310, 320–1
infrastructure, 179, 243, *see also* railways
Inquisition, 97–8
Institut d'Égypte, 218
Institute of Languages, 165
interest charges, 209, 241, 252, *see also* banking
Interior, Ministry of the, 20, 272, 277n
Internet, Umm Kulsoum website, 329
investment, 179, 229, 338
Iranian Revolution, 337
Irrigation, Ministry of, 20, 273
Isis, 4–5, 48, 50
Islam, 68, 235–43, 245–62; changes, 209; control of appointments, 20, 242–3; puritan tendencies, 66, 71; relics, 142, *see also* Muslims; Shi'ism; Sufism; Sunnism

Islamic education, 238–9, *see also madrasas*
Islamic fundamentalists, 162, 195, 200, 216, 223, 234, 246–57, 338, 340, *see also* Muslim radicals
Islamic law, 61, 69, 209, 225, 238, 240–1, 293; employment, 112; of inheritance, 110, 137, 209, 284; property, 110–11, 112, 284, *see also* law
Islamic League, 248–9
Islamic Museum, 124n, 302
Ismahan, 331, 332
Ismail Pasha, Khedive of Egypt, 167–71, 292
Ismaili Shi'ites, 101, 124
Ismailia Quarter, 148, 174, 291–2
Ismailia (Suez Canal), 198
Israel: and the occupied territories, 337; the October War, 229; provocations, 201; Sadat's peace treaty, 228; Six Day War, 221–3; Suez crisis, 201, *see also* Jews
Israel-Arab War (1948), 194–5, 215
Ittifaq, Abyssinian slave, 284

al-Jabarti, Abd al-Rahman, 70–1, 152, 154–6
Jabes, Edmond, 186
Japan, aid to Egypt, 243–4
Jedda, 85
Jerusalem, 124–5, 127, 222
Jesus Christ, 50
Jews: aftermath of wars with Israel, 202; communists, 216n; departure of, 196, 200–2; in Fustat, 92–6, 97–8, 100–1; Iraqi sects, 93n; Karaites, 93n; and King Farouk, 195; *mawlids*, 63n; synagogues, 92–3, 181, 202, 295; turbans, 115, 132; under the British, 177, 181, 186; under the Mamluks, 130–1, *see also* Hebrews in Egypt; Israel
Jitney cabs, xv, 232, 339, *see also* taxis
jizya see taxes
John, king of Cyprus, 116
Julius Caesar, 8, 48
July coup *see* officers' coup (July 1952)
Justice, Ministry of, 273n
justice system: 20th century, 272–4, 323; medieval, 130, 270–1, 272–3, 323, *see also* law; Islamic law
juvenile delinquency, 287–8

Kaaba, Mecca, 322
Kafre *see* Chephren
Kamil, Mustafa, 207
al-Kamil Sha'ban, Sultan, 284
Karnak, 46
Khaemwes, high priest, 46
Khan al-Khalili, 69n, 99
Khan, Muhammad, 336
Khatun, Zaynab, treasure of, 301–2
khawagāt see Europeans
Khay, 270
Khedivial Club, 179

Khedivial Geographical Society *see* Geographical Society
Kher'aha, 5–6, 12
Khufu, pharaoh *see* Cheops
Khusraw, Nasir, 98
Kinglake, Alexander, 84, 120
Kipling, Rudyard, 166n
Kit Kat Casino, xv, 191
Koran, 237, 240, 262, 312, 313, 314, 323; chanters and readers, 21, 57, 72, 84, 109, 112, 239, 330; *dhikr* singers, 65; exegesis of, 214–15; illuminated, 137, 140, 141
Kuchuk Hanem, 165
Kufa, 316

Labrunie, Gérard *see* Nerval, Gérard de
lakes, seasonal, xiv, 117
Lampson, Sir Miles, 189, 190, 193
land and property, 20, 110–11, 127, 161, 170, 180–2, 196, 213, 218, 220, 225, 229
Lane, Edward, 63, 70–1, 113–14, 163–4, 252, 310
Lane-Poole, Stanley, 178
law: Bar Association, 336; family, 225; labour, 215, 217; Napoleonic Code, 170; press law (1933), 213–14; under the British, 174, 175; *see also* Islamic law; justice system
Layali al-Hilmiyya (TV series), 320
Le Bon, Charles, 168
Lehner, Mark, 289
Leo Africanus, 113, 117–18, 137–8, 270
Lesseps, Ferdinand de, 167
Levy, Isaac, 187
libraries, 21, 133, 134, 149, 155, 168, 336
limestone *see* Muqattam limestone
literacy, 187, 213, 214, 223
literature, 29, 44, 211, 214, 236–7, 335–6, *see also* writers
Loti, Pierre, xiv–xv
Louis IX, of France, 73
Lower Egypt, 6, 9, 29
Luxor, 210

Maadi, 7, 181, 291
ma'assil, 297
Machiavelli, 136
McPherson, Joseph, 45n, 64
madrasas, 15, 57, 136, 146, *see also* colleges; Islamic education; schools
Madrasat al Mushāghibīn (drama), 333
Mahdist revolt, 149
Maher, Ahmed Pasha, 192
Mahfouz, Naguib, x, 123n, 199, 275, 295, 307, 322–3, 324, 335
Maimonides (Maimoun Ibn Musa), 95, 101, 133
Mali, 99, 106–7
Malik ibn Anas, 61
Maltese Bathhouse, The (film), 255–6

Mamluks, 39n, 72–87, 106, 126–32, 310; army, 126, 128, 138–142, 144, 152–3; building boom, 127; court of, 107–9; dress, 115; and intellectual decline, 135–8; slaughter of, 160–1; under Ottoman rule, 144–5, *see also* Turks
Mansa Musa, king of Mali, 106
manufactures, 96, 128–9
al-Maqrizi: on the Black Death, 82–3; on cemeteries, 57; on famine, 80; on Ittifaq, 284; on medieval Cairo, 103–22*passim*, 132, 281, 324; on the Sphinx, 39n, student of Ibn Khaldun, 136, 138
al-Maridani mosque, 105
Mariette, Auguste, 43, 166–7, 170
Mark, the Evangelist, 50
markets: animals, 26–7, 52–3, 58; books, 133; camel market, 21; hashish, 122; humour and, 317; medieval Cairo, 105–6; slaves, 105–7, 110; street, 26–7, 52–3, 294–5, *see also* bazaars; shops and shopping
marquetry, 137, 293
marriage, 113–14, 225, 244–5, 257, 275–6
Ma'ruf Street, 279
Marzouk, Hagg Mustafa, 295
Mason Bey, 149
masons *see* stonemasonry
al-Mas'udi, 116
mathematics, 137
Matisse, 211
mausoleums *see* tombs
mawlids, 45n, 59–60, 62–6, 84, 242, 298, *see also* entertainments; festivals and feasts
Mecca, 35, 60, 85, 127, 162&n, 322
media, 318–21; state control, 319–21, *see also* press, the; Radio Cairo; television
medicine: at Al-Azhar, 238; decline in interest, 137, 146; deteriorating services, 231; doctors, 95, 100, 110, 119, 133, 149, 166, 226; midwives, 112, 166; the professionally sick, 264–6; research grants, 133–4; *see also* health; hospitals
Medina, 127, 162
Meidum pyramid, 30
Memphis, 22, 23, 236, 289; bureaucracy, 273; burial customs, 53–5; cosmopolitan nature of, 46–7, 49; court cases, 270; Greek and Roman, 47–50, 104; growth and decline, 9–12, 13–14, 45, 51–2; in myth, 4–5; necropolis at, 28–30, 34–5, 39–40, 41, 43, 46, 52; refuse problems, 121n
Mena House Hotel, conference, 190
Menelaus, king of Sparta, xiii

Menes, unifying pharaoh, 9–10, 28
Menkaure, *see* Mycerinus
metro line, 243, 252, 272, 324
Middle Egypt, 46
military parades, 116, 138–40
military technology, 72, 128, 130, 141, 152–3, *see also* firearms
minarets, 12, 15, 74, 76, 86, 293
Misr, 21
Misr al-Fustat *see* Fustat
Misr al-Qadima, 14n, 102
Modern Art Museum, 336
Molière, 207
monasteries: Christian, 37, 92; dervish, 27, 110, 136
Mongol hordes, 75, 85, 126, 311
Morris, William, 211
morticians *see* burial customs
Mose, 270
Moses, found in bullrushes, 92
mosques, xi, xii, xvi, 15, 17, 20, 35, 38, 83, 86, 92, 110, 124, 137, 143, 181, 240, 271, 290, 293; 20th century, 210–11, 246, 254, 291; funerary, 57, 62, 70, 71, 85–7, 89, 163, 168; Muhammad Ali and, 161, 163, *see also* shrines
Mother of the World, xi, 147
moulids see mawlids
Moyne, Lord, assassinated, 192
al-Mu'ayyad Sheikh, Sultan, 110, 131
Mubarak, Ali Pasha, 146, 168
Mubarak, Husni, President, 243
muezzins, 21, 235–6
mufti: dress, xi, 151, 228, *see also* grand mufti
Mugamma', building, 232
Muhammad, Prophet, 237, 310
Muhammad V, king of Granada, 135
Muhammad Ali Pasha, 160–3, 165, 193, 293
Muhammad Ali Street, 143, 264
Muhandisin district, 286–7, 290
Muhieddin, Dr Ala', 248–9
al-Mu'izz li Din Allah, 68, 99, 290, 292
Mukhtar, Mahmoud, 210
al-Mulik, Nizam, 72
mummies: dance of the dead, 88–9; healing powers of, 40; mummification, 54; plunder of, 40–2
al-Muqaddasi, 15
Muqattam cliffs, 26, 28, 32, 34, 92, 125, 238, 242
Muqattam limestone, 31, 32, 34, 35, 76, 252
Murad, Leila, 211–12
museums *see* under individual names
music, 21, 116, 117, 185, 211–12, 220, 230, 328–32, 336; censorship, 321; heavy-metal, 325, 326
Muski district, 16
Muslim Brotherhood, 195, 198,

199, 214, 216, 217, 225, 227
Muslim radicals, 191, 225, 325, *see also* Islamic fundamentalists; Muslim Brotherhood
Muslims: Arab conquest of Egypt, 14–15; and the Inquisition, 97; piety of, 237–8; relations with Christians, 131–2, *see also* Islam
al-Mustansir, Caliph, 80, 119, 309
al-Mutanabbi, Abu Tayyib, 316
al-Mutawakkil, Caliph, 55, 139, 142–3
Muwaffaq al-Din ibn Uthman, 69
al-Muwaylihi, Muhammad, 326–7
Mycerinus, 32, 33, 38, 39, 289
myths: Egyptian, xv, 3–6; Greek, xiii, 47

Naguib, President Muhammad, 216–17
al-Nahas, Mustafa Pasha, 189, 198
Nahum Effendi, Senator Chaim, 186
Napoleon Bonaparte, 42, 121, 134, 151–7, 242–3, 295, *see also* France
Nariman, Queen, 196–7
Nasir al-Din Balisi, 99
al-Nasir Muhammad, Sultan, 84–5, 106, 107–9, 127
al-Nasser, Gamal Abd: President, 201, 217–27; social contract, 231, 232; the soldier, 195, 227; funeral of, 89, 226–7, 260, 334
National Democratic Party, 337
National Guidance, Ministry of, 219
National Library, 149, 336
nationalism *see* Egyptian nationalists
nationalization, 217, 219–21
Nazli, Queen, 195
Nebuchadnezzar, 44n, 93
Neferrehu, priest, 283
Nehru, Pandit, 218
Nelson, Admiral Horatio, 156
Nerval, Gérard de, 157–69, 163, 165, 174
Nesedil, concubine of Ismail Pasha, 170
New Kingdom: poetry, 23; tomb builders, 37, 46
Niebuhr, Carsten, 112, 146–7
nightclubs, 21–2, 230
Nile, 25; barrages, 19, 43; breeeze, 25–6; Delta, ix, 5, 6, 9, 14, 16, 46, 51; failure to flood, 79–82; floods, 6, 8, 10, 14, 32, 79, 116, 267; monuments, 219; source of, 92, 149, 151, 167; steamboats, 19, 159
Nilometer, 10, 79, 91, 116
Nkrumah, Kwame, 218
noise, 17–18, 27
Nubarian, Nubar Pasha, 174

al-Nugūm, 255
Nuqrashi, Mahmud Pasha, 195

obelisks, 3, 42, 44–5, 245
Octavian *see* Augustus Caesar
October War, and its aftermath, 229
officers' coup (July 1952), 200; effects of, xi, 205, 216, 283, 319
oilfields, 222
Old Kingdom: inscriptions, 37; reliefs, 22–3, 34
Omar, Caliph, 51
On, 3–4, 7–9, 11–12, 16, 44, 245, *see also* Heliopolis
Opera House, 168, 169, 171, 175, 185–6, 205, 244n; New Opera House, 243–4, 308–9, 333
Opera Square, 174, 198, 211, 303
opium, 117, 144, 288, 295
Osiris, 4–5, 50
Osman, in the Baybars stories, 311–12, 314
Ottoman Empire: decline of Egypt and, defeat Mamluks and conquer Egypt, 141–7; and the French, 157; Ismail Pasha and, 171; Muhammad Ali and, 162; World War I policy of, 182, *see also* Constantinople
Ottoman Turks, 83, 85, 87–8, 115; army, 140–3, 144

palaces, xii, 15, 46, 85, 91, 153–4, 293, 294; built under Ismail, 168, 169; of Fatimid caliphs, 123n, 124, 125, *see also* Citadel
Palestine, 157, 162; War (1948), 194–5, 215
Palestinians, 194, 331
Paris, 43, 167–8, 262
parliament, 170, 184, 215; Speaker assassinated, 250
Pedro of Seville (the Cruel), 135
'People of the Cave', 326n
Per-hapi-on, 49, *see also* Babylon
persecutions: by the Catholic Church, 97, 101; by the Romans, 51; of Coptic Christians, 131–2; of Ismaili Shi'ites, 101
Persians, 39–40, 44n, 46–7
Peruw-Nefer port, 46, *see also* Bon Voyage port
Petrie, Sir W M Flinders, 272
pharaohs, 11, 289, *see also* individual names
philosophy, 133, 136, 152, 209, 215
pigeon post, 128–9
pilgrimage sites: Christian, 50; Muslim, 57, 71
Pilgrimage to Mecca, 106, 115–16, 136
pilgrims, 99, 102, 106, 116
Piloti, Emmanuel, 103
Pinon, Carlier de, 88
Piperno, M, 150
plagues, 82–4, 84n, 85, 89, 103, 127, 195, *see also* diseases
Plato, 11, 132, 133, 135

playing cards, 128
poetry, xiv, 23, 137, 259–60, 318
Poliakov, M, 185
police, 178, 272; Central Security, 234, 247; in Imbaba, 287; maintenance of order, 179, 183, 272; massacre of at Ismailia, 198; and reverse gravity, 282–3; and Sadat's critics, 228; secret, xi, 216, 218–19, 226, 335; shooting of strikers, 216; traffic police, 304–5; uniforms, 218–19
politics, 20, 214, 216–17, 228, 276–7; demonstrations, 89, 210, 320; Nasserite socialism, 219–21, 223, 224–6, 231, 239, 244
Pollock, Jackson, 300
pollution, 17–18, 119–21, 340
polo, 74, 115
Popular Quarters, 287–9
population: of modern Cairo, 19; in 1930, 187; of Memphis, 10; density in medieval Cairo, 103–4; effects of growth, 16–19, 186–7, 213, 215, 220, 228, 230, 232, 233–4, 290–1
post office, 175, 272
pottery, neolithic, 7
poverty, 187–8, 266–9, 275–8, 285, 287–8
press, the, 20, 21, 170, 186, 208, 211, 215, 233, 255, 314–15, 319–20; Press Syndicate, 336, *see also* media
printing, 134&n, *see also* publishing
Prolegomena (Ibn Khaldun), 135, 136, 137
property: confiscation of, 202; development, 180–2, 335
prostitution, 117, 164, 171, 176, 177–8, 182, 219, 288
protection rackets, 113, 145
Ptah, 4, 11, 23, 35
Ptahshepses, high priest, 282
Ptolemaic rule, 29n, 47–9, 104
Ptolemy, 133
Ptolemy Soter, 47
Public Instruction, Ministry of, 179, *see also* education
Public Works, Ministry of, 179
publishing: and censorship, 322–4, *see also* printing
Pulli, Antonio, 195
Pyramid Texts, 8
pyramids, 4–5, 11, 12, 13, 29–34, 37, 289; fables and fantasies, 33–4; stone plundering, 38–9, 43; and tourism, 160, *see also* tombs
Pyramids, Battle of, 152–3
Pythagoras, 11

al-Qahira, xv, 67, 82, 94, 102, 125, 290, *see also* Cairo
qahwas see coffee houses; cafés
Qalawun, Sultan, 77–8, 110, 230
Qalyubiyya Governorate, 272
Qamhiyya *madrasa,* 136
Qasaba, 102, 104, 111, 116,

120, 123n, 139–41, 230, 290, 293
Qayt-bay, Sultan, 76, 242
Qina province, 310
al-Qinawi, Izzat, 308–9
quarrying, 27–8
Qubba Gardens, 180

Ra, 29, 44
rabies, 166
Racine, 208
radh, 318
Radio Cairo, 219, 221, 236, 319, 320–1, 329–30; Listeners' Committee, 321, 330–1, *see also* media
ragpickers, 268–9, 303
railways, 149, 165, 170; Railway Museum, 218; sabotaged, 183, *see also* infrastructure
Ramadan, 114, 144, 236, 253, 269, 296, 309, 320, *see also* fasting
Ramses II, pharaoh, 34n, 37, 46, 52
al-Rashid, Caliph Harun, 143
Rasim, Ahmed, 186
al-Razi, Abu Bakr, 133
real estate *see* land and property
Reason *see* Philosophy
Rebecca cypher, 191
Reesha, Farid, 259–60
refuse: collection and recycling, 267–9; non-collection of, 121, 147; *see also* sewage
relief carvings, 22–3, 34, 38, 39, 54, 272
restaurants, 17, 154, 160, 185, 203, 219, 244, *see also* cafés
revolution of 1952 *see* officers' coup (July 1952)
Rigoletto (Verdi), 170n
al-Rihani, Naguib, 211
riots: (1919), 183, 209; Black Saturday, 197–200; bread, 232–3; inter-communal, 234
roads, 168, 179, 223, 230
Roberts, David, 164
Rhoda island, 49, 79, 81, 116
Roger II, king of Sicily, 99
Rome, conquest and occupation of Egypt, 14, 42, 47–51
Rommel, Field Marshal Erwin, 190, 191
Roosevelt, Franklin D., 190
Rose al-Yusuf, weekly journal, 330
Rosetta stone inscription, 42–3, 48

Sabri, poet, 259–60
al-Sadat, Anwar: in World War II, 191n, 227; and the officer's coup, 200, 227; President, 227–34, 260; and Arabism, 227–8; economic policy, 231; makes peace with Israel, 228; rediscovered roots, 228; tomb of, 36, 89
Safran, Nadav, 315n
Sahure, Pyramid of, 39
St Simeon, Cathedral of, 238
saints: days, 115; female, 74; worship of, 61–2, 64, 71; *see also* shrines; tombs; *mawlids*
Sala, Contessa della, 169, 170

Salah al-Din (Saladin), 38, 68–9, 101, 125, 135
al-Salih Ayyub, Sultan, 72–3, 74
al-Salih Ismail, Sultan, 284
Samaritans, 115
Sandys, George, 88–9
Saphir, Jacob, 91–3
Saqqara, 12, 13, 22, 28–9, 30, 31, 34, 37, 39, 41, 46, 47, 282; bureaucracy, 273; catacombs of the sacred baboons, 53; reliefs, 54, 270
Sarapis, 48, 50
Sarghatmish *madrasa,* 136
al-Saud family, 162n
Saudi Arabia, 162n, 245; TV, theatre, film and, 321, 322, 333n, 334
al-Sayyid, Afaf Lutfi, 318n
al-Sayyid, Dawud Abd, 336
Schnitzer, Eduard *see* Emin Pasha
schools: curriculum, 217–18; foreign religious, 176; Islamic, 238, 293; Jewish, 202; private, 202–3; state secular, 162, 165, 170, 179, 213, 215, 218, 231, 234, 238, *see also madrasas*
science, at Al-Azhar, 238
secularism, and traditional values, 210–15, 216, 225, 245, 254, 324–5, 327–8
Seila pyramid, 30
Selim I (the Grim), Sultan, 119, 135n, 140–2
Seneferu, pharaoh, 30–1, 39
Serageddin, Fouad, 198
Serapis *see* Sarapis
Sesostris I, pharaoh, 44–5
Seth, 4–6, 14
sewage, 213, 223, 230, 243, 273, 287, *see also* refuse
Shaarawi, Hoda, 208
Shaarawi, Sheikh Muhammad Mitwalli, 235, 237
shadow puppets, 118–19
al-Shafi'i, Imam Muhammad Ibn Idris, 60–1, 69, 71, 92
Shagar al-Durr, Sultana, 73–5, 77
Sham al-Nissim festival, 45n
Sharia *see* Islamic law
Sharif, Omar, 220
Shaykhun, amir, 271
Shenouda III, Coptic pope, 238, 253
Shepheard's Hotel, xv–xvii, 159, 179, 182, 188, 198, 199, 200, *see also* hotels
Shi'ism, 61–3, 67–9, 80, 100, 101, 124, 125, 135, *see also* Fatimid Empire; Islam
shops and shopping: medieval Cairo, 104–5; 19th century, 159, 174; 20th century, 175, 184, 195, 199–200, 244, 286, 291, 292, 294–5, 339, *see also* bazaars; markets
shrines, 60, 61, 62, 68, 69, 71, 75, *see also* mosques, funerary
Shubra district, 16, 177, 233–4, 240, 253
Sidi Uqba, tomb of, 60n
Sinai Peninsula, 222

Six Day War, and its aftermath, 221–4
slaves: in *Aida*, 169; Crusaders, 35; Islam and, 241; Ismail Pasha and, 170–1; markets, 105–7, 110, 158; purchase of, 95, 105–6; revolt of, 105, *see also* Mamluks
soap operas, Egyptian, 21
Sokar, 28
solar boat, 12n, 23
solar calendar, 8–9
Solon, 11
Sosigenes, 8
Soviet Union, and Egypt, 219, 223, 228
Speke, John Hanning, 92, 167
Sphinx, xiv, 39, 160, 243
spice trade, 15, 99, 129, 143, 146
spies, 191, 195, 201
squatters, 233–4, 289
Stanley, Henry M, 149&n
Step Pyramid, 13
stock exchange, 174, 180, 187, 338
stonemasonry, 27–8, 29, 38
Story of Isa bin Hisham, The (al-Muwaylihi), 326–7
storytelling, 230, 308–12, 315
Strabo, 33, 45, 49
street names, changes, 217
street vendors, 104, 278, 291, 292, 296, 320
strikes, 183, 198, 210, 216, 320
Styx, river, modelled on Memphis, 47
Sudan, 149, 162
Suez Canal: British troops and, 183, 197, 198; nationalized, 201, 218; and the October War, 229; opening of, 167–8; sale of Egypt's share in, 171; and the Six Day War, 222–3, *see also* canals
Suez crisis of 1956, 201
Sufism, 69–71, 135; Brotherhoods, 62, 65; coffee and, 241; convents, 112; dancing, 260–1; Ibn Farid controversy, 242; Ibn Khaldun and, 136, 242; iconoclastic zeal, 39; suppression of, 225; turbans, 115, *see also* Islam
sugar industry, 180
Sulayman the Magnificent, 119
Sunna, the, 237
Sunnism, 63, 67, 68–9, 80, 125, 126, 135, *see also* Islam
Supreme Cohen of Jerusalem, 95
Synod Toulouse (1229), 97
Syria, 123, 125, 162

Tafur, Pero, 271
Tahra the Pure, 261–2
Tahrir Square, 217, 231, 232, 274, 329, 335
Takla brothers, 170
Tanis, 22
taverns, 117, *see also* bars
Tawfiq, Khedive of Egypt, 171–2
taxes: on baldness, 138; on commerce, 129; French occupation and, 156; Ismail

Pasha and, 171; Mamluk beys and, 145; on non-Muslims, 98, 99–100, 165–6; on prostitution, 117; on wine, 117
taxis, x, xiii, 251–2, 340, *see also* Jitney cabs
Taymur, Muhammad, 327
al-Tayyib, Atif, 336
Tefnut, goddess of moisture, 4
Tel al-Armana, 46, 267
Tel al-Kabir, Battle of, 172
telegraph services, 165; sabotaged, 183
telephones, 179, 223, 230–1, 243
television, 21, 230, 244, 309, 318–21; religious, 237, 238, 245, 254; satellite, 21, 333, *see also* media
Temple of Ptah, 35, 40, 46, 48, 49, 51, 52, 236, 270
Temple of the Sun xv, 11, 40, 42, 44
Temples: desecrated by Christians, 51; plundered by Egyptian rulers, 43
textile industry, 129, 180, 339
theatre, 21, 118–19, 168, 207–8, 211–12, 220, 230, 321, 336
Thevenot, Monsieur de, 41
Thompson, Jason, 114n
Thoth, 5, 34, 44
Thousand and One Nights, xi, 23–4, 96, 158, 159, 310, 317, 322
Timmerman, Herr, 149
Tito, Marshall, 218
tobacco, Islam and, 241
tombs: Ancient, 11, 22, 27–35, 37, 46; architecture, 60, 76; Islamic, 35–6, 56–9, 63, 68–70, 72, 74–8, 85–7, 110, 112, 127, 145; looting of, 40–3; modern, 36, 89, 210; and the Nile, 79; plunder of, 40–3; quarried for stone, 36–9; reliefs, 54–5; of saints, 75; of Sufi *walis*, 70; tomb dwellers, 58–9, 202, 341–2; Umm Kulsoum, 329; and women, 112; *see also* catacombs; cemeteries; City of the Dead; pyramids
tortures, 270–1
tourism, 180, 229, 338
tourists: Arab, 21, 57, 78, 230; Turkish, 117; western, xv, 6, 19, 78, 159–60, 244, 250, *see also* Herodotus
Toynbee, Arnold, 136
trade, 85, 95–7, 99–100, 103, 107–9, 129, 146, 170, 174
trade unions, 207, 215, 216, 277
traders, foreign *see* business, foreign control
traffic: medieval, 120; 19th century, 148, 151; 20th century, 230, 243, 272, 279, 303–4, 333, 335, 340
tramways, 175, 179, 187, 220
treasure, 301–3
Tripoli, 85
Tumanbay, Sultan, 119
Tunis, 332, 333

Tunisia, 309
turbans: sectarian colours, 115, 132, 139; and the tax on baldness, 138; on women, 111
Turf Club, 179, 191, 198, 199
Turks, 71–2, *see also* Mamluks; Ottoman Turks
Tutankhamun, 22, 46, 210
Tutmosis III, pharaoh, 42
Tutmosis IV, pharaoh, xiv

'ulema, the, 61, 134–5n, 241, 256n
Umm Ahmad, 275–6
Umm Ali, 73, 74
Umm Hashim's Lantern (Haqqi), 327–8
Umm Kulsoum, x, 58, 230, 255, 298, 328–31, 334, 337
undertakers *see* burial customs
United States *see* America
universities, 20, 21, 281, 293; American University, 277; 'Ayn Shams University Faculty of Medicine, 264–6; al-Azhar, 225, 238, 241, 253, 293, 313, 323; Cairo University, 207, 210, 215, 221, 278–9, 312; *see also* al-Azhar, college; education
Upper Egypt, 6, 9, 10, 20, 29
Upper Egyptians, 177, 317–18
Urabi, Colonel Ahmad, nationalist revolt, 172, 207
Urban II, pope, 124
Uruba Palace, 180n
usury, 209, 241, 252
utilities, 168

Valle, Pietro della, 41
Valley of the Kings, 210
veils, 111, 130, 184, 185, 208–9, 213, 256–7
Verdi, Giuseppe, 169–70n
Versailles Peace Conference, 183
veterinary science, 137
villas, 148, 168, 174, 211, 229
Virgin Mary, 50, 239–40, 253

al Wahab, Muhammad Abd, 211, 331
Wahbi, Yusuf, 211
Wahhabis, 162n
waqf endowments, 110–12, 146, 161, 242, 279
war memorial, 36
warfare *see* military technology
water carriers, 293
water pipes, 177, 191, 264, 297, 298
water supply, 20, 104, 168, 188, 213, 230, 234, 243, 244, 272
Weinstein Stationery, 291
Weret, Queen, jewellery of, 22
Wikalat al-Balah, 294
Wilkinson, Sir Gardner, 64, 271
William of Tyre, 124
wine, 100, 117, 159, 170, *see also* alcoholic drinks
Wingate, Colonel F. R., 149
women: and chastity, 112;

Copts, 213, 256; and equal rights, 208–9; 225–6, 331; female circumcision, 241; female saints, 75; and French troops, 154; fundamentalism and, 252; in the harem, 107, 113–14, 130; in medieval society, 111–14; in modern society, 274–6; and nationalism, 183; as rulers, 73; and veils, 111, 130, 184, 185, 208–9, 213, 225, 256–7
work, government promises of, 231, 232, 244
World War I, 182–3
World War II, 188–92, 227
writers, 211, 226, 254, 315, 322–4, 334; Writers' Union, 336, *see also* literature

Yashbak, amir, 294
Yazid, Caliph, 61
Young Egypt Party, 227
Young Men's Muslim Association, 195

Zabbālīn see ragpickers
Zaghloul, Saad, 89, 183, 208, 210
al-Zahiri, Khalil, 102
Zaluski, Count, 149, 151
Zamalek district, 20, 291
Zaynab Khatun *see* Khatun, Zayrab
Zaynab, Sayyida, 64–6, 327–8
Zaytun, 239
al-Zaytuni, Badr al-Din, Sheikh, xiv
al-Zimam, Kafur, 316
Zionists, terror attacks by, 192
zoo, x
Zoser, pharaoh, 29–30
Zuhayri, Kamil, 292